Hacking Firefox™

Hacking Firefox™

More Than 150 Hacks, Mods, and Customizations

Mel Reyes

Wiley Publishing, Inc.

Hacking Firefox™: More Than 150 Hacks, Mods, and Customizations

Published by
Wiley Publishing, Inc.
10475 Crosspoint Boulevard
Indianapolis, IN 46256
www.wiley.com

Copyright © 2005 by Wiley Publishing, Inc., Indianapolis, Indiana

Published simultaneously in Canada

ISBN-13: 978-0-7645-9650-6
ISBN-10: 0-7645-9650-0

Manufactured in the United States of America

10 9 8 7 6 5 4 3 2 1

1B/SR/QX/QV/IN

For general information on our other products and services or to obtain technical support, please contact our Customer Care Department within the U.S. at (800) 762-2974, outside the U.S. at (317) 572-3993 or fax (317) 572-4002.

Wiley also publishes its books in a variety of electronic formats. Some content that appears in print may not be available in electronic books.

Library of Congress Control Number: 2005017558

About the Author

Mel Reyes, a veteran of technology and programming, is an avid fan and user of Firefox and all its predecessors. He programs in several languages, works with a variety of technologies, and runs MRTech.com, which provides free technology news, support, tips, and software. He works in several industries helping clients with web, desktop, and database application development. Mel can be reached by e-mail at mel@mrtech.com.

Credits

Executive Editor
Chris Webb

Contributing Writers
Phil Catelinet
Alex Sirota
Aaron Spuler
Terren Tong

Technical Editors
David Gegenheimer
James Russell

Development Editor
Marcia Ellett

Copy Editor
Maarten Reilingh

Production Manager
Tim Tate

Editorial Manager
Mary Beth Wakefield

Vice President and Executive Group Publisher
Richard Swadley

Vice President and Publisher
Joseph B. Wikert

Project Coordinator
Erin Smith

Graphics and Production Specialists
April Farling
Jennifer Heleine
Stephanie D. Jumper
Erin Zeltner

Quality Control Technicians
Amanda Briggs
Jessica Kramer
Carl William Pierce
Charles Spencer

Proofreading and Indexing
TECHBOOKS Production Services

Cover Design
Anthony Bunyan

To my loving and caring family—Wendi, Samantha, and Skylher

Foreword

If software is an art—and I think it is—then I must be the only artist in the world who advocates defacing his own work. But if ever there was a product designed for hacking, Firefox is it. Because Firefox is an open-source project, its lifeblood—its source code—is available to hackers the world over. And I do mean *hackers*. These guys ship software before they put on pants.

What separates Firefox from other open-source projects is that it isn't designed for a technical community. Products like Linux are generally regarded as being "by geeks, for geeks," but with Firefox it's more like "by geeks, for grandmas." We focus obsessively on the user experience so that everything *just works*, right out of the box. Indeed, you may find that when you first start Firefox, you don't *need* to hack it. This odd sensation will be accompanied by symptoms of hacker withdrawal, including, in severe cases, a sudden willingness to go outside. You'll find yourself scoffing at certain parts of Firefox just to feel as if you have something to hack ("Pfft, I could hack a *much* cuter fox for their logo").

No worries: Shortly thereafter, your geeky sense will begin tingling again. Think back to *The Matrix*. Where most of the world saw a vibrant 3-D reality, Neo and his crew saw an endless stream of flashing green code. Okay, so real life (if this *is* real life) isn't *quite* that cool, but you and I see technology through a different lens than Grandma. She isn't going to notice—or care—if her toolbar buttons are five pixels apart instead of seven, but I am, and I want to fix it. Because we are empowered to change anything, we notice everything.

Besides, hacking isn't just about fixing what's wrong. It's also about making what already works *work for you*. Sure, traditional, rectangular context menus work well enough, but wouldn't pie menus be better? And yeah, it's easy enough to click that back button, but it's ever so far. . . Why can't I make a quick gesture with my mouse to go back, wherever it happens to be? Well enough, good enough—"enough" does not exist in the hacker vocabulary. There is only an escalating sense of "better."

I began work on Firefox two years ago, when I was 17, and I'm still hacking on it right now in another window. Firefox is not a business. It is a passion. It is the product of a global community of developers fueled by their own drive to *create*, and no matter how hard we try to polish it for Grandma, our roots shine through. We urge you to join us; our art is yours.

Blake Ross
Co-creator of Firefox
www.blakeross.com

Acknowledgments

First and foremost, I thank the most profoundly beautiful, incredibly understanding, rock and foundation, love of my life—my wife, Wendi. Without her superhuman efforts to manage day-to-day things, I don't think this book would have been possible. To my loving daughter Sammi B., whose smiling pictures and letters gave me the energy on those extremely long and late nights to continue writing. To my younger and vibrant daughter, Skylher B., for making sure I didn't miss any of those important moments in the first year of her life. And to the new addition who adds a delightful finish to this whole process.

To Can and Bry for being the best babysitters, in-laws, and friends a person could ever have. Thanks also to the rest of my family, friends, and coworkers for lending an ear and for the words of encouragement.

Special thanks to the great efforts and massive contributions made to this book and for the expertise supplied by Phil Catelinet, Alex Sirota, Aaron Spuler, and Terren Tong. Thanks, guys!

Finally, I thank Chris Webb and Marcia Ellett of Wiley for their patience, indulgence, and the opportunity they have afforded me with this endeavor.

Introduction

"And so at last the beast fell and the unbelievers rejoiced. But all was not lost, for from the ash rose a great bird. The bird gazed down upon the unbelievers and cast fire and thunder upon them. For the beast had been reborn with its strength renewed, and the followers of Mammon cowered in horror."

from *The Book of Mozilla, 7:15*

Assumptions

To use this book and reap its benefits, you should have a solid foundation in using Windows/ Linux and Mozilla Firefox. This book covers basic to advanced hacks, the majority of which are compatible with any platform that the Firefox 1.0 official release currently runs on.

Using This Book and What You Will Find Here

To use this book, all you need to do is have a basic understanding of how Firefox works, how to install it, and how to find files on your computer. As you read, you will begin to unravel the marvels of coding for Firefox using the basics of Cascading Style Sheets (CSS) and JavaScript and then later diving into XML User Interface Language (XUL) and the Cross Platform Component Object Model (XPCOM). The final goal is being able to create extensions that will allow you to customize Firefox to your heart's content.

This book starts by giving you a brief overview of how to hack manually, how to hack with extensions, and then a quick glance at what you will need to do to back up critical files so that you can practice safe hacking.

Then it breaks down each of the individual components of Firefox from interface to rendering to privacy and walks you through hacking and modifying key files to apply tons of possible interface and functionality changes. It also includes a great list of proven extensions with which you can modify core features of Firefox, as well as the look and feel of the interface.

In addition, this book covers the grassroots efforts that Mozilla and Firefox have become known for among developers—the ability to use the highly extendable Mozilla programming language and interface to modify any aspect of the browser by creating extensions, and also how you can change the appearance of the browser by creating themes.

Conventions Used in This Book

As you read this book, you will find boxed icons that highlight additional information of interest. The informational icons include the following:

This icon indicates special information relating to the current section that you may find useful.

This icon indicates information that explains the best way to do something or alerts you to special considerations you should be aware of when performing a routine task.

This icon indicates a reference to related information in another chapter.

This icon indicates cautionary information, alerting you to potential hazards encountered within the tasks at hand.

Being a Part of the Community

The Mozilla initiative, in existence for more than seven years now, is the divine spawn of the Netscape Corporation. Several years spent in planning and restructuring have lead to some incredible products, including the Mozilla Suite, Firefox, Thunderbird, and many other smaller projects. Several of these projects are currently official releases, with Firefox being the flagship, standalone browser. The key to the Mozilla community is that it is now an official nonprofit international organization with many volunteers who help in debugging, hacking, and documenting the interface and features.

The community of people who use and create for Mozilla is tremendous, and as large as it is, it still requires the assistance of all users, basic or experienced, to find and submit bugs that may come up or to submit requests for options that are currently not available.

While you might hear a lot about the Mozilla organization, this book also covers the other supporting sites and individual initiatives, such as the XULPlanet, MozillaZine, MozDev, Extension Room, and Extension Mirrors sites. All of these help users and programmers support the Mozilla efforts by hosting web forums, extension homepages, and independent projects.

Searching and Submitting Firefox Bugs

The Bugzilla site (`http://bugzilla.mozilla.org`) is the core management center for tracking and communicating bugs and requests for enhancements (RFEs), and to check on the latest development efforts for future releases.

Your first visit to Bugzilla might be a little daunting, but, as you read this book, you should be able to understand and maybe even help with issues in the currently released builds by searching and submitting your findings and bugs to the Bugzilla site.

Though registration is not required for searching, you should register and get a Bugzilla user account to help communicate bugs and workarounds and to receive patch status on bug reports you submit. The key thing to remember when submitting a bug is that you should thoroughly search the Bugzilla database using different permutations of keywords that can describe your problems. For example, suppose this was the issue at hand: "My browser crashed during an online SSL secure transaction at MyRustyRedChevyTruck.biz." Before submitting a bug, do some digging, check to see if it is a bug with *any* secure site or just the one you had a problem with. Once you have deduced whether it involves all secure web sites or just this site, you can go into the Bugzilla database. You can search to see whether this is a known bug, if a future major release includes the fix, or if there is a workaround.

The initial search that you should do would be for "MyRustyRedChevyTruck.biz." If this search does not bring back any results, do additional searches for "SSL crash" or "browser crash secure site." Each permutation of searches you do will help in removing duplicate bug reports, which, in the end, will reduce overhead in managing, categorizing, and tracking bugs.

If, after thorough researching, you conclude that yours is a unique bug, go ahead and submit a new bug by selecting the correct form entries on the Bugzilla site. Pay close attention when classifying your submission, as doing so will expedite your request and remove the categorization burden from the developers. If you are confused about classifying the bug, just do your best; the category owners will sort it into the correct bucket. After submitting a bug, you will receive communication from the Mozilla team and possibly other users who will confirm or resolve the issue. If your submitted bug is a legitimate bug, it will be queued for further testing and troubleshooting.

Contents at a Glance

Contents

Part III: Hacking Menus, Toolbars, and the Status Bar

Part IV: Hacking Navigation, Downloads, and Searching

Part VI: Creating Extensions and Themes

Basic Hacking

Hacking Firefox Boot Camp

Gearing up to hack Mozilla Firefox is as simple as understanding some basic Internet browser features, installing some tools, and being able to find files on your computer system. Then it gets just a tad more complicated. This chapter starts things off by discussing the different methods for hacking Firefox that are covered in this book and how things will progress. Try not to get bogged down with the onslaught of topics that are covered here, because many of them are covered in depth throughout the book.

If you understand some basic web programming tools, such as CSS, JavaScript, and XML, you are one step ahead of the game. Conversely, if you are not well versed in these technologies, you will find plenty of examples and references to guide you along your hack training.

First, we cover some of the key tools you should use to get an edge when hacking Firefox. Tools covered include the Document Inspector, basic text editors, and JavaScript Console. A good portion of this chapter helps you find your personalized Firefox settings in your Profile directory and then highlights the key features of most of the files. As you continue to read this book, you will tap into many of the key components of your profile. Then we will approach the different methods of hacking the browser using some of the functionality included with the browser, such as about:config and the JavaScript Console. Finally, you'll learn the basics of changing your preferences and interface by manually hacking the prefs.js, user.js, userChrome.css, and userContent.css files. After getting all your gear, you will begin your quest to understand the core technologies involved in hacking just about every aspect of Mozilla Firefox.

by Mel Reyes

in this chapter

- ☑ Installing the Document Inspector
- ☑ Editing text tools
- ☑ Using the JavaScript Console
- ☑ Your profile explained
- ☑ Backing up before hacking

Installing the Document Inspector Gadget

Out of the box, the Firefox Installer has two installation modes: Standard and Custom. If you have already done a Standard installation, you will be missing a key hacking and programming component: the Document Inspector, or DOM Inspector.

The Document Inspector extension is a development tool used to analyze the Document Object Model (DOM) of web pages or the Firefox interface, and is very useful in digging deeper into the core structure of web pages, the Firefox browser window, and browser elements. Currently, this browser development tool is available only from Firefox's main installation process. Later in this chapter and throughout the book, you will begin to see how web page document model standards fit into Firefox's interface customization.

So you want to install the Document Inspector (also called the DOM Inspector), but you already have Firefox installed? No problem. Simply reinstall Firefox, but instead of choosing the Standard installation type, choose the Custom installation type.

Follow the prompts until you get to the Select Components screen. Select Developer Tools, by clicking the checkbox as shown in Figure 1-1, to install the Document Inspector tool.

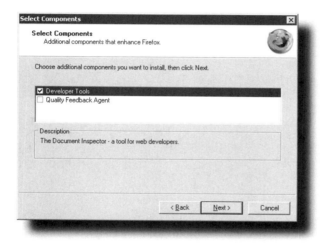

FIGURE 1-1: Install the Document Inspector tool

Once you have completed this installation or reinstallation, you will notice the DOM Inspector in your Tools menu is now available to all profiles on the system. You can use this tool as a resource for dissecting bits and pieces of web pages and the Firefox interface. Figure 1-2 shows the DOM Inspector view of a web page that is currently loaded in the main browser. Note that the hierarchy for the currently loaded web page is displayed in the left-hand panel, with each level or node grouped by the HTML-defined hierarchy and code. Additionally, details on the currently selected node are displayed in the right-hand panel; this panel becomes useful when hacking the Firefox interface.

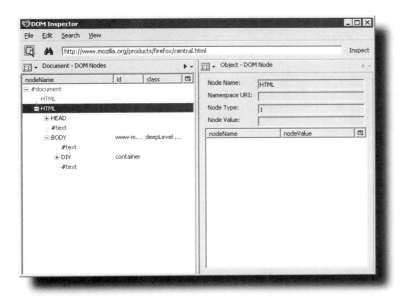

FIGURE 1-2: DOM Inspector document tree and object properties

Occasionally, I have noticed that running the DOM Inspector on a fresh install or reinstall did not yield the desired results or did not work at all. To correct this, I have tried either uninstalling Firefox and then reinstalling with the Developer Tools option enabled, or creating a new Firefox profile. Unless you are running an older version of Firefox that prompts you if you want to delete all the program files, the Firefox uninstaller retains all the supporting plugins and other files that it might need. If prompted to delete all Firefox program files, do not confirm this prompt; doing so will require reinstallation of plugin support for features such as Macromedia Flash, Shockwave, QuickTime and/or RealPlayer. Historically, uninstalling and reinstalling and/or creating a new profile have been the two methods that I have used to resolve mysterious Firefox issues when I could not consistently reproduce them.

Note   For information on how to use the Profile Manager to create a new Firefox profile, visit the incredibly useful MozillaZine Knowledge Base at `http://kb.mozillazine.org/Profile_Manager`.

While having a pretty hierarchy tree of your HTML is nice, the real benefit of the DOM Inspector is using it to hack Firefox itself. Firefox is built on a cross-platform extensible user interface language called XUL, which is based on XML standards and was created to support Mozilla applications. The user interfaces for the Mozilla Suite, Firefox, Thunderbird, and Sunbird all use XUL to create and display the user interface. This interface foundation is the core element that helps all these programs run on different operating systems. The interface is a collection of object definitions used to create each of the elements on the screen.

Using the DOM Inspector can easily help you walk through the hierarchy used to create the actual windows displayed by Firefox. To load the browser window's XUL hierarchy, just follow these steps:

1. In the main browser window navigate to any external web site, such as `http://www.mrtech.com`.

2. Open the DOM Inspector from the Tools menu. At this point, the web site opened in the previous step will be parsed.

3. From the File menu, choose the entry from the Inspect a Window menu option that corresponds with the site opened in the first step, in this case, "MRTech.com - Mozilla Firefox."

After following these steps, the nodes or page elements for the main browser window are loaded and available for visual inspection, as shown in the left-hand Document - DOM Nodes panel of Figure 1-3. For future reference, you can use the following location or URL for the main Firefox browser window to quickly browse the node tree: `chrome://browser/content/browser.xul`.

After you have the nodes listed in the left panel for the browser.xul page, just click on Inspect to the right of the location bar to open a window to browse the actual page on the bottom half of the screen (also shown in Figure 1-3).

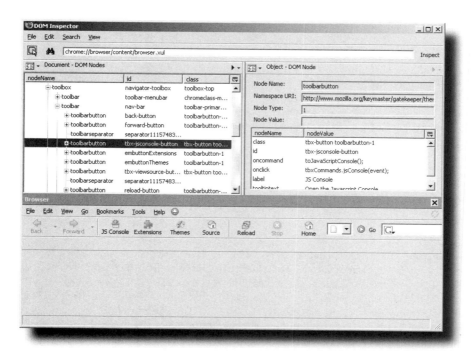

FIGURE 1-3: DOM Inspector with Firefox's browser.xul loaded

To find the internal name or id of a specific Firefox window element, I like to use the Select Element By Click option from the Search menu. Once you have selected this, you can click on any of the screen elements on the bottom half of the window and the DOM Inspector jumps to the actual definition for that element within the hierarchy. There you can easily access the internal id associated with the element and use that for future coding or manipulation.

Note The Select Element By Click option works only after you have clicked on Inspect next to the location bar.

Using the DOM Inspector and Figure 1-3, I will now explain how XUL is used to build the main Firefox browser window. As you see from this figure, there is a XUL object or node called toolbox with an id of navigator-toolbox. This object defines the top-level toolbar container on the main browser window. This container holds the three individual toolbar objects that are visible in the main window. They are toolbar-menubar, nav-bar, and PersonalToolbar. Digging deeper, the nav-bar toolbar object has a toolbarbutton object defined as back-button. This object holds the object information for the Back button, which is displayed on the browser window's navigation toolbar, and the fun continues from there with the rest of the interface XUL definitions.

All in all, the DOM Inspector is the most useful tool to begin digging around and understanding the interface elements that make up the Firefox windows.

Editing and Programming Text Tools

Another tool you will need is a good text-file editor. While the basic text editor that comes with the operating system works for some people, I have found that more functionality is desirable when working with web or Firefox files. Choose an editor with good code syntax highlighting or with other advanced options.

Key attributes to look for in a good programming editor or interface include the following:

- Is it actively developed?
- Can it support Windows, UNIX, Mac OS, and Unicode text-file formats?
- Does it have customizable tab stops or multi- or tabbed-file support?
- Is it free?

Using the editor provided by your operating system may work for you for now, but you may find yourself being a little more productive if you opt for a more up-to-date editor. Several good freeware text editors are actively developed and contain features that even the most diehard vi expert could grow to appreciate and love. Additional coverage on better programming editors is available in Chapter 16. One text editor that I have used in the past is EditPad, which works on Windows and Linux-based systems. I have also used the following Windows-based editors: Notepad++, PSPad, and the quick and simple Win32Pad.

You also have a few options for Linux distributions, including KDevelop, Nedit, Kate for KDE, or GEdit for GNOME. Apple Mac users have a lot of options for editors, including BBEdit, jEdit, and Mellel.

Tip In addition to these editors, you can download and install the chromeEdit extension, featured in Chapter 2, for basic editing of the user.js, userChrome.css, and userContent.css files. For more information or to download chromeEdit, visit `http://cdn.mozdev.org/chromedit/`.

To download any of the aforementioned editors, just visit their sites:

- **BBEdit:** `http://www.barebones.com/products/bbedit/`
- **EditPad:** `http://www.just-great-software.com/`
- **jEdit:** `http://www.jedit.org/`
- **Kdevelop:** `http://www.kdevelop.org/`
- **Mellel:** `http://www.redlers.com/`
- **Nedit:** `http://www.nedit.org/`
- **Notepad++:** `http://notepad-plus.sourceforge.net/uk/site.htm`
- **PSPad:** `http://www.pspad.com/en/`
- **Win32Pad:** `http://www.gena01.com/win32pad/`

Tip For more options and information on programming editors and software, visit `http://www.thefreecountry.com/programming/editors.shtml`.

Using the JavaScript Console

The JavaScript Console is a very handy debugging tool, is a built-in feature of Firefox, and does not require special installation. If you are a web developer or are planning on creating Firefox extensions, the JavaScript Console is the tool that you want to tap into to make sure you use the proper JavaScript syntax and to help you find your coding bugs.

To open the console, select JavaScript Console from the Tools menu. The console shows you three different types of information: Errors, Warnings, and Messages.

When first opened, JavaScript Console shows all messages for your current browser session, as illustrated in Figure 1-4. The console shows errors only if there are any; this includes errors for all sites visited since Firefox was last opened up. If there are no messages displayed, Firefox has not encountered JavaScript errors on any of the pages you have navigated to so far.

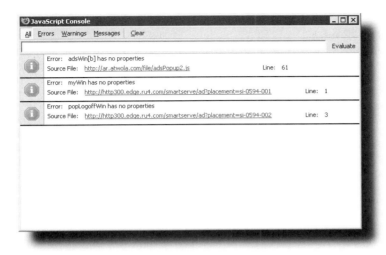

FIGURE 1-4: JavaScript errors displayed in console window

A key feature of the console is its ability to jump to the offending code if you click the Source File: link just below the error message. Doing so opens the View Source window directly to the line number referenced in the message, as shown in Figure 1-5.

```
var url=adsHt+"/html/"+MN+"/"+adsScr+"/"+adsExt+"?"+adsNMSG+"&height=

// *******************************************************************
// Open a window with the correct built URL and the correct window pe
// Make it a popunder (Netscape 6 and 7 don't allow blur so we must f
// *******************************************************************
adsNPopup = window.open (url, 'adsNPopup', a)
if (adsUA.indexOf("Netscape")!=-1) {
    window.focus()
} else {
    adsNPopup.blur()
}

// *******************************************************************
// We have shown a popunder so write a cookie in the domain of the pe
// is set in the beginning) and with the path=/ (unless set in the be
// a value (and an expires date) of the cookieTimeInHours from now.
// *******************************************************************
if (cookieDomain==""){
  var h=location.hostname,q=h.lastIndexOf('.'),ld=h.substring(q+1,h.l
  if (ld.indexOf("com")!=-1){
      dm="."+sd+"."+ld
  }
  else(
      var z=h.lastIndexOf('.',y-1),td=h.substring(z+1,y)
```

FIGURE 1-5: Source code of offending JavaScript code

Chapter 15 dives deeper into using the console and covers how to enable some of the advanced debugging preferences. The chapter also shows you how the JavaScript Console is a good area to display status messages while debugging and creating your extensions.

What and Where Is My Profile?

Your settings are stored in a Firefox directory or profile, which Firefox creates right after your first install. Your profile contains all your Firefox-specific settings, including but not limited to the following:

- Extensions
- Themes
- Bookmarks
- Saved form values
- Saved passwords

Additionally, your profile contains any imported settings from Internet Explorer, Netscape 6/7, or Mozilla browsers.

Losing any part of your profile can be extremely annoying; Chapter 2 covers how to hack settings in your Firefox profile.

To work with your current profile manually, you first need to find the root directory where your personal settings are stored. To do this, you must follow the directions specific to your operating system, shown in the next section. This operating system–dependent "settings" directory is referred to as your %UserPath% as we continue. From there, you will be able to find the path and directory structure in which Firefox has stored your user profile.

Finding Your User Path

Each operating system has a different directory to which it saves your user settings. Most applications take advantage of this operating system "user path" to store their settings, so as not to collide with other users who might log into the same computer. Firefox does the same; it uses this directory to create the user's profile. The challenge is that each operating system uses a different naming and directory structure to store these files and settings. Making life even more complicated, different versions of the same operating system (for example, Windows) use different structures. Peruse the following subsections to find the operating system you are currently using, and read how to find your user path.

Firefox Profile Name History Lesson

Throughout its development cycle, Firefox has been through a few changes. Earlier development and testing builds saved the profile and settings to the following Phoenix directory:

```
%UserPath%\Phoenix\Profiles\
```

Phoenix was the original name for the Mozilla browser–only project; this made perfect sense for the profile directory name. Even though the project name changed to Firebird for legal reasons, the Phoenix Profile directory persisted. Finally, after additional legal and copyright wrangling, the name Firefox was born. Not too long after this, the development version of Firefox included an automated migration of most of the profile entries and files from the Phoenix directory to the Firefox directory:

```
%UserPath%\Firefox\Profiles\
```

But it did not end there. The final decision made was that for new installations the root profile directory should live in harmony with the core common Mozilla directory structure and eventually become the following:

```
%UserPath%\Mozilla\Firefox\Profiles\
```

So if you have been testing Firefox for a long time now, you may have two or three directories, but only one is your current working Profile directory.

Using Windows?

If you are using Windows, your user directory should look similar to this:

- **Windows 2000/XP:** C:\Documents and Settings\<LOGINNAME>\Application Data\
- **Windows NT:** c:\Windows\Profiles\<LOGINNAME>\
- **Windows 9x/ME:** C:\Windows\Application Data\Mozilla\Firefox

Note The drive (C:\ above) and location of the default Windows directory may vary based on your custom installation.

Using Linux/UNIX?

If Linux/UNIX is your modus operandi, you should expect to find your Firefox profile in a directory similar to ~/.mozilla/firefox.

Using Mac OS?

Finally, for all you Apple aficionados, your directory structure should be something similar to ~/Library/Application Support/Firefox.

Now that you have found your user directory, this will now be referred to as %UserPath% and will be used to track down where Firefox has stored your profile.

Note

For official information on locating your Firefox profile, visit `http://www.mozilla.org/support/firefox/edit#profile`.

Express Pass to Your Profile Path

One nice feature that Firefox finally enabled is human-readable settings for the profile.ini file with the direct or relative path to the current profile(s). Prior to this, profile information was stored in binary format only, and automating and scripting Firefox profiles was difficult to do. The profiles.ini file lives in the now common path for Firefox Profiles, which is as follows: %UserPath%\Mozilla\Firefox\.

The profiles.ini file will look similar to the following if this was the first time you installed Firefox:

```
[General]
StartWithLastProfile=1

[Profile0]
Name=default
IsRelative=1
Path=default\zsryldfv.slt
```

In this first example, notice that the `IsRelative` setting is equal to 1, which is a Boolean toggle for true. This means that the path is relative to the common Mozilla Firefox path of %UserPath%\Mozilla\Firefox\, so the full directory path would look something like %UserPath%\Mozilla\Firefox\default\zsryldfv.slt.

Note that `zsryldfv` in the path is a randomly generated directory name and varies from system to system. If you had previously installed earlier builds of Firefox that stored the profiles in other places, the profiles.ini file might look something like this:

```
[General]
StartWithLastProfile=1

[Profile0]
Name=default
IsRelative=0
Path=%UserPath%\Firefox\Profiles\default\zsryldfv.slt
```

Moreover, you will notice that `IsRelative` is zero or false, so the Path entry in the file reads as-is, or absolute, and that is where you will find your current profile.

Unhide Your %UserPath% and Enable File Extensions for Windows

For Windows systems such as Windows 2000 and XP, the %UserPath% may be hidden, and a file's extensions may not be visible. To correct this situation on these systems, just follow these steps:

1. Open Windows Explorer by selecting the Run option from the Start menu.

2. Enter **explorer.exe** and press OK.

3. On the menu bar, select Tools ⇨ Folder Options, and in the View tab uncheck the "Hide extensions for known file types" option.

4. Then check the "Show hidden files and folders" option and click OK at the bottom of this dialog box.

At this point, the file listing should refresh, and hidden directories and file extensions will be available within all application and file/folder dialogs.

Backing It Up Before Hacking It Up

As with any hack or modification to a program, being able to restore to a previously working state is critical. Luckily, Firefox hacking and modifications are primarily text file based and can usually be restored very easily. For the most part in this book, we will not be hacking the binary or low-level executables of Firefox. However, you are introduced to hacking several key text files to either hack or repair your system.

This section prepares you to prepare your system for hacking and quickly points out how to back up your extensions, themes, and critical files such as your profile, and so on.

Saving the Installer, Extensions, and Theme Files

In preparation for any hacking adventure, make sure if you have to rebuild that you have all the necessary files that you previously used.

1. Make sure you create a Backup directory in a reliable location. Best practices dictate that you create a Backup folder either on your desktop or in a common backup location. This is where you want to store backups of your preferences, extensions, and any other supporting files.

2. Make sure you save the original installation file for Firefox. This will come in handy when you want to reinstall a fresh copy of the base application. Even though you probably will not do this often, there are some sections in this book where you will want to reinstall.

3. Review your currently installed extensions by going to the Extensions manager in the Tools Menu (choose Tools ⇨ Extensions). If you have none, you are all set. If you do have extensions installed, you should do the following.

   a. Go down the list of extensions in the Extensions window, right-click each extension, and choose Visit Home Page from the right-click menu.

   b. Almost every extension's support page should allow you to download the XPI or extension file by right-clicking on the download or install links and saving the file to the Backup folder you created in Step 1.

   c. Some sites use JavaScript code to install their extension. For these, you will just have to bookmark the site and revisit them in case of emergency.

4. Do the same thing for Themes that you did for Extensions. Just open the Themes window (choose Tools ⇨ Themes), run down the list of Themes, right-click each extension and choose Visit Home Page from the right-click menu for each theme, and save all of the individual Java Archive (JAR) or themes files to the backup directory.

Backing Up Critical Files

Now that you have all the core installation files backed up, you can proceed by backing up your profile. To ease into hacking Firefox, I recommend using the free MozBackup tool for Windows systems, shown in Figure 1-6, to back up and then restore your Firefox profile. Linux and Mac users should focus on finding and backing up the profile directory completely, which is also an option for Windows users. Chapter 2 covers the use for some of the files that are nicely packaged by MozBackup, and below is a list that describes some of the key files.

FIGURE 1-6: MozBackup backup selection screen

Note For more information or to download MozBackup, visit `http://mozbackup.jasnapaka` `.com/`.

Some of the critical profile files include the following:

- **bookmarks.html:** Where all the bookmark entries are stored and can be viewed with any browser.

- **cookies.txt:** Contains all cookies currently stored for all sites.

- **pref.js:** Contains all of the Firefox settings and customizations that you have made — for example, changing the homepage, location of last download folder, and so on.

- **hostperm.1:** Contains cookie and image permissions that have been enabled.

- **formhistory.dat:** Contains autocomplete data for form fields on web pages.

- **user.js, chrome/userContent.css, and chrome/userChrome.css:** Are not created by default and should be backed up if you have created or modified them.

To make a backup of your Firefox profile on Windows systems using MozBackup, follow these steps:

1. Download and install MozBackup.

2. Close all Firefox windows and run MozBackup.

3. Click Next on the Welcome screen.

4. Select the "Backup a profile" option if not already selected and the Mozilla Firefox listing at the bottom of the Operation Type screen and then click Next.

5. Select the profile you want to back up. (Most installations will have only one profile listed.) You can also select a different path to save the file and then click the Next button.

6. Choose whether you want the backup password protected, and follow the prompts if you do.

7. Select the components that you want backed up. To save space and time, leave the Cache entry unchecked and then click Next.

At this point, the backup begins and a PCV file is created with the date as part of the filename — Firefox 1.0.3 (en-US) - 7.10.2005.pcv, for example. One reason I like this tool is that it uses standard ZLib or Zip file compression to bundle the files, not a proprietary format. This means that the file is compatible with any extraction program that supports Zip files. You can open the file directly in your compression program of choice, or just rename the file extension from .pcv to .zip and quickly scan through and extract specific files.

Additionally, you can run through the MozBackup file to selectively restore any of the files that have been bundled by selecting Restore a Profile from the Operation Type screen. On the next screen, you select the profile and the backup file to restore from and then proceed by picking the files to restore.

If you use a Linux or Mac system, or you just want to cover all bases, make sure that you can find your profile and make a complete backup of the profile directory before proceeding. Chapter 2 covers how to find your profile, or you can visit the MozillaZine Knowledge Base article here at `http://kb.mozillazine.org/Profile_Folder#Firefox`.

While there are other, less critical files that you might want to back up in the installation path for the main application, the files covered here are really the core user files for running Firefox; the rest are plugins and additions that are covered in Chapters 11, 13, and 14.

So now you are ready to hack, right? Keep in mind that the backup that you just completed is an early cut of your profile. You will go through several iterations, hacks, and modifications throughout this book, and you may eventually want to revert to a previous version. Keeping backups of major milestones and achievement points will help you restore to one of your more recent working profiles. I can't stress enough how annoying it is to lose months' worth of bookmarks, hacks, installed extensions, and settings because I was too lazy to do a backup.

 Cross-Reference Chapter 14 gives you some additional tools and methods for backing up, which should make life a little easier.

Summary

This chapter is geared to help set the foundation for the rest of the book. To do so, I wanted to focus on having an understanding of some of the basic tools, such as the DOM Inspector and JavaScript Console, which will be referenced throughout the chapters. Additionally, the purpose of a profile was explained, as well as how to find it. Finally, the importance of backing up installation files, extensions, and your profile before you begin hacking was stressed. With this quick run-through of Firefox basics, we can now move on to bigger and better things.

Hacking Around Manually

Here is where we will lay the groundwork for what will be an exciting adventure into hacking Firefox. The about:config screen and the prefs.js and user.js files are covered here. We won't be taking it for a hair-raising ride yet, just kicking the tires for the time being. This chapter covers the fundamentals around the prefs.js file and user.js file. These files are critical to your settings; please do not try to edit them until you have created a backup of your profile, which is explained in Chapter 1.

Using Hidden about:config to Hack

about:config is one of the many hidden gems that you will find in Firefox. What about:config does is give you a visual interface where you can find the name of a preference and see or change its current value. You can also add new or hidden preferences via this interface. To open the about:config page, all you have to do is type **about:config** in the location bar (this is where you would normally type a web address) and press Enter.

The basic layout of the about:config screen is a list with the following four columns:

- **Preference Name:** This column is the actual preference name used by Firefox.
- **Status:** The Status is one of two different values: default or user set. This is what you use to determine whether a preference has its original or modified values.
- **Type:** This column lists the type of preference, Boolean, integer, or string. These help Firefox understand how to use the preference.
- **Value:** The value for the preference correlates to the preference name and type.

Figure 2-1 shows about:config in action.

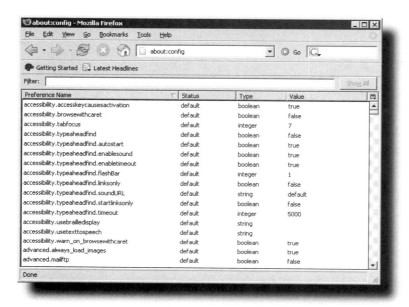

FIGURE 2-1: The about:config preference editing screen

To update or modify a value just double-click on the row. Boolean values will automatically toggle, and integer/string values will bring up a prompt. You can also right-click on the list to accomplish any of the following:

- Copy a name or value.
- Create a new/missing preference.
- Toggle to another value or reset back to the default value.

To further aid in finding preferences, you can use the Filter location bar just above the list; type in any part of a preference name, and the list will automatically filter down to preference names that contain that value. Just delete the typed filter or click Show All on the right-hand side to show all preferences again.

Typing in a filter of "throbber" brings up the browser.throbber.url preference, which just so happens to be the only preference entry with "throbber" in it, as shown in Figure 2-2.

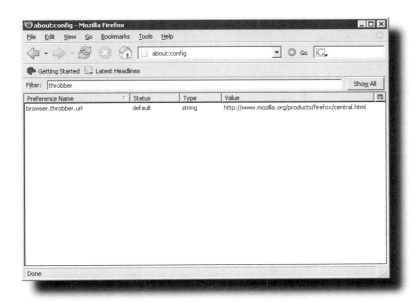

FIGURE 2-2: Results of searching for "throbber" in about:config

One excellent reference for preference names and descriptions is available on the Preferential Extension web site. This extension and web page, though somewhat dated, contain names and descriptions for the Mozilla Suite, Firefox, and Thunderbird preferences that you can tweak and hack. You can find the web site at `http://preferential.mozdev.org/ preferences.html`.

Hacking Your Profile Settings

This section covers how to manually make setting changes to your Firefox profile using the prefs.js and user.js files. Both files are plain text files, but only prefs.js is created with a default installation. The syntax used in each file is the same, is very strict, and is covered here, but make sure to carefully review manual changes to either before hacking away.

Hacking the prefs.js File

Firefox uses a file called prefs.js to store customized preference settings in a name-value pair function in the root of your profile directory. This name-value pair directly coincides with the Preference Name and Value on the about:config screen, covered in the previous section. Key features available via the Tools ⇨ Options menu, plus customizations such as homepage and extension settings, are stored in this file.

The foundation for these settings is a JavaScript call to user_pref with a key and a value. The basic format of this call is as follows:

```
user_pref("SystemPreference") = "MyValue";
```

The preference key is SystemPreference, and the key's associated value is MyValue. The prefs.js file may contain a small number of preference entries or quite a few if you have customized several browser options or installed any extensions. Figure 2-3 shows the prefs.js file open in a standard text editor.

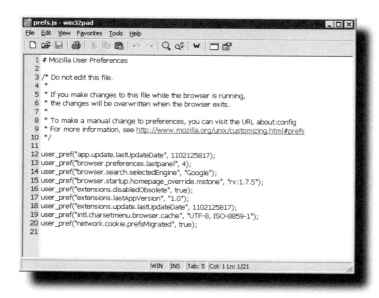

FIGURE 2-3: Default prefs.js created with a new profile

Customized variables from the prefs.js are populated only once, when the browser starts up, and are saved only when Firefox is completely shut down. Keep this in mind, because manually modifying the prefs.js file while Firefox is open will nullify your prefs.js hacking efforts. This is because the file is overwritten with what Firefox has in memory when it shuts down. Each customized preference entry is stored one per line in this file. In the case of a browser crash, any recent preferences changes are lost. Firefox has built-in default values, which are used if a preference setting is not explicitly included or modified in the prefs.js file.

Here is a basic example of how to modify the prefs.js file. In the about:config search example illustrated in the previous section, you found browser.throbber.url as the Preference Name when searching for "throbber." The *throbber* is your activity indicator; it is the moving status icon on the top-right side of the browser window. The throbber URL or web page loads if you click on the throbber at any point. Please note this is different from your homepage, which is associated with your startup page, new window, and so on.

Keeping in mind that you have to close out all your Firefox browser windows, you can now drill into the %UserPath% and Profiles directory structure to find and open the prefs.js file. The basic format that you want to use is to mimic the name/value keys format as follows:

```
user_pref("browser.throbber.url") =
"http://www.hackingfirefox.com/";
```

Note that this is actually one continuous line, although it appears on two lines here.

Once you have opened up the prefs.js file in your editor, you can do a search for throbber to see if that entry already exists and change it. If the entry does not exist, you can manually type it in, or you can go directly to the end of the prefs.js file and add your entry there. Adding an entry to the bottom of the prefs.js file works very well because Firefox reads this file in sequentially and the last key-value association is the pair that is used. While there is extreme merit in forcing yourself to find and manually update the actual entry needed, I have found myself with prefs.js files as large as 500 to 700 lines long depending on how many extensions or options I have played around with. Hunting and pecking for multiple preferences is not at the top of my list. Call it laziness or call it genius for tapping into the quick-turnaround techniques of copy and paste, but you know which one I prefer; now you can decide for yourself.

For example, you can see in the following that the prefs.js already has a custom entry for the throbber:

```
user_pref("browser.throbber.url") =
"http://www.hackingfirefox.com/";
user_pref("SystemPreference1") = "MyValue";
user_pref("SystemPreference2") = "MyValue";
user_pref("SystemPreference3") = "MyValue";
user_pref("SystemPreference4") = "MyValue";
```

Then you can just add the new entry to the bottom, like this:

```
user_pref("browser.throbber.url") =
"http://www.hackingfirefox.com/";
user_pref("SystemPreference1") = "MyValue";
user_pref("SystemPreference2") = "MyValue";
user_pref("SystemPreference3") = "MyValue";
user_pref("SystemPreference4") = "MyValue";
user_pref("browser.throbber.url") = "http://www.mrtech.com/";
```

When Firefox initially reads in the prefs.js it sets the browser.throbber.url preference equal to http://www.hackingfirefox.com/. Then it continues parsing the additional entries and finds that browser.throbber.url preference value is now equal to http://www.mrtech .com/, so the earlier value is negated. When Firefox shuts down, it writes a single row for each preference with the latest value; in this case, browser.throbber.url is equal to http://www .mrtech.com/. Future startups will not mention the http://www.hackingfirefox .com/ site again.

Hacking the user.js File

The user.js file is very much like the prefs.js file in format and functionality. The key difference is that the user.js file is used to set or reset preferences to a default value. Upon restarting the browser, the user.js settings supersede the stored values of the prefs.js file. The user.js file is static and does not get manipulated by Firefox; it is used only to set or reset values in the prefs.js file. So, using this file you can easily deploy a common set of hacks to all users in an organization or to your friends. The user.js file is not initially created with the default profile settings and must be created when needed. For example, if I had five computers on which I wanted to synchronize some basic Firefox preferences, I would create one user.js file and add entries such as the following:

```
// Set link for Throbber icon click
user_pref("browser.throbber.url") = "http://www.mrtech.com/";

// Turn on Find As You Type (FAYT)
user_pref("accessibility.typeaheadfind", true);

//Autostart FAYT
user_pref("accessibility.typeaheadfind.autostart", true);

// Search all text with FAYT
user_pref("accessibility.typeaheadfind.linksonly", false);

// Set FAYT Timeout in Milliseconds
user_pref("accessibility.typeaheadfind.timeout", 3000);
```

Once the user.js file is created, I can close Firefox and copy the file to the profile directory on each computer. The next time and every time the browser is loaded after that, these settings will supersede the values that are stored in the prefs.js file, even if the user manually changed the prefs.js, used about:config, or changed the preferences in the Tools ⇨ Options menu. Making preference changes that conflict with values in the user.js within a browsing works only for the remainder of the time the browser is opened; closing and relaunching Firefox forces the user.js settings to be reapplied.

A key thing to remember is that removing values from the user.js file will not automatically remove them for the prefs.js; you must do this manually Therefore, if you want to reset or remove a preference you should include a line with the original default value in the user.js, as follows:

```
user_pref("SystemPreference") = "DefaultValue";
```

Or, optionally, you should make sure that the values are completely reset, close Firefox, and remove the setting from both the user.js and the prefs.js files. While theoretically you can use the user.js file as a one-time feature to set values, I have always been concerned with third-party tools or extensions tapping into specific preferences. For this reason, I always collect my defaults and have the user.js apply these defaults each time. This way, I am assured that my settings and preferences are strictly adhered to and applied every time I start up Firefox.

Note For more speed, performance, security, and other hacks visit MR Tech's Mozilla, Firefox & Thunderbird Hacks at `http://www.mrtech.com/hacks.html`.

Hacking Browser and Web Page Content

This section explains how to modify the browser's interface and manipulate content. The userChrome.css and userContent.css are Cascading Style Sheet files that use specific rules to manipulate many visual aspects of the browsing experience. Some aspects include menu or web page font sizes, spacing around toolbar icons or web page images, and hiding menus or menu options or other screen elements. The userChrome.css file is used to manipulate the Firefox interface, while userContent.css is used to manipulate actual web pages.

Note For official Mozilla examples for customizing the userChrome.css or userContent.css files, visit `http://www.mozilla.org/unix/customizing.html`.

Hacking the userChrome.css File

This section gives you a fundamental understanding of how to use userChrome.css to modify your browser's appearance. Examples that are more advanced and more details on how to modify this file appear in coming chapters. The userChrome.css file is located in the chrome subdirectory of your profile; on default or new builds, this file does not exist. A sample file called userChrome-example.css comes with new installations of Firefox and contains some basic examples. To test the examples in this section, you can edit the userChrome-example.css file and copy it into the chrome directory in your profile folder as userChrome.css.

The userChrome.css file is really a Cascading Style Sheet (CSS), very much like those that you use for normal HTML web pages. Where a style sheet on a web page usually modifies visual elements of the page, such as graphics, colors, placement, and so on, the userChrome.css file modifies visual elements of the entire Firefox interface, what we like to call *chrome*.

How is this possible? you may ask. Well, this is just one of the many fundamental differences between the Mozilla base code and other browsers, let alone other development platforms. Since shortly after Netscape began the Mozilla project, the Mozilla has aimed to create core low-level components with top-layer user interfaces that are cross-platform compatible. This cross-platform focus spawned the ability to create a customizable and extensible user interface. This customizable user interface initiative led to the creation of Mozilla's XML User Interface Language (XUL), as well as CSS support for interface and dialog presentation. Later chapters dig into the browser's user interface model and dissect a few of the key screens.

To continue with a simple example, assume that we know that the id or name for the throbber icon is throbber-box. Now that we have that, you can change the display property of this element to either hide it or to change its visual properties, such as space padding and so on.

To hide the throbber on the browser chrome, the entry in the userChrome.css file would look like this:

```
#throbber-box {
    display: none !important;
}
```

When you restart the browser, you will notice that the throbber is gone. Using common CSS techniques, the default style of the throbber box has been overwritten to change its presentation.

For a good list of interface ids that are available and that are accessible via userChrome.css customizations, visit http://www.extensionsmirror.nl/index.php?showtopic=96.

This next example changes some of the properties around the throbber box instead of hiding it. The basic properties we will modify are border, margins, and padding. Where the border is drawn around the object, padding is added within the boundaries of the border, and margins are added outside the border boundaries:

```
#throbber-box      {
    border: 1px solid BLUE !important;

    padding-left: 5px !important;
    padding-right: 5px !important;

    margin-left: 20px !important;
    margin-right: 20px !important;
}
```

Additionally, let's increase the width of the search bar by adding the following code:

```
#search-container, #searchbar {
    -moz-box-flex: 300 !important;
}
```

This change just about doubles the current width of the search bar for easier viewing of long search strings.

Figure 2-4 shows Firefox without customizations.

FIGURE 2-4: Plain throbber in top-right corner

Figure 2-5 shows Firefox with throbber and search-bar customizations.

FIGURE 2-5: Throbber with border, spacing, and margin customizations, and wider search bar

What you should notice is a blue 1-pixel border around the throbber, with 5 pixels of padding space to the left and right inside the border, and 20 pixels of margin spacing outside the border. Additionally, the search bar is now wider and will resize dynamically if the window becomes smaller. The properties that are included here are standard Cascading Style Sheet properties.

Note For full CSS Level 1 standards and documentation, visit `http://www.w3.org/TR/REC-CSS1/`. Additionally, for CSS Level 2 standards, visit `http://www.w3.org/TR/REC-CSS2/`.

Hacking the userContent.css File

Much like userChrome.css, the userContent.css file uses CSS standards to allow you to manipulate properties. The key difference is that userContent.css alters the style or layout of the web page content instead of user interface elements. The userChrome.css file is also located in the chrome subdirectory of the profile, and a sample userChrome-example.css file is included with new profiles. To test the examples in this section, you can edit the userContent-example.css file and copy it into the chrome directory in your profile folder as userContent.css.

Later in the book, you see how to use the userContent.css file to block unwanted advertisements. This section includes a basic example of how to manipulate the browser's content to show a red dashed border around links that target a new window. The changes applied in this example modify web page links with targets of _new and _blank. These targets tell the browser to open a new window with the content from the link when clicked.

The syntax for this customization is much like that of the previous userChrome.css example:

```
/* Put dashed red border around links that open a new window */
:link[target="_blank"], :link[target="_new"],
:visited[target="_blank"], :visited[target="_new"] {
    border: thin dashed red;
    padding: 2px !important;
}
```

Both the border and padding property should look familiar and behave the same as in the previous example. The key difference here is that the intended object is a link that has a target of either _blank or _new.

Notice the dashed borders (they will appear red on your screen) around links on the page shown in Figure 2-6.

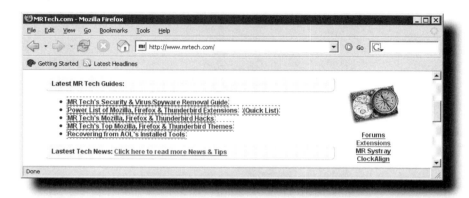

FIGURE 2-6: Customizations applied by userContent.css to a page

Alternatively, you can split the style, one for a normal link and one for a visited link, where the visited link would have a different-colored border, in this case blue:

```
/* Put dashed red border around links that open a new window */
:link[target="_blank"], :link[target="_new"] {
    border: thin dashed red;
    padding: 2px !important;
}

/* Put dashed blue border around visited links that open a new
window */
:visited[target="_blank"], :visited[target="_new"]{
    border: thin dashed blue;
    padding: 2px !important;
}
```

Basic Hacking with Extensions

Using extensions can lead to some of your best hacking. The concept of extensions is straightforward, and the availability and diversity of extensions are incredible. The extensions discussed in this section have excellent features and each is briefly covered with references to the key features that will help you in hacking your browser experience. While hacking extensions themselves is covered in Chapter 3, this section covers basic extensions that you can use to hack preferences, settings, and the Firefox interface. The chromEdit extension is best suited for editing the user.js, userChrome.css, and userContent.css files, while Configuration Mania and Preferential extensions are great tools for tweaking preferences and settings. These extensions are tried and true and have become indispensable tools in my everyday hacking.

Hacking with the chromEdit Extension

When working with the four key files that Firefox uses for customization, you may quickly find it an annoyance to have to browse over to a separate editor and then load up the file you need. Whether it is the userChrome.css, userContent.css, or user.js file, chromEdit gives you an editing environment right in a browser window (see Figure 2-7).

The chromEdit extension creates a multitab window with editing capabilities for each, except prefs.js, which is available only in this screen in read-only mode. Because the prefs.js file is overwritten when you close your browser, it really does not make sense for this editor to allow modifications to the file while the browser is open. It does let you view it, though, so you can reference existing preferences that are already set in the file.

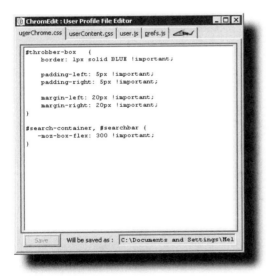

FIGURE 2-7: The chromEdit window with edit tabs

Note For more information or to download chromEdit, visit `http://cdn.mozdev.org/chromedit/`.

When changing any of the files, make sure you click Save on each window to ensure your changes are applied. Much like editing these files manually, the changes will not take effect until the next full browser restart.

> **Tip** By default, chromEdit is opened in a separate window. To have it open in a tab instead, just add the following user preference to the user.js file:
>
> ```
> user_pref("extensions.chromedit.openintab", true);
> ```

Hacking with the Configuration Mania Extension

The Configuration Mania extension allows you to tweak several of the preferences that are not available via the standard Preferences screen (see Figure 2-8). Given the incredible flexibility of Firefox, this tool really comes in handy when you need to change the low-level settings to improve performance, usability, or navigation, or for development purposes. Each section has several options, which are categorized by the following:

- Browser
- HTTP Network
- Chrome Uninstaller
- Mouse Wheel
- Keyboard Navigation
- Master Password
- Debug

This extension is a good way to get around having to find preference names and values to tweak your browser and can be used to get your feet wet with hacking Firefox preferences and tweaking hidden settings.

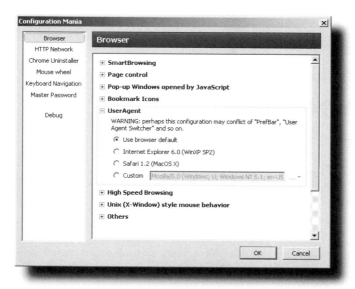

FIGURE 2-8: Configuration Mania window with several tweaking and hacking options

Note You can find the Configuration Mania homepage at `http://members.lycos.co.uk/ toolbarpalette/confmania/index_en.html`.

Hacking with the Preferential Extension

The Preferential extension, while dated, offers an incredibly easy interface to view all current and available preferences in a hierarchical mode, as shown in Figure 2-9. Once the interface has been opened and after each of the categories has been populated, you can peruse each setting by expanding and collapsing each key in the hierarchy. Preferential creates a hierarchical view based on the groupings and separation of preferences by the period(s) in the preference name. Preferential builds a hierarchy tree where, for example, browser.throbber.url would have a top hierarchy level of browser, a subhierarchy level of browser.throbber, and one property of browser.throbber.url, as shown in Figure 2-10. The number of levels is driven by the number of period-separated values in the preference name. So a preference such as font.default would have one level only, font, and a preference such as sessionsaver.static.default.cookies would have a hierarchy tree of three levels: sessionsaver, then sessionsaver.static, and then sessionsaver. static.default. The final level would be the value of sessionsaver.static.default.cookies.

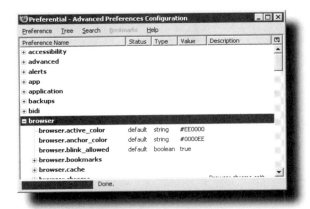

FIGURE 2-9: Preferential window with top-level browser tree expanded

One great benefit of this extension is that it can show you a description for many of the common preferences. However, because the extension is not actively being maintained, some descriptions may be blank. Another great feature is that you can delete a preference tree without having to search through files or other dialogs. All you have to do is click on the tree level that you want to remove and then right-click and delete. To accomplish this with about:config, you would have to reset each individual setting. For example, suppose you just installed the Session Saver extension and after using it realized that you really didn't want it, so you uninstalled it. While uninstalling removes the files and the extension information from your profile, it does not remove your customized settings from your prefs.js file. Typically, you would have to close Firefox, open the prefs.js file, remove the sessionsaver entries, save the file, and relaunch Firefox. Optionally, you could open the about:config tool from the main browser window, apply a filter of "sessionsaver," and then right-click and reset each value, which for this extension could total over 30 entries. Using Preferential you avoid all this; you quickly peruse your setting and just delete the top-level hierarchy of sessionsaver, and all 30+ settings would be removed without your having to restart Firefox or reset each value.

When launching this extension (by choosing Tools ➪ Advanced Preferences . . .) you see the progress dialog showing you the status as it populates the whole tree.

Figure 2-10 shows the Preferential window with an expanded preference view.

Note For more information or to download Preferential, visit `http://preferential.mozdev` `.org/`.

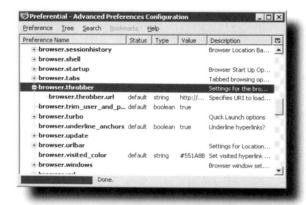

FIGURE 2-10: **Preferential window with top-level "browser.throbber" tree expanded**

To edit the preference, just right-click and choose Edit Selected from the context menu. Most interface preferences changes take effect on restart; although some should be available immediately.

Note You may receive a misleading warning when launching Preferential which states that it needs to "launch an external application." This is a false-positive warning and should be ignored. Press OK or Cancel; neither option will launch an external application.

Hacking an Extension's Options

When you install an extension, an entry gets created in the Extensions manager (see Figure 2-11), which can be opened up from the Tools menu. Several extensions have additional customizations and properties that you can tweak. To open up the options for an extension (if any), just select the extension desired and click the Options button or right-click to bring up the context menu.

FIGURE 2-11: Extension Manager window with right-click context menu

Remember that not all extensions have an option dialog, but many do. The Options button is grayed out unless options are available for the extension. Additionally, each extension that does have an options dialog varies in size and options.

For example, Figure 2-12 shows the options dialog for the Bookmark Backup extension.

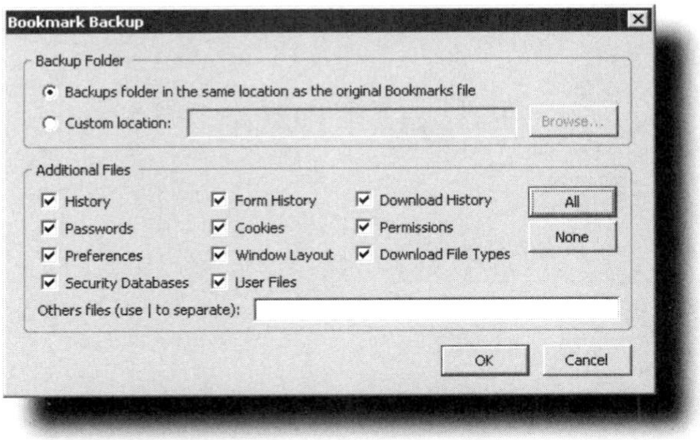

FIGURE 2-12: Bookmark Backup allows you to modify the default files to back up.

The Bookmark Backup extension options illustrated here create copies of the select files to either the default directory or to a custom directory each time you close your browser. The files are saved in directories by weekday: one for Monday, one for Tuesday, and so on.

Summary

This chapter begins the whirlwind of hacking Firefox by introducing the about:config functionality that is built into Firefox, then jumping right into ways of hacking the profile settings. You met the prefs.js, user.js, userChrome.css, and userContent.css files, and learned how to best use each one to get started with hacking Firefox. Finally, this chapter introduced three great hacking extensions: chromEdit, Configuration Mania, and Preferential.

Hacking Extensions

Folks who hopped on the Mozilla bandwagon early enough have seen a monstrous coding effort with regards to locking down the interface and developing methods of enhancing or extending the browser. Seeing the changes firsthand has given me a true appreciation for the Mozilla movement and the developers behind the curtains. From version to version prior to the 1.0 release of Firefox, there were numerous changes to the backend calls that were available, as well as many refinements to how the browser handled, stored, and installed extensions. This combined with the fundamental differences between how the Mozilla Suite and Firefox handle extensions has led to some major hacking by extension developers and users, yours truly included. While the concept and approach for creating extensions for Mozilla and Firefox are similar, there are some basic differences. These differences and the need to port or convert Mozilla Suite coding efforts to Firefox may warrant actual hacking of Firefox's base extension install file or the cross-platform installer (XPI) to get them working properly.

Tip Despite the .xpi file extension, the basic file format of an extension is a standard compressed ZIP file.

The following section covers what you might have to do to get an abandoned or older extension working for you in the latest release. This chapter is also a good primer for understanding the fundamentals of extensions, from how they are packaged to how to quickly get older extensions and functionality back up and running. Later in this chapter, I'll walk you through the process of cleaning up your profile and references to older extensions so that you have a clean slate to start installing extensions and themes again.

Understanding Older versus Newer Extensions

If you were an early adopter of Firefox, you know that the old method of managing extensions was completely revamped and moved from the Tools ⇨ Options submenu to a new interface called the Extension Manager, shown in Figure 3-1. This move, coupled with the changes in the format of the definition file embedded within each XPI, temporarily caused some major bumps in the road for users due to version incompatibilities, installation issues, and profile corruption. These were eventually smoothed out with updates from the extension developers. Some of the reasoning behind the changes included a need to track, disable, uninstall, and provide additional extension options for users.

FIGURE 3-1: Firefox's new Extension Manager window

Prior to the 1.0 release, Firefox development went through several version milestones (such as version 0.8 or 0.9). In the later development cycles, the formatting for how to package an extension changed, and a new standard was set specifically to help better manage compatibility, installation, and so on. There were several ways of recovering from older released builds and extensions—for example, by just upgrading an extension or hacking the original extension installer. Others required an outright fresh start. Because of the number of changes from earlier builds, it is always recommended that you create a new profile to correct legacy issues, but I do not subscribe to that school of thought. I've always wanted to know what was going on underneath that I could hack around and fix.

Recovering from Disabled Older Extensions

When upgrading from one of these earlier builds, access to older extensions was no longer available because the interface was removed from the Tools ⇨ Options submenu and only newly formatted extensions were listed in the Extension Manager. If you planned it right, you could have modified the disabling of obsolete extensions by changing the `extensions.disabledObsolete` hidden preference from true to false in your prefs.js or user.js file prior to upgrading and would have saved yourself some time.

```
user_pref("extensions.disabledObsolete", false);
```

If you make this change prior to upgrading to a newer version of Firefox, your extensions are not automatically disabled. This does run the risk of making Firefox crash or become inoperable and should be used cautiously. (Making backups of your profile is always recommended.) Because this is a hidden preference and information on it is difficult to find, we now come to the reason to hack the XPI file or to use extensions such as Show Old Extensions and Extension Uninstaller. With these extensions, you have a fighting chance of recovering or cleaning up your profile without having to scrap all the stored settings by creating a new one. In my experience, well over 90 percent of the extensions worked perfectly. They simply lacked the 1.0 version label updated in the install.rdf or installer manifest file that is embedded within the XPI file.

When first upgrading to one of the builds with the newer Extension Manager, one of my most used extensions was probably Show Old Extensions. It allows you to see older extensions in your Extension Manager. This was very important because several extensions had not been updated to support this newer format and this was the only way to access the options for an older extension, let alone see what version you had installed without having to dig into the chrome directory or the chrome.rdf file.

Note

You can download the Show Old Extensions extension at `http://www.pikey.me.uk/mozilla/`.

In Figure 3-2, you see that using Show Old Extensions shows the Extension Uninstaller extension with a bright red icon, which denotes that it is an older extension. Without the Show Old Extensions extension, none of the older extensions installed would show up on the list.

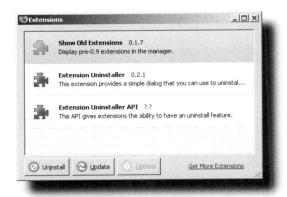

FIGURE 3-2: Extension Uninstaller as displayed by Show Old Extensions

Note

If it is installed, you will need to disable the Slim List Extension extension for Show Old Extensions to work properly.

Removing Older Extensions

Now that you can see your old extensions, you can use this tool to get back up and running. When upgrading from versions 0.8 through the 0.9 Preview to version 1.0, all extensions that were not 1.0-compatible were automatically disabled unless you had the `extensions` `.disabledObsolete` preference set to false. During the upgrade, some extensions were checked against the Mozilla Update site to find upgraded versions, but the site usually did not have an update. If no compatible update was found, it was left as a disabled extension. So you now had two issues: The extension was disabled, and if you did not have Show Old Extensions installed, you were not able to access them. With Show Old Extensions installed, you could try to enable the extension and see if it would work as is; at the very least, you had some information as to the extensions you had installed. So you could move on to upgrading and uninstalling older versions.

While some have had little to no luck with Extension Uninstaller, my experience has been positive in using this to clean house with both Firefox and the Mozilla Suite. This extension adds a submenu to your Tools menu called Extension Uninstaller that, when launched, pops up a custom dialog listing all old extensions. Because Extension Uninstaller is in the older extension format, you can see how to uninstall it using its own features.

Figure 3-3 shows that installing Extension Uninstaller also installs a supporting extension called Extension Uninstaller API. This is an advanced programming interface that allows others to tap into common uninstall functionality. To open the window, select Extension Uninstaller from the Tools menu.

FIGURE 3-3: Main Extension Uninstaller dialog

All old extensions can be uninstalled at the same time. After restarting Firefox, you should not see a reference to them in the Extension Manager.

To uninstall an extension, follow these steps:

1. Select it from the list.

2. Click Uninstall.

3. Confirm the "Are you SURE..." dialog by clicking OK.

4. Close the confirmation dialog.

Repeat these steps until you have uninstalled all of your older extensions and then restart your Firefox. When uninstalling the Extension Uninstaller, you'll notice that the option is removed from both the Extension Manager and the Tools menu.

Tip In the irony of all ironies, you can uninstall the Extension Uninstaller using itself. Just follow the steps above and select the Extension Uninstaller and API entries to uninstall and restart your browser.

Note You can download the Extension Uninstaller extension at `http://www.mozmonkey.com/extuninstaller/`.

Starting Over without Losing All Your Settings

Starting over using the steps listed in this section is the easiest way to remove all old references and still keep your settings, saved login, cookies, and so on. What you want to do is remove the files and directories associated with the old and new extensions and themes. I have personally done this more times than I really want to admit to, but here goes. Using the location of your profile that you found from Chapter 1, you will now dig in and find the items to delete.

Tip If you plan on reinstalling extensions and themes immediately afterward, skip to the "Listing Your Extensions and Themes" section in this chapter to make sure you have all the names and links you will need to easily and quickly rebuild.

Step 1

First, you want make sure that you close Firefox completely and make a backup of your profile before you continue. Closing Firefox completely assures that any files that are in use are not locked for backing up and also makes sure that files like prefs.js, bookmarks.html, and formhistory.dat files are properly flushed and saved to the hard drive. In this example, my profile is saved to C:\...\Firefox\Profiles\default\zsryldfv.slt\.

Taking it from there, find and open the chrome directory (see Figure 3-4). At this point, you want to remove all the files and directories *except* for the following (if they exist):

- userChrome.css
- userContent.css

Tip   Extensions such as BugMeNot and Sage create noncritical temporary files in the chrome directory, which are re-created when reinstalling and using them for the first time. These are safe to delete.

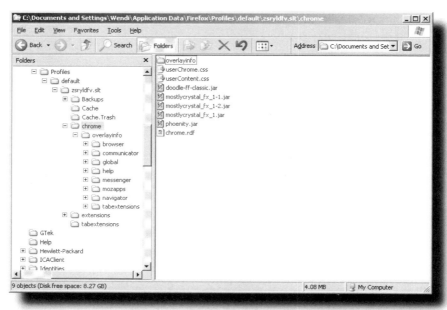

FIGURE 3-4: Firefox Profile directory before cleanup; under Windows XP

Step 2

Remove the extensions directory located in the Profile directory. This is the location for all of the newer extensions and themes and should probably be cleaned up every now and then anyway.

Step 3

Firefox creates a fast load file that is located in the root of your Profile directory and is called either xul.mfl or xul.mfasl, depending on your operating system. This file is a compilation of the currently install browse interface or XUL customizations. It is refreshed or re-created when Firefox closes, but it is imperative to remove it if you have completed Steps 1 and 2, as references to extensions that the XUL cache file contains will be invalidated by these steps.

That's it. You are now ready to reopen Firefox, and you're back to your original clean slate with regards to extensions and themes. Firefox recovers itself by re-creating all the necessary files and directories it needs to continue loading. Your preferences and other settings are still intact, and you can proceed with rebuilding your arsenal.

Why Won't Some Extensions Install?

Have you ever tried installing an extension from a site only to find that the extension will not install as promised? Were you able to figure out how to install it? This section covers why some sites do not install properly and how to get around these limitations.

There are two ways that an extension can be properly installed from a web server. One is by having the web server send the correct Mime Type associated with the extension file; the other is by using the built-in JavaScript functionality available to Mozilla applications. Some web-hosting providers and some extensions developers still do not properly handle extensions, leaving it up to the user to figure things out. From the web-hosting standpoint, all the developer or hosting provider has to do is add an XPI mime-type to the server's configuration.

 Chapter 11 contains more information on Mime Types.

The entry below can be easily added to Apache .htaccess or httpd.conf files to add prompt Mime Type support for XPI file extensions that are associated with Firefox Extensions:

```
AddType application/x-xpinstall .xpi
```

This Mime Type can also be added to Microsoft IIS web server by selecting the MIME Map or MIME Types options from the IIS Manager's Properties dialog for the site in question.

Despite the ease of this step, some web-hosting providers may not allow changes to site settings, leaving the developer with no quick server-based solutions. Knowing this, developers should use the standard JavaScript functionality to prompt Firefox to download the file as an extension, but they fail to do that as well. So that leaves you downloading an XPI file to your hard drive and not knowing what to do with it.

Developers who want to add Extension JavaScript installation support to links can use the following code:

```
<a href="extension.xpi" onClick="if(typeof(InstallTrigger)!=
'undefined') {var InstallXPI = {'Extension Installation':
'extension.xpi'}; InstallTrigger.install(InstallXPI); return
false;}" type=" application/x-xpinstall">Install Extension Here</a>
```

This code gives both support for left-click installation as well as for right-click and "Save Link As" support.

The following is an explanation of how to install an extension remotely (or from a site that does prompt you), and how to install an extension locally from your hard drive. Where and how an extension is saved to your profile is also covered.

Installing Remotely versus Locally

Installing remotely is virtually a no-brainer, thanks to the beauty of Firefox. If everything is as it should be, you simply click on the install or extension link. You get a time-delayed confirmation screen, as shown in Figure 3-5. Click OK, and the extension adds itself to your list and is available when you restart your browser.

FIGURE 3-5: Firefox Extension Install prompt

Easy, right? But what do you do when it prompts you to download? The best thing to do is to save the file to a common location such as your desktop. Then all you have to do from within Firefox is open the file.

1. Select File ⇨ Open File.

2. Navigate to your desktop or the directory you saved the file to.

3. Type ***.xpi** and press Enter in the File name: input box.

4. Select the XPI extension file you just downloaded and click Open.

At this point, Firefox displays the standard installation dialog. Alternatively, you can open the Extension Manager and drag the extension file into that window to achieve the same results.

Tip

Another great drag-and-drop tip is that you can drag and drop multiple extension files to the main browser window or Extensions Manager window to install more than one extension at a time.

Keep in mind that drag-and-drop extension functionality is not available on all operating systems.

Using MR Tech's Local Install Extension

One thing that really bothered me with regards to the Extension and Theme Managers was the inconsistency between Firefox and other products such as Thunderbird and, most recently, NVU in providing an Install button in the manager window. So I hacked together MR Tech's Local Install (see Figure 3-6), whose roots started with the Install New Theme extension by Bradley Chapman.

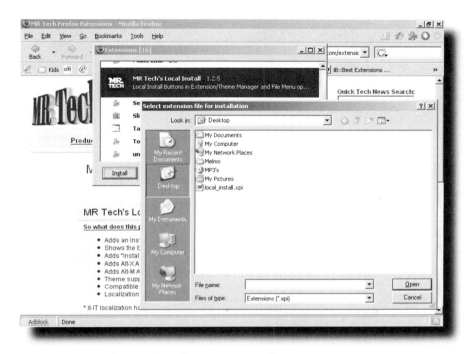

FIGURE 3-6: MR Tech's Local Install extension installation

Originally, I wanted just to mirror for the Extension Manager the Install button functionality that Bradley had created for the Theme Manager. Version 1.0 was quickly built and released. Since then, File menu, shortcut keys, and international localizations have been added.

More features are planned for the future. The basic idea is that you can now easily choose local copies of extensions and themes. For extensions, it automatically defaults to a *.xpi file type, and for themes, it defaults to a *.jar file type, making it easier to distinguish those files from others you might have saved in the same directory.

Note   For more information or to download MR Tech's Local Install, visit `http://www.mrtech`
`.com/extensions/`.

Where Did It Get Installed?

Firefox uses an XML-based file to store a listing of extensions and themes; the file is formatted to Resource Description Framework (RDF) specifications. The Extensions.rdf file is located in the extensions directory of your profile, as shown in Figure 3-7. The new standard in creating and installing an extension is to assign your extension or theme a unique 32-character Globally Unique Identifier (GUID). GUIDs are generated using a combination of variables to create a globally unique id. For example, the GUID for MR Tech's Local Install extension is

{9669CC8F-B388-42FE-86F4-CB5E7F5A8BDC}. Now all you have to do is find the directory corresponding to that GUID in the extensions directory to find the supporting files for my extension.

Note To create a GUID for your own testing or development, visit http://www.hoskinson .net/webservices/guidgeneratorclient.aspx.

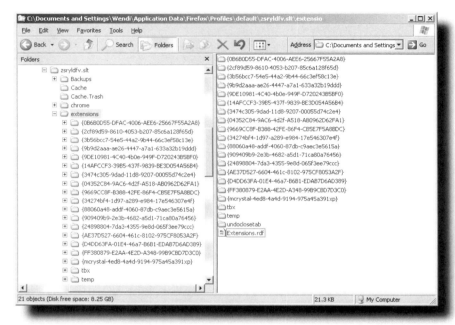

FIGURE 3-7: Firefox's extension directory

When you add a new extension or theme, a temporary copy is placed in the temp folder under the extension directory. When you restart, the extension is installed or reinstalled in its prospective directory.

Hacking Older Extensions

Hacking an extension, old or new, is relatively easy; all you really need is a decent compression program that handles ZIP files and a decent text editor. Despite the file extension of .xpi, an extension is really just a standard ZIP file. So you can easily open or extract the contents using any common compression program.

Changing Supported Version Number

You might come across an extension that you believe will work well with the latest release of Firefox but just has not been updated to include the 1.0 versioning in the install.rdf file embedded within the XPI. That is when you whip out your compression tools. (My preference on Windows systems is 7-Zip.) Using 7-Zip to update an extension's supported Firefox version numbers is a breeze; but first, let's configure it properly to make it easier to use.

Note You can download 7-Zip at `http://www.7-zip.org/`.

To configure 7-Zip for easy access to all archives, just make sure you have Shell Integration enabled by following these steps:

1. Open the 7-Zip Manager program.

2. Select Tools ➪ Options.

3. Click on the Plugins tab.

4. Click on the Options tab (see Figure 3-8).

5. Make sure that the Integrate 7-Zip to shell context menu is enabled.

FIGURE 3-8: 7-Zip Plugin options configuration window

Optionally, you can also have it as a Cascaded context menu so you don't clutter up your right-click menu with too many options.

At this point, all you have to do is find the extension you saved locally and choose Open archive from the right-click menu. If you enabled the cascaded context menu option, Open archive will be under a 7-Zip submenu. Figure 3-9 displays the contents of the extension.

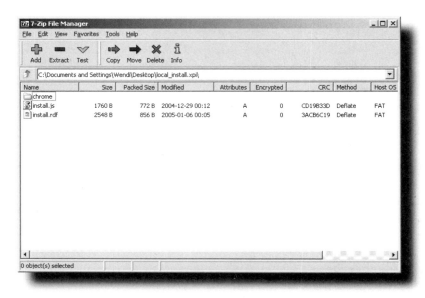

FIGURE 3-9: 7-Zip File Manager window

Now you just have to select the install manifest or install.rdf file and either press the F4 function key or choose the File ➪ Edit submenu to load the file for editing. Once opened, look for the `maxVersion` string, which should look similar to this:

```
<em:targetApplication> <!-- Firefox -->
    <Description>
        <em:id>{ec8030f7-c20a-464f-9b0e-13a3a9e97384}</em:id>
        <em:minVersion>0.7</em:minVersion>
        <em:maxVersion>0.9</em:maxVersion>
    </Description>
</em:targetApplication>
```

Now you can change the `maxVersion` line value of 0.9 to 1.0, save the file, and exit your text editor. The 7-Zip Manager detects that you have updated the install.rdf file and prompts you to update the extension file with the change you just made. Confirming this dialog posts your updated file into the XPI file, and now you are ready to install it.

Note The left and right tags that compose the `maxVersion` line are standard XML encapsulation tags, where the `em:` prefix is the encapsulating namespace used to group elements and attributes for the Extension Manager properties in the install manifest.

Modifying Code within an Extension

One of the beautiful things with having extensions packaged as standard Zip files is that you can easily uncompress, modify, and repackage them to review the code or fix any lingering issues you may have found. That said, let's briefly look at the anatomy of an extension so that you will know what you will see once you extract an extension file.

Internal Extension Structure

The basic structure of an extension, as shown in Figure 3-10, requires at a bare minimum for 1.0 support an install.rdf file. This file is the manifest detailing the information the Firefox extension installation process needs to install your extension.

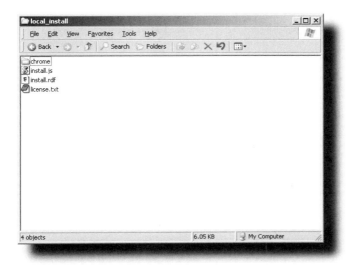

FIGURE 3-10: Extracted contents of the Local Install extension

The install.js and license.txt files are optional. The install.js file is required only if your extension needs to support Firefox versions prior to 0.9. Versions prior to 0.9 used the original extension installation process, so install.js is no longer required to support newer versions of the browser. The license.txt file is primarily there for informational purposes and is not used by the extension; you may choose to omit or remove it.

Once you have extracted the main XPI file, you will have one additional file to extract: a JAR file, which is located in the chrome directory. Once again, much like the XPI file, the JAR file is a ZIP file. The JAR file contains the actual content and code for the extension and may contain several subdirectories. Figure 3-11 shows the JAR file for the Local Install extension, as well as the contents extracted with its subdirectories. Just as you opened the XPI file to view the contents, you can extract the contents of the JAR file in Windows by right-clicking the JAR file and selecting Extract to NAME\ (where NAME is the name of the JAR file). I find extracting the contents to a subdirectory makes it easier for me, but you can also choose the Extract Here option.

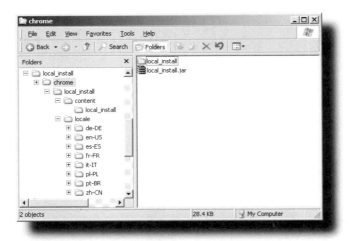

FIGURE **3-11: Extracted contents of the JAR file in the extension's chrome directory**

Note 7-Zip is not the only compression tool for Windows that has viewing, editing, or extracting features; however, it is a fast and free alternative.

The primary structure of an extension may consist of the following directories:

■ content

■ locale

■ skin

While the exact role each of these directories plays is further covered in Chapters 16 and 17, the directories are briefly covered here. As you can see from Figure 3-12, the content directory is the primary location for the extension's code, whether that is JavaScript, XUL, or other supporting files.

The locale, skin, defaults, or components directories and content are supporting features to an extension and may not exist in all extensions. The most common directories that you will see are locale and skin, which are discussed here. The defaults and components directories are primarily used for advanced extension programming and are covered in Chapter 17.

The locale directory exists with extensions that offer translations or locale-specific text. Firefox checks to determine if there is a match between the local system's locale and one found in the install.rdf manifest file. If no match is found, it should default to en-US or the English translation. Many extensions offer a multitude of translations, but this varies from extension to extension.

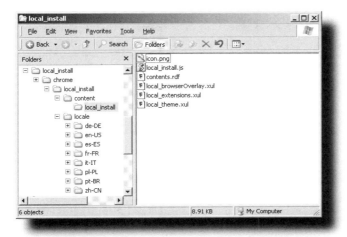

FIGURE 3-12: File listing of the content directory

The skin directory exists if the extension is using any Cascading Style Sheets or images to alter an existing Firefox window or to define the style of an extension-created window.

Basic Methods for Modifying Content

With an understanding of the basic structure of an extension, you can begin perusing the code and making changes or fixing bugs. While Chapter 17 covers how to officially package an extension and its contents, you can use one of the following two methods to make quick changes to files within the XPI archive:

- **You can use the File ⇨ Edit features of tools** such as 7-Zip, WinRar, or WinZip to edit files within the XPI or JAR files. This is probably the easiest approach because most compression tools detect changes to the edited file and prompt you to update the main extension file. This is the same method you used in the previous section to edit the Firefox maxVersion number in the install.rdf file.

- **You can extract and edit the files into directories** as you did through this section to view the contents. Then you can drag the file(s) into the appropriate directory within your compression tool. While most tools offer drag-and-drop functionality, some may not, and you should revert to the previous method for quick edits.

The methods described in the following sections are basic and may be seem very elementary, but they are the quickest way to update extensions when needed. More advanced methods are covered in Chapter 17.

Hacking the Extension Manager

The Extension Manager is the hub for managing all of your installed extensions. This section covers ways to enhance its functionality by documenting your installed extensions and themes, changing the visual appearance of the window, or adding needed functionality. ListZilla and Info Lister both provide an interface for you to document the extensions or themes you have installed, each with great features. Slim Extension List and EMbuttons both modify the extension or themes manager and add functionality. Local Install provides additional local installation support.

Listing Your Extensions and Themes

After using and adding different extensions and themes to my daily arsenal of tools, I started to get frustrated with a few things, such as tracking the extensions and themes I had installed, making the extension list easier to read, and adding toolbar buttons for both extension and theme managers. That's where ListZilla, InfoLister, Slim Extension List, and EMButtons come in handy. While ListZilla and InfoLister have similar features, some find InfoLister a little more feature rich.

Using the ListZilla Extension

Once installed, ListZilla creates a ListZilla option in the Tools menu. Selecting the menu allows you to save a list of your Extensions or Themes to the following formats:

- HTML
- Text
- vbCode

Each option prompts you for a file location and name and saves the corresponding file. Figure 3-13 shows an example of the HTML output generated by the Export Extension List option.

Tip One nice feature that both the ListZilla and InfoLister extensions have is the ability to create links to an extension's homepage when choosing HTML for your output.

Note For more information or to download ListZilla, visit `http://roachfiend.com/archives/2005/03/03/listzilla/`.

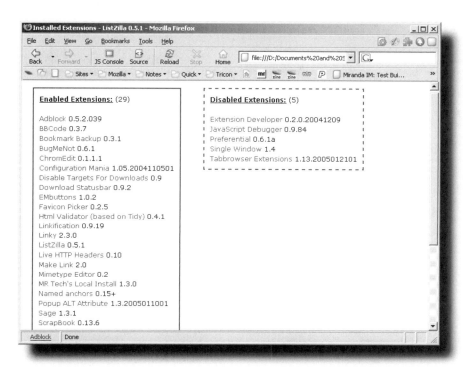

FIGURE 3-13: Sample HTML output using ListZilla

Using the InfoLister Extension

Much like ListZilla, the InfoLister extension allows you to save a list of extensions and themes, but it also goes beyond this with features such as the following:

- Plugin information
- Current Firefox build version
- Autosave functionality
- Output format customization
- FTP capabilities

Figure 3-14 shows sample HTML output generated by InfoLister. Additionally, Figure 3-15 shows the Customize Output options available.

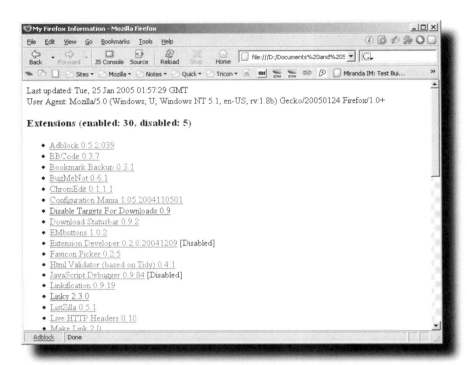

FIGURE 3-14: Sample HTML output using InfoLister

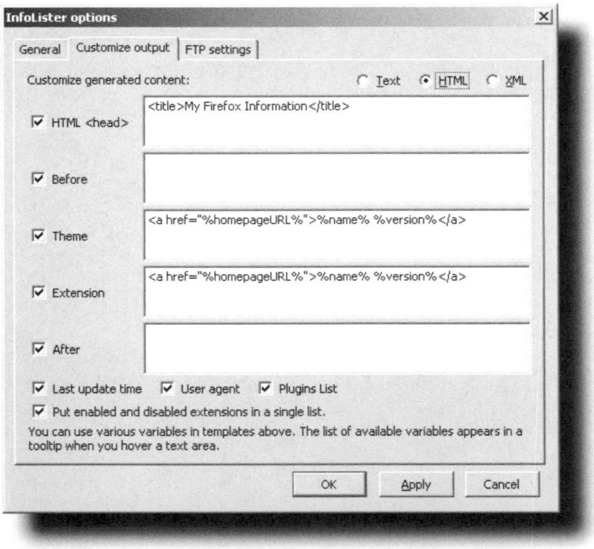

FIGURE 3-15: Customize Output options in InfoLister

Note For more information or to download InfoLister, visit `http://mozilla.klimontovich` `.ru/infolister/`.

Hacking with the Slim Extension List Extension

This extension does two simple things: It decreases the amount of space each listing needs, and it sorts the list alphabetically. In Figures 3-16 and 3-17, you see the before and after results of using this extension.

FIGURE **3-16: Before installing Slim Extension List**

Note For more information or to download Slim Extension List, visit `http://v2studio.com/` `k/moz/`.

Hacking with the EMbuttons Extension

EMButtons brings with it a mixed bag of options. Its key feature is the ability to add toolbar icons for the Extension or Theme Manager windows, but it also has some nice hidden features that are accessible via the Options window. The Options window, as shown in Figure 3-18, has preferences to sort the Extension or Theme Manager entries. It additionally has an enhancement for the Extension Manager to increase the response time in showing the listed extensions and one to collapse the listing even tighter than Slim Extension List does.

FIGURE 3-17: After installing Slim Extension List

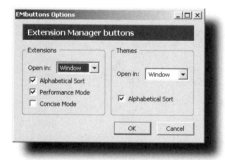

FIGURE 3-18: EMbuttons options menu

Note   For more information or to download EMButtons, visit http://moonwolf.mozdev.org/.

Recommended Extensions by Category

Table 3-1 provides a list of my recommended extensions by category. These are listed in the forums on my site at http://www.mrtech.com/, as well as Mozilla Updates and several other major Mozilla extension sites.

Table 3-1:   Recommended Extensions

Category	Description
General Enhancements	
AdBlock	Blocks virtually (99.9%) all banner ads
Alt-Text for Link	Shows links' destination URL in tooltips
CuteMenus	Adds icons to most menu items
Grease Monkey	Allows you to add or modify web page behavior
Launchy	Opens links/mailtos with external apps
Linkification	Highlights and linkifies plain text link
Linky	Opens/downloads all or selected links, and so on
MR Tech's Local Install	Theme/extension local install options
Popup ALT	Shows legacy image alt tag tooltips
Reload Every	Schedules reloading of a web page
RIP	Helps remove unwanted content from a web page
Sage	Lightweight RSS and ATOM feed aggregator
ScrapBook	Saves web pages and easily manages notes
Slim Extension List	Makes items in extension list shorter
TargetAlert	Tries to append an icon to link
URLid	Creates URL-specific style customizations
WebMailCompose	Makes mailto: links load your webmail
Download Extensions	
Disable Targets For Downloads	Disables download targets by extension
Download Manager Tweak	Downloads manager options
Download Sort	Download files and sort them into specific directories
Download Statusbar	Shows download info on the status bar
FlashGot	Customize support for download with external applications

Continued

Table 3-1 (continued)

Firefox Hacking Extensions	
Bookmark Backup	Backs up bookmarks and other core files
ChromEdit	Edits your Mozilla configuration files
Configuration Mania	Allows you to configure hidden preferences
Extension Developer	Extension Development Tool
Extension Uninstaller	Uninstalls older extensions
Preferential	Accessible GUI tree for preferences
Information Extensions	
Listzilla	Creates list of current themes and extensions
InfoLister	Creates list of current themes and extensions
Status Bar Extensions	
Download Statusbar	Shows download info on the status bar
ForecastFox	Highly customizable weather forecasts
FoxyTunes	Adds Audio Playback options to status bar
Gmail Notifier	Allows checking for new Gmail messages
Statusbar Clock	Adds the date/time to your status bar
Tab-Browsing Extensions	
Single Window	Basic tab-browsing options
Tab Mix	Great compilation of tab browser tweaks
Tabbrowser Extensions	Adds tons of tab-browsing options/tweaks
Tabbrowser Preferences	Adds GUI options for hidden tab browser
undoclosetab	Allows you to open recently closed tabs
Toolbar Extensions	
EMbuttons	Adds themes/extensions buttons and options
Firefox UltraBar	Search engine and blog toolbar
GoogleBar	Adds a Google toolbar to the browser
Toolbar Enhancements	Adds useful toolbar buttons and options
Yahoo! Companion	Adds Yahoo! Companion toolbar

Web Programmer Extensions	
BBCode	Context menu access to BBCODE/HTML code
EditCSS	On-the-fly editing/testing of page style
Html Validator	Checks HTML pages for correctness, based on Tidy.
Live Http Headers	Adds HTTP header to page info tab
Make Link	Builds html or bbcode links in clipboard
Mime Type Editor	Mozilla's Mime Type helper application
Named Anchors	Shows Named Anchors on Page Info window
ScrapBook	Save and manage web sites and notes easily
User Agent Switcher	Changes agent string sent to web sites
View Cookies	New cookies tab in the Page Info dialog
Web Developer	Adds many useful Web developer features

Summary

Personally, I think that extensions are the most significant enhancement to web browsing that has come out in a very long time. Dedicating an entire chapter to understanding how Firefox handles extensions and how to hack them was easy for me to envision. Add to that the customization options available to the extension manager and a nice list of extensions to wrap things up, and you have a chapter chock full of goodies.

Hacking Themes and Icons

by Mel Reyes

One of the great features of Firefox is its ability to dynamically render the interface, or chrome, using Cascading Style Sheets to overlay the screen's style. The browser's interface is created using Extensible User-Interface Language (XUL), which is an extremely powerful and robust markup language that allows you to create all the elements of a screen or dialog using standards such as XML, JavaScript, CSS, and internal calls.

Themes are small files installed in Firefox that modify its interface without affecting any functionality. Themes do this by referencing an XUL window and then the individual object names defined in the XUL file to assign or change the layout, images, or presentation style associated with objects defined in the XUL window. Each object (button, label, and so on) has an id assigned to it and is defined in the file. For the main browser window, this XUL file is called browse.xul and is located deep in the browser.jar in the chrome subdirectory where you installed Firefox.

As in the previous chapter, this chapter tackles issues that may arise when installing themes. Like extensions, themes have undergone similar transformations because of changes in the way later versions of Firefox install them. These changes, coupled with changes to graphical interface elements and styles throughout the development cycle prior to the 1.0 release, may cause themes to lack proper support for their final released builds. This chapter demonstrates some basic techniques to modify the interface, provides assistance in rebuilding or recovering from older themes, and shows you other techniques to hack the interface.

Note For more information on Cascading Style Sheet standards and implementation documentation, visit `http://www.w3.org/Style/CSS/`.

in this chapter

☑ **Hacking the interface**

☑ **Hacking themes**

☑ **Hacking web site icons**

☑ **Recommended themes**

Changing the Window's Background Color

Although changing the background color of the Firefox browser window seems trivial, it does allow you to dive a little deeper into some of the defined elements of the main browser window while providing another example of how to use the userChrome.css file, Cascading Style Sheets, and some creativity. This example highlights the specific ids and names assigned to the browser elements as they are defined in the main browser.xul. Starting from a clean slate, Figure 4-1 provides a reference for the original color scheme for a standard Windows installation.

FIGURE 4-1: Standard window showing window, menu, and tabs

The next step in this process is to begin identifying the XUL id of each of the screen components. Again, the focus of these early exercises is not to fully elaborate on how to get the ids, but how to hack them. Later, in Chapters 16–18, you have the chance to dive through the whole object model for Firefox. The initial focus is on the background color for the menu bar, toolbar, and the status bar, which have ids of `menubar`, `toolbar`, and `statusbarpanel`, respectively.

Now you need to focus on creating a range of colors that you can access. Luckily, you can reference standards at web sites such as `http://www.w3.org/TR/2001/WD-css3-color-20010305#colorunits` for color selection and support for CSS syntax. You want a standard Red-Green-Blue (RGB) representation of the color of choice, which you can refer to by a name such as silver, in the hexadecimal format, #C0C0C0, or by allowing the browser to extract the RGB values using the following syntax: `rgb(192,192,192)`. Once you have determined what color you want to use, you can pull together the code needed to assign the background color. For this example, I wanted to go a little lighter than silver, so I chose #E0E0E0.

Note Comments in Cascading Style Sheets files are blocked out with slashes and asterisks, like this: /* MY NOTE HERE */. Also, if there is an existing userChrome.css with a @namespace line, as in the following example, all plain text has to be pasted below this line.

```
/* Change Main Window Colors */

menubar, toolbar, statusbarpanel {
    -moz-appearance: none !important;
    background-color: #E0E0E0 !important;
}
```

When we break out the syntax, you see the basic structure defining the elements `menubar`, `toolbar`, and `statusbarpanel` and then associating a style using CSS code. Standard CSS formatting calls for curly braces to delineate the beginning and end of formatting.

The first line within the brackets has a property of `-moz-appearance` with a format of none followed by a key instruction of `!important`. This line tells the browser that the default style for objects with ids of `menubar`, `toolbar`, and `statusbarpanel` should be ignored and that this style should be used. This style change works because of the CSS instruction of `!important` used on each line. As defined by CSS standards, the original style definition takes precedence over a user-defined style of the same name. With the `!important` style instruction in place, Firefox implements the user-defined style instead of any previously defined style with the same name. I like to do this to clear the formatting. Doing so ensures that I have a clean slate, even if I am using a custom theme that might otherwise alter the appearance.

To apply these changes, you can either edit the userChrome.css manually from your profile\chrome directory or use an extension such as ChromEdit to easily access this file and paste the lines in. Once you have updated and saved the userChrome.css, you need to restart the browser for the changes to take effect. Figure 4-2 displays the updated browser window after the background style changes have been applied.

One of the first things that you might notice after the initial joy of updating colors is that not all browser window elements are updated to reflect the color changes. Because we defined only the menu bar, toolbar, and status bar panel in the userChrome.css for changes, several other elements, such as menus, tabs, dialogs, and so on, are not updated, as shown in Figure 4-3.

FIGURE 4-2: Main window updated with new color scheme

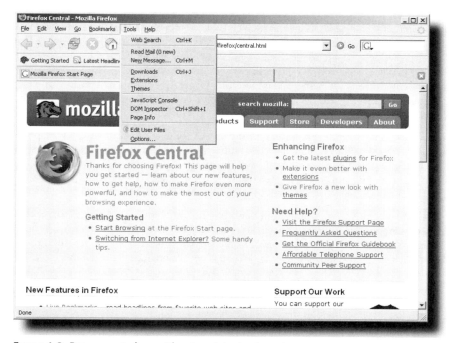

FIGURE 4-3: Browser window with mismatched color schemes

As you can see, a few more objects and ids need to be added for full colorization. For simplicity's sake, these are given to you here. Now we can add menus, popups, dialog boxes, tabs, sidebars, and other ids to cover the full range of elements that need updating. Again, just edit the userChrome.css file by replacing the previous snippet you pasted in with the following one and restarting Firefox:

```
/* Change Main Window Colors II:  adding tab area, toolbar menus,
right-click menus and other screen elements */

menus, menubar, toolbar, statusbarpanel,
.tabbrowser-tabs, tab:not([selected="true"]),
menupopup, popup, dialog, toolbox,
window, page, vbox, button, caption,
sidebarheader, prefwindow {
    -moz-appearance: none !important;
    background-color: #E0E0E0 !important;
}
```

One key entry that should stand out in this list is `tab:not([selected="true"])`. This entry is a variation on a plain `tab` element; it causes the tab that is selected to stand out for easier visibility. Without this entry, it would be difficult to determine which tab is active. This entry causes the active tab, the "Mozilla Firefox Start Page" tab, to retain your system default colors while the background tabs have the color change applied, as shown in Figure 4-4.

FIGURE 4-4: Main window after updating menus, tab bar, and so on

You can play with the color, font, and font size of the active tab by adding the following before or after the snippet you just added:

```
/* Change visual appearance of selected tab */

tab[selected="true"] {
   -moz-appearance: none !important;
   background-color: #F0F0F0 !important;
   font-family: Arial, Helvetica, sans-serif !important;
   font-size: 110% !important;
   font-weight: bold !important;
}
```

To vary the background tab appearance even more, you can change the opacity, font, and font size with the following code. Remember that most text background style changes that you can make using Cascading Style Sheets can also be implemented to browser window elements. For best results and easier reading, add this code above or below the two example CSS definitions that we just covered:

```
/* Change visual appearance of background tab(s) */

tab:not([selected="true"]) {
   -moz-appearance: none !important;
   -moz-opacity: 0.6 !important;
   font-family: Arial, Helvetica, sans-serif !important;
   font-size: 90% !important;
}
```

These changes are illustrated in Figure 4-5. Notice that distinguishing between active and background tabs is much easier.

Note You may have to add or omit some of the style entries in the preceding examples, depending on the theme you are using or the extensions you have installed because of the changes that they might apply.

Using a Tiled Image for the Window's Background

While the following basic example is readily available on the Mozilla.org site (specifically from the Mozilla Firefox FAQ page at http://www.mozilla.org/support/firefox/tips), this section shows you how to extend it to your liking and to get it to work for you.

```
/* Use a background image for the toolbars:
   (Substitute your image file for background.gif) */

 menubar, toolbox, toolbar, .tabbrowser-tabs {
   background-image: url("background.gif") !important;
   background-color: none !important;
   }
```

The beauty of this hack is that it shares the same screen elements as the previous section, where you modified the background colors, so all you have to do is mock up the same ids and screen elements to your liking.

FIGURE 4-5: Main window with tab after enhancing the tab appearance

Before hacking the style and adding screen elements, though, you need to know how to reference the image so that Firefox knows where to read it. The `background-image` CSS property uses a Uniform Resource Locator (URL) to find the file. While typically one would relate a URL with a web site, this is merely a way of specifying the path to the file.

The easiest way to have the userChrome.css file find the image is to save it to the same directory as the userChrome.css, which is under your profile's chrome directory. You can, however, hardcode the full path to the file if you want to. Additionally, any image or background that you find can be used for the window background, but you may want to avoid images that are not specifically meant to be tiled, as they may not be visually appealing.

Note To save an image from a web page, just right-click on the page, select View Background Image, and then save the image locally. You can also search the Internet for "web page background images," and tons of sites come up.

Using the basic example from the Firefox FAQ page mentioned earlier, we will fill in some of the missing pieces. In reality, the example is not missing anything; it just makes for a better experience if not just the primary elements on the page have a background image. The following example is a mirror copy of the background colors example with the addition of style changes from the previous Firefox window color background example. Figure 4-6 displays a beautiful lavender marble background that is applied to the main browser window.

```
/* Using a Tiled Image for Window's Background and more */

menus, menubar, toolbar, statusbarpanel,
.tabbrowser-tabs, tab:not([selected="true"]),
menupopup, popup, dialog, toolbox,
window, page, vbox, caption,
sidebarheader, prefwindow {
    -moz-appearance: none !important;
    background-image: url("lavender.jpg") !important;
    background-color: none !important;
}
```

FIGURE 4-6: Main window with background image

As in the background color examples, you need to enter and save this code into your userChrome.css file and restart Firefox. For this example, I pulled an image from a background-testing page that I created back in the Netscape 2.0 era: http://www.mrtech.com/backgrounds/. Specifically, I picked image number 14 or 14.jpg and saved it in my profile's chrome directory as lavender.jpg. You can use this same page to test how different font colors display using a unique array of background image colors and textures.

Tip

One cool trick you can do is break up the elements and give them different background images.

Reducing Space around Toolbar Icons

One of my pet peeves with many themes is the amount of space padding around toolbar icons when using the text label on the toolbar. Most theme layouts are geared toward using the standard icon size without text, but I prefer using small icons with text descriptions—and most themes, including the default theme, do not have optimal spacing in this mode. Whether you have selected Icons and Text or Text with or without Use Small Icon, Firefox adds just a bit too much spacing, which bloats the toolbar.

Tip

To customize your toolbar, right-click on the toolbar and choose Customize from the popup menu.

Once again, to apply this example, enter the following in your userChrome.css, save, and restart Firefox:

```
/* Reducing Space Around Toolbar Icons */

.toolbarbutton-1,
toolbar[mode="text"] .toolbarbutton-text {
  padding: 3px 3px 0px 3px !important;
  margin: 0px 0px 0px 0px !important;
  min-width: 0px !important;
  display: -moz-box;
}

.toolbarbutton-menubutton-stack,
.toolbarbutton-menubutton-button,
.toolbarbutton-menubutton-stack:hover,
.toolbarbutton-menubutton-button:hover,
.toolbarbutton-menubutton-stack:hover:active,
.toolbarbutton-menubutton-button:hover:active {
  padding: 0px 0px 0px 0px !important;
  margin: 0px 0px 0px 0px !important;
  min-width: 0px !important;
  display: -moz-box;
}
```

Note

A larger space gain is realized when you have toolbar text labels enabled.

Figure 4-7 displays the default theme with toolbar text enabled. Figure 4-8 shows the effects of applying the toolbar style changes with small icons.

FIGURE 4-7: Main window with small icons and toolbar text enabled

FIGURE 4-8: Main window with toolbar-spacing hack applied

To achieve the tightest fit, you can override the padding, margin, and minimum width for the toolbar buttons by setting most to zero and tweaking some of the padding. To do this, you have to change the properties for all toolbar button types and any associated actions such as `hover` and `active`. The `toolbar[mode="text"] .toolbarbutton-text` line handles spacing when in text-only mode.

Hacking Themes

This section dives into what you will need to know to accomplish the following:

- Enable dynamic theme switching
- Install older unsupported themes
- Install extensions locally
- Extend some popular extensions
- Clean up web icons or favicons

Reenabling Dynamic Theme Switching

One nice feature that was disabled during one of the late pre-1.0 builds was the ability to dynamically switch the browser's theme without restarting. The decision to disable this by default was made to allow more time to resolve some chrome refresh switching issues. Fortunately, there is a hidden preference to reenable this feature, if you dare. Why such an ominous tone? Well, historically, dynamic theme switching support has been very spotty; in the final Firefox 1.0 release, it was disabled as a default and will be revisited for a future release. Depending on the theme installed, userChrome.css customizations, and other considerations, enabling this feature may cause temporary toolbar, menu, or page misalignments, all of which are quickly resolved by closing and relaunching Firefox.

Because it is a hidden preference, my approach is to add the modified preference to the user.js file to make it easier to manage any additional hacks that I want. This approach also helps with remembering hacks long after you have applied them.

Note

The user.js file is in your profile directory.

Add the following code to the user.js file. Once you have saved the entry, you must restart Firefox, and dynamic theme switching will be enabled. You may experience some browser display issues when switching, but mainstream and updated themes generally seem to handle this feature well.

```
// 1.0 Preview disables dynamic theme switching,
// this re-enables dynamic theme switching.
user_pref("extensions.dss.enabled", true);
```

Note In JavaScript or .JS files, double forward slashes (//) denote a comment.

Additionally, you can edit the `extensions.dss.enabled` preference using the about:config utility (just type **about:config** in the location bar).

Hacking Older Themes

Themes suffer from the same versioning issue that plagues extensions when it comes to supporting older versions. This is not an issue per se; it's simply something that you might have to address when working with older themes and extensions. These controls were put in place to assure proper support in the event that the underlying core code was changed for any reason; they make the browser as stable as possible relative to third-party extension or theme code.

Firefox themes are images packaged with code and bundled into a JAR file. JAR files are compressed files that use ZLIB or the standard ZIP file compression format to store files together. To begin hacking them, you must download the JAR file locally. Most sites will give you an Install and/or an alternate download link; in either case, you can try right-clicking and saving the JAR file locally.

Embedded in the root of the theme's JAR file is the install.rdf file, which holds installation information and, more important, the minimum and maximum supported browser versions. Using any ZIP-supported compression program, you can open or extract the contents of the theme JAR file. The entries you are looking for are usually formatted as follows:

```
<em:minVersion>0.8</em:minVersion>
<em:maxVersion>0.9</em:maxVersion>
```

This tells Firefox that the current theme supports earlier versions of Firefox only, versions 0.8 through 0.9, which are pre-1.0 release builds. Similarly, you may experience this issue with future releases of Firefox 1.1, 1.2, 2.0, and so on, and may need to hack a theme to support them accordingly while you wait for the theme developer to come out with an update.

As discussed in Chapter 3, any ZIP-supported tool can be used to edit a theme. Running under Windows, 7-Zip is my tool of choice. Figure 4-9 shows the contents of the ever-so-beautiful Phoenity theme. From here, you can easily edit the install.rdf file, and after you close your editor, 7-Zip prompts you to update the JAR file.

To edit the install.rdf, follow these steps:

1. Highlight the install.rdf file in the main 7-Zip window.
2. Choose File ⇨ Edit or press the F4 key.
3. Apply your changes and close your editor.
4. Confirm updating of the theme jar file.

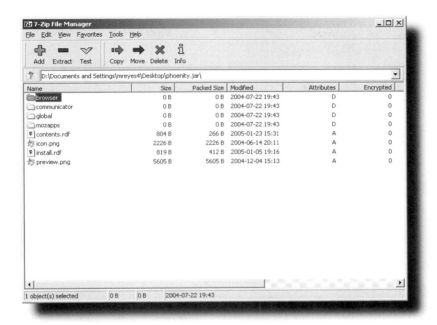

FIGURE 4-9: Phoenity theme contents viewed in 7-Zip

At this point, you are ready to install the theme and have Firefox properly recognize it as compatible with your version. The only possible drawback to hacking a theme is when it does not support all of the newly added screen elements. This happens when a new feature, toolbar, or screen has been added to Firefox, and third-party themes do not have associated graphics. The most common example of this is the Mozilla Update graphic indicator that shows up next to the browser's throbber on the right side of the Firefox window. Because this feature was introduced later in the pre–1.0 release era, some themes do not contain the images needed to display properly. Minor inconsistencies like these are the things that you may or may not be able to live with when hacking different themes.

Recovering from Disabled Older Themes

Much like installing extensions, installing a newer version of Firefox may disable some of your themes. This is a built-in feature to protect you from unsupported older code and to assure a clean, stable environment.

Unlike extensions, there are really no tools or hacking extensions to recover from the truly old themes easily. You can try hacking the theme's JAR file, as described in the previous section, or checking the Mozilla Update site or the theme developer's web site.

If you want to keep your existing profile and would like to clean up the directory and manually remove any lingering theme or extension files, just hop on over to the "Starting Over without Losing All Your Settings" section in Chapter 3.

In my experience, doing this cleanup every now and then yields the best experience without having to completely rebuild features such as password prompts, hacks, and so on.

Tip   Because of several changes made from earlier builds, it is highly recommended that you create a new profile if you had previously tested development versions of Firefox.

Why Won't Some Themes Install?

Have you ever tried installing a theme from a site only to find that the theme will not install as promised? Were you able to figure out how to install it? This section covers why some sites do not install properly and how to get around these limitations.

Much like many extensions, many themes suffer from poor installation support from web pages. To alleviate this issue, use the standard Mozilla JavaScript functionality to prompt Firefox to download the file as an extension. Developers should have set this up for you, but because some do not, you may end up downloading to your hard drive a JAR file that you may not know what to do with. Read on to learn how to install a theme remotely or from a site that does prompt you, but, more important, how to install a theme locally from your hard drive. Where and how a theme is saved to your profile are also covered.

If you want to add JavaScript theme installation support to links that you develop, you can use the following code:

```
<a href="theme.jar" onClick = "if (typeof(InstallTrigger) !=
'undefined') {InstallTrigger.installChrome(InstallTrigger.SKIN,
'theme.jar', 'Theme Installation'); return false;}"
type="application/x-zip-compressed">Install Theme Here</a>
```

The code above gives support for left-click installation as well as right-click and Save Link As support.

Installing Remotely versus Locally

Installing remotely is virtually a no-brainer, thanks to the beauty of Firefox. If everything is as it should be, you simply click on the install or theme link, which produces a confirmation screen, as shown in Figure 4-10. Click OK, and the theme is added to your list and is available for use immediately.

FIGURE 4-10: Firefox theme install prompt

Tip

If you enabled the Dynamic Theme Switching hack described earlier in this chapter, you can switch to the new theme without having to restart.

Easy, right? But what do you do when it prompts you to download? The best thing to do is save the file to a common location such as your desktop. Then all you have to do from within Firefox is open the file. To open the file, follow these steps:

1. Select File ➪ Open File.

2. Navigate to your desktop or the directory you saved the file to.

3. Select the JAR theme file you just downloaded and click Open.

Firefox displays the standard confirmation prompt. You are now set to install extensions, no matter how a site delivers them to you.

Tip

Another way to open downloaded JAR files is to open the Theme Manager and drag the JAR file into its window.

Using the Local Install Extension

On thing that really bothered me with regards to the Extension and Theme Managers was the inconsistency between Firefox and other products such as Thunderbird and, most recently, NVU in providing an Install button in the manager window. So basically, I hacked together MR Tech's Local Install, shown in Figure 4-11, which has its roots in the "Install New Theme" extension by Bradley Chapman.

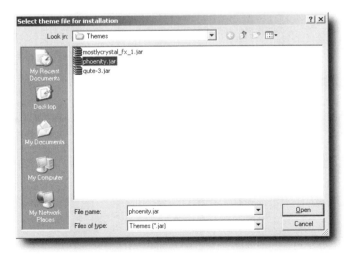

FIGURE 4-11: MR Tech's Firefox Local Install theme installation

Originally, I just wanted to mirror for the Extension Manager the Install button functionality that Bradley had created for the Theme Manager. Version 1.0 was quickly built and released. Since then, File menu, shortcut keys, and international localizations have been added.

The basic idea is that you can now choose how you can install local copies of extensions and themes. For extensions, it automatically defaults to an *.xpi file type, and for themes, it defaults to a *.jar file type, making it easier to distinguish those files from others you might have saved in the same directory.

Note   You can download the Local Install extension at `http://www.mrtech.com/extensions/`.

Hacking via userChrome.css

Earlier in this chapter we introduced the manual steps for creating your own style sheets to change the appearance of the main browser windows and supporting screens. This section dives into how to use customizations already packaged with some very popular themes.

Several themes have *subskins*, style sheet modifications that are wrapped up into a CSS file, which is then bundled within the theme's JAR file. Doing this makes certain features optional and allows the themes themselves to be hacked from the userChrome.css.

A generic example of a userChrome.css entry that uses a subskin looks like this:

```
@import url("chrome://global/skin/subskin/round.css");
```

This tells the browser to look for the round.css file in the registry theme's chrome path of `://global/skin/subskin/`.

If you switch themes and no round.css file is found, the browser continues without failure. Remember that in your userChrome.css file, all `@import` lines for subskins or other features need to be put above the `@namespace` line, if it exists.

You have to check each individual theme to see if it has subskins and determine the exact path- and filenames needed to take advantage of the modifications. The following sections cover some of the popular themes and some of the available hacks.

Hacking Aaron Spuler's Themes

Aaron Spuler's collection of themes is by far my most recommended and best-loved collection of themes under one roof. The style and consistency within each theme is something most users will appreciate. That coupled with timely updates makes for a great set of themes to adopt as your primary set.

Themes featured on his site include the following:

- Apollo
- Atlas
- Blue
- iCandy Junior
- Mars

- Neptune
- Playground
- Pluto
- Rain
- Smoke

Two of the several hacks that are available with most of these themes are brushed metal background and Safari-style tabs, as shown in Figure 4-12.

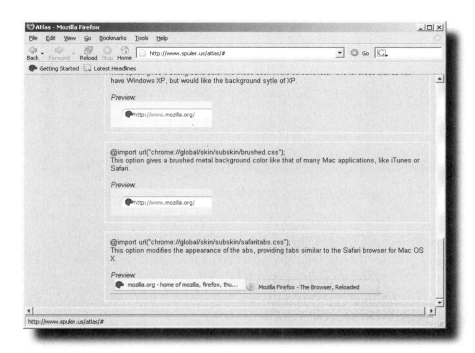

FIGURE 4-12: Aaron Spuler's theme hacks

To apply the brushed metal background hack shown in Figure 4-13, just add the following line to your userChrome.css, save, and restart Firefox:

```
@import url("chrome://global/skin/subskin/brushed.css");
```

To apply the Safari-style tabs, add the following line:

```
@import url("chrome://global/skin/subskin/safaritabs.css");
```

Tip To download or install any of Aaron's themes, visit `http://www.spuler.us/`.

FIGURE 4-13: Aaron Spuler's Atlas theme with the brushed background subskin applied

Hacking the Mostly Crystal Theme

Another great theme that can be hacked with subskins is Mostly Crystal. Mostly Crystal is based on Crystal SVG (for Linux) icons created by Everaldo (http://www.everaldo.com). Several nice features of Mostly Crystal subskins allow for rounded corners, toolbar tweaks, and using menu icons, as shown in Figure 4-14.

Here are just some of the great hacks you can apply that are specific to the Mostly Crystal theme, as shown in Figure 4-15:

```
/* Use SMALL throbber image regardless of toolbar size. */
@import url("chrome://global/skin/subskin/throbber-sm.css");

/* Change the Plain Dropmarkers for address bar and menulists to
images. */
@import url("chrome://global/skin/subskin/dropmarker.css");

/* Show icons for menuitems (English only). */
@import url("chrome://global/skin/subskin/menuitems.css");

/* Use stylized address and search bars. */
@import url("chrome://global/skin/subskin/rounded.css");
```

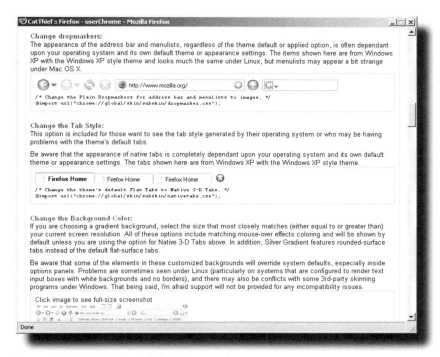

FIGURE 4-14: Mostly Crystal subskins samples

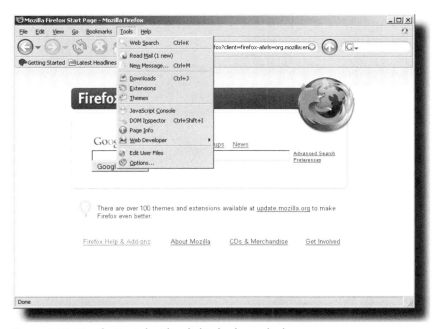

FIGURE 4-15: Mostly Crystal with subskin hacks applied

Tip To download or install the Mostly Crystal theme, visit `http://www.tom-cat.com/mozilla/firefox.html`.

Hacking the Phoenity Theme

Phoenity has become my theme of choice for several reasons, but mostly because of its small, simple icons. Besides its support for extensions with icon functionality, it boasts support for several other applications and has its own Firefox subskins.

These are just some of the multitude of great options that you have with regards to being able to hack the Phoenity skin, as shown in Figure 4-16.

Use this snippet to apply Phoenity icons to the menus:

```
@import url("chrome://browser/skin/subskins/cutermenus.css");
```

To update the icons used by buttons, add this to the userChrome.css:

```
@import url("chrome://browser/skin/subskins/cutebuttons.css");
```

For smooth, rounded corners around the location and search bars, use this line:

```
@import url("chrome://browser/skin/subskins/roundedbars.css");
```

Note To download or install the Phoenity theme, visit `http://phoenity.com/firefox.html`.

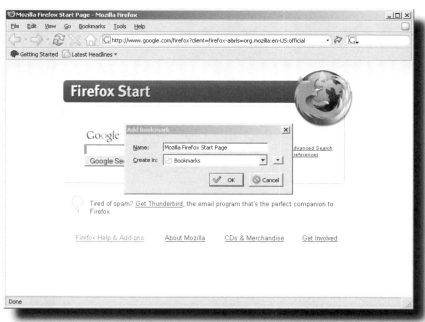

FIGURE 4-16: Phoenity theme with subskin hacks applied

Hacking Website Icons

A web site icon or *favicon* is a 16 × 16 pixel icon that is viewable on the location bar of most browsers; Firefox also has the capability of displaying this icon as the bookmark's icon. This section covers how to make sure that you have favicon support enabled; how to remove it manually; and, briefly, how to use the Delete Icons extensions.

Enabling Icons for Bookmarks and Websites

By default, Firefox tries to load a site's favicon to display it on the location bar and as the bookmark's icon. The standard favicon format is an ICO or icon file, but Firefox also supports GIF, JPEG, PNG, MNG, XBM, and BMP formatted icons. The default file that Firefox looks for, if it is not specified in the web page, is favicon.ico on the root of the web server the page is being loaded from.

Note While the default display of icons is 16 × 16 pixels, Firefox resizes icons to display properly in the location bar and bookmarks. Additionally, the maximum size for icons to be saved with bookmarks is 16K.

Some tweaking extensions allow you to enable or disable the loading of favicons by modifying the following preferences listed. My preference is to have both entries in my user.js file to make sure they are always set to my preferred setting of `true`.

```
user_pref("browser.chrome.favicons", true);
user_pref("browser.chrome.site_icons", true);
```

Sites can specify the name and the location for their favicon file with HTML entries such as the following:

```
<link href="favicon.ico" rel="SHORTCUT ICON">
<link rel="icon" href="favicon.ico" type="image/x-icon">
<link rel="shortcut icon" href="favicon.ico" type="image/x-icon">
```

Note In Firefox, favicon.ico can be replaced with any GIF, JPEG, PNG, MNG, XBM, or BMP formatted icon (for example, favicon.gif and so on).

Tip For a web service to create favicons from your own pictures, visit `http://www.html-kit.com/favicon/`.

Removing Favicons Manually

While this task seems trivial, it does involve some digging into the bookmarks.html file. This file is formatted as a standard HTML file with specific syntax to allow Firefox to parse it properly. This file is loaded once on startup and saved when the browser shuts down. Special attention should be made to close all Firefox windows before editing it, as all changes will be lost if

Firefox is left open. You can use this to your advantage if sites have malformed or corrupt favicons, or if the bookmark file becomes corrupt. Additionally, if sites update their favicon, the favicon will not get updated in the bookmarks.html file.

Tip The bookmarks.html file is located in the root of your profile directory and should be backed up before editing.

The bookmark file uses a standard HTML link to store the information for each bookmark with special properties, as illustrated in the following:

```
<A HREF="http://www.spreadfirefox.com/" LAST_CHARSET="UTF-8"
ID="rdf:#$4wPhC3">
```

Additional properties that are stored within the link tag, if available, include:

- `LAST_VISIT`
- `LAST_MODIFIED`
- `SHORTCUTURL`
- `ICON` or favicon

The `ICON` property holds a base64 or text equivalent of the binary icon file that is downloaded from the site. Because of this conversion, the `ICON` property's value is very long. A bookmark that contains an icon image will look similar to the following link:

```
<A HREF="http://www.mozilla.org/products/firefox/central.html"
ICON="data:image/png;base64,SNIPPED" LAST_CHARSET="ISO-8859-1"
ID="rdf:#$GvPhC3">
```

Note For the sake of keeping the preceding example short, 778 characters were removed where you see `SNIPPED` in the `ICON` property of the link.

To remove the `ICON` or favicon, just follow these steps:

1. Close all Firefox windows.
2. Make a backup of bookmarks.html.
3. Load the bookmark file from your profile directory into any text editor, preferably one with HTML syntax highlighted to make it easier to read.
4. Page through or do a search for the offending web address.
5. Scroll over to the `ICON` property for that site and remove all values within the quotes for the `ICON` property, including the `ICON` tag.

The resulting tag should look like this:

```
<A HREF="http://www.mozilla.org/products/firefox/central.html"
LAST_CHARSET="ISO-8859-1" ID="rdf:#$GvPhC3">
```

The next time you visit that link in your bookmarks, the favicon will be fetched again and saved to your bookmarks.

Removing Icons with the Delete Icons Extension

If you want to facilitate removing bookmark icons, this is the extension you want to try. This extension adds a Delete Icon property to the right-click context menu for bookmarks and a Delete Icons entry to the Tools menu. The bookmark option removes just the individual icon that was right-clicked; the Tools menu option can remove all icons and allow you to start over. As a proponent of housecleaning, I like to do a full sweep every now and then, and this extension makes it very easy.

 Note   To get Delete Icons, visit `http://www.gozer.org/mozilla/extensions/`.

Recommended Themes

I use several criteria used to make theme recommendations, including frequency of updates, extendibility, and version compatibility. Keeping themes updated is critical, considering the multitude of options as well as updates that are made to the underlying rendering code. The following extensions have historically been very good in maintaining compatibility and providing extended features such as subskins and support for popular extensions:

- **Atlas:** `http://www.spuler.us/atlas/`
- **Doodle Plastik and Doodle Classic:** `http://home.student.uu.se/dana3949/doodle/`
- **iCandy Junior:** `http://www.spuler.us/icandyjr/`
- **Lila:** `http://www.deviantart.com/deviation/12834861/`
- **Mostly Crystal:** `http://www.tom-cat.com/mozilla/`
- **Noia 2.0 Lite:** `http://www.deviantart.com/deviation/5706856/`
- **Noia 2.0 eXtreme:** `http://www.deviantart.com/deviation/12834861/`
- **Phoenity:** `http://www.phoenity.com/firefox.html`
- **Playground:** `http://www.spuler.us/playground/`
- **Pluto:** `http://www.spuler.us/pluto/`
- **Qute:** `http://quadrone.org/graphics/`
- **Toy Factory:** `http://www.projectit.com/freestuff.html#toyfactory`

Summary

This chapter is a good primer for theme development and understanding some of the fundamentals of how themes work. The chapter highlights different approaches to hacking the Firefox user interface with colors, background images, and changing the spacing around icons. It also taps into installing themes remotely and locally, then moves right into applying hacks to themes that support subskins or Cascading Style Sheet modifications. Finally, it tackles how to manually hack favicons or website icons, as well as how to hack them with the Delete Icons extensions.

Hacking Performance, Security, and Banner Ads

part

Performance Tweaks and Hacks

Hack it, tweak it, and make it scream down the information highway. This chapter covers several of the much-touted hacks that you will find on the Internet, as well as some other less popular but very useful hacks. You will get the skinny on the what, how, and why of them. More important, you'll see how to customize them to fit your current setup and situation. The primary method of hacking for this section is adjusting key hidden preferences.

by Mel Reyes

Deviating from RFC Specs

Warning: The following hacks may make your browser download faster than your eyes can handle. Okay, kidding aside, the following hacks are a set that has generated a lot of controversy because it breaks away from industry standards. Based on RFC specification numbers 2068, 2616, and others, the defined and recommended maximum number of simultaneous connections using HTTP/1.0 Internet protocol is four. For HTTP/1.1, the defined and recommended number is two. These hacks bump this number up; they also increase the number of connections per server. If you are using dial-up access, these hacks will be marginally beneficial and are really geared more for DSL, cable, and corporate networks; customizing these settings is covered in the "Bandwidth and Processor-Specific Optimizations" section later in this chapter.

 Note — RFC stands for Request for Comment. These specifications are published to create technology standards for communication protocols and other application implementations.

These RFC standards are in place to balance a web server's performance under heavy traffic by providing a certain level of quality of service for all users. However, as many users have realized, leeching and improved download performance are necessary when cruising through the net or downloading large files. This, coupled with the fact that the RFC was originally published in 1997, really begs for some radical changes to be taken. So you deal with the problem directly by increasing the number of concurrent connections made to a server for a page request.

Note A request is any communication from Firefox to a web server; such requests include the call to download the page and each element that the page refers to (for example, graphics, JavaScript files, Cascading Style Sheets, and so on).

Hacking Simultaneous Connections

To edit these settings, you can use the built-in about:config utility, add the entries to the bottom of your prefs.js, or add them to the user.js file. My preference is the latter because it makes it easier to update and manage all my tweaks and hacks without having to weed through all the other settings or screens. Figure 5-1 displays the defaults for the four settings that we hack in this section.

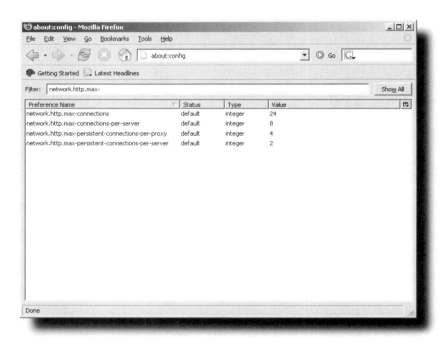

FIGURE 5-1: The about:config utility with the network preferences

While performance is genuinely good for single-page browsing with default settings, loading multiple pages or loading pages with tons of supporting content, such as thumbnail images, may take some time to queue up and download. Moreover, if you have created a multipage bookmark or homepage or, like me, have JavaScript-triggered buttons to blast open 4 to 12 sites in tabs simultaneously, you know the importance of downloading all pages and page elements as fast as possible.

Here is the code you can add to the user.js file:

```
user_pref("network.http.max-connections", 96);
user_pref("network.http.max-connections-per-server", 32);
user_pref("network.http.max-persistent-connections-per-proxy",
24);
user_pref("network.http.max-persistent-connections-per-
server", 12);
```

Tip

The faint of heart can modify these settings with the Tweak Network Settings extension, which can be found at `http://www.bitstorm.org/extensions/`.

The network.http.max-connections hack increases the number of total connections that the browser will make at one time. The network.http.max-connections-per-server hack breaks this down to the maximum number of connections per server.

Tip

For additional networking preferences, default values, and notes, visit `http://www` `.mozilla.org/quality/networking/docs/netprefs.html`.

Persistent connections are implemented with HTTP web protocols and allow fewer TCP/IP calls to be initiated to a web server when making multiple requests. This is also known as *keep-alive*, because it reuses the active connection to communicate additional requests. The `network.http.max-persistent-connections` settings bump the number of simulta-neous requests that can be made, in effect forcing the download of as many of the page ele-ments at the same time as possible.

Note

For more information on HTTP/1.1 Persistent Connections standards, visit `http://www.w3` `.org/Protocols/rfc2616/rfc2616-sec8.html`. For HTTP/1.1 performance informa-tion, visit `http://www.w3.org/Protocols/HTTP/Performance/`.

Pipelining Hacking

A key feature called *pipelining* was incorporated into the HTPP/1.1 standard. While this fea-ture does give a boost to communication between the browser and server, there are some web servers and proxy servers that may not fully support its use. Pipelining takes several requests and submits them to the server back to back without waiting for a response, with the expecta-tion of receiving the requested objects back in the order submitted. The benefit is gained in the fact that there is less chatter and delay between the browser and server because the browser is not waiting for a response from the server for the first request before making the next, and so on.

```
// Enable Improve Pipelining
user_pref("network.http.pipelining", true);
user_pref("network.http.proxy.pipelining", true);
user_pref("network.http.pipelining.firstrequest", true);
user_pref("network.http.pipelining.maxrequests", 8);
```

Note network.http.pipelining.maxrequests is capped at eight, and setting this value to anything higher will be ignored. The default is four.

Though it is not recommended, I have suffered no ill effects from using `network.http` `.pipelining.firstrequest`. It is not recommended, because Firefox has yet to determine if the server can handle pipelined requests.

Tip For more information on HTTP pipelining, visit `http://www.mozilla.org/projects/` `netlib/http/pipelining-faq.html`.

Other Hacks

The following tweaks increase the amount of time and number of entries for which the browser remembers the Domain Name Server (DNS) resolution information. DNS servers are the bridge between a website's named address and the TCP/IP address assigned to it. Increasing the DNS expiration and the number of entries reduces the number of times Firefox needs to poll to gather this information.

The FTP idle and keep-alive settings use a default of 300. Lowering these shortens the amount of time that the browser waits before giving up and timing out for FTP connections and keep-alive callbacks.

```
user_pref("network.dnsCacheExpiration", 86400);
user_pref("network.dnsCacheEntries", 256);
user_pref("network.ftp.idleConnectionTimeout", 60);
user_pref("network.http.keep-alive.timeout", 30);
```

Note These hacks help with browser responsiveness but may have some side effects, including premature timeouts. Use these hacks with this understanding and modify or remove them if you experience any unforeseen issues with website name resolution, FTP idle connections, and so on.

Optimizing Page Rendering

Page rendering is handled by the internal core technology, called NGLayout, or by Mozilla's layout engine. By tweaking the NGLayout paint delay setting, you reduce the amount of time that the browser waits before it begins rendering a page while downloading, which achieves some marvelous visual performance. I like this a lot because it enables me to know exactly what is downloading and to enjoy its rendering in real time without having to wait for all the content to load. This does take its toll on central processing unit (CPU) utilization, but with today's high-end processors and systems, this is less of a factor.

Tip Using tab browsing usually requires less CPU time and memory; pages load faster because Firefox does not have to render a whole new window. Additional tab browser tweaks and settings can be found in Chapter 10.

Hacking Page Rendering

Most of these hacks are scattered all over the Internet, but most take snippets from several key sources, including the Firefox Tuning information posted in the Firefox Features forum on MozillaZine.org forums. To access the healthy discussion on tuning Firefox, visit http://forums.mozillazine.org/viewtopic.php?t=53650.

The TweakFactor.com site summarizes these hacks in a nice clean page, which can be found at http://www.tweakfactor.com/articles/tweaks/firefoxtweak/4.html. However, in my experience, the following tweaks are really the core tweaks that help in rendering and page timing for display purposes:

```
user_pref("nglayout.initialpaint.delay", 0);
user_pref("content.notify.ontimer", true);
user_pref("content.interrupt.parsing", true);
user_pref("content.notify.interval", 100);
user_pref("content.notify.threshold", 100000);
user_pref("content.notify.backoffcount", 200);
user_pref("content.max.tokenizing.time", 3000000);
user_pref("content.maxtextrun", 8191);
```

The nglayout.initialpaint.delay tweak shown in the preceding code modifies the amount of time Firefox waits before it begins rendering a page, where the default is 250 (milliseconds). The rest of the content hacks alter the timing for internal reflow and page generation.

The "content.notify.ontimer" is on by default, but I always like to include it just in case. This turns on the timer-based reflow management used for rendering. Users upgrading from pre-1.0 releases may have this preference disabled; setting it to true should rectify this.

The "content.notify.interval" preference sets the amount of time allowed between reflows and is measured in microseconds, where the default is 250000. Some have balked at setting this to such a low number, but I have yet to suffer from doing so.

The "content.notify.backoffcount" sets the number of reflows to do before waiting for the rest of the page to arrive.

The "content.max.tokenizing.time" was implemented to give the user interface responsiveness while parsing a page. The default for this setting is three times the "content.notify.interval". This is the amount of thread processing time to use before releasing controls to the user interface.

The "content.maxtextrun" preference by default is 8191, but in builds prior to 0.9.5, it was 8192, and the one-digit difference, based on the notes in the Bugzilla posting, made a huge difference in rendering due to buffer thrashing and overallocations. This hack is included just in case you are still on an old build or this setting has not been properly updated. For more information on this fix, visit https://bugzilla.mozilla.org/show_bug.cgi?id=77540.

The combination of these hacks should yield a very nice experience when downloading larger pages or pages with complicated table structures.

Unblocking Error Dialogs

One annoying feature that really is not a rendering-specific issue is the browser's popping up a modal dialog warning that there is an error while connecting to a site. A typical modal dialog blocks background activity until you respond to its question, usually in the form of an Are-you-sure-you-want-to-exit? type of dialog. What this tweak does is replace a failed URL's modal dialog prompt with an error page. Having used this hack for a long time now, I have found it to be most useful if you are loading several pages at the same time. In this instance, the error dialog actually holds up the whole browser from downloading other background content. Using this tweak allows the other pages and page elements to load without the lockup.

```
user_pref("browser.xul.error_pages.enabled", true)
```

One side effect of using this hack is that the displayed URL in the location bar is a pointer to the internal XUL page that is used to generate and display the error. To rectify this situation, you can install the Show Failed URL extension, which does as it says; it shows the URL in question in the location bar. This extension can be downloaded from `http://www.pikey.me.uk/mozilla/#sfu`.

Tip For more information on why this preference is not enabled by default, visit the Bugzilla site at `http://bugzilla.mozilla.org/show_bug.cgi?id=28586`.

Disabling Smooth Scrolling

Smooth scrolling may be a nice feature, but I can never tell the difference when it is enabled. However, I have noted a slight performance hit on older computers that have it enabled.

```
user_pref("general.smoothScroll", false);
```

My preference is to tweak as much power and performance as possible out of the browser and forgo most of the frills, so this feature ends up getting disabled on my systems.

Bandwidth and Processor-Specific Optimizations

When originally learning these connection, rendering, and pipelining hacks for the Mozilla Suite and Firefox, I did my own performance testing. I did this at probably just around the same time other sites had been doing it, but my findings were a little different. My original approach was to bump up each of the settings by some factor, starting with a factor of 10, and then work my way down from there. I monitored the following key issues:

- CPU utilization
- Browser responsiveness
- Failed sites
- Broken images

While in the end they do not share the same factor, my findings were that the max-connec-tions settings worked well at four times their default and the persistent-connections worked well at six times their default. After some testing, 96, 32, 24, and 12 were the magic numbers for me and so far have proven to be accepted by many users. Table 5-1 shows the test systems used.

Table 5-1   Test Systems

Computer Type	DSL (256k)	Cable (1MB)	T1	Installed Memory
Intel Pentium II 400 MHz			✓	1GB
Intel Pentium III 500 MHZ	✓			256MB
Intel Pentium III 1133 MHz Mobile		✓	✓	512MB
Intel Pentium 4 2.8 GHz			✓	768MB
AMD Athlon 1000	✓	✓		512MB
AMD Athlon XP 2000+	✓	✓		1GB
AMD Athlon 64 3000+	✓	✓		512MB

Based on these system configurations, you can see that the connection hacks suggested work with a wide range of speed and memory amounts. Despite the fact that newer computers can render content much faster, I am amazed by the incredible performance of Firefox using the same settings as older systems. However, you may experience some hiccups and may need to modify these settings. So here are some suggestions.

As mentioned earlier, there are several sites and forums with recommended values and settings based on your computer and connection speed. At just about every one of these cyberplaces, you find a mixed bag of results and recommendations. Because of the many variables that can affect how you connect and how your system performs, I steer clear of recommending all the tweaks mentioned on those sites. Instead, I rely on the settings that I have used successfully and modify those accordingly for my recommendations.

The key to testing is to gauge how your system and connection react based on the changes you make. In keeping with the factor testing methodology, modem users and others can test the suggested tweaks and conduct some initial testing to pinpoint what works best. One page that I use for testing contains a form submit button that is tied to a JavaScript function to blast open four to eight pages at a time, preferably into tabs. This page can be found at `http://www.hackingfirefox.com/blaster.html`.

Cross-Reference   Chapter 10 covers several tools for customizing your tab browser settings.

This page helps you gauge how your system and connection handle downloading of multiple pages and graphics. Again, key factors to monitor are broken pages or images, timeouts, and CPU utilization. For example, a modem user on a fast computer may want to try a factor of 1.5 or 2 times the default values for simultaneous connections.

```
user_pref("network.http.max-connections", 48);
user_pref("network.http.max-connections-per-server", 16);
user_pref("network.http.max-persistent-connections-per-proxy",
8);
user_pref("network.http.max-persistent-connections-per-
server", 4);
```

Additionally, for users on a slow computer, modifying the content rendering should help with CPU utilization:

```
user_pref("nglayout.initialpaint.delay", 125);
user_pref("content.notify.ontimer", true);
user_pref("content.interrupt.parsing", true);
user_pref("content.notify.interval", 300000);
user_pref("content.notify.threshold", 300000);
user_pref("content.notify.backoffcount", 10);
user_pref("content.max.tokenizing.time", 2000000);
user_pref("content.maxtextrun", 8191);
```

There really is no smoking gun when it comes to calculating the best fit for all the PC and connection speed permutations, but playing around with these settings will help you pinpoint what works best for you.

Tip Visit `http://www.tweakfactor.com/articles/tweaks/firefoxtweak/4.html` for some examples of settings and tweaks based on computer and connection speeds.

To conduct some nonscientific performance testing, take the following steps:

1. Apply the tweaks that fit your system best.

2. Clear the browser's cache.

3. Exit and restart the browser.

4. Make sure you have JavaScript links set to open into tabs.

5. Open the blaster page at `http://www.hackingfirefox.com/blaster.html`.

6. Select one of the tests provided—four, six, or eight pages.

7. Monitor CPU utilization, page rendering, broken images, and so on.

Additionally, you can test for browser responsiveness by switching tabs while the pages are loading. To further stress-test these settings, try scrolling the foreground page with your mouse wheel while the content is downloading.

Tip

You can add a Clear Cache toolbar button, as well as other useful buttons, by installing the Toolbar Enhancements extension from `http://clav.mozdev.org/`.

Optimizing Disk and Memory Cache

The following hacks are targeted to help you decide where and how much disk and memory to allocate for Firefox to use. While changing these settings may seem mundane and trivial on some systems, they can really make a difference on others. Cache, whether disk or memory, is a local buffering zone that holds a copy of content that has been downloaded and viewed. Disk Cache is persistent between browsing sessions and stored on the hard drive, which assists the browser in not having to download content each time it is accessed. Memory Cache is session-based — that is, once you close Firefox, the memory cache or local buffer is cleared.

Note

If Firefox happens to crash, the entire disk cache is cleared out automatically.

Changing Disk Cache Location

Modifying the location of the disk cache can have a side benefit of freeing up space without having to repartition or remap directories at the operating-system level. The best benefit, though, comes if you happen to have two physical hard drives installed. In my experience, moving a system's paging file and Firefox's disk cache to a secondary drive helps performance by balancing disk reads and writes across both drives.

Tip

Before applying this hack, clear your cache directory.

By default, newer computers come with one hard drive and one partition. This, coupled with the fact that newer hard drives are very fast, means that this hack is not a top priority for very fast computers. If you are on an older system with a second hard drive or would like to repoint the disk cache to a RAM drive, this tweak is for you. Here's how to modify this setting:

```
// Sample for Windows Users
user_pref("browser.cache.disk.parent_directory",
"d:\\temp\\");

// Sample for Unix/Linux/Mac Users
user_pref("browser.cache.disk.parent_directory", "/tmp");
```

Note

A subdirectory of cache is created in the directory you choose.

If the path you have chosen does not exist, Firefox creates it the next time you open it up. Windows users should make sure that this value has double slashes, as displayed in the preceding code; not including these causes internal parsing errors and possible preference-file corruption. The only exception to this rule is if you are adding this value via the about:config screen, in which case, you should not use the double slashes — single slashes will automatically get converted to double.

Viewing, Changing Size, and Cleaning Your Disk Cache

This first section is more for informational purposes and to point you to your disk cache for cleaning. As you can see from Figure 5-2, typing **about:cache** in your browser's location bar and pressing Enter brings up the memory and disk cache statistics with the capability of drilling in and inspecting the entries stored. The first piece of information that you can use is your current memory and disk cache settings and utilization. The memory cache optimization hack in the next section and the disk cache size customization that follows give you an indicator of how efficiently you are allocating this space by analyzing the "Storage in use" figures.

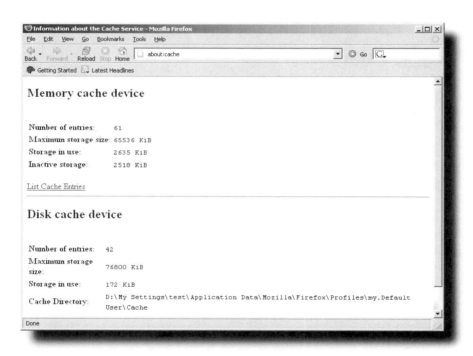

FIGURE 5-2: The Information about the Cache Service page

To change the amount of disk space allocated for disk caching, you can modify the following preference:

```
user_pref("browser.cache.disk.capacity", 76800);
```

The preceding value sets your disk cache to 75MB (75 × 1024KB), where the default is 50,000, a tad less than 50MB. By monitoring your disk utilization from time to time, you can see how effective this setting may be. You can also see from Figure 5-2 that the location of your disk cache is listed, making it easier for you to locate and clean up manually.

As for the memory optimizations, using the about:cache statistics, you will be able to determine after a period of sustained browsing if the Bugzilla-recommended update of 64 megabytes is enough for your needs. (See next section.) For some applications or websites, if they are heavy with DHTML or graphics, monitoring and updating the memory cache may make a huge difference.

Increasing Memory Cache Size

This hack helps by retaining objects from visited sites in memory so they do not have to be reloaded from a site or from disk. Memory cache can be populated by either disk cache or recently downloaded content and is used for browsing history, the Back button, or any similar feature. Based on Bugzilla bug id # 105344, which you can find at `https://bugzilla .mozilla.org/show_bug.cgi?id=105344#c26`, the default memory cache allocations are listed in Table 5-2.

Table 5-2   Memory Cache Allocations

Installed RAM	Automatic Cache Allocation
32MB	2MB
64MB	4MB
128MB	8MB
256MB	14MB
512MB	22MB
1024MB	32MB
2048MB	44MB
4096MB	58MB

While this is a nice allocation for circa 1990, today's memory prices have yielded default memory configurations of 512MB to 1GB for most systems and warrant a revisit to the default allocation. After some testing, I have noticed no load or performance hit by allocating more than the recommended memory for Firefox. Add to this that there are no apparent preallocation memory increases, and this hack is a no-brainer.

```
// Amount of per session memory cache to use:
// -1 = dynamically allocate (default),
// 0 = none, n = memory capacity in kilobytes
// If you have the memory to spare, enabling this
```

```
// will run things a little smoother.
// 65536 = 64MB, drop this down you can not spare the RAM
// 32768 = 32MB, etc.

user_pref("browser.cache.memory.capacity", 65536);
```

Caution   Do not get overzealous with this hack. There is only so much content one can visit in a day, and reserving too much memory could possibly lead to unforeseen issues.

Windows Memory Optimization Hack

Windows NT–based operating systems such as Windows NT 4.0, 2000, XP, and 2003 Server have a built-in feature of clearing or trimming the working set of memory pages when you minimize a window. Windows does this to clear up used memory and to allow more memory for other applications. This memory technique usually yields a memory usage reduction of 50 to 95 percent when minimizing a window (or the last window, if several windows are open) and applies to any program. Figures 5-3 and 5-4 display the significant drop in memory allocation with the default window minimize behavior.

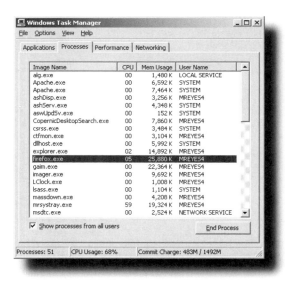

FIGURE 5-3: Memory utilization before minimizing

So why is this memory trimming so bad for Firefox? Because Firefox renders just about every visual component and element of the browser, trimming memory used by the browser forces Firefox to reallocate and rerender all visual elements on the browser as well as the web page that is loaded, causing some grief and possible hard drive thrashing.

```
// Allows Firefox to maintain its GUI memory
// so that the browser window will snap right back
// after being minimized.
user_pref("config.trim_on_minimize", false);
```

FIGURE 5-4: Memory utilization after minimizing, without this hack

Note

For more information and history on this feature, look up Bugzilla bug number 76831 or visit `https://bugzilla.mozilla.org/show_bug.cgi?id=76831`.

When you modify this preference, Firefox minimizes a window without trimming the memory usage when running under Windows NT–based systems. The upside is that the Firefox window will definitely snap back without a delay; the downside is that memory usage will stay the same, and you do not benefit from having Windows trim the memory pages.

Tip

For more information about how Windows trims memory or how to avoid this in your programs, visit the following knowledge-base article: `http://support.microsoft.com/kb/293215`.

Venturing into Optimized Third-Party Builds

Despite the blazing speeds you have already achieved, there are additional, processor-based optimizations you can attempt. Both Intel and AMD have a core set of features and routines that are used to handle the operating system's needs. With the advent of multimedia enhancements and instruction sets such as MMX, 3dNow, SSE, SSE2, and SSE3, optimizing Firefox to your specific processor type and instruction set helps with responsiveness and page-rendering speeds. A great resource for choosing a build for your specific operating system and system type is the MozillaZine.org website at `http://forums.mozillazine.org/viewtopic.hp?t=203504`.

How do you determine which enhanced instruction sets your system is capable of? For Windows users, you can check your system settings from the Control Panel. A more informative and reliable tool is CPU-Z, from `http://www.cpuid.com/`. As shown in Figure 5-5, this program gives you an immediate look into what your processor's capabilities are.

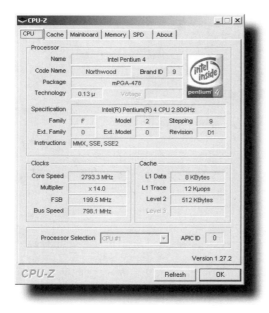

FIGURE 5-5: Main CPU-Z information screen

The Instructions field in the middle of the CPU-Z screen contains the information on which you need to focus. Using this, you can see that this system's maximum supported instruction set is SSE2 and that it's an Intel Pentium 4–based processor. Armed with this information, finding a compatible, optimized build is a snap. The real question is which customized build to use, and there really is no easy answer to that.

Linux users can issue the **cat /proc/cpuinfo** command in a console window to yield results similar to the following:

```
processor : 0
vendor_id : GenuineIntel
cpu family : 6
model : 13
model name : Intel(R) Pentium(R) M processor 1.60GHz
stepping : 6
cpu MHz : 1601.033
cache size : 64 KB
fdiv_bug : no
hlt_bug : no
f00f_bug : no
coma_bug : no
fpu : yes
fpu_exception : yes
cpuid level : 2
wp : yes
flags : fpu vme de pse tsc msr mce cx8 apic sep mtrr pge mca cmov
pat clflush dts acpi mmx fxsr sse sse2 ss tm pbe tm2 est
bogomips : 3170.30
```

The key elements to look for when running the Linux cpuinfo program are the values from the `flags` line, which will contain CPU information for processor support such as `sse sse2` in the preceding code. If the flags are too difficult to decipher, just rely on the model name, which here is Intel Pentium M processor 1.60GHz.

Most builders provide release versions of their optimized builds, also known as *branch* or *milestone* versions. These are usually in line, feature for feature, with the officially released Mozilla builds, with the exception of some builders who may include fixes to annoying or trivial issues. Additionally, many builders also create trunk or nightly builds; these builds are literally bleeding-edge-technology versions of all recent code changes submitted for the next major milestone version. For the most part, these trunk builds have historically been relatively stable, with the exception of a few times when sweeping changes and new functionality were introduced. In these times, trunk builds are not the most pleasant to use. So if you want to dive into the custom builds arena but do not have the time to rebuild your profile, you may want to stick with the branch or milestone optimized builds.

Tip

For daily updates of optimized builds, visit the MozillaZine Third Party/Unofficial Builds forum at http://forums.mozillazine.org/viewforum.php?f=42.

Most customized builds come packaged as ZIP and 7z compressed files or self-extracting executables. What this means is that they do not have an official installer, and they need to be extracted before you use them. On the upside, this means that you can keep your current installed version and still do testing with newer versions. For ZIP or 7z packaged builds, you need to use tools such as 7-Zip, WinZip, ungzip, and so on to extract their contents. Some builders provide self-extracting executables for Windows-based systems that automatically extract to a Firefox directory.

Note Always make a backup of your profile directory or any critical files before running any newer official or optimized build.

From past and present testing of builds, I recommend the following four optimized builds:

- **MOOX:** Getting and using MOOX builds is as easy as visiting the build definitions page, `http://www.moox.ws/tech/mozilla/mdefs.htm`, and seeing which build you want. These builds are not processor-specific; they are processor feature or instruction set–specific and are easy to pinpoint from the definitions page. For more information and downloads, visit `http://www.moox.ws/tech/mozilla/firefox.htm`.

- **MMOY:** These branch and trunk builds are superoptimized with patches not found in any of the official Mozilla builds. They are not processor-specific, but they are instruction set–specific. Some enhancements include faster hash algorithms, improved JPEG rendering, and others. For more information and downloads, visit `http://forums.mozillazine.org/viewtopic.php?t=54487`.

- **stipe:** These branch builds are instruction set–specific and in the past have gotten very good results and feedback from users. For more information and downloads, visit `http://forums.mozillazine.org/viewtopic.php?t=215104`.

- **BlueFyre:** These are trunk builds and are AMD processor–specific, supporting only Athlon XP and later. For more information and downloads, visit `http://forums.mozillazine.org/viewtopic.php?t=92495`.

Note Third-party builds use customized application icons for the main application window because of restrictions in icon and logo usage and to help users know when they are running official builds versus third-party builds.

After extracting these builds, just find and launch firefox.exe and sit back and enjoy. If Firefox does not come up properly or you are not happy with it, you can simply close it and remove the directory you extracted. Your main installed version should still be working properly.

Tip Recent changes in extension and theme processing for Firefox 1.1 may make 1.0 and 1.1 version switching a hassle. To minimize your headaches, make sure to install new extensions, themes, and updates with your 1.0 builds.

Spring Cleaning

One of the most recommended fixes for issues that may arise is "Create a New Profile." While a lot of users do that, my preference is to dig a littler deeper and try to clean house myself. While some fixes in the past were preference related, most for me have been file and legacy configuration issues, mostly with themes and extensions.

Refreshing Your XUL Cache File

As mentioned in Chapter 1, XUL is a cross-platform extendable language used to create the browser's interface. Additionally, it is the language used by extensions to overlay or modify the existing Firefox interface. The XUL cache is a collection of these XUL modifications that hold options, dialogs, and overlays for extensions and created pages. The XUL cache is used to increase the load and speed of applying extension hacks and rendering the main Firefox interface. My experience has been that extension changes and updates may not clean up discontinued XUL cached pages, and I most often find myself using this tweak when the process of upgrading extensions takes a turn for the worst.

To remove the XUL cache file, just follow these steps:

1. Close Firefox.
2. Find your profile directory (discussed in Chapter 1).
3. Delete the xul.mfl or the xul.mfasl file.

Note   The size of the XUL cache file increases with the number of extensions you have installed.

This file may range from a few hundred kilobytes to close to a few megabytes. If you are fearful of any losses, just rename it, but do not worry; the XUL file is re-created the next time you launch Firefox.

Just to be safe, you should do this every time you upgrade an extension that may have gone through a lot of feature enhancements or fixes, and after uninstalling any extension. My preference is to do so any time I have to dive into the profile directory.

Note   You can disable the XUL cache, but doing this may cause several issues with extensions. Do this only if you are an extension developer and follow the steps detailed in the MozillaZine knowledge-base instructions at `http://kb.mozillazine.org/Dev_:_Tips_:_Disable_ XUL_cache`.

Cleaning Up after Uninstalling or Upgrading

For the sake of not repeating the "Starting Over without Losing All Your Settings" section in Chapter 3, I will just mention this subject here and explain its importance as it relates to performance. Performance issues may arise when upgrading extensions, themes, or the main browser itself. Using the instructions in Chapter 3, you have a much better chance of being able to recover your profile's usability without having to create a new one.

The key areas where Firefox configurations usually benefit from cleaning up are as follows:

- Configuration issues with extensions, overlays, and upgrades in the Chrome\Overlayinfo directory

- Older theme JAR files that get copied to the chrome directory instead of the extensions directory

- Cleanup of some minor extension installer configuration settings or install.rdf properties

- Cleanup of extensions listed in the Extensions.rdf file

- Cleaning up XUL cache file in the main profile directory

After cleaning up your profile, Firefox should return to its default appearance, sans any extensions and themes, allowing you to begin rebuilding your settings.

Summary

This chapter taps into increasing browser performance, decreasing response time, and tweaking the most out of the Firefox browsing experience. Hacks to the connection, page rendering, disk and memory caches, and memory usage enhance performance greatly. Additionally, the chapter covers the use of third-party builds that offer extended fixes and optimizations specific to your computer's processor capabilities; these builds offer improvements in rendering images and core browser functionality, tweaking even more performance in the long run. Finally, the importance of cleaning up the profile to remove any lingering issues or junk that may have been left behind by extensions, hacks, and normal use is covered.

Hacking Security and Privacy

L et's face it: Privacy and security are two very real concerns. Most people don't like to think about them very much. Fortunately, you're using Firefox, so you are already on the right track. Windows users out there who previously used Internet Explorer are already significantly safer just by switching browsers. And while Linux folks traditionally tend to be very knowledgeable when it comes to security concerns, and most Mac users are generally used to being safe and secure due to their minority, Firefox takes security and privacy one step further.

by Aaron Spuler

The default settings in Firefox are good at protecting your privacy and security. But you can make some modifications to protect yourself even more. If you're ready to lock down your browser tighter than Fort Knox, let's get started.

Concerns with Saving Form or Login Data

Firefox has the ability to store commonly used form elements and login credentials. I find this behavior to be incredibly convenient. If you're using a public computer, however, or are looking at sensitive information, turning this option off, either temporarily or permanently, is easy.

To access the settings for form or login data, you must open the Options window and access the Privacy settings. To do this, select Tools ➪ Options. If you are using Linux or a Mac, select Edit ➪ Preferences. Then select the Privacy button on the left side of the Preferences window.

There are six items available in the Privacy section, but the one we're concerned with right now is the second from the top. To expand this section, click on Saved Form Information to access more options. Figure 6-1 shows this window. (My theme, Neptune, is shown in the screenshot, so your screen may differ slightly depending on the theme you are using.)

FIGURE **6-1:** Privacy settings for Saved Form Information

To purge any previously saved form data, click the Clear button. You will not be prompted to confirm this action, and there is no reversing this action, so be absolutely sure you want to clear any saved form data before proceeding. To prevent Firefox from saving any sort of form data in the future, uncheck "Save information I enter in web page forms and the Search Bar."

To manage login data, expand the Saved Passwords section. Figure 6-2 shows the options available. Again, the process is similar to management of saved form data. To purge all previously stored login credentials, click the Clear button. Unlike the Clear button for saved form data, you will be prompted with a dialog to confirm your request. To prevent Firefox from saving any login credentials, uncheck "Remember Passwords."

With saved form data, it's all or nothing, but Firefox allows you to selectively manage passwords. The Password Manager allows for fine-grained management of passwords. Clicking on the View Saved Passwords button brings up the Password Manager, as shown in Figure 6-3.

FIGURE 6-2: Privacy settings for saved passwords

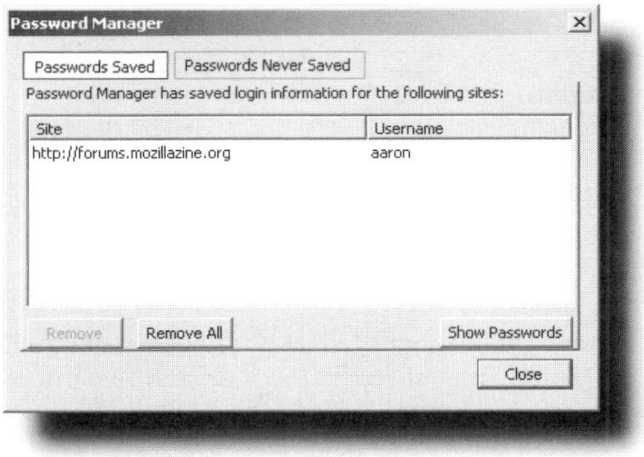

FIGURE 6-3: The Password Manager

The Password Manager allows you to view any passwords that you've previously told Firefox to save. If you want to view passwords, click the Show Passwords button. If those passwords are confidential, I recommend hiding them again after viewing; simply click Hide Passwords. You have the ability to remove individual sites or remove all sites from the list. Login credentials for sites that you told Firefox to never save are listed in the Passwords Never Saved tab, with the option to remove them individually or remove all from the list.

Creating a Master Password

A Master Password protects access to your stored passwords in the Password Manager. When you have set a Master Password, you are prompted to enter it before access to the Password Manager is granted. To create a Master Password, click the Set Master Password. . . button (shown in Figure 6-2). Be sure to select a Master Password that you will be able to remember, because if you forget it, there is no way to retrieve that information. Figure 6-4 illustrates the Change Master Password window.

FIGURE 6-4: The Change Master Password window

Covering Your Tracks

Now that you know how to manage form and login data, let's talk about how can you further protect yourself. In general, you should not give any sort of confidential or sensitive information out to any website unless that site is using encryption to mask the data from third parties. To notify you of encryption status, all themes provide a visual clue in the URL bar. Generally, the URL bar turns from white to yellow and displays a padlock on the right side. Different themes do things slightly differently — most themes do not stylize the URL bar, but all of my themes utilize the rounded URL bar, and so do themes by CatThief, Lynchknot, and others. Figure 6-5 displays the secure-site indicator in the URL bar in both the default theme and my Neptune theme.

FIGURE 6-5: Secure-site indicator in URL bar

If you wish to remove all traces of information that Firefox has collected during your browser history, you can do so with one click. Referring to the Privacy settings shown in Figures 6-1 and 6-2, the Clear All button in the bottom-right corner will completely cover your tracks. When you click Clear All, you are presented with a confirmation dialog in case you accidentally clicked it. After confirming that you wish to clear all data, the following information will be removed:

- Browsing history
- Cache
- The list of recently downloaded files
- All saved form information and searches
- All cookies
- Saved passwords

Cleaning Up Browsing History

If you were not already aware, Firefox and all other browsers keep track of what sites you have visited in an effort to make pages load faster. Firefox stores records of the browsing history in three ways:

- A list of sites you have visited called the History
- A list of files downloaded called the Download History
- A temporary storage area for web page files called the cache

Cache

Pages you view are stored in a special temporary folder so that next time you visit the page, it loads faster because the entire page does not need to be downloaded again—only the portions of the page that have changed. Firefox allows the specification of a maximum size for the cache folder and the option to delete the contents of that folder. The cache is an all-or-nothing type of item. You are not allowed to selectively remove items from the cache, but you can remove all items with the Clear button, as illustrated in Figure 6-6.

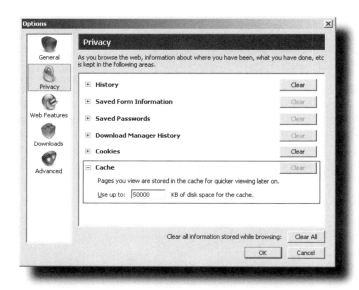

FIGURE 6-6: Privacy settings for cache

Download Manager

The Download Manager stores information about which files you have saved from the Internet. You can access options for how Firefox should remove items from the Download Manager History in the Privacy Settings window, shown in Figure 6-7.

Before pressing the Clear button, be entirely sure that you want to remove all items, because you are not prompted for confirmation.

If you wish to remove individual items from the Download Manager History, you can do so in the Downloads window, shown in Figure 6-8. To open this window, choose Tools ➪ Downloads. Removing an item is as simple as clicking Remove, which appears next to the item's name in the list. There is no confirmation—once you've clicked Remove, the entry is gone, and there is no way to get it back. The Clean Up button in the Downloads window has the same function as the Clear button in the Download Manager History section of the Privacy Settings window.

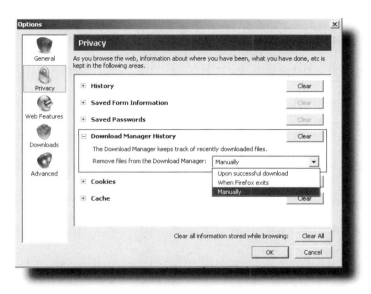

FIGURE 6-7: Privacy settings for Download Manager History

FIGURE 6-8: The Downloads window

History

The History is a list of every website you have visited, along with the time of visit. As with the Download Manager, there are two options to consider in the Privacy Settings window (see Figure 6-9): You can set the number of days that Firefox stores items in the list of pages visited, and you can clear the list. You will not be prompted for confirmation when pressing the Clear button.

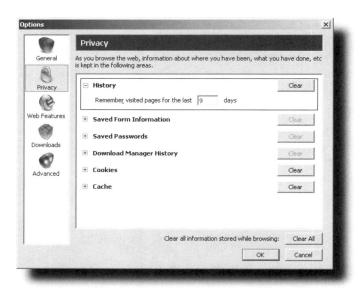

FIGURE 6-9: Privacy settings for History

To view and delete individual items from the History, you must view the History from within the main browser window. You can open the History in two ways: by selecting Go ⇨ History or selecting View ⇨ Sidebar ⇨ History (see Figure 6-10). Once the History is visible, you can perform searches to find individual items. To delete an item, either right-click the item and select Delete or highlight the item and press the Delete key.

FIGURE 6-10: The History sidebar

Blocking Unwanted Cookies

You probably are already familiar with the term *cookie*. If not, here is a quick explanation. A *cookie* is a file created by an Internet site to store information on your computer, such as your preferences when visiting that site. When you visit a site that uses cookies, the site might ask Firefox to place one or more cookies on your hard disk. Later, when you return to the site, Firefox sends back the cookies that belong to the site. This allows the site to present you with information customized to fit your needs. Cookies cannot gather any personal information that you do not provide, and websites cannot read cookies set by other sites. Figure 6-11 displays the cookie preferences.

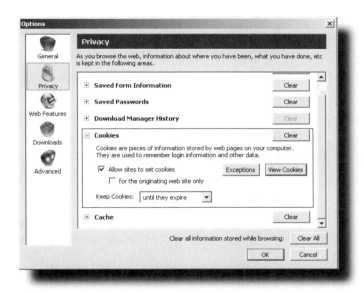

FIGURE **6-11: Privacy settings for cookies**

From here, you can set preferences such as the length of time cookies are allowed to stay on your computer, whether any sites are allowed to store cookies on your computer, and whether cookies from sites other than the originating site are allowed. The latter case warrants some explaining: If you are visiting a site, such as http://www.cnn.com, that is partnered with an advertising site, such as http://www.doubleclick.net, which provides the ads on the original site, only http://www.cnn.com will be allowed to store cookies on your machine; http://www.doubleclick.net will not. If the option to limit cookies to the originating site only is not selected, both sites will be able to store a cookie on your computer, and then http://www.doubleclick.net would have some information about the site you visited because its cookie would store some information stating that you had requested the cookie from http://www.cnn.com—this is how some ad agencies on the Internet are able to track an individual's behavior.

Reviewing Stored Cookies and Removing Them

If you wish to find out what cookies are stored on your computer or remove some cookies, click on the View Cookies button (shown in Figure 6-11). That opens the Stored Cookies window, shown in Figure 6-12.

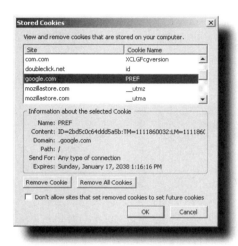

FIGURE **6-12: The Stored Cookies window.**

Selecting a cookie from the list at the top displays its information in the lower pane. To remove a single cookie, highlight it and click the Remove Cookie button. To remove all cookies, click the Remove All Cookies button. To prevent a removed cookie from coming back, make sure to check the box beside "Don't allow sites that set removed cookies to set future cookies."

Preemptively Blocking Known Undesirable Cookies

What if you know that you don't ever want to receive cookies from a specific site? Firefox has the ability to preemptively block any cookies in a list. Click the Exceptions button (shown in Figure 6-11). In the Exceptions window, you can list what sites are always or never allowed to store cookies. Figure 6-13 shows the Exceptions window. Simply type the address of the website in the text box at the top and then click the Block button. From now on, Firefox will never allow that website to store a cookie on your computer. (If you already have cookies stored from that site, you will have to remove them using the Stored Cookies window, shown in Figure 6-12.)

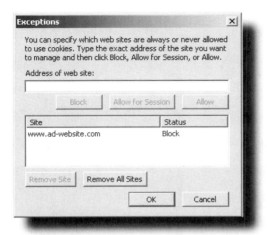

FIGURE 6-13: The Cookie Exceptions window

Using the Mozilla Update Service

The Mozilla Update service allows you to update the extensions and themes installed, as well as the Firefox program itself. The easiest way to use the update service is to select Advanced from the list on the left of the Options window, click Software Update, and then click the Check Now button, as shown in Figure 6-14.

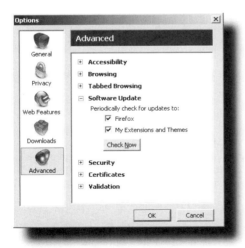

FIGURE 6-14: Advanced settings for updating software

After you click the Check Now button, Firefox checks for any updates and presents a list if any are found, as shown in Figure 6-15.

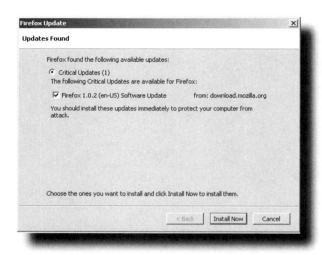

FIGURE **6-15: The Firefox Update window**

From here, you can select which updates you wish to install and then click the Install Now button. Updates to extensions and themes sometimes take effect immediately. If not, the updates take effect after Firefox is restarted. Firefox updates require the browser to be shut down while updating files.

There are several other ways to check for updates:

- Extensions only
- Themes only
- Update notification service

For updates to themes or extensions, there is a button in the individual Extensions and Themes windows for this purpose, as shown in Figure 6-16. The Update Notification Service is the only way to check for updates to Firefox, themes, and extensions at the same time. The Update button in both the Extensions and Themes windows checks for updates only for extensions or themes.

The final method for receiving updates is through the Firefox update notification service. Different themes do this in different ways. I chose to use the same icons as the default theme for update notification, while some themes use custom icons. I elected to make the update notification icons invisible unless there are updates available, while some themes, including the default, always show the update notification icons. As shown in Figure 6-17, the update notification icon is the circle with an up arrow inside it, to the left of the throbber. There are three different states for update notification:

- A green circle means that everything is up to date.

- A blue circle means that extension(s) and/or theme(s) require updates.

- A red circle means that there is an update to the Firefox browser.

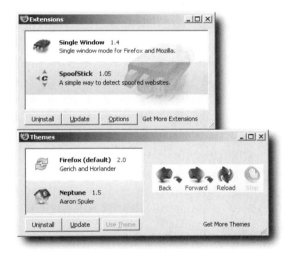

FIGURE 6-16: Extensions and Themes updates

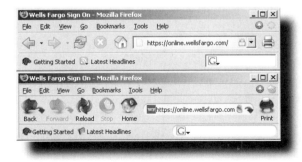

FIGURE 6-17: Update notification on the menu bar

Disabling Extension Installation

One of the greatest security advantages of using Firefox over Internet Explorer is the way Firefox handles autoinstallation. While Internet Explorer allows websites to automatically install items, Firefox never allows anything to be installed unless requested. Before installing any extensions, you are prompted to ensure that you really want to install. If you'd like to fine-tune that behavior even further, you can disable extension installation altogether. In the Options window, under Web Features is where you can find these settings, as shown in Figure 6-18.

FIGURE 6-18: Web Features in the Options window

You can view and modify which sites are allowed to install extensions without any additional confirmation by clicking the Allowed Sites button. To disable extension installation entirely, simply uncheck "Allow web sites to install software."

Disabling Suspicious JavaScript Features

Sometimes, websites can do tricky things with the JavaScript code embedded in their pages. You can disable JavaScript completely, but doing so can break the functionality on some websites. To disable JavaScript, simply uncheck "Enable JavaScript." You can still use JavaScript but disable suspicious behaviors by clicking on the Advanced. . . button next to the JavaScript checkbox. I personally allow some of the suspicious behaviors but disable others. My configuration is shown in Figure 6-19.

FIGURE 6-19: The Advanced JavaScript Options window

Disabling Windows shell: Protocol

The Windows shell: protocol is a very dangerous security risk. This protocol affects only Windows systems, so Linux and Mac systems are safe from this sort of attack. Using the `shell:` prefix (instead of the `http:` prefix) allows access to the files stored on your computer. If pointed to a nonexistent file, Firefox does not know what to do and eventually crashes. This problem was discovered and fixed with the release of Firefox 0.9.2. If someone gained access to your computer, the protocol could be reenabled. To check and see whether you are safe, type **about:config** in the address bar. In the filter bar, type **shell**.

If the `network.protocol-handler.external.shell` option is set to `false`, as in Figure 6-20, you are safe. If it is set to `true`, you can right-click on it and select Reset; this deactivates the shell: protocol.

FIGURE 6-20: Disabling the Windows shell: protocol

Anti-Phishing Measures and Tools

Phishing is an attempt to steal personal information to be used for identity theft. Generally, an email is sent that looks like a valid site asking you to update personal information. The website that is linked in the email is actually a fake site that looks identical to the real site and even has what looks like a valid URL in the address bar. There are ways to tell that the site is fake, however.

Traditionally, no valid website would ask you to update personal information such as bank-account numbers, Social Security number, or credit card information via email. If you get such an email, do not update your information with the link provided!

Phishing scams usually involve some form of spoofing, masking the true URL of a site and making it look like something else. A spoofed site could make the URL in the address bar say http://www.mozilla.org, but you could actually be on another site, such as http://www.spoofed-mozilla.com, for example.

The other way to tell that the site is fake is a little harder, because it involves detecting the site's fake URL. The best way to detect a faked URL is by using the Spoofstick extension. Spoofstick always displays the domain name of the site that you are currently viewing. For example, if you were at http://www.corestree.com/spoofstick/, Spoofstick would say "You're on www.corestreet.com," as shown in Figure 6-21.

FIGURE 6-21: Spoofstick tells you where you are.

If things are not going right—that is, if you're on a spoofed site—the URL in the address bar and the Spoofstick will not match. That's your cue that things have gone awry. The Spoofstick extension always shows the real URL that you are visiting and cannot be spoofed with any sort of trickery.

You can find this extension at http://www.corestreet.com/spoofstick/, along with a great example of a phishing scheme foiled by Spoofstick. After installing the Spoofstick extension, simply right-click on the toolbar and select customize. Then you can drag the Spoofstick button to the location you desire. In Figure 6-21, I hid the Spoofstick button by going into the Spoofstick configuration.

Summary

This chapter covers several topics that should help you achieve the level of security you desire in your browsing. Topics covered include form and login data, Master Passwords, cookies, update service, JavaScript features, and phishing. General information is covered on all aspects of privacy in Firefox. This chapter does not aim to show every possible combination of settings—just the range of options available. You can use the information provided to customize the security preferences to your liking.

Hacking Banner Ads, Content, Images, and Cookies

by Terren Tong

Benjamin Franklin once said, "Nothing in life is certain except death and taxes." In the Internet-pervasive world, we can make an amendment to those immortal words—"Nothing is certain on the Internet except ads and more ads." For better or worse, the Internet has grown into a largely commercial medium. Many nonmerchant commercial web sites rely on advertising as a primary source of income. While one of the main goals of advertising is to get the attention of consumers, it also serves to raise the ire of users. Many advertisements are distracting at best and annoying at worst. Firefox includes several tools that help the user fight the deluge of ads that intrude on the Internet experience. One of the default weapons in the Firefox repertoire is the built-in popup blocker, which suppresses one of the most aggravating advertising techniques. While this is a great feature, this still leaves banner ads, offensive images, cookies, and JavaScript and DHTML tricks that some sites employ to get around.

This chapter covers some features of Firefox that can reduce the number of displayed ads. We also cover the Ad-Block extension, which provides a bit more flexibility than what is included in Firefox. Beyond annoying display elements is something still linked to advertisements but unseen: cookies. Cookies can be useful—they allow websites to place a small piece of information on your computer to remember who you are. This is great for things such as forums, so that every visit does not require the user to log in again, or for e-commerce sites to keep track of items in the shopping cart. The gray area of cookies comes when marketers use them to track what sites you have visited and use that information to build a profile of your web browsing habits or send you targeted advertising. In addition to blocking banners and images, we will look at various methods of blocking cookies.

It is important to note that a lot of nonmerchant web sites do rely on advertising as an important source of revenue. Blocking all ads from your favorite web sites is probably not the best way to show appreciation for the content they produce. A web master of a large web site noted dryly, "Users are always saying, 'Why are they forcing ads down our throats? We can just go elsewhere.' But if that is really the case, why do people try so hard to block ads instead of going to the theoretical elsewhere?"

So you should realize that the Internet is an advertisement-subsidized medium, much like television and most printed media; it would be a good idea to continue supporting sites that you do appreciate and frequent on a regular basis by being a bit selective with the techniques covered in this chapter. As repugnant as advertising is at times, the Internet as it is now is probably preferable to a subscription-based model where users would have to pay for each individual site they visit.

Using the Block Image Function

In addition to popup blocking, which by default is turned in with a standard Firefox installation, Firefox includes a feature that enables the user to block images from specific domains. This allows users to filter out images from domains that they do not want to see images from, including sites known for advertising and/or graphic content. However, life is not black and white, and neither is image blocking. There are caveats to the domain filtering method of image blocking, as a site may host images you do and do not want to see. Despite the potential for problems, the block image function is easy to use, available without additional Firefox extensions, and effective at filtering out the more egregious domains you definitely do not want to see.

The first method of blocking images is very easy. Fire up a web page, preferably one that is graphically heavy. Put the mouse cursor over any image and right-click on the image. A menu like that shown in Figure 7-1 should appear.

FIGURE 7-1: The Block Images command through a right mouse click

Highlighting and clicking Block Images from examplewebsite.tld blocks all images from that particular web site. (The text of this option always reflects the loaded web site.) Refreshing the current page should result in a drastically different looking web page without much of its graphics. If you just blocked images from your favorite web page, don't worry; later in this section, we go through the process of undoing the change. Even if you blocked an actual domain that you really do not want to see images from, you should not skip this next part, as there are some important points about the block image function that we examine.

There are people who do not want images loaded at all; maybe they are on a very slow dial-up Internet connection, or they think that a thousand words are worth more than a picture. Those who are interested in a text-only browser can feel free to check out `http://lynx.browser.org`. However, Firefox has the ability to perform a similar function. Select Tools ⇨ Options, and an Options window like that shown in Figure 7-2 appears. Load Images is checked by default—turning this off removes all graphical elements from web pages indiscriminately. The indented suboption "for the originating web site only" is far more interesting. Checking this removes from a web page graphical elements that are not part of the same domain. Suppose that examplewebsite.tld has advertisements displayed from exampleadvertisers.tld embedded on its web site. Enabling the "for the originating web site only" option strips images such as those from exampleadvertisers.tld and any domain other than examplewebsite.tld. Referencing a subdomain, such as images.examplewebsite.tld, does not seem to be affected.

FIGURE 7-2: Loading Images for the originating web site only

Most advertisements are delivered through an ad server and reside on a different domain from the content web site, so this technique serves to block many image-based ads. This is still not the magic solution, however, as this has negative effects in scenarios that do not involve advertisements. One example would be an auction site that has several accompanying pictures to show off the product. If the auctioneer decided to host pictures on his own personal web space or through one of the many photo hosting services that are springing up, the images would not display for someone with the "for the originating web site only" option enabled. Clearly, this blanket option is not ideal for the majority of users, but fortunately it can be fine-tuned, so please keep this option turned on as we continue.

Referring to Figure 7-2, note the Exceptions button beside Load Images. Open up the Options dialog again, and give that a click. This should bring up the dialog shown in Figure 7-3.

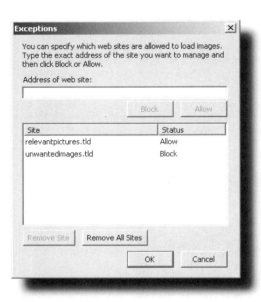

FIGURE 7-3: Image exceptions to allow and block specific sites

If you participated in the earlier exercise of blocking images, now you have the opportunity to restore images to the site that you experimented on. Simply highlight the web site that should be restored and click the Remove Site button. When you refresh that particular web page, all the picture elements should be restored.

As previously mentioned, the "for the originating web site only" option generally blocks too much, although it does a good job of removing the majority of advertisements. The Exceptions dialog allows just that—sites that should always be allowed to display pictures can be listed, as well as sites that you would never want to see pictures from. Think of the "originating web site only" option as the paranoid approach; with this on, it is up to users to specify sites that they explicitly allow to pull in third-party pictures. This still does not guarantee that advertisements or inappropriate images will not sneak in—somewebsite.tld might still pull in ads from ads.somewebsite.tld, which we already mentioned is not blocked, and visiting inappropriatewebsite.tld will still load inappropriate images from that particular domain. Leaving off the "originating web site only" option would be a more optimistic approach, and instead of the white list approach previously outlined, this still requires the user to maintain a blacklist of what sites to block. Neither approach is perfect, and both approaches require a fairly significant amount of vigilance on the part of the user, but they do offer a start in filtering unwanted images.

Using Built-in Content Handling to Block Ads

Blocking out advertisements based on very specific criteria, such as through a domain name, is a very low-level approach. While using lists to filter out domains is effective for some larger advertisers, maintaining a list for the hordes of smaller sites is a daunting proposition. I call this *a low-level approach* because it requires personal attention and manual implementation. On the flip side, I consider blocking advertising with the originating web site option *a high-level approach* because it relies on the program to target the fact that advertisements are generally delivered through a different domain from the one on which the content is hosted. The problem with this approach is that a lot of legitimate images get filtered out, and the user is still faced with the low-level problem of having to specify sites to allow. Both the blacklist and the whitelist approach have their uses, but clearly the devil is in the details; in this case, the small sites require more work than most users would probably like to put in.

Beyond the fact that most advertisements are delivered by a foreign domain, ads possess other properties that you can take advantage of from a high-level perspective. For example, advertisements share a lot of attributes, and you can take advantage of this to attack and remove ads on a more generic basis than filtering through domain names. Taking advantage of share attributes is somewhat complicated and requires some understanding of HTML and Cascading Style Sheets (CSS) but is more versatile than the image blocking tricks covered in the previous section.

Once again, users should navigate to their profile directory folder. Two subfolders are important here: the chrome folder and the US/chrome folder.

In the US/chrome folder, there should be two files; userContent-example.css is the one that we are interested in, and this should be copied to the chrome folder and renamed userContent.css. Using your text editor of choice, you can open up the userContent.css file that should now be inside the chrome folder. This file contains the following partial snippet:

```
/*
 * Edit this file and copy it as userContent.css into your
 * profile-directory/chrome/
 */


/*
 * This file can be used to apply a style to all web pages you view
 * Rules without !important are overruled by author rules if the
 * author sets any. Rules with !important overrule author rules.
 */
```

Currently, there is nothing active in the userContent.css file. Everything surrounded by "/* */" is commented out, meaning that it serves just as annotation for the author and anyone reading through the file and is not parsed by Firefox. A long discussion of CSS is beyond the scope of this book, but in short, CSS allows a user to define a set of rules to manipulate HTML elements. (Those who are interested in pursuing the subject further are encouraged to check out http://www.w3.org/Style/CSS/.)

For more on CSS, see *CSS Hacks and Filters: Making Cascading Stylesheets Work* by Joseph W. Lowery (Wiley, 2005).

As we continue scrolling through the userContent.css file ,there are a few additional CSS examples, none of which is directly pertinent to image blocking. However, they do provide a look at the structure of a CSS rule statement, which is made up of three components in the following format:

```
selector { property: value}
```

The `selector` is the HTML element that the rule will be applied to, while the `property` refers to what specific component is being modified, and the `value` is what the `property` will be set to.

For functionality equivalent to disabling Load Images (as shown in Figure 7-2), you can add the following to the bottom of the userContent.css file:

```
IMG { display: none ! important}
```

For the selector, we are targeting the HTML tag `IMG`, the property that we are modifying is `display`, and the value that it is being set to is `none`, meaning that no images will be displayed. `! important` specifies that this particular rule supersedes anything that is listed in the CSS of the web page. Saving the file and restarting Firefox should implement loading no images through the userContent.css file. However, this does not put us in any better position than what we could achieve inside the Options dialog. Nonetheless, this is a great example of how the default behavior of a web site can be changed, and it highlights the power of userContent.css.

CSS allows for a more specific selector statement that includes more than one type of HTML tag, and instead of strictly `IMG` tags, we can throw something in front such as the following:

```
A:link[HREF*=".banner"]
```

Instead of filtering all images, this line will filter only those images that point to a URL with the string `.banner` embedded somewhere. Other key substrings include `ad.`, `ads`, and `?click`. All these can be daisy-chained to the original CSS IMG rule to form something like this:

```
A:link[HREF*=".banner"] IMG,
A:link[HREF*="ad."] IMG,
A:link[HREF*="ads."] IMG,
A:link[HREF*="?click"] IMG { display: none ! important }
```

Now instead of filtering all images, this code will filter only hyperlinked images with specific substrings inside the URL. Because these strings are relatively common within links to advertisements, these lines will filter out a lot of ads without affecting as many legitimate pictures. Several commercial software programs try to filter out URL image links with the word banner in it, but with free (and easy) methods like this, there really is very little incentive to purchase a product that is functionally equivalent.

A former Netscape employee and current Mozilla contributor, Joe Francis, has a great userContent.css file that is reproduced here:

```
/* You can find the latest version of this ad blocking css at:
 * http://www.floppymoose.com
 * hides many ads by preventing display of images that are inside
 * links when the link HREF contains certain substrings.
 */

A:link[HREF*="addata"]  IMG,
A:link[HREF*="ad."]  IMG,
A:link[HREF*="ads."]  IMG,
A:link[HREF*="/ad"]  IMG,
A:link[HREF*="/A="]  IMG,
A:link[HREF*="/click"]  IMG,
A:link[HREF*="?click"]  IMG,
A:link[HREF*="?banner"]  IMG,
A:link[HREF*="=click"]  IMG,
A:link[HREF*="clickurl="]  IMG,
A:link[HREF*=".atwola."]  IMG,
A:link[HREF*="spinbox."]  IMG,
A:link[HREF*="transfer.go"]  IMG,
A:link[HREF*="adfarm"]  IMG,
A:link[HREF*="adserve"]  IMG,
A:link[HREF*=".banner"]  IMG,
A:link[HREF*="bluestreak"]  IMG,
A:link[HREF*="doubleclick"]  IMG,
A:link[HREF*="/rd."]  IMG,
A:link[HREF*="/0AD"]  IMG,
A:link[HREF*=".falkag."]  IMG,
A:link[HREF*="trackoffer."]  IMG,
A:link[HREF*="tracksponsor."]  IMG { display: none ! important }

/* disable ad iframes */
IFRAME[SRC*="addata"],
IFRAME[SRC*="ad."],
IFRAME[SRC*="ads."],
IFRAME[SRC*="/ad"],
IFRAME[SRC*="/A="],
IFRAME[SRC*="/click"],
IFRAME[SRC*="?click"],
IFRAME[SRC*="?banner"],
IFRAME[SRC*="=click"],
IFRAME[SRC*="clickurl="],
IFRAME[SRC*=".atwola."],
IFRAME[SRC*="spinbox."],
IFRAME[SRC*="transfer.go"],
IFRAME[SRC*="adfarm"],
IFRAME[SRC*="adserve"],
IFRAME[SRC*=".banner"],
IFRAME[SRC*="bluestreak"],
IFRAME[SRC*="doubleclick"],
IFRAME[SRC*="/rd."],
IFRAME[SRC*="/0AD"],
```

```
IFRAME[SRC*=".falkag."],
IFRAME[SRC*="trackoffer."],
IFRAME[SRC*="tracksponsor."]  { display: none ! important }


/* miscellaneous different blocking rules to block some stuff that gets through
*/

A:link[onmouseover*="AdSolution"] IMG,
*[ID=inlinead],
*[ID=ad_creative],
IMG[SRC*=".msads."] { display: none ! important }


/* turning some false positives back off */

A:link[HREF*="thread."] IMG,
A:link[HREF*="download."] IMG,
A:link[HREF*="netflix.com/AddToQueue"] IMG,
A:link[HREF*="click.mp3"] IMG { display: inline ! important }

/*
 * For more examples see http://www.mozilla.org/unix/customizing.html
 */
```

Joe's userContent file aims to minimize the hassle of wrongly blocked content while maintaining a very effective rate of ad blocking. Many other userContent.css files found on the Web look like they are derived from this one. If you just want something that works without a huge time investment, definitely check it out.

Note   The latest version of the userContent file shown in the preceding code can be found at `http://www.floppymoose.com/userContent.css`. On the main page, Joe discusses the goals behind his implementation of his blocking rules, as well as some more great snippets for blocking Flash ads.

As well as this method works, it requires users to pore through HTML or to have some knowledge about which string combinations are frequently used by advertisers. This does require significantly more technical knowledge on the user's part than the simple image blocking method described earlier. Another concern is that advertisers are aware that keyword filtering is catching on, and there are sites that are avoiding keywords such as `banner` so they will still slip through CSS filters. Nonetheless, this method is much more effective than just simple image blocking, and with more conservative substrings used in the CSS, this should avoid a lot of false positives. Maintaining the userContent file is much less tedious than the white/black lists that would have to be used with the default image blocker. A final thing to note is that CSS controls the way that content is displayed, which means ad content is still being downloaded.

Blocking Rules with the Adblock Extension

We have now gone through two methods of blocking advertisements. The first is through the built-in image blocker, and the second is through the userContent.css file. Both have their advantages and drawbacks. The image blocker is initially very easy to use but becomes daunting when many sites are taken into account. The userContent.css file is very effective when specific HTML and text elements are filtered out. However, it requires more technical savvy and some familiarity with CSS. It may also require the user to dig through the HTML of web pages to find what specific elements are responsible for triggering advertisements.

We will now look at a tool that is not included with the standard Firefox installation to fight advertising: the Adblock extension.

Grab the Adblock extension from `http://adblock.mozdev.org/`. Be sure to close down all instances of Firefox and restart it to load the extension.

Adblock is described as a "content filtering plug-in" that is "more robust and more precise than the built-in image blocker." This is promising, as these are the exact criticisms of the image blocker.

Blocking Nuisance Images

As with the other methods covered, Adblock does require user configuration to work effectively. At first glance, Adblock seems as though it can be used just like the image blocker that was covered earlier in this chapter. Fire up any web site with graphical elements. Right-click on any image on the web page, and at the bottom of the context menu, there should be a new menu item, Adblock Image, shown in Figure 7-4.

FIGURE 7-4: Adblock Image appears on the context menu.

Click on Adblock Image, and a dialog similar to the one shown in Figure 7-5 should appear. The differences between Adblock and the Block Images command should be readily apparent.

FIGURE 7-5: Adding a new Adblock filter through the right-click menu

Notice that Adblock is not blocking all images from the web site, as Block Images does; instead, Adblock is targeting one specific image element, as shown in the text box. In fact, you can target every element on a web page that may be an ad without having to go through a web page's source code, if you choose Tools ⇨ List All Blockable Elements, which brings up a dialog like that shown in Figure 7-6, with a fairly large list of elements.

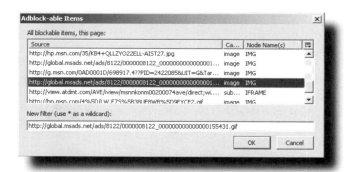

FIGURE 7-6: Listing page elements that are blockable through Adblock

This functionality is important because there are undesirable elements on a web page that you cannot see without either going through the code or bringing up the Adblock-able Items menu. One example is something called a *web bug*, which is a small embedded image used to monitor who has visited a specific page.

Tip

The Electronic Frontier Foundation (www.eff.org) has a great FAQ entry on web bugs. It's available at http://www.eff.org/Privacy/Marketing/web_bug.html.

Although this functionality is great when you need it, let us return to our quest for a robust, general, low-maintenance solution to blocking many ads, not just a single image.

Using Simple Blocking Rules

Wildcards are interesting and useful. Wildcards in a poker game represents any card and can be substituted for any specific other card. In computer jargon, wildcards represent the same concept. In coding, the asterisk (*) is widely understood to mean any string. Wildcards are tied closely to the concept of substrings, which we brought up earlier when discussing the userContent file.

```
A:link[HREF*="?click"] IMG { display: none ! important }
```

In essence, what is being said here is "Find images that are hyperlinks where the hyperlink itself has the substring ?click embedded, and do not display it." This relates to wildcards because this statement implies that you don't care what text is before or after ?click as long as ?click is somewhere in there. A wildcard has been used indirectly here; unlike the case-specific block rules used previously, this particular rule is applicable to a wide range of images that fits the blocking criteria.

Using the example in Figure 7-5, we might want to ignore all images that are inside the /ad/ subdirectory. This can be done by deleting sm_bl_logo.gif from the end of the statement. There is another implied wildcard here: ignoring everything in the /ad/ directory without having to specify the name of each image is another example of a wildcard statement. While this certainly offers more control over blocking ads than Firefox's image blocking function, this will affect only one specific web site, and this is not an effective use of wildcards. You can, however, apply some of the same principles that were used for some of the userContent files to make Adblock more effective. Assuming that a lot of web sites use a subdirectory /ads/ to deliver ads, you could start by filtering out everything that is in an ad directory with the following:

```
*/ad/*
```

Through the use of wildcards, we are saying, "Filter out any image element on any web site that has the substring /ad/ in it," which shows the power of wildcards over the relatively inflexible nature of the Block Images command. If you navigate to Adblock's Tools menu and bring up the submenu, you should see the following options:

- List All Blockable Elements
- Overlay Flash (for left-click)
- Preferences

Click on Preferences. A dialog like the one shown in Figure 7-7 comes up.

FIGURE 7-7: The Adblock Preferences dialog

Under the main text area you should see the specific directory that was blocked with the Adblock functionality and also the */ad/* for users who gave that a try. Each rule can be removed by highlighting the specific rule, right-clicking, and then selecting Delete. There are several other things of note here, starting with the New Filter text box. If you know some filters that should work pretty well, you can enter them directly here. A couple of simple blocking rules can include */ads/* and *banners*. Blanket statements can also be applied here; *swf*, for example, will filter out all Flash elements on all web pages.

There are two radio buttons at the bottom: Hide Ads and Remove Ads. Hide Ads is functionally similar to CSS rules, as the content is still downloaded but is not displayed, while Remove Ads will not download the images. The latter will save bandwidth, but the former gives the impression that the ad is still being downloaded, which may be important to some web sites.

Wildcards do give us much more flexibility in image blocking than we used to have. And compared to creating CSS rules and throwing them into the userContent.css file, they are relatively easy to use. There are more advantages to the Adblock extension than just wildcards: Enter regular expressions, discussed in the following section.

Note An efficient Adblock filter list is of high importance. Each Adblock element needs to be compared to a filter rule. If there are x number of Adblock rules and y number of Adblock elements on a web page, there can be x*y comparisons, which in computer science terms is more or less the worst-case scenario as far as algorithmic efficiency goes. When the number of rules is small, this may not matter much; as the rule list gets large, however, the scaling efficiency progressively gets worse, and a page takes longer to render.

Understanding Regex Pattern Matching

The power of regular expressions *(regex)* is pattern matching. As powerful as wildcards are, they are not always enough, and this is where regular expressions come in. Regex is a way of denoting a pattern within a string without the need to actually specify the pattern directly. You briefly saw the power of wildcards used in conjunction with Adblock. Regex can be thought of as advanced wildcards combined with some control elements. Being able to represent any string with an asterisk (*) as a wildcard in the previous section is a powerful concept, but to be able to represent the alphabet only or numbers only is more useful and more precise. While regex does offer more flexibility than a simple wildcard statement, it comes at the cost of additional complexity. We do not go here into an all-encompassing look at regex syntax—only the more relevant elements for ad blocking are covered.

Note In regex, * no longer represents the universal wildcard.

Here is a quick rundown of regex syntax:

- `.` (a period): The universal wildcard in regex. denoting any single character
- `\w`: An alphanumeric wildcard that includes A–Z, 0–9, and underscore (_)
- `\W`: A nonalphanumeric wildcard including symbols (for example, \, ., and @)
- `?`: Zero or one instance of the search pattern to the immediate left
- `*`: Zero or more instances of the search pattern to the immediate left
- `+`: One or more instances of the search pattern to the immediate left
- `()`: Denotes a specific substring within the regex expression
- `[]`: Denotes any one specific letter or element within the set
- `|`: Denotes or (for example, `(a|b)`, meaning a or b)

If the regex syntax and explanations don't seem intuitive right now, be patient. Most of these elements are applied in an upcoming example that should help clear things up. Again, this is just a subset of the regex syntax. There are ways to express numerals only, negation statements, and several other things, but a discussion of this at this point will likely lead to more confusion. Readers who feel they can handle a bit more are encouraged to look at one of the many regex sites on the Internet. A programming language that is renowned for its close integration with regex is Perl, and many sites that offer tutorials on regex often refer to Perl. Nonetheless, many of the lessons are applicable to what we hope to accomplish with Adblock, as regex expressions are generally portable between languages.

Note A couple of my favorite regex sites are `http://www.troubleshooters.com/codecorn/littperl/perlreg.htm` and `http://www.regexlib.com/`. Neither focuses specifically on ad blocking, but both provide solid examples of how to use regex efficiently, which can be then applied to Adblock.

Starter Regex Samples Expression Rules

Previous examples in this chapter noted that filtering elements that can be very effective are the words `ad` and `ads`. With regex, it is possible to express this as a single pattern instead of two. We do need some sort of base for regex, and in this instance, using the string `ad` as a base to work from is a good start. With Adblock, a regex expression has to be bound by `/[regex]/`, where `[regex]` is the regular expression. The forward slash lets Adblock know that we are indeed intending this to be a regular expression and not a simple pattern-matched rule.

`/ad/`

This short snippet is our base for a more selective regex expression. As it stands, it is essentially the same filter as `*ad*`, which removes any advertising element with the substring `ad` in it. This is an imperfect solution, though, because it filters out an image called jimsd**ad**.jpg or any other substring with `ad` in it. Ads do occur in subdirectories though—`www.somesite.tld/ad/` might be a subdirectory that should be filtered and shopping_ad.jpg is something else that is undesirable, but `www.somesite.tld/addons/` is something you want to avoid filtering. For ad subdirectories, you don't need to specify the first forward slash, you can simply catch the tailing one. The preceding code snippet can be refined to be more selective.

First, assume that any letter in front of the string `ad` will make it something that you want to keep. Therefore, any nonword alphanumeric character is suspect. Any nonalphanumeric characters are denoted with `\W`—this can be thought of as a wildcard specific to symbols.

`/\Wad/`

This can be read as "a substring that contains `ad`, and immediately in front of it is something that is not part of the alphabet and is not a number." Note that the backslash escapes the `W`; therefore, it is not a literal. `\W` is case sensitive, as the lowercase `\w` means that it is an alphanumeric, which is not what is desired here.

Note The preceding expression can be rewritten as `/(\W)ad/` to improve readability. Readability is an integral part in keeping regex manageable, and brackets should generally be used liberally to help with this process.

Unfortunately, because of the quirks of regex rules, the underscore is grouped alongside alphanumeric characters. We have to amend the regex rule to read "a substring that contains `ad`, and immediately in front of it is something that is not part of the alphabet and is not a number, OR it is an underscore."

`/(\W|_)ad/`

This will now filter out elements such as shopping_ad.jpg. However, we can still do better, as this does not account for anything to the right of `ad`. Elements such as `www.regex.tld/additionalexamples/` will be filtered out because they still fit the criteria we set, but we also want to be able to spot something like ads.advertising.tld or `www.advertiser.tld/ads/`, so a little more creativity is in order. The following example uses another nonalphanumeric wildcard so that any long phrases will not be filtered out:

`/(\W|_)ad\W/`

This means that while `ads` will still not be filtered out, we will not get a false positive with something like additional examples. We can refine this some more to include the optional `s`, as follows.

```
/(\W|_)ad(s)?\W/
```

The `?` symbol means that the preceding character or string will appear once or will not appear at all. Isolating the `s` within the brackets specifies that it is the character we are interested in; without the bracket, it will be searching for the entire string `ads`, which is not what we are looking for.

We now have a robust regular expression for filtering the `ad` substring, and because of all the extras we have put into constructing the search pattern, we avoid a lot more false positives than a generic `*ad*` filter that is dumped straight into Adblock.

A second example would be `banner`. As previously mentioned, some advertisers are catching on that there are software solutions that automatically filter the word `banner`, assuming that it is an advertisement of some sort. Suppose they try to be tricky, and instead of `banner`, the site has a script that varies the number of occurrences of the letter n in `banner` to throw simple filters off. Again, regex allows us to work around this.

```
/banner/
```

This is no different from a nonregex simple `*banner*` filter. Say the site we are looking to work around only increases the number of occurrences of n and will not have `baner` as a variant. We can express any number of additional ns like this:

```
/bann(n)*er/
```

The `(n)*` means that there can be zero to any arbitrary number of the letter n following the string `bann` and before the string `er`. This will filter `banner`, `bannner`, `bannnnnnnnner`, and so on.

It is undeniable that regex is very powerful and allows for a lot of flexibility, far more than the methods previously covered. It meets the criteria of being general and is fairly low maintenance when applied across a variety of sites once the expression is written. Unfortunately, regex is also the most complicated and likely to have the steepest learning curve of the techniques covered here.

Note The Adblock Project forum (`http://adblock.mozdev.org/forum.html/no_wrap`) is a great resource for more ad-specific examples of regex, but some care and scrutiny are required, as not all regex statements are constructed carefully. In a worst-case scenario, a lot of legitimate elements can be filtered out.

You can find a thread that may be particularly useful at `http://aasted.org/adblock/viewtopic.php?t=45`.

A site with constantly updated Adblock filters, including some fairly complex regex expressions, is located at `http://www.geocities.com/pierceive/adblock/`.

A great program to test your freshly constructed statements or to verify someone else's work is The Regex Coach, donationware located at `http://www.weitz.de/regex-coach/`. You can enter the regex and a target string to see what is being matched. Do not start and end regex expressions inside the Regex Coach with `/ /`; this is a requirement of Adblock, *not* general regex.

Blocking JavaScript and DHTML Tricks

The techniques that make web pages serve dynamic instead of static content are collectively known as *dynamic HTML (DHTML)*. Pictures (and therefore ads) can be served up without extensions such as .jpg, .gif, or .png through a script. This can make it more difficult to block ad elements if the site chooses to use keywords that are not covered with the ones that are commonly identified. Again, the use of Adblock, and especially the List All Blockable Elements command, helps the user find occurrences of such problems.

JavaScript is responsible for the popups, so it is desirable to block it. Most JavaScript elements can be blocked with the all-encompassing wildcard filter, `*js*`. Again, this has the problem of blocking what could be a legitimate nonadvertising use of JavaScript. We can be more specific and practice some regex to block JavaScript elements with the .js extension along with some keywords such as ad(s), pop, and popups. Scripts that reference a remote file that does not end in .js cannot be blocked with a general expression either; they will also squeeze by js filters, both through simple wildcard blocking of the `ad` string and even the fancy regex blockers. Most of these scripts are recognized by Adblock and can be seen with the List All Blockable Elements command, and this is another instance where a very specific filter should be used. Unfortunately, with version 0.5 of Adblock, inline JavaScript (meaning the JavaScript code is embedded directly in the HTML file) that does not link to a .js file cannot be blocked. Ideally, paranoid users may want to just turn off JavaScript completely, but some good sites (for example, maps.google.com) do rely on JavaScript and will not work without it.

Blocking Cookies Options and Tools

All efforts so far have been aimed at filtering visual elements, which are generally just an inconvenience, but there is the unseen privacy risk that has not yet been addressed. The focus now is on cookies.

Cookies are little pieces of information that are left on your computer by web sites. A developer thought that little pieces of information left were a lot like leaving cookie crumbs on the kitchen counter, so the name stuck. Maybe it is because the name is so innocent sounding that it does not inspire the sense of alarm that is usually triggered by terms such as *advertising* and *spyware*. Nonetheless, cookies can be more malicious and more valuable to advertisers in the long run than a displayed ad.

Cookies do have legitimate uses. Message boards use them so that a forum member does not have to log in every single time he visits. Merchant sites use cookies to keep track of what is being added to shopping carts, because the HTTP protocol is *stateless,* meaning that web pages do not remember what has transpired on a previous page without some help. Cookies can also store a database session or some other piece of information that allows the web site to know what has previously transpired. The downside of cookies concerns your privacy. An advertiser can place a cookie on your computer that can then be read by someone else with a commercial interest; that third party could generate a database of your particular surfing habits based on cookies stored on your computer. Besides unwittingly giving up demographic information about yourself to a third party who has zero accountability, you make yourself a target of advertising that is tailored specifically toward you. Clearly, the privacy implications of cookies are huge, and Internet users should be concerned.

Firefox allows the user to choose how cookies are dealt with under the Tools ⇨ Options ⇨ Privacy menu, shown in Figure 7-8.

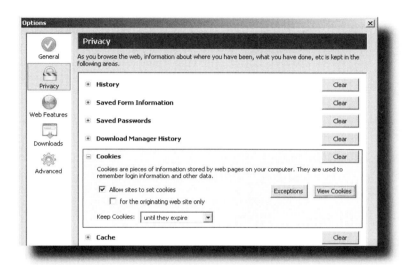

FIGURE 7-8: Cookie handling in Firefox

Several things can be done to improve the default settings for allowing cookies. The "for the originating web site only" feature should probably be turned on; this will block web bugs from setting cookies and will allay many privacy concerns. Cookies have expiry dates that are determined by the site; after that particular date, cookies expire and are deleted. Firefox can flush cookies every time the browser closes down, or users can set the date on which they want the cookies to expire. Like JavaScript, cookies can be disabled entirely. However, many sites require cookies to function properly, and this approach would be very limiting. Unlike images, however, maintaining a whitelist for cookies is not nearly as daunting as for Block Images. There will be sites that you will want to allow cookies for; these may include message boards that you frequent regularly, a gaming site that lets you choose an alternative color scheme, or your bank's web site that needs cookies to let you do online banking. But cookies are probably not relevant to many web sites that you visit. Maybe you visited a funny site mentioned by a friend; you're not coming back, and that site does not need to set a cookie. In fact, the majority of sites that are visited probably do not need to set a cookie, as far as the user is concerned. In all likelihood, it is on the message board, the gaming site, and the banking site where cookies are important for the user. It is easy enough to set these few sites as exceptions so the shopping cart at your favorite online store will work for you. This is fairly low-maintenance and less intrusive than having to address each individual cookie specifically.

Tools for Cleaning Unwanted Cookies

The built-in tool for cookie removal in Firefox is good and may be sufficient for most users. The easiest way to perform this chore would be to clear all cookies and start from scratch. But this can be a problem if you want to clear out some cookies and save some others. For example, I allow cookies for the message board sites I regularly frequent. Unfortunately, I get too creative with passwords on some of the web sites, and because I am automatically logged in, I tend to forget passwords. As long as the cookies are working for the site, I can log in without remembering my password. But when my cookies get wiped, I can't get in without my password. Fortunately, the Stored Cookies dialog, shown in Figure 7-9, allows me to select which cookies I'd like to remove.

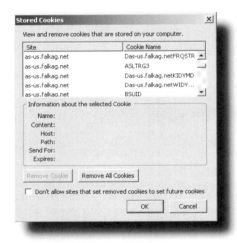

FIGURE 7-9: The Firefox Stored Cookies list

For those that are still allowing cookies to be set by default, the checkbox at the bottom of the Store Cookies dialog, "Don't allow sites that set removed cookies to set future cookies," will be of interest; highlight the cookies that are never allowed to make an appearance again, check the box, and click on the Remove Cookie button—these cookies will be added to a domain black-list for cookies.

An interesting extension is CookieCuller, which has a Protect Cookie options; the cookie for yourfavoritemessageboard.tld can be protected so that it does not get deleted accidentally. A second benefit is that an icon to access cookie options can be dragged onto the Firefox toolbar so you no longer need to navigate through the Tools menu.

Note   CookieCuller can be downloaded at `http://cookieculler.mozdev.org`.

Summary

This chapter covered many techniques to filter or block ads, including the domain whitelist/blacklist image block included within Firefox, taking advantage of the userContent to change the way that ad elements are displayed, and a more aggressive approach with the Adblock extension that allows for powerful regular expressions to be used to be more selective about what is being blocked. The issue of cookies and privacy was addressed, along with Firefox's ability to deal with cookies. Unlike images and ad blocking, maintaining a whitelist for cookies is not nearly as complex, and we took a quick look at identifying what sites a user would choose as candidates for a cookie whitelist. Those who want slightly greater control over cookie management were also introduced to CookieCuller, a third-party extension that provides slightly more functionality.

While advertising is an important facet to keeping a subsidized Internet alive without having to resort to subscriptions to every nonmerchant web site, aggressive marketing practices, including in-your-face banner ads and intrusive popups, have caused a backlash against advertisers in general. Again, it should be stressed that while the topics covered in this chapter are a powerful arsenal against advertising, some discretion should be used in blocking ads, as they do hurt independent web sites.

Hacking Menus, Toolbars, and the Status Bar

part

Hacking Menus

An application is analogous to a workspace — while there might be a lot of similarities between two cubicles in the same office, it does not necessarily mean that they are set up the same. Yes, there is a chair in both cubicles, there is a desk, and there is a similar computer, but the pens, books, or the general arrangement of each cubicle may be different. An effective workspace is arranged in such a way that it helps its occupant be more efficient and comfortable in performing tasks. If an application is like a workspace, the ability to rearrange elements in an application is arguably as important as being able to choose where to place a mouse in relation to the hand. For right-handed people it makes sense to have the mouse to the right of the keyboard, but this arrangement makes less sense for someone who is left-handed. The concept behind customization is that one size does not fit all.

An effective GUI allows the user to maximize the usefulness of an application and its features. However, a GUI is targeted at a general populace and not the individual user. Consider cookies, the management of which we cover in Chapter 7. A person who is unconcerned about cookies and privacy is unlikely to be concerned that there are several menu layers that have to be navigated through in order to manage cookies; the power user, however, may want to be able to get at this functionality with a single button.

This chapter covers the power to change Firefox's interface to suit the needs of a specific user. Despite assertions to the contrary, looks do matter if the number of skins and themes for different applications is any indication. The more superficial changes, such as customized menu icons, are discussed, along with some more useful tips, such as changing the displayed menu options and menu spacing. Several methods of changing the interface are also discussed, from editing Firefox files directly to hacking with extensions.

Hacking Menus Manually

The most basic way to change the look of the menus requires nothing more than the trusty text editor, which, by the time you get to this chapter, should be getting a lot of use. The file that we are going to edit is not created by default. Depending on the version of Firefox, you may or may not have a US\chrome directory with a userChrome-example.css file in it. (Version 1.01, which I have done a clean install with, does not seem to have it.) The .css file extension should be setting off light bulbs — the syntax used for the userChrome file will be very similar to that of the userContent.css file, which we cover in Chapter 7. For those who are interested in the userChrome-example file that does not come with the current Firefox installation, here are the contents:

in this chapter

☑ Hacking menus

☑ Hiding menu options

☑ Hacking menu spacing

☑ Hacking menu fonts and style

☑ Menu extensions

☑ Hacking menu icons

☑ Theme-supported icons

```
/*
 * This file can be used to customize the look of Mozilla's user interface
 * You should consider using !important on rules which you want to
 * override default settings.
 */

/*
 * Do not remove the @namespace line -- it's required for correct functioning
 */
@namespace url("http://www.mozilla.org/keymaster/gatekeeper/there.is.only.xul");
/* set default namespace to XUL */


/*
 * Some possible accessibility enhancements:
 */
/*
 * Make all the default font sizes 20 pt:
 *
 * * {
 *    font-size: 20pt !important
 * }
 */
/*
 * Make menu items in particular 15 pt instead of the default size:
 *
 * menupopup > * {
 *    font-size: 15pt !important
 * }
 */
/*
 * Give the Location (URL) Bar a fixed-width font
 *
 * #urlbar {
 *     font-family: monospace !important;
 * }
 */

/*
 * Eliminate the throbber and its annoying movement:
 *
 * #throbber-box {
 *    display: none !important;
 * }
 */

/*
 * For more examples see http://www.mozilla.org/unix/customizing.html
 */
```

Note that the same structure (following) is used for the example rules shown here:

```
selector { property: value}
```

Note Readers are encouraged to take a closer look at Chapter 7, where the topic of CSS is covered in more detail.

Hiding Menu Options

Power users are always concerned about desktop real estate. Personally, I do a lot of ridiculous things to squeeze in an extra row here or there, including using autohide with the task bar in Windows. Generally, this is more difficult to do at the application level. Some applications do allow the user to hide a status bar or title bar, or sometimes even all the menus, but generally they allow very little customization. The userChrome.css file, however, does enable us to remove specific menu items.

Note Toolbar items can be added and removed by right-clicking on the toolbar area and selecting the Customize Toolbar option. A dialog with various icons should pop up, and these can be dragged to the position of your choice on the toolbar, as shown in Figure 8-1. Conversely, toolbar items that are of little value to you can be dragged onto the dialog, and they will be removed. One example of wasted toolbar space is the long white strip at the top, which serves as a buffer.

FIGURE 8-1: Add to and remove items from the toolbar. Menu items, however, cannot be simply dragged off.

As the stereotypical guy, the first thing that I will remove using the userChrome file is the Help menu. This is probably a safe choice for you too, as readers of *Hacking Firefox* are the type who should be resourceful enough to find help on the Internet. If the userChrome.css file does not yet exist, it needs to be created in the profiles/chrome directory.

The code for removing the Help menu is straightforward:

```
menu[label="Help"] {
    display: none !important;
}
```

Save to the userChrome file and restart Firefox. The Help menu should be gone, as shown in Figure 8-2.

FIGURE 8-2: With the userChrome.css file, the
Help menu has been removed.

Note
The code is case sensitive—`label="help"` is *not* the same as `label="Help"`. The former will have no effect, while the latter will remove the menu.

The same procedure can be done for every other menu item simply by replacing `Help` with the appropriate menu item. Removing multiple menu items at once can be done in one of two ways. You can duplicate the Help removal code and change the menu item specified in `label`, or you can expand upon the CSS statement a little bit more and keep the code a bit cleaner. The following will remove both the Edit and the Help menu:

```
menu[label="Edit"],menu[label="Help"] {
    display: none !important;
}
```

The keyword `menu` removes the entire tree specified, and sometimes this functionality may not be desired. Submenu items can also be removed using the same technique, but with `menuitem` as the keyword instead of `menu`. One of the menu items that I have little use for is Reload, as I always use the keyboard shortcut, so I will remove it along with the Help and Edit menus. The View menu should look like Figure 8-3 after this has been applied:

```
menuitem[label="Reload"], menu[label="Edit"],menu[label="Help"] {
    display: none !important;
}
```

FIGURE 8-3: Reload usually sits under Stop but has been removed as a menu item.

Removing unwanted menus and menu items is a straightforward task when compared with some of the tricks and work that were involved in ad blocking in Chapter 7. Customizing the menus and items that are displayed should be quick work through the userChrome file.

Hack Menu Spacing

Beyond removing different menus from the toolbar, the spacing between the various elements can also be changed. It may be the case that more free space is desired up there, or perhaps there is too much free space and you want the menus to be spread out over the bar area.

In the userChrome file, add the following:

```
/* default: 4 6 4 6 - top right bottom left */
menu {
     padding: 4px 6px 4px 6px !important;
}
```

The first line is commented out. It is good practice to comment code, as several months down the road, when the userChrome file is being revisited, it may be hard to discern at a glance what the code is doing. Restarting Firefox should net no difference because these are the default values for menu spacing. As the code suggests, the first value is the spacing on the top; the second value, the amount of space to the right of the menu; the third value, the space below; and the fourth value is the amount of padding on the left. With an average resolution of 1024 × 768, a one- or two-pixel increment represents a relatively minor change. The horizontal change may be more noticeable as each button is changed by the number of pixels specified. The total change in spacing will be a multiple of the value entered for the left and right values, as shown in Figure 8-4.

FIGURE 8-4: A change of only a couple pixels on the horizontal span is fairly subtle.

To get a better idea of how each element affects the overall positioning, try exaggerated values, such as 50, to see where the spacing is going for each value. Astute readers may notice that menu is also the selector used for hiding menus, except that we were a little bit more specific on what was being hidden. (We specified the particular menu to be removed.) Right now, the spacing is being applied globally to all the menu items, but this does not need to be the case. With the following code snippet, the File menu will look like that shown in Figure 8-5, wider while every other menu remains the same:

```
menu[label="File"] {
     padding: 4px 20px 4px 20px !important;
}
```

FIGURE 8-5: Increasing the width of only
one item

Specific menu spacing items override global ones. For example, if widths of 10 were specified for the left and right padding for the menu as a global, but there is also the extra wide File listed in the userChrome file, the File-specific instruction will override the global value.

While changing the horizontal component does not affect the other items in the menu, changing the vertical components does. The example of changing either one of the top or bottom fields to something that is immediately obvious will show the menu to be offset vertically, but the other menu fields will be centered as a sum of both vertical components. This is better illustrated with the following code and Figure 8-6:

```
menu[label="File"] {
      padding: 4px 6px 25px 6px !important;
}
```

FIGURE 8-6: An offset File menu

Different values are used for the top and bottom fields, resulting in an offset File menu in comparison to other menus. Note that the vertical padding of the other menus is still affected, although only a different set of spacings is specified for the File menu.

Note The same principles of adjusting individual or global settings apply with `menuitem`. For those who like the large-button approach of Windows XP, try a larger value (around 15) to give menus a buttonlike feel.

Hack Menu Fonts and Style

Now that the menus and menu items have been changed around a bit, it is time to change menu fonts. Once again, for a global effect, the selectors involved will be `menu` and `menuitem` — the first property that will be modified is the actual font and then the size, resulting in the menu shown in Figure 8-7:

```
menu {
  font-family: "Neuropolitical" !important;
  font-size: 5mm !important;
}
```

FIGURE **8-7: A changed menu font. Notice that embedded menus inside the top-level menu are considered a menu and not a menu item.**

The CSS code should be fairly straightforward. The following preceding changes the font for the menus to Neuropolitical and increases the font size to 5 to increase the readability. If you also wanted menu items to share a font, you could change the code slightly:

```
menuitems,menu {
    font-family: "Neuropolitical" !important;
    font-size: 5mm !important;
}
```

Some other interesting properties that can be changed include the following:

- `font-weight`: Values include `bold` or `100` to `900` in increments of 100 to denote the level of boldness.
- `font-style`: Values include `italic` and `oblique`.
- `color`: Values include hex codes (e.g., `#abcdef`, `111222`) and color names (`blue`, `green`, `red`).

This is by no means an extensive list of CSS functionality, but merely the tip of the iceberg. Besides the ability to customize the look of Firefox, there can be some interesting applications. Bolding or otherwise changing specific menus and menu items so that they stick out could be used for tutorial purposes to bring attention to certain features.

Note

For a complete list of available font modifications with CSS, refer to `http://www.w3.org/TR/REC-CSS2/fonts.html`.

Hacking Menus with Extensions

There are extensions that provide similar functionality to some of the topics just covered. The first one is Compact Menu, which provides options to remove menus, as we did in "Hiding Menu Options," earlier in this chapter.

Note

The Compact Menu extension can be downloaded from `http://cdn.mozdev.org/compact/`.

Go ahead and install the extension, then restart Firefox. If you right-click on the toolbar now and choose the Customize option, there will be a couple of subtle changes that you can see in Figure 8-8.

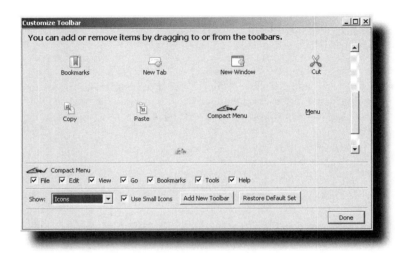

FIGURE 8-8: The Compact Menu extension adds two menu items, Compact Menu and Menu, as well as the Compact Menu checkboxes.

Deselecting the checkboxes shown underneath the items removes those items from the toolbar. One of the benefits of using Compact Menu to do this instead of altering the CSS file as we did earlier is that Firefox does not need to be restarted for the Compact Menu changes to take effect.

Note   The userChrome.css file takes precedence over the Compact Menu extension—if a menu was specified to be hidden with the userChrome file, having the checkbox checked on Compact Menus will *not* override the userChrome setting.

The additional functionalities that are not possible with userChrome are the Compact Menu and the Menu icons. (They are functionally equivalent.) If the Compact Menu icon is dragged onto the toolbar, all the menu items are replaced by Compact Menu, and all the default menus are listed under it instead. This has the dual benefit of freeing up toolbar space and keeping all the functionality intact; the same thing cannot be said about the userChrome method of hiding menu items. For an example of Compact Menu in action, see Figure 8-9.

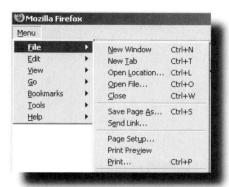

FIGURE 8-9: No functionality is lost with Compact Menus, as all menus are still accessible. Note that userChrome rules are still in effect; File alone is in bold, as specified with the CSS.

The next extension, Menu Editor, provides some functionality that has not been covered yet. Instead of changing around elements of the toolbar menu, it allows the right-click context menu on a web page to be changed around. The ordering of the menu items can be changed, and some items can be removed.

Note   The Menu Editor extension can be downloaded from `http://menueditor.mozdev.org/`.

Posted installation instructions for Menu Editor are a bit spotty. Menu Editor can be accessed by entering the following URL into the location bar:

```
chrome://menuedit/content/menueditprefs.xul
```

The window shown in Figure 8-10 should come up.

For me, the Back, Forward, Reload, and Stop options are not very useful, because I tend to use extra mouse buttons or keyboard shortcuts, so those have all been axed along with the separator directly below them. Those still leery of playing with the regex discussed in Chapter 7 may be interested in moving the Adblock items farther up on the context list.

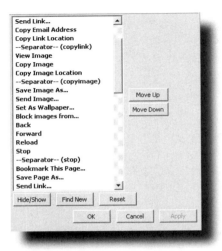

FIGURE 8-10: The Menu Edit page allows right-click context menu items to be reordered and removed. In larger browser windows, some of the buttons will show up to the extreme right.

Hacking Menu Icons

So far, this chapter has dealt with textual elements, having modified the menus in various ways both through CSS and through extensions. Several of the hacks covered were practical. Menus that were not needed were suppressed. Emphasis could be put on certain menus or menu items with bolding or other text tricks. What we have not yet modified is the graphical aspect of Firefox, a project that definitely appeals more to vanity than to useful purpose. Yet *skinning*, the term for applying a theme to an application, is immensely popular, as seen through the thousands of skins available for something like WinAmp or, on an even more basic level, the myriad wallpapers that populate each desktop. While themes and icons cannot compensate for a poorly designed GUI, a nice-looking theme can enhance the appeal of an application.

Theme-Supported, Customized Menu Icons

Themes modify the GUI more extensively than just strictly icon replacement; they change the look of the application in various ways. Tabs may look different; mouseovers may react differently. The extent of these changes is dependent on the theme.

Mostly Crystal Theme

The Mostly Crystal theme should look familiar to Linux desktop users, as the icons are based on the Crystal theme (http://www.everaldo.com/crystal.html) of KDE fame. The Mostly Crystal icon set is bright and cohesive — the art is consistent throughout, which is something that not every theme or icon set can always claim. The theme is similar in style to the default Internet Explorer theme in Windows XP. The icons have a shaded 3-D look and tend to appear more user friendly than the default Firefox theme.

Note The Mostly Crystal Theme is hosted by its author, CatThief, and it can be downloaded from http://www.tom-cat.com/mozilla/firefox.html.

A sample of the menu icons is shown in Figure 8-11.

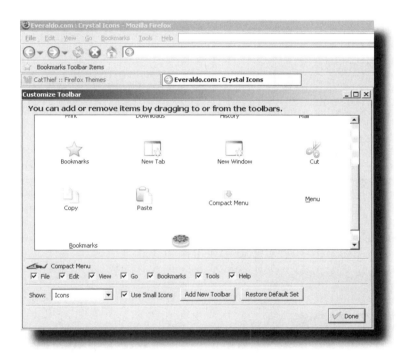

FIGURE 8-11: A view of the replaced icons, courtesy of CatThief's Mostly Crystal icon theme. Note that the appearance of the tabbed windows has also changed.

There are some more subtle changes, including the one shown in Figure 8-12 — instead of the Bookmark item's having a raised effect during a mouseover, the lettering now turns blue on screen.

FIGURE 8-12: Mouseovers on bookmarks cause the text to turn blue instead of having the raised effect of the default Firefox theme.

The Mostly Crystal theme can be customized through the userChrome file. For those who do not like the new bookmarked item icon, it can be changed back to the old style page. The same rule applies to the new tab style. Other options from a very extensive list include the ability to round address and search bars.

Note   You can find a thorough listing of what changes can be made to the Mostly Crystal theme at `http://www.tom-cat.com/mozilla/firefox/userchrome.html`.

Aaron Spuler's Menu Icons

Unlike the Mostly Crystal theme, Aaron Spuler's Menu Icons is not just a single theme, but a collection of ten themes. Each of the themes has its own distinctive style and is far more than a simple color change. Some that stand out particularly are the very artsy Apollo theme, the bright yellow Mars theme, and the subtle Smoke theme. The majority of Spuler's themes have a rounded location bar.

Note   Aaron Spuler's themes can be found at `http://www.spuler.us/index.html`. (JavaScript needs to be enabled, for those who may have turned it off.)

Figure 8-13 shows the Mars theme.

FIGURE 8-13: Aaron Spuler's Mars theme: Round and yellow is the theme here. Notice the rounded location bar, which looks more like a Mac application than a Windows-based one.

As with the Mostly Crystal theme, Aaron Spuler includes some lines that can be included in the userChrome file to change icons and even the shading style of the Firefox browser frame. With the following code in the userChrome file, the browser window and the look of the tabs change dramatically, as shown in Figure 8-14:

```
@import url("chrome://global/skin/subskin/brushed.css");
@import url("chrome://global/skin/subskin/safaritabs.css");
```

FIGURE 8-14: The browser window with the brushed.css subskin and Safari-style tabs enabled through the userChrome.css file

Note

Subskins are *not* global, as suggested by the preceding code. (For example, the code added to the userChrome file will have no effect when you are using themes other than Aaron Spuler's.)

A few extra settings and options are covered in the Theme Options link at the bottom of the theme pages that users will likely find useful.

Finding More Icons

Although the themes previously introduced are of high quality, there will still be those who crave more choices. Here is a listing of several other web sites that have a good collection of themes to go through:

- `https://addons.update.mozilla.org/themes/?os=Windows& application=firefox`: An aggregation of themes straight from Mozilla
- `http://beverlyhills.web.infoseek.co.jp/themes.html`: A collection of high-quality themes like Aaron Spuler's
- `http://www.saegepilz.de/Themeseite/`: Links and previews of themes
- `http://lynchknot.com/ffthemes.html`: A small collection of themes

Another site that is definitely worth checking out is `www.deviantart.com`. Though a lot of things are mixed in along with the skins, there are some definite gems buried there. Users are also encouraged to do a simple search on Google for "Firefox themes," as the number of theme sites is plentiful.

Hacking with the CuteMenus Extension

So far, the themes that have been explored change only the main toolbar and the associated icons. Here, we look at how to add icons to the right-click context menu with a pair of extensions.

Using the CuteMenus Extension

The original CuteMenus extension adds the icon set from the original Firefox theme to the popup context menus.

Note Grab the CuteMenus Extension from `http://cute.mozdev.org/`. (This example uses v0.4 XPI.)

Figure 8-15 shows CuteMenus in action.

FIGURE 8-15: The CuteMenus icons liven up the right-click context menu and add some flair where there is usually only text.

Unfortunately, this version of CuteMenus does not allow for the modification of the icon set being used. Users employing the default Firefox skin will be content with CuteMenus, but others who have adopted another theme might consider this limitation a fashion faux pas requiring remedy.

Using Aaron Spuler's Hacked CuteMenus Extension

Aaron Spuler has a version of the CuteMenus extension that is more versatile than the one found at the CuteMenus URL, as it allows the icon theme for the right-click menu (aka context menu) to be changed.

Note Two versions of the modified CuteMenus extension are available. The newer one (v 0.3.8) is on Aaron Spuler's site at `http://www.spuler.us/extensions/cutemenus.htm`. If you have the original CuteMenus theme installed, remove it first, because there will be a conflict if the hacked CuteMenus extension is installed directly on top; neither version will function. For those who have accidentally done this, go to the Firefox profiles/chrome directory and remove the CuteMenus Themes folder as well as cutemenus.jar. This should allow the new version of CuteMenus to install properly.

Bring up the configuration dialog for the new version of CuteMenus by right-clicking on a web page area to bring up the context menu. While holding down the Shift key, move the mouse around; an additional menu, CuteMenus Config, should pop up at the bottom of the menu, as shown in Figure 8-16.

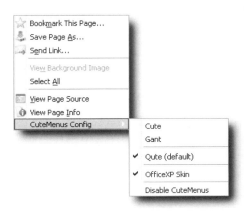

FIGURE 8-16: The CuteMenus variant allows the user to change CuteMenus themes and to disable CuteMenus without uninstalling the extension.

The OfficeXP Skin that is checked overrides any subskin settings that may be in effect; in this particular case, the context menu does not inherit the settings from brushed.css. CuteMenus themes are not nearly as plentiful as themes for Firefox, although there are some out there. Aaron Spuler has an associated CuteMenus theme for each one of his Firefox skins, so users who found a theme to their liking on his web site can use his hacked CuteMenus.

Summary

This chapter explored ways to customize the menus in Firefox, from removing unwanted menu items to changing spacing and fonts. Remember when using the userChrome.css file that settings can be applied at a global level to an entire set of widgets or to individual, specific items. The font for example, can be changed for all the menus, but you can choose to bold just the File menu. A lot of the text and menu customization focused on how to increase the amount of usable toolbar space.

The Compact Menus extension provides a second method of hiding menu items. Beyond hiding menus, Compact Menus allows every menu to be listed under a single global menu — a handy feature for those who value toolbar space.

The Menu Editor function provides some useful functionality, including the ability to reorder and hide items. Examples of items that are redundant in the right-click context menu are Back and Reload, which a lot of users will trigger using keyboard shortcuts.

The chapter also looked at obtaining themes for Firefox. Outstanding themes discussed included the Mostly Crystal menu icons theme and Aaron Spuler's collection of themes. These accomplish changes in icons as well as more subtle changes, including the way that tabs look and the way that mouseovers are handled with bookmarks. With both sets of themes, additional customization is available through the userChrome file.

The final topic covered was changing the right-click context menu with two variants of the CuteMenus extension. The simpler version of CuteMenus adds the default Firefox icons to the right-click menu for those who are content with the original theme but would like a touch of pizzazz. A further developed version of CuteMenus allows modification of context menu themes, adding additional customization possibilities for the discerning user.

Although many useful customizations are possible with Firefox, it is safe to say that Firefox is not all work and no play. Themes definitely make the diminutive browser anything but dull.

Hacking Toolbars and the Status Bar

The next two areas of Firefox customization we tackle are the processes of hacking the toolbar and status bar. As mentioned briefly in Chapter 8, there is a lot of valuable application real estate that can be reclaimed through the removal of toolbar items. Conversely, there are buttons that are worth adding, including a button for the Compact Menus extension. Beyond the default toolbar items, one of the areas that has not been touched yet is the status bar, which is generally underused; that, we shall remedy.

by Terren Tong

Removing and Changing Toolbar Buttons

In Chapter 8, we briefly went over how to add items to and remove items from the toolbar. A context menu, like the one shown in Figure 9-1, can be brought up by right-clicking on the toolbar area (anywhere above the bookmarks).

FIGURE 9-1: Toolbar context menu

The navigation toolbar is the entire row beneath the menus, while the bookmarks toolbar is the row just above the tabs. By default, both the navigation toolbar and the bookmarks toolbar are on. However, navigation keyboard shortcuts will still work with the navigation toolbar off. For example, pressing Ctrl+L on a Windows machine brings up an Open Location dialog; with the navigation bar on, the focus changes to the location bar. Users should preferably start with the Customize option, as there is a finer level of control available instead of having to remove an entire toolbar at once.

The customize option is interesting because it allows you to remove only certain elements of the toolbar. Again, any item on the toolbar can be removed through the Customize option except for the text menus; the process of removing these was covered in detail in Chapter 8.

There are several things of note in Figure 9-2, the most important being the Customize Toolbar window and the navigation toolbar. Items in the navigation toolbar can be rearranged; items that the user deems unnecessary can be dragged to the Customize Toolbar area, and they will be removed. Conversely, icons in the Customize Toolbar menu can be dragged and added to the navigation toolbar.

FIGURE 9-2: The Customize Toolbar menu. Items can be dragged from the toolbar into this dialog, and vice versa.

If none of the toolbars has been turned off, there are three areas to which toolbar items can be dragged: the main menu toolbar, the navigation toolbar, and the bookmarks toolbar. As previously mentioned, the only toolbar that cannot be turned off is the main toolbar on top. One of the interesting items in the Customize Toolbar menu is Flexible Space, which expands to take up all the gray space in a given row. It appears in the top row to the right of the text menus. If the Flexible Space were to the left of the menu, the menu items would be forced to the right side of the browser window.

Note One of the reasons we advise the user to keep the navigation and bookmarks toolbars on at least temporarily is that the navigation and bookmark elements are not accessible in the Customize dialog when they are hidden; this would mean, for example, that the location bar cannot be moved.

Toolbar items can be moved in several ways. Items can be moved between different toolbars, and they can be removed by dragging them into the Customize Toolbar dialog. As noted in Chapter 8, a significant amount of space wasted with the flexible space that eats up all the extra room in the main menu toolbar. Removing that allows the user to place other items there, including larger ones like the location box. Remember that removing an item does not remove that functionality from Firefox; if you choose to remove the Reload Page button from the navigation toolbar, the Reload Page keyboard shortcut, the right-click context menu, and View ⇨ Reload will still allow for a page refresh. This is especially important to keep in mind for a customized kiosk browser or a locked-down version of Firefox that may be used in the workplace.

I tend to take the new tab keyboard shortcut for granted, so that is not particularly important for me, but some newer users may find that useful. If you are ambivalent about keyboard shortcuts and want to add a lot of icons to the toolbar menu, you might want to consider the Add New Toolbar button This will add a new toolbar between the navigation toolbar and the bookmarks toolbar. All the items that are not used by default can be dragged onto this toolbar without having to modify the existing ones. Note that if this toolbar has no items, it does get deleted and will not show up on the main page.

There are a few restrictions with the Customize Toolbar functionality. One of these restrictions is that no items can be dragged to the right of the bookmarks toolbar Items icon — only to the left.

The other option available is the ability to modify the way that the toolbar items are displayed; the checkbox controls sizing, and the drop-down box controls labels and icons. Both should be self-explanatory, so exploration will be left up to the user.

Showing System Icons

We now move on to system icons, which are located on the status bar at the bottom of the browser window. System icons include page security, live bookmarks, and the popup blocker. Unlike the toolbar, which is mostly static except for the times that it is being modified, the status bar is dynamic. The icons, as shown in Figure 9-3, are not in set positions.

FIGURE 9-3: The Security button and the Live Bookmarks icon appear only on certain pages. The layout of the status bar is not static, like that of the toolbar.

You can, however, force the system icons to appear on every single page. Unfortunately, there is no content menu here that you can access from inside Firefox, so once again, you must fire up the trusty text editing utility and point it toward the userChrome.css file.

The first step is to force on the Security button, which can be accomplished with the following:

```
#security-button {
 list-style-image:
url("jar:resource:/chrome/classic.jar!/skin/classic/browser/Security-
broken.png");
 min-width: 20px !important;
-moz-box-direction: reverse;
 display: -moz-box !important;
}
```

While this forces the Security button on, it will always display with the broken security sign (a slash across the lock) regardless of the security level. Because of this, you need to add more specific cases to handle the different levels of web page security. In addition to the preceding code, you need the following:

```
#security-button[level="high"] {
 list-style-image:
url("jar:resource:/chrome/classic.jar!/skin/classic/browser/Secure.png")
!important;
 display: -moz-box !important;
}
```

```
#security-button[level="low"] {
 list-style-image:
url("jar:resource:/chrome/classic.jar!/skin/classic/browser/Secure.png")
!important;
 display: -moz-box !important;
}
```

```
#security-button[level="broken"] {
 list-style-image:
url("jar:resource:/chrome/classic.jar!/skin/classic/browser/Security-
broken.png") !important;
 display: -moz-box !important;
}
```

You now have CSS rules for three specific cases: high-level encryption, low-level encryption, and no encryption. Pages that are digitally signed will have the lock icon at the bottom, and the rest will have the lock with the slash. Notice that there is no separate icon for the low-grade encryption pages, so it is still up to the user to check how secure a site is before submitting personal information. Whipping up a different icon for the low-level encryption would be a quick and useful exercise in further customizations. Figure 9-4 shows the no-security icon that will appear on most web pages.

FIGURE 9-4: Most web pages are not digitally signed, and the slashed-lock icon will be shown. This should generally not be a concern unless the site in question is an e-commerce site.

The popup blocking functionality in Firefox is buried under Tools ➪ Options ➪ Web Features ➪ Allowed Sites, which is quite a bit of clicking. The popup blocker in the status bar shown in Figure 9-5 can be enabled with this bit of code:

```
/* Always display the Popup Blocker Button in the status bar. */
#page-report-button {
list-style-image:
url("jar:resource:/chrome/classic.jar!/skin/classic/browser/Info.png")
!important;
 min-width: 20px;
 display: -moz-box !important;
}
```

Allow popups for www.cnn.com
Edit Popup Blocker Options...
Don't show info message when popups are blocked
Show 'http://www.cnn.com/virtual/editions/europe/2000/roof/change.pop/frame...

FIGURE 9-5: Allowing popup options is a lot quicker with an easily accessible button in the status bar.

The final system icon that will be added is the live bookmark. Live bookmarks are a neat bit of functionality. On sites that provide RSS feeds, the live bookmark shows up as a folder with all the current RSS items showing as a direct link. As with the different encryption levels for the security icon, there is only a single icon that represents live feeds, and the only way to tell if a page supports it is through a tooltips dialog. The code to enable live bookmarks on all pages follows:

```
#livemark-button {
 -moz-appearance: none !important;
 list-style-image:
url("jar:resource:/chrome/classic.jar!/skin/classic/browser/page-livemarks.png")
!important;
 min-width: 20px;
 display: -moz-box !important;
}
```

An example of the tooltips and a set of live bookmarks are shown in Figure 9-6.

Note Figure 9-6 shows all three of the system icons. When all three are enabled, the positions are static. Regardless of the order of the code in the userChrome file, the system icons will appear in this order.

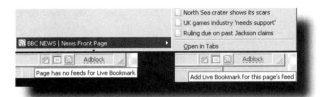

FIGURE 9-6: A live bookmark of the BBC RSS service is shown at the top of the image. Notice that the live bookmark acts as a folder, and news articles act as bookmarked links. These change as the BBC page changes. The Live Bookmark icon does not differentiate between pages with feeds and those without feeds; users will have to rely on tooltips.

Show Mozilla Update Icon

The one system icon that we will add to the toolbar is the Mozilla Updates button. This icon is not available directly from the Customize Toolbar menu, but it requires that only a couple of lines be added to the userChrome.css file:

```
/* Always display the Mozilla Updates in the toolbar. */
toolbarbutton[type="updates"] {
 visibility: visible !important;
}
```

Once the file has been saved and Firefox restarted, the button with the up arrow shown in Figure 9-7 should appear in the toolbar. (The button will be green on your computer screen.) A single button click checks the Mozilla web site for updates to Firefox, as even Firefox is not immune to the occasional security update. Unfortunately, the update icon cannot be moved or repositioned.

Mozilla Updates button

FIGURE 9-7: The Mozilla Updates button can be forced on through some userChrome code, but unlike the other toolbar items, it cannot be moved.

Adding Customized Toolbar Buttons

Through the use of two extensions that will be introduced here, additional buttons can be added to the toolbar, much like what you saw with Compact Menus in Chapter 8. You saw the benefits of having the popup blocker reside in the status bar; it is immediately accessible instead of requiring four levels of menu navigation.

The EMButtons Extension

With EMButtons, icons for the Extension Manager and the Theme Manager will be available from the Customize Toolbar dialog.

Note The EMButtons extension is available at `http://moonwolf.mozdev.org/#embfx`.

Besides the ability to add the two manager icons to the toolbar, the EMButtons extension creates shortcut keys to access both menus, so the time spent cleaning up the tool will not suddenly be rendered moot. It is worthwhile to add at least one of the buttons to the toolbar at least temporarily, because some additional functionality is available through EMButtons. Right-clicking on either the Themes or Extensions icon brings up a context menu with a few new items. The one that we are interested in is EMButtons Options, which brings up the dialog shown in Figure 9-8.

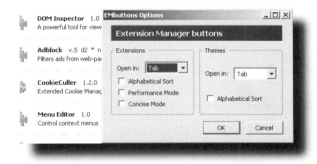

FIGURE 9-8: The Extension and Theme Managers can be forced
into a browser window instead of popping up as a dialog.

Note The keyboard shortcuts added by EMButtons are Ctrl+Shift+E/T/O for the Extension Manager, the Theme Manager, and the Options dialog, respectively.

The first option is the ability to force the Extension and Theme Managers to either open up in the current browser window or have them show up as a sidebar like the history window. With dual monitors, dialogs appear in strange places at times, and having the manager windows open up in the browser makes a lot more sense to me personally.

The Alphabetical Sort is also a nice option to have, especially for those who have a lot of themes or extensions installed. Items are otherwise in chronological order, not usually the most efficient sorting method when you are looking through a larger list. The other two checkboxes are Extension Manager–specific. Performance Mode removes some formatting that is supposed to speed things up; I have a smallish list of extensions installed, so the benefits are not readily apparent to me. Concise Mode removes the descriptions and icons for extensions so a larger list can be displayed at once.

The Toolbar Enhancements Extension

The Toolbar Enhancements extension builds on the same idea of adding more useful buttons to the main toolbar.

Note

Grab the Toolbar Enhancements extension from `http://clav.mozdev.org/#tbx`.

Toolbar Enhancements makes available a different set of toolbar buttons than EMButtons. Figure 9-9 shows the buttons that are enabled through this extension.

FIGURE **9-9: The toolbar icon set that the Toolbar Enhancements extension enables. Note that no Themes or Extension Manager icon is included here; that functionality remains with the EMButtons extension.**

Here is a quick summary of the function of each item (listed in order from left to right, beginning with the top row and then moving to the bottom row):

- **Source:** View page source
- **JS Console:** Brings up the JavaScript console
- **Full Screen:** Puts Firefox into Full Screen mode (different from maximize window, same as F11)
- **Clear Cache:** Clears the disk cache
- **Info:** Brings up the Page Info dialog box
- **Bookmarks . . .:** Brings up the Bookmark Manager window
- **JavaScript:** Enables/disables JavaScript in the current tab
- **Redirections:** Enables/disables meta-redirections in the current tab

- **Options:** Brings up the Options dialog usually found under the Tools menu
- **Images:** Enables/disables images in the current tab
- **Bookmark:** Bookmarks the current page
- **Plug-Ins:** Enables/disables *all* plugins in the current tab

While some of the items described help reduce navigation issues, four items in particular are very interesting, as they provide additional functionality; they are the JavaScript, Redirections, Images, and Plug-Ins buttons. The ability to disable JavaScript, redirects, images, and plugins in a specific tab or window is unique to the Toolbar Enhancement extension. Previously, these options could be applied only globally to all windows and all tabs. This makes it possible to allow a favorites-type site to run with all the bells and whistles; at the same time, another browser window can act as a sandbox, with everything locked down when you are visiting sites of dubious origin.

Besides adding buttons to the toolbar, Toolbar Enhancement adds some more customization features. While the Customize Toolbar dialog is open, right-clicking on the toolbars brings up the menu shown in Figure 9-10.

FIGURE **9-10: Toolbar-specific options are available through the Toolbar Enhancement extension.**

Again, options are available at the specific toolbar level and are not necessarily applied across the entire toolbar. Because most users are likely to be familiar with the default toolbar icon set, text descriptions for those may be removed, while the unfamiliar ones from the Toolbars Extension can be labeled. Full-Screen mode hides some of the toolbars, and this dialog allows the user to choose which additional ones will be shown. The final set of controls is for the alignment of the toolbar and offers several other positions:

- **Top:** The default area
- **Below Tabs:** Moves a toolbar below the tab area
- **Left and Right:** Orients the toolbar elements vertically along either edge of the browser window
- **Bottom:** Adds a toolbar above the status bar on the bottom of the screen

Adding Useful Toolbars

After all the hard work of deciding which buttons to ax from the toolbar, we now focus on a few extensions that place on the toolbar additional buttons that go beyond navigational shortcuts.

Using the Googlebar Extension

My absolute favorite tool for Internet Explorer was, without a doubt, the Google toolbar. Although long-term Firefox users may take popup blocking and an integrated Google search box for granted, it was something novel on the Internet Explorer side when it was first released. So the Googlebar Extension for Firefox seems a bit redundant, as two of the major selling points of the IE version are already included in Firefox. Or are they?

 Note   Grab the Googlebar extension at `http://googlebar.mozdev.org/`.

The basic search box is shown in Figure 9-11. Despite some similarities with the built-in Firefox search box, the Googlebar menu expands to include direct links to some of the specific Google searches, including Google Images and Google Groups. The Googlebar extension options can also be changed here.

FIGURE 9-11: The Googlebar search box is more robust than the built-in Firefox search dialog. With no search parameters, the G button redirects the browser window to the main Google page. With search parameters entered, a search is launched.

The Googlebar search dialog is integrated closely with the rest of the toolbar; we will refer to this as we discuss the functions of some of the other buttons.

Figure 9-12 shows the next group of buttons as we traverse the Googlebar.

The first icon is Site Search: this does a search only on the site that is being browsed. For example, you may want to find out what is being said about Firefox on Microsoft's site only. If you navigate to `http://www.microsoft.com`, type **Firefox** as the search term, and hit the Site Search button, pages that refer to Firefox on the Microsoft site will be brought up.

 Note   Site search functionality is also available through the following syntax: `site:www` `.targetwebsite.tld searchterm`.

Site Search

I'm Feeling Lucky

Google Groups

Google Directories

FIGURE 9-12: The Googlebar includes Site Search, I'm Feeling Lucky, Google Groups, and Google Directories as part of the default set of buttons

I'm Feeling Lucky takes the user directly to a web page based on the search term and is functionally equivalent to the button found on the main Google page. The groups and directory search buttons do searches in Google Groups and Google Directories, respectively.

Figure 9-13 shows the next set of buttons, the Googlebar Options, and a set of additional specialized searches.

Googlebar Options

Specialized
Google Searches

OS-specific Searches

University-specific
Searches

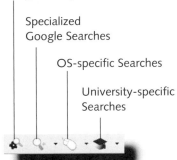

FIGURE 9-13: From left to right, Googlebar Options, specialized Google searches (big drop-down menu), OS-specific searches (BSD, Linux, MacOS, Windows), and university-specific searches.

We're going to skip some of the navigation buttons. (They are useful, however; the up one directory feature is arguably faster than deleting parts of the URL manually.) The last item, the highlighter, is the most underrated item on both the Internet Explorer and the Firefox side. Once again, the highlighter ties back into the Googlebar search dialog — words that are entered there can be highlighted on a web page. One of my coworkers remarked that Firefox already has similar functionality through the Find in Page dialog, but that is not completely true. The Googlebar highlighter allows for multiple, independently searchable, highlighted terms, while Find in Page treats text entered as a single string. Figure 9-14 shows the highlighter in action.

FIGURE 9-14: There are four highlighted terms: Firefox, browser, web, and security. Clicking on the word in the Googlebar finds the next instance of that particular word. By contrast, the Firefox search can search for a single term only.

Performance can be an issue with the highlighter; when it is activated before a search term is entered into the Googlebar search dialog, it processes each character as it is being entered, resulting in pauses as the Googlebar parses the page. For example, if you are searching for Firefox; it will first attempt to highlight *f*, then *fi*, then *fir*, and so on. Every time a letter is entered, the search string is treated as a new string, and the highlight process restarts. Users on slower computers are advised to turn off highlighting before entering a new term in the search bar.

The only caveat with the Googlebar extension is its relative inflexibility. Googlebar buttons cannot be added to other toolbars, and you cannot add other toolbar buttons to the Googlebar. Nonetheless, it does offer many useful features, none of which have functional equivalents in a default Firefox installation.

Using the Yahoo! Toolbar Extension

Unlike the Googlebar extension that was written by volunteer developers, Yahoo! has gone ahead and created an in-house version of its toolbar for Firefox. The Yahoo! Toolbar is best suited for those who make extensive use of the Yahoo! portal; the default layout at first glance is merely a lot of navigation shortcuts, as shown in Figure 9-15.

The Yahoo! Toolbar for Firefox can be downloaded from `http://toolbar.yahoo.com/firefox`.

FIGURE 9-15: The Yahoo! Toolbar is similar to the Googlebar. Most of the extra items on the default toolbar point to specific locations in the Yahoo! portal.

The Yahoo! Toolbar, like most of the other toolbars out there, allows customization. Where it differs is that Yahoo! remembers toolbar settings across different computers. There is no option to customize a single computer only; all changes require a Yahoo! account, which may be a deterrent for some users.

Once an account has been created and the user has logged in, the toolbar changes quite drastically, and elements on the toolbar become user configurable. One of the very useful options is the ability to save bookmarks on the Yahoo! Toolbar. This means that something bookmarked at home can be brought up at a remote location that has the Yahoo! Toolbar installed.

Under the pencil icon is an Add/Edit Buttons option, and most users will want to pick and choose what elements they display on the Yahoo! bar. The toolbar buttons available are generally shortcuts to different parts of the Yahoo! site, but a lot of the items also act as drop-down menus, so they are more useful than just a simple bookmark. News, in particular, is very nice, as it is also an integrated RSS reader that grabs the Yahoo! news portal headlines.

The Yahoo! Toolbar allows two non–Yahoo!-related buttons to be defined by the user with the Your Own Button function. Unlike bookmarks toolbar items, these are visible on all computers with the Yahoo! Toolbar extension installed.

Note Changes made to the Yahoo! bar need to be flushed out with the Refresh Toolbar command found under the pencil icon.

The Yahoo! Toolbar is interesting because of the online memory component that transports settings and personal items such as bookmarks across multiple computers. For people who make extensive use of the Yahoo! portal, this is a very good tool that makes navigating between different parts of Yahoo! a breeze. Unlike the Googlebar, though, it does not offer tools like the highlighter; the focus is clearly on users who use many computers and would like a consistent interface that does not need to be synchronized manually.

Using the Web Developer Extension

Changing gears, we move away from search-based toolbars and look at a toolbar that is aimed at web development but should also be of interest to anyone who is interested in how a site is constructed: the Web Developer extension from Chris Pederick.

The Web Developer extension can be downloaded from `http://www.chrispederick` `.com/work/firefox/webdeveloper/`.

Some very powerful tools are available with Web Developer, but we will go through just a handful. A screen shot of it in action is shown in Figure 9-16.

FIGURE 9-16: The Web Developer extension hides a lot of functionality under each button.

The Disable menu allows various page elements to be turned off. Options are applied globally. Some of the more interesting uses include disabling cookies and JavaScript to see if a page still functions normally. Again, it is important to note that the functionality differs somewhat from the Toolbar Enhancements extension, as that applies settings to specific tabs and not on a global basis, like the Web Developer extension.

The Images menu has a lot of helpful functions that can summarize a lot of information about the graphical aspect of a page very quickly. In particular, the Display functions are very neat — they include a tooltips-like icon that pops up beside each graphical icon with the associated statistics (image size, dimensions, or the path of the image).

Those who are curious about why certain pages are not loading correctly in Firefox can take web masters to the task with the Tools menu, which can validate CSS and HTML according to w3.org specifications.

Hacking the Status Bar

With a bit of code earlier on in the chapter, some persistent system icons have been added to the status bar, but a lot of the real estate down there remains unused. Although we have looked at several extensions that add functionality to the toolbar, we have not yet looked at any that spice up the status bar. The sections that follow examine several extensions for the status bar to complement the changes made to the toolbar.

Current Date/Time with Statusbar Clock Extension

One of the simplest and most useful extensions is the Statusbar Clock extension, which simply adds the date and time to the bottom of the Firefox window.

Note The Statusbar Clock extension is written by Momokatte, whose site can be found at `http://www.cosmicat.com/`. The version of the Statusbar Clock extension from his site, however, will not install in Firefox 1.0. Extensions Mirror has a modified version that removes version restrictions and is available to download at the following location: `http://www.extensionsmirror.nl/index.php?showtopic=105&hl=`.

Options are kept simple; the choice of the display elements such as the day, month, year, and whether this should be presented numerically or spelled out completely is configurable by the user. The position in the status bar is configurable and is based upon the relative location of other elements. Figure 9-17 has a shot of the Statusbar Clock in action.

FIGURE 9-17: The Statusbar Clock. The formatting in this example has been modified—the day has been removed, and the date and time ordering has been reversed.

Display the Weather with ForecastFox

Living in the Pacific Northwest and being on two wheels during the warmer months means that I tend to make several visits to the weather site each day so I know whether to make a bee-line for home after a day in the office or whether it will remain pleasant enough to go for a quick spin up the coastline. ForecastFox grabs its weather feeds from the Weather Channel, so it also works for those of us not based in the United States. After the installation and restart of Firefox, the installation dialog shown in Figure 9-18 will appear.

Note ForecastFox can be downloaded from `http://forecastfox.mozdev.org/`.

You must specify a Forecast Location in the Code field. That is easy for U.S. citizens, as that is simply the zip code you would like weather information from. Everyone else must use the Find Code function. The Unit of Measure radio buttons allow you to specify the units of measure for temperature and wind speed. For American, this is Fahrenheit and MPH; for English, it is Celsius and MPH; and for Metric, this is Celsius and KPH. Although ForecastFox sits in the status bar by default, it can be moved to another position on the browser window. Its position on the status bar can also be manipulated — with the default Always Last option it appears in the far-right corner. Enabling the Specific Position option and setting lower values forces ForecastFox to the left of the status bar; 0 forces it to the extreme left.

The flexibility with the display configuration is also very impressive. A mix of icons and text can be independently set for Current Conditions, Today's Forecast, and Extended Forecast. Figure 9-19 shows some of the customizations possible.

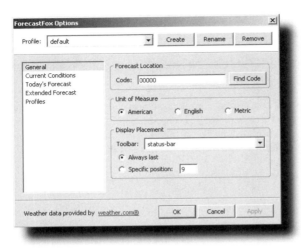

FIGURE 9-18: The ForecastFox setup dialog appears after the first restart of Firefox after the installation of the extension.

FIGURE 9-19: ForecastFox allows the choice of icons, label, or icons and labels for six distinct elements.

For the current conditions, I have chosen icons and labels. The labels that you want displayed can also be specified; in this particular case, for the first element, I've chosen the current weather condition and the temperature along with the current weather icon. The display elements in tooltips for the current conditions can also be specified, and I chose to include more detail here, including wind condition and the location of the forecast. The next element over is the overall forecast for the day. Again, both icons and labels are enabled, but this time, the option chosen for the label is temperature and the chance of precipitation. The final item shown is the extended forecast, set to display the icon only. The number of extended forecast days can be between 0 and 9.

ForecastFox is a very well developed extension, and for anyone who is slightly concerned about weather conditions, it's an absolute must-have.

Playing Music with the FoxyTunes Extension

For those who are not using a multimedia keyboard, it can be distracting to switch from the work application to the media player to play songs. On the lighter side of things, let's take a look at the FoxyTunes extension, which adds multimedia buttons to Firefox's status bar.

> **Note** The FoxyTunes extension can be downloaded from `http://www.iosart.com/foxytunes/firefox/`.

FoxyTunes hooks into a variety of media players and displays the song name along with navigation buttons, as shown in Figure 9-20.

FIGURE 9-20: FoxyTunes in action on the status bar. ID3 tag information is displayed, along with a standard set of multimedia navigation buttons.

Some of the more interesting buttons include the ^ button, which brings the media player to the forefront. This is a useful alternative to Alt-tabbing or searching the taskbar for the application. The colored note icon (farthest to the left) brings up the main menu for FoxyTunes. Some of the options include keyboard shortcut definitions for the multimedia application. A couple of additional features that are very nice are the sleep timer and the alarm function; FoxyTunes can stop the media player after a given amount of time or start playing music at a given time. This is helpful, as some applications, such as Apple's iTunes, do not have a plugin system like Winamp to add such functionality, and this is a unique way to sidestep that limitation.

FoxyTunes has a good number of customization options; much of the interface can be hidden, and it can even be skinned.

> **Note** Skins for FoxyTunes can be downloaded from `http://www.iosart.com/foxytunes/firefox/skins/`.

On-the-Fly Proxy Switching with the SwitchProxy Extension

The SwitchProxy extension allows users to switch between different proxy servers quickly. The Connection Settings dialog in Firefox allows for only a single proxy to be specified, while SwitchProxy can remember and manage several.

Note The SwitchProxy extension can be downloaded from `http://mozmonkey.com/ switchproxy/`.

SwitchProxy is not strictly a status bar extension; the default install also throws up a toolbar. The status bar portion of the extension is useful enough so that the toolbar portion does not have to stay on. A context menu of the SwitchProxy status bar is shown in Figure 9-21.

FIGURE **9-21: The context menu from the SwitchProxy status bar. Proxies can be quickly selected from this list.**

The interface for adding a proxy through SwitchProxy is essentially the same as the one inside Firefox, except that added proxies can be named and saved. SwitchProxy allows for two types of proxy management: the traditional one, where a single proxy, aptly named Standard, is used; and a more complex type, called Anonymous, where the user enters a list of proxies and a rotational interval to switch between them. With cookies turned off, rotating proxies breaks any sort of tracking attempts that a web site may try to use.

Note Jeremy Gillick's MozMonkey site has a forum thread that maintains a list of active proxies for those looking for something more than the single proxy supplied by an ISP. The list can be found at `http://forums.mozmonkey.com/viewtopic.php?t=19`.

The StockTicker Extension

During my first programming job, my boss enjoyed monitoring his stocks on a little Yahoo! stock ticker. I remember him saying, "Every time this beeps, it means I am losing money." Every time I think about real-time stock monitoring, that story gives me a good chuckle. For the part-time day trader looking for a stock utility that is a little bit more subtle than my boss's ticker, there is the StockTicker extension, which sits right in the Firefox status bar, as shown in Figure 9-22.

Note The StockTicker extension is available at `http://mozmonkey.com/stockticker/`.

FIGURE 9-22: The StockTicker extension in the status bar.

A list of stock symbols can be entered into the StockTicker list, and it will scroll through each symbol. The user can specify the amount of time that the ticker spends on each symbol and how often prices should be updated. A different color scheme can also be used — maybe dropping stock prices are less stressful if they are colored in blue. Details about each symbol can also be requested that will take the browser window to the stock listing page of choice. By default, it is finance.yahoo.com.

For those who have a big list of stocks and just cannot wait for each list item to scroll past, the View All Stocks function brings up the window shown in Figure 9-23.

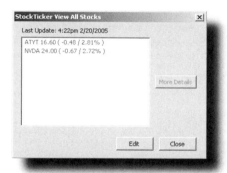

FIGURE 9-23: A dialog with all entered stock symbols can be brought up.

Summary

While the subject of toolbar modification was touched upon before, this chapter provided a more thorough look at how both the toolbar and status bar can be modified to improve and extend the Firefox interface. Starting simply with adding and removing buttons through the Customize Toolbar dialog, it quickly moved on to a discussion of forcing on system icons through the userChrome file before exploring a wide variety of extensions that streamlined the Firefox interface. One of the most useful system icons enabled is the popup blocker.

The first extension explained was the EMButtons extension, which added two new icons to the Customize Toolbar dialog and single-click access to the Extension and Themes Managers menus. More important, it added keyboard shortcuts so navigating through several layers of menus was no longer necessary.

The next set of extensions focused on extending toolbar functionality with a wider scope than navigation shortcuts. The Googlebar extension emulates and extends upon Google's hugely popular Internet Explorer toolbar. The strength of the Yahoo! Toolbar bar is that it is a network application; bookmarks and settings are saved online and on any browser with the Yahoo! bar loaded. The final toolbar enhancement introduced is the Web Developer extension, which provides a rich set of tools that can be used to scrutinize or debug web sites.

The chapter then discussed the underused status bar. One of the simplest extensions is the Statusbar clock, which adds a clock and date to the status bar. ForecastFox and FoxyTunes are two extensions that are more complex. ForecastFox pulls in feeds from Accuweather.com for a user-specified location and displays weather information in the toolbar. FoxyTunes is a hook for a large number of media playback applications and adds a set of multimedia buttons to the status bar, as well as the ID3 tag of the currently playing song. The SwitchProxy extension should be appealing to privacy buffs; it streamlines and extends functionality already found in Firefox by providing an easy method to switch between proxies, both manually and automatically through proxy lists. The final extension looked at is the StockTicker extension, which pulls your favorite stock symbols and displays their rise and fall every few minutes.

The topics covered in this chapter should give you a good idea of how you can maximize the usability of the Firefox toolbar and status bar. A balance of GUI improvements and the introduction of fantastic new functionality add another dimension to Firefox, far beyond its being just another browser.

Hacking Navigation, Downloads, and Searching

part

IV

Hacking Navigation and Tab Browsing

The great thing about Firefox is the ability it provides to customize the browser to suit your personal preferences. You can start the browser with one, two, five, ten, or as many tabs as you like, each with a different web site. You can alter the look and behavior of those tabs in just about any way you like. Did you just close a tab accidentally? No problem. You'll learn how to reopen it. Don't like the tab bar at the top of the browser? Move it wherever you like. Once you start using mouse gestures, you'll wonder how you ever browsed without them. This chapter is all about getting around in Firefox and making it easier for you to find what you're looking for quickly and comfortably.

by Phil Catelinet

Setting Your Home Page

When you first install Firefox, the default home page is http://www .google.com/firefox. You don't have to change it if you like starting from a clean, quick-loading page every time, but you probably have a favorite web page that you like to read when your browser starts up. Firefox makes it easy to set the home page to anything you like.

Specifying a Single Home Page

Browse to your favorite web site, select Tools ➪ Options, and the first item you see on the General window is Home Page. Figure 10-1 shows the options in the General window. Click the Use Current Page button to set the home page to the site you're currently viewing.

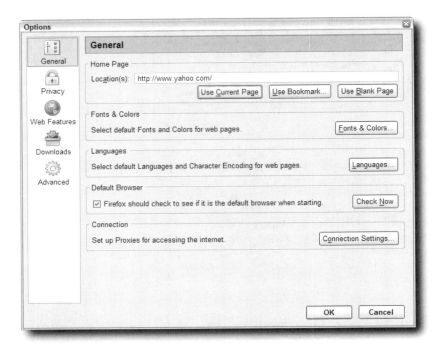

FIGURE 10-1: Set the home page to the current page.

Specifying Multiple Home Pages

So far, Firefox is no different from any other web browser when it comes to the home page. However, what if you visit several different web sites every day, throughout the day? Normally, you'd select these sites from your bookmarks or from the links on the Personal toolbar. After a while, that can be a lot of clicking and browsing. Firefox makes it easy for you to open multiple web pages at startup, each one in its own tab. This way, you can read one of your favorite sites in one tab while another site waits in another tab, ready whenever you are.

As with nearly everything in Firefox, there are several ways to set up multiple home pages.

The Easy Way

Suppose you want to load three different web sites when Firefox starts. Open three new tabs and in each tab browse to one of your three favorite sites. Figure 10-2 shows Firefox with three tabs, each with a different site.

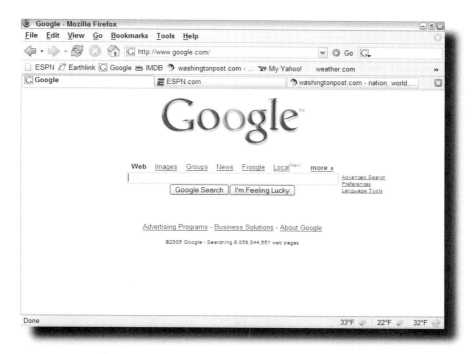

FIGURE 10-2: Firefox with three browser tabs in use.

Now, go back to Tools ⇨ Options ⇨ General. The Use Current Page button now has become the Use Current Pages button. When you click the button, your previous single URL is replaced with three URLs, each one separated by the pipe character. You can see how this new configuration looks in Figure 10-3.

To add another web site to your set of home pages, click the Home button, then open another tab and browse to a new site. Return to the Tools ⇨ Options ⇨ General window and click Use Current Pages again. Firefox appends the new site to your existing set of home pages.

The Easier Way

Browse to each site you want to have in your set of home pages, and bookmark them in a new folder. (Call it "Home Pages" so you won't confuse it with your other folders.) When you've assembled all of your home pages in the folder, go back to the Options window and click on the Use Bookmark . . . button. A new window with all of your bookmarks pops up (as shown in Figure 10-4), and you can select your Home Pages folder from the list. The set of home pages fills in the Location(s) field, and the next time you start Firefox your set of home pages opens in tabs. You can do this with any of your existing bookmark folders as well.

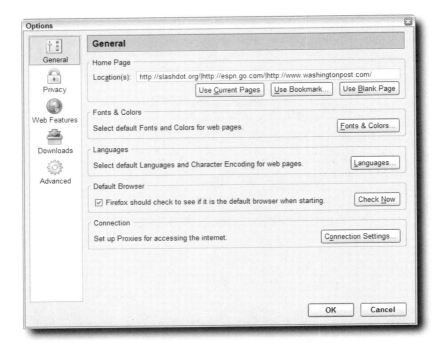

FIGURE 10-3: Firefox's General options showing three home pages.

FIGURE 10-4: The Bookmarks window lets you select a bookmark or folder to use for your home page(s).

The Hard Way

Now that you've seen how Firefox parses individual web sites as multiple home pages, you can add additional web site tabs manually by typing them in the General Options Location(s) box. Separate each URL with a pipe and no spaces. Your Location(s) box should look like this:

```
http://www.google.com/|http://us.imdb.com/|http://start.earthlink.net/
```

To add another tab with another web site, type another pipe after the last slash, then type the full URL, including `http://`. When you restart the browser, the new tab appears to the right of the other sites. The sites always open in the same order as the URLs in the Location(s) box.

Opening New Windows

Tabbed browsing is perhaps the greatest innovation in web browser technology since the invention of the browser itself. Prior to tabbed browsing, if you wanted to look at multiple web sites at the same time you had to open a new browser window for each site. If you were looking at only two or three sites, it wasn't so bad, but any more than that tended to clutter up your screen too much to get anything done. With tabbed browsing, you can open as many sites as you like and browse them all in one application window. Tabbed browsing has become so ingrained for me that I have trouble using other browsers and programs. I find myself using the key combinations and mouse clicks that open new tabs, but instead produce unintended results in the wrong applications.

Speaking of other applications, Firefox's default behavior when you come to it from links in other programs (such as your e-mail application) is to reuse the last browser window. The effect is that the new link loads in place of the previous page opened in that window. Sometimes you don't mind, but often you kept that other browser page loaded for a reason, and now it's gone. The Back button might bring it back for you, unless it was a special window that did not have any browser buttons, such as a media player or video presentation. Firefox provides several options just for these situations:

- Open links from other applications in the most recent tab/window (the default setting).
- Open links in a new window.
- Open links in a new tab in the same window.

You can choose among these options on the Advanced window of the Options menu, under Tabbed Browsing (see Figure 10-5). Select the "a new window" option to order Firefox to open a new window for any links from other applications, and you won't overwrite existing windows with new pages.

Note On MacOS, this is Firefox ⇨ Preferences . . ., then the Advanced tab on the Preferences sheet.

FIGURE 10-5: Native options for tabbed browsing.

You can also adjust some of the other default behaviors of tabs from this same menu. By default, when you open a link in a new tab, Firefox loads that tab in the background. The "Select new tabs opened from links" and "Select new tabs opened from bookmarks or history" options open new tabs in the foreground. "Warn when closing multiple tabs" generates a popup window warning you if you try to close more than one tab at a time by right-clicking on the tab bar and selecting "Close Other Tabs," or if you try to close a window with multiple tabs open.

Because tabbed browsing is one of the most popular features of Firefox, it's also popular with extension writers and hackers. The next section explains how you can alter the behavior of tabs well beyond the original scope of the feature.

Tab Browsing Hacking

By default, Firefox hides the tab bar when only one tab is open. You can change that setting from the Tabbed Browsing window by unchecking "Hide the tab bar when only one web site is open." You can then double-click on the empty space next to a tab to open a new, blank tab.

You can see more of Firefox's tabbed browsing attributes in about:config. Filter the list with the string `browser.tabs` and the list of adjustable tab settings appears. For example, when you open a folder of bookmarks in tabs, Firefox overwrites any open tabs with the new ones from the folder. However, if you change the following to `false` and open a folder in new tabs (right-click on the folder and select "Open in Tabs"), the new tabs are appended to the existing tabs.

```
Browser.tabs.loadFolderAndReplace
```

Note Explanations of about:config settings can be found at `http://preferential.mozdev`
`.org/preferences.html`.

Using userChrome.css to Hack Tabs

You've already seen the power of modifying the userChrome.css file to alter the appearance of other Firefox elements. Now the focus is on what you can do with the look and feel of tabs.

By adding code to the userChrome.css file, you can move the tab bar to the left, right, or bottom of the browser window. For example, to put the tab bar at the bottom of your Firefox window, add this line to your userChrome.css file:

```
#content > tabbox { -moz-box-direction: reverse; }
```

Restart Firefox and your tab bar appears at the bottom of the screen, as shown in Figure 10-6.

Firefox provides a default busy icon for tabs that are loading pages, but you might want to give yourself a clearer indication of what's going on with your tabs. To change the colors of normal, active, and loading tabs, add these lines of code to your userChrome.css file:

```
/* Change Tab Colors */
/* Change color of active tab */
tab[selected="true"] {background-color: rgb(222,218,210) !important; color:
black !important;}
/* Change color of normal tabs */
tab {background-color: rgb(200,196,188) !important; color: gray !important;}
/* Tab while loading */
tab[busy] {color:gray !important;}
```

Remember that you can undo all of these changes by deleting the lines from userChrome.css and restarting Firefox.

Tip You can see other examples of tab bar appearance tricks at `http://www.mozilla.org/`
`support/firefox/tips#app_tab`.

FIGURE 10-6: Firefox with tab bar at the bottom of the screen.

Bring Back Those Lost Tabs

I don't know what I'd do without tabbed browsing. I like to browse with many tabs open all the time. I'm constantly opening links in new tabs and closing old ones. Occasionally, I'll close the wrong tab by accident. At times like that, I used to be stuck: what site was in that tab and how did I get to it? Luckily, the SessionSaver extension restores closed tabs, bringing back those sites that might still need your attention. After you install SessionSaver, you see a menu for it under Tools. If you haven't closed any tabs yet, you'll just see the SessionSaver option by itself. From here, you can capture your open tabs as a session and restore them at any time, as shown in Figure 10-7. It's similar to bookmarking a group of tabs in a folder and reopening that folder's bookmarks in individual tabs.

The real power of SessionSaver is its ability to restore your closed tabs. After you close a tab, SessionSaver puts a new option on the Tools menu, Snapback Tab, along with a menu of recently closed tabs. Figure 10-8 shows an example of the Snapback Tab menu. Select any of these items and the closed tab fades in as a new tab to the left of any currently opened tabs. As you restore closed tabs, SessionSaver removes them from the menu so you always have a list of closed tabs.

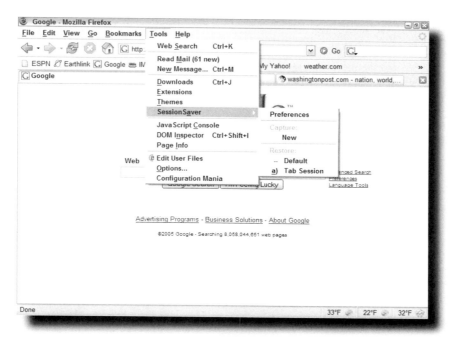

FIGURE 10-7: SessionSaver's Capture function lets you save open tabs.

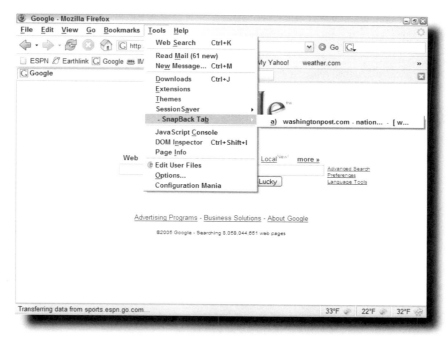

FIGURE 10-8: SessionSaver's Snapback Tabs menu brings back your closed tabs.

SessionSaver includes one other feature not specifically related to tabbed browsing. On SessionSaver's Preferences menu, you have the option to save your browser session each time you close the browser. This feature can be both good and bad. If Firefox crashes or you close the entire browser window by accident, SessionSaver remembers your opened tabs and sites and brings them back exactly as they were. This setting overrides Firefox's home page setting, so you won't see your favorite sites when the browser starts. If you were in the middle of some hard-core browsing, you'll be right back where you were. However, it restores the web sites as they were when the browser closed, without reloading them from the Internet. So, if you were looking at an up-to-date news site, you'll see the news as it was then, not now. A click of the Refresh button reloads the site, of course, but it can be a little disconcerting the first time you see old news if you're not expecting it. You can disable this feature and restore your usual home page settings by unchecking the option on the SessionSaver Preferences menu.

Note SessionSaver is available at `http://www.pikey.me.uk/mozilla/#ss`.

Using Extensions to Hack Tab Browsing

When it comes to tabbed browsing, there are so many different ways of doing things that it makes perfect sense to use extensions to hack them. Consider these two powerful extensions for configuring tabs:

- Tabbrowser Preferences
- Tab Mix

These two extensions overlap in terms of the features they handle. They can be used together or separately, as you prefer, though you might want to use only one of the two. If you install both extensions and make changes using one of them, the other might override your changes with its own settings.

Tabbrowser Preferences

Unlike other extensions, which create separate items available under the Tools menu, Tabbrowser Preferences menus appear as the Tabbed Browsing item in the main Options window, as shown in Figure 10-9. The "Load external links in:" setting at the top replaces the Tabbed Browsing settings that were under the Advanced button before you installed the extension. The selections you made regarding new window and tab behavior for external application links carry over to the Tabbrowser Preferences extension.

Using Tabbrowser Preferences, you can accomplish some of the tasks you previously learned how to do through the userChrome.css file. The extension provides the option to move the tab bar to the bottom of the browser window. Under the Features expandable menu item, check the "Place the tabbar on the bottom of the window (requires restart)" checkbox and restart Firefox. To undo the change, uncheck the box. If you don't like getting your hands dirty with CSS code, the checkbox method gives you an easy way to move the tab bar.

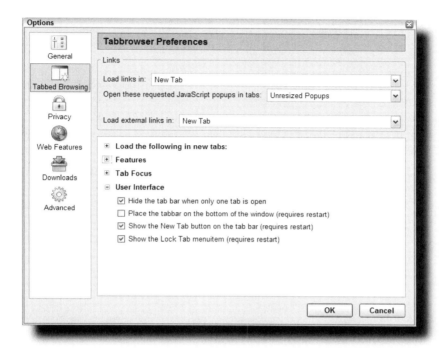

FIGURE 10-9: The Tabbrowser Preferences window.

Tabbrowser Preferences also gives you different ways to adjust how Firefox handles new windows and popups. Under Links at the top of the Tabbrowser Preferences window, you can use the JavaScript popups option to change how Firefox handles new windows loaded by JavaScript code. Instead of letting the web designer dictate how new windows operate, you can decide to open those windows in tabs if you like.

The "Load the following in new tabs:" expandable menu gives you the ability to open searches and typed URLs in new tabs, instead of opening them in the current tab or window. It even lets you open them in the foreground or background, whichever you like.

The Tab Focus options change how new windows behave when used in combination with the preceding settings regarding those windows. If you change the options at the top to force new windows into new tabs instead, Tab Focus lets you tell Firefox to open those new tabs in the background. And the "Select tabs when the mouse is moved over them" checkbox puts tab switching into the palm of your hand (assuming you're using that hand to control the mouse).

Note You can get the Tabbrowser Preferences extension from `http://www.pryan.org/mozilla/site/TheOneKEA/tabprefs/`.

Tab Mix

While Tab Mix duplicates most of the features of Tabbrowser Preferences — in fact, it's based in part on an earlier version of Tabbrowser Preferences — it provides some additional options that the other extension does not have. Tab Mix uses a separate tabbed window to show off its abilities. You can see this window in Figure 10-10. Unfortunately, the only way to reach this menu is by opening the Extensions window, selecting the Tab Mix extension, and clicking the Options button.

The Link tab shows you the options for new window and links behavior that you've already seen twice before.

The Tab tab lets you change the focus of newly opened tabs from links, bookmarks, and the browser history. It also has an option to reopen closed tabs, similar to SessionSaver. The difference is that Tab Mix's feature puts the Undo Close Tab item in the context menu of the tab bar, rather than under the Tools menu of the browser itself (see Figure 10-11). Depending on your browsing habits, this location might be more convenient for you when you need to bring back that tab you just closed. To enable Tab Mix's tab restore feature, check the box under Tab Features, and then check the Undo Close Tab box on the Menu tab. If you want to see a list of closed tabs, check the box next to Closed tab list, as well.

FIGURE 10-10: The Tab Mix menu window.

Tab Mix has another advantage over Tabbrowser Preferences: it lets you move the tab bar to the bottom of the browser window without restarting the browser. Check out the Appearance tab for this option. You can also add a progress bar to your tabs instead of the throbber icon, for a better visual representation of pages loading.

FIGURE 10-11: Tab Mix can restore closed tabs too.

Finally, the Mouse tab lets you drag tabs to change their order and select tabs by moving the mouse over them. You can adjust the delay when changing the focus from tab to tab as you move the mouse, giving your eyes a chance to catch up with your hand.

Get Tab Mix from `http://tab-mix.info.tm/`.

Better Browsing through Better Mousing

Firefox doesn't include much in the way of enhancements for your mouse. There are a few settings you can configure yourself, but, aside from adjustments to scroll behavior, the mouse behaves the same in Firefox as it does in any other application. Once again, extension writers have stepped in to improve what Firefox includes and to port features from other browsers and applications to make it easier for you to browse without leaving the page window.

This sections looks at several different features:

- Changing how your mouse scrolls.
- The different things your mouse scroll wheel can do.
- Mouse gestures that let you "draw" your way around the Internet.

Let's start with hacking your mouse scroll feature.

Firefox includes a feature called *smooth scrolling* that lets you see just how much of the page goes by when you use the Page Up or Page Down keys or your mouse scroll wheel. Without smooth scrolling, Firefox jumps up or down a page when you scroll, but, with this feature turned on, the browser glides up and down the page. With the mouse wheel and smooth scrolling, the amount of scroll depends on how fast you flick the wheel, but the visual effect is the same. You can turn off smooth scrolling in the Options window under Advanced.

Firefox's default scroll effect with the wheel alone is three lines on the web page. You can alter the scroll wheel behavior by holding down certain keys while using the wheel:

- Alt+scroll wheel cuts the amount of scroll per wheel notch to one line.

- Ctrl+scroll wheel increases or decreases the size of the type on the web page.

- Shift+scroll wheel moves forward or backward in the browser history for the current tab or window.

These settings can be changed via about:config. Type **mousewheel** in the Filter field to narrow the focus to just the default mouse settings. Figure 10-12 shows the mousewheel settings in the about:config window. You can alter any of the settings by double-clicking on them.

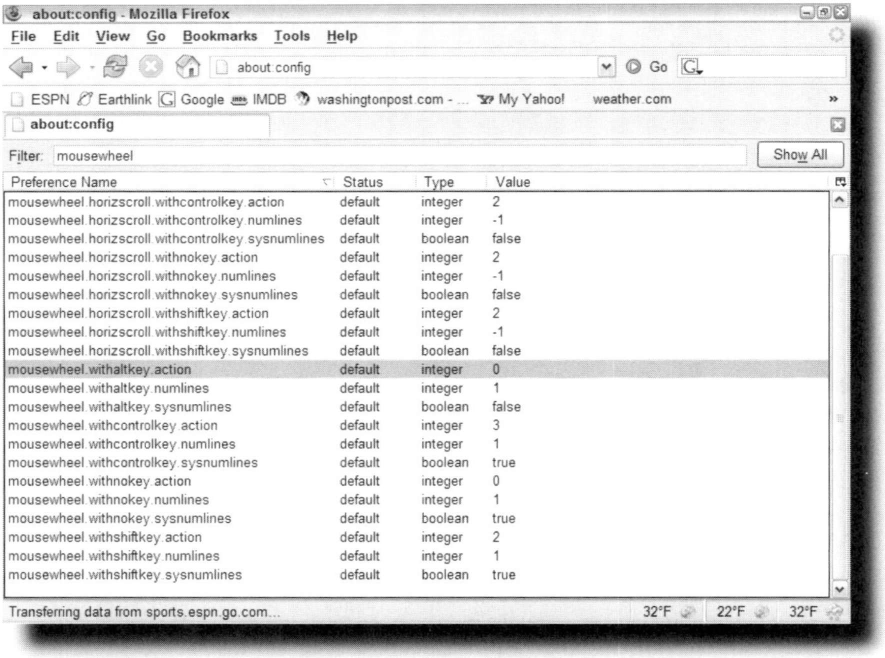

FIGURE 10-12: The mousewheel options in about:config.

You'll need to keep these action variables in mind:

- 0 is scroll by lines of text in the browser window.
- 1 is scroll by pages of text in the browser window.
- 2 is move forward or backward in browser history.
- 3 is make the page text larger or smaller.

For example, if you want to change the Shift+scroll wheel behavior to scroll a page at a time, double-click on the line

```
mousewheel.withshiftkey.action
```

and change the number in the popup window to 1. The change takes effect immediately.

To increase the number of lines that the scroll wheel scrolls to 10, double-click on the following and change the number in the popup window to 10:

```
mousewheel.withnokey.numlines
```

You'll also need to double-click on

```
mousewheel.withnokey.sysnumlines
```

to change the setting from true to false. Otherwise, Firefox ignores your other change and sticks to the browser's default of 3 lines of scroll. Again, these changes take effect right away, so you can switch to another window or tab and see if you like the effect. To change the settings back to their defaults, right-click on the ones in boldface and select Reset from the menu.

Using Configuration Mania to Adjust Your Mouse Scrolling

If you don't like editing your preferences through about:config and having to remember variables, extension writers provide easy windowed methods of adjusting these settings. The Configuration Mania extension lets you tinker with many different Firefox features, among them mouse behavior. After you install the extension, you can access it through an entry on the Tools menu. Open the Configuration Mania window and select Mouse wheel from the list of items on the left (see Figure 10-13).

Any changes you made to the scroll settings through the about:config menu carry over to Configuration Mania. Here, instead of keeping track of obscure variables, you can select the mouse wheel and key combination and change their functions as you like. To change the way mouse scrolling behaves when the Shift key is pressed, select Shift from the modifier drop-down list, then adjust the settings appropriately. To change the number of lines that a particular scroll setting scrolls on the page, uncheck the "Use system default" box if it is checked and change the number in the field. As with changes made with about:config, Configuration Mania's changes take immediate effect.

Note You can get Configuration Mania from `http://members.lycos.co.uk/toolbarpalette/confmania/index_en.html`.

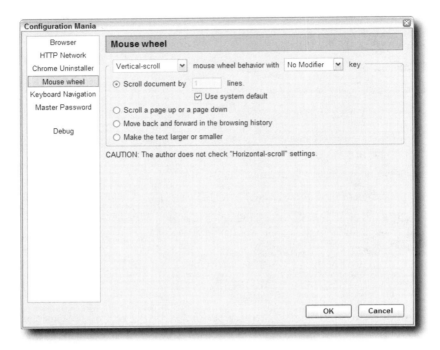

FIGURE 10-13: Configuration Mania's Mouse wheel options.

Show Your Artistic Side with Mouse Gestures

Navigating web sites usually means a lot of clicking on various browser buttons and menus as you look for the information you want. Mouse gestures make it easier for you to keep your mouse where it belongs — in the web browser window itself — by turning the functions of the browser's menus into figures you trace with your mouse. You hold down a mouse button and drag the mouse in a two-to-five line design, and the browser performs the action associated with the gesture. To go back in the browser's history, you would hold down the right mouse button and move the mouse from right to left across the web page. To close the browser window, hold the right button and move the mouse down and to the right. You can assign mouse gestures to nearly any browser feature.

There are several mouse gesture extensions out there, but the easiest one to configure and use is probably All-in-One Gestures. It provides detailed windows for its features and a well-designed interface listing the predefined mouse gestures and methods for creating your own. Figure 10-14 shows All-in-One Gestures' list of predefined gestures.

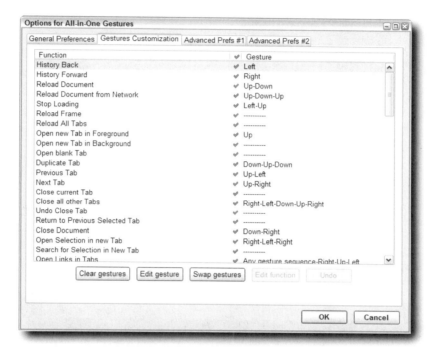

FIGURE 10-14: The list of mouse gestures provided by All-in-One Gestures.

The artistic aspect of mouse gestures is in how they can be displayed on screen. All-in-One Gestures shows you a thin red line that follows your cursor as you perform a gesture (see Figure 10-15). The line lets you see exactly which way you moved the mouse, and you see the letters corresponding to the gesture in Firefox's status bar.

Mouse gestures take a little adjustment, but once you get used to them you'll find you want to use them in all of your applications. If you're new to the concept, I suggest learning the following simple gestures first:

- History Forward
- History Back
- Next Tab
- Previous Tab
- Reload page
- Close Tab/Window

Once you're adept at these gestures, try some of the more complex ones or make your own. Soon, they will be like tabs: you will wonder how you ever used a browser without them.

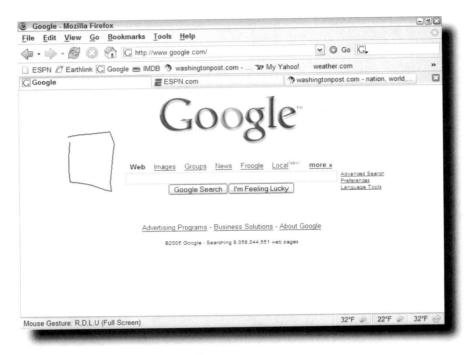

FIGURE 10-15: Mouse gestures in action.

Summary

There are many ways to customize Firefox to suit your personal browsing habits and tastes. You can open any number of web sites as your home page, using a tab for each site. Tabs can be styled however you like, with icons and progress bars to tell you which ones are active. And mouse gestures and scroll enhancements let you keep the control of your browsing in the palm of your hand.

Download and Plugin Hacks

A side from browsing, downloading is probably the most important feature to most users, and hacking that experience is what this chapter is all about (that and, of course, plugins). One of the best enhancements that Firefox introduced over its predecessors was a unified and configurable Download Manager window. As you can see from Figure 11-1, the Download Manager window consolidates what used to be individual download status dialogs for each download and displays them in one list. All of the options available in the original download status dialogs, such as Pause, Resume, Open, and so on, are also available in the new unified window. Additionally, the ability to open the default downloads location by clicking the location label next to "All files downloaded to" and cleaning up the download history by clicking on the Clean Up button are available here.

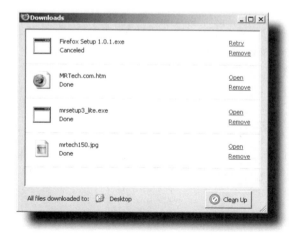

FIGURE 11-1: Default Download Manager window

To change the default download location, hop over to the Downloads section from the Tools ➪ Options menu, as shown in Figure 11-2, which also shows the other options available.

Note In Mac OS X, the command is Firefox ➪ Preferences.

FIGURE 11-2: Download preferences available from the Tools ➪ Options screen

While the Download Manager is a great tool, some may want additional features when it comes to downloading, such as displaying downloads in the status bar, sorting downloads into directories, and other tweaks. The following hacks and extensions allow you to customize your download experience to your liking.

Hacking Download Behavior

The default download experience using Firefox is pretty good. This section shows you how to hack the basic internal options to your liking, such as clearing your download history, configuring download alerts, and other useful hacks.

Clearing Download History

With the advent of security and privacy issues, many users want to make sure that downloads are not tracked well after they have closed Firefox. Figure 11-3 shows that Firefox 1.0 has a configurable interface to manage the Download Manager History from the Tools ➪ Options menu in the Privacy section.

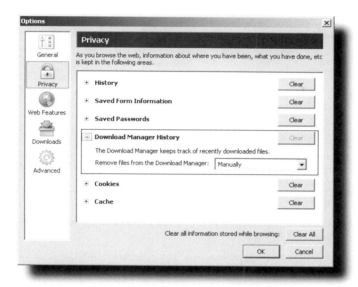

FIGURE 11-3: Download Manager History settings in Firefox 1.0

Figure 11-4 shows the Firefox 1.1 redesign of the Options screen.

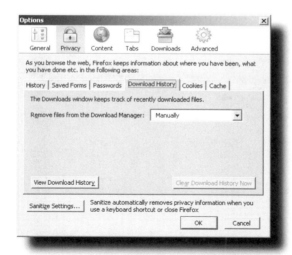

FIGURE 11-4: Download History Privacy settings in Firefox 1.1

Despite the provision of this interface, my preference is to manually add settings to the user.js file to guarantee the setting is merged back into my preferences upon restart. To do this, enter one of the following settings into your user.js file, depending on which history method you prefer.

- To remove downloads from the history when they complete successfully, use the following entry. Keep in mind that cancelled downloads are not removed.

```
user_pref("browser.download.manager.retention", 0)
```

- To remove all downloads when you close your instance of Firefox, use this setting. Keep in mind that downloads will persist in the Download Manager for the whole session that you have Firefox open and are not cleaned out until you exit.

```
user_pref("browser.download.manager.retention", 1)
```

- To keep a history of all downloads and to allow yourself to manually prune the list, just add the following to your user.js file.

```
user_pref("browser.download.manager.retention", 2)
```

Figure 11-5 shows the Download Manager options via the about:config utility.

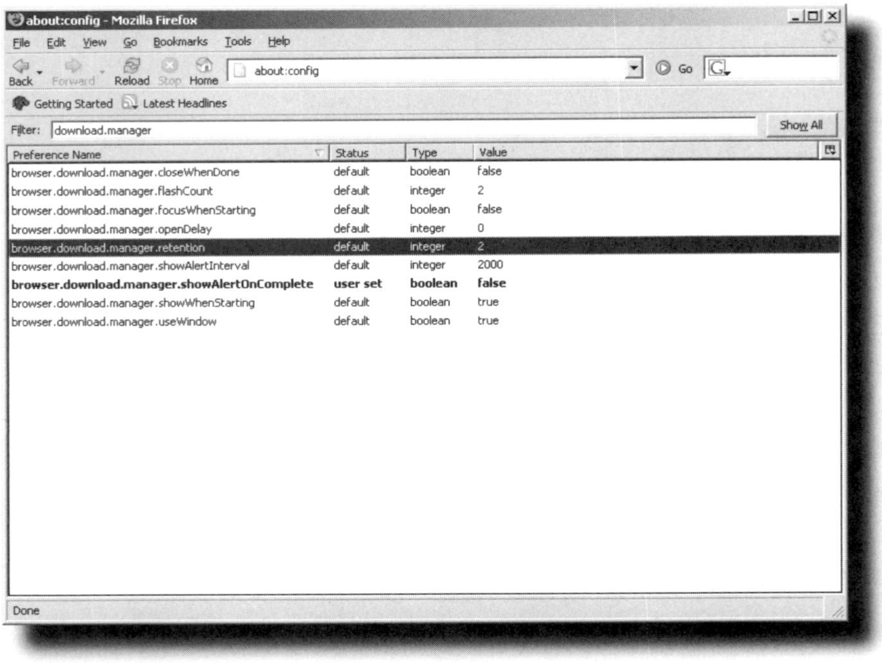

FIGURE 11-5: The about:config tool with Download Manager retention setting highlighted

Tip

To get more documentation on preferences that you can change, with their associated values and descriptions, visit this great MozillaZine Knowledge Base article: `http://kb.mozillazine.org/Firefox_:_FAQs_:_About:config_Entries`.

In Figure 11-6, you see that Firefox 1.1 introduces a Sanitize option to the Tools menu. This feature can be configured from the Privacy section of the Options screen and allows you to manually choose which settings to clear when shutting down Firefox.

FIGURE 11-6: Sanitize options introduced with Firefox 1.1

While the final version of Firefox 1.1 was not officially released during the development of this book, intermittent test builds were. These builds provided insight into interface and feature enhancements, as well as into changes that were being coded and planned for the final release. These test builds, which are known as *trunk builds*, are usually compiled and made available on a daily basis and on some servers on an hourly basis. They usually provide fresh, bleeding-edge copies of code changes introduced throughout the previous day's efforts of coding and fixes. For information or to download trunk builds or to see the progress of outstanding bugs and fixes that have been checked, visit the Firefox Builds forum on MozillaZine.org at `http://forums.mozillazine.org/viewforum.php?f=23`.

Other Useful Hacks

You can add the hacks in Table 11-1 to your user.js or prefs.js file to allow further customization of the Download Manager settings without having to install an extension.

Each preference listed in the following table should be formatted as follows and saved to either the prefs.js or user.js file:

```
user_pref("name", value)
```

Optionally, you can modify them using the about:config functionality built into Firefox.

Table 11-1   Customizing the Download Manager Settings

Preference Name	Description	Value
browser. download. manager. closeWhenDone	Use this to close the Download Manager window when it finishes downloading.	true/false
browser. download. manager. focusWhenStarting	Use this to focus the Download Manager window when a download starts.	true/false
browser. download. manager. openDelay	This is the number of milliseconds that Firefox waits before displaying the Download Manager. Setting this to 2000 will have it wait 2 seconds before opening the manager window. This is useful if you are downloading a bunch of small files and do not want the Download Manager to keep popping up.	integer
browser. download. manager. showAlertOnComplete	Use this to enable/disable the download complete alert window that pops up on the bottom-right side of the browser.	true/false

Tip To change a preference back to the default, just remove the entry from the user.js file, if it exists; then open about:config, select the preference, right-click, and select the Reset option from the context menu. This will set the value back to the default value.

Hacking Downloads with Extensions

Hacking the download experience with extensions is the most useful way to personalize downloading, whether it is showing the download status in the status bar, tab, or in the sidebar. Additionally, eliminating annoying situations such as blank new windows on file downloads and sorting downloads into different directories based on their file extension can really come in handy. This section covers them all and what options work best with each.

Showing Downloads in the Status Bar Using the Download Statusbar Extension

One of the most useful extensions that I have found to minimize the impact of downloading files, while maintaining a keen eye on progress and download throughput, is the Download Statusbar extension. While the title might imply that the default status bar is modified, in reality, what it does is build a custom download status bar that it places temporarily above the official status bar area extension, as shown in Figure 11-7.

Tip

To maximize Download Statusbar's effectiveness, disable Firefox's built-in Download Manager window from popping up. Do this in the Downloads section of the Tools ↪ Options menu.

FIGURE 11-7: Download Statusbar extension, with Firefox download complete and Thunderbird download paused

When Download Statusbar is in action, you will see a new bar open up above the status bar with the progress and information about each of the current downloads. To pause a download, left-click it and then click it again to resume. A red band appears around paused downloads. Additionally, right-clicking a download shows a context menu with different options based on active, paused, or completed downloads. Figure 11-8 displays the different configuration options available with this extension.

Note

For more information about the Download Statusbar extension, visit `http://downloadstatusbar.mozdev.org/`.

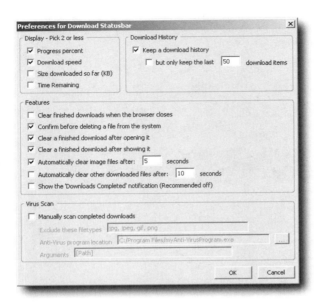

FIGURE 11-8: Download Statusbar extension options window

Showing Download Manager in the Sidebar or Tab with Download Manager Tweak Extension

On the surface, this extension appears to be a cute overlay to the internal Downloads Manger, as shown in Figure 11-9, but when you dig into the options, you'll find that there are a few other interesting tweaks and possible hacks that you can apply. Nice hidden features include the following:

- Specify Download Manger window open delay.

- Specify buttons to show in the Download Manager window.

- Move the toolbar in the window and other minor tweaks.

Another nice customization is placement of the Download Manager — whether you want it in a new window, in the sidebar, or in a tab. The basic features fit the extension's name aptly but don't do it justice with respect to what it really provides.

There are three ways to get to the Download Manager Tweak options and settings. You can:

- open the Extension Manger and double-click on the extension's entry on the list.

- click the Options button on the Download Manger's toolbar.

- access it via the Tools ⇨ Options menu in the Downloads section by clicking the Download Manager Tweak Options button there.

Figure 11-10 displays the options available for this extension.

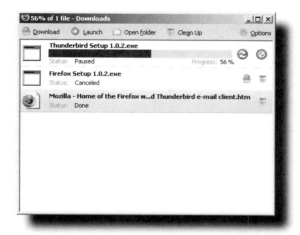

FIGURE 11-9: Download Manager Tweak customized version of the Download Manager

FIGURE 11-10: Download Manager Tweak options and settings

Tip

For more information on the Download Manger Tweak extension, visit `http://dmextension.mozdev.org/`.

Disabling Blank Download Windows with the Disable Targets for Downloads Extension

One of the most annoying things about downloading files off the Internet is the insistence of web masters, HTML coders, and automated download sites on adding a target field to a file's download link. You have probably seen this — for example, you click to download myhack.zip, and when you do, a new blank window opens and then download begins, leaving behind the blank window after the file has completed. As mentioned on this extension's web site, this issue has been officially filed as Bug #241972, which can be found here: `https://bugzilla .mozilla.org/show_bug.cgi?id=241972`. Most users would like a resolution sooner rather than later, and that is where the Disable Targets for Downloads extension comes in.

This extension removes targets only from active hyperlinks, not those wrapped in JavaScript code, and so on.

A normal link may look like this (shameless plug):

```
<a href="http://www.mrtech.com/mrsetup3_lite.exe">Download
Here</a>
```

But a link with a target will look similar to the following:

```
<a href="http://www.mrtech.com/mrsetup3_lite.exe"
target="_blank">Download Here</a>
```

This extension disables the link's additional `target` property so the browser handles the link normally and opens it in the current window.

By default, this extension disables new windows for links with targets for the following file-name extensions: .zip, .rar, .exe, tar, .jar, .xpi, .gzip, .gz, .ace, and .bin.

While this extension covers the majority of common filename extensions, I tend to add a few more potential culprits, including .7z, .cab, .msi, and .pdf.

Figure 11-11 shows the Disable Targets for Downloads Options window.

For more information or updates for the Disable Targets for Downloads extension, visit `http://www.cusser.net/extensions/disabletarget/`.

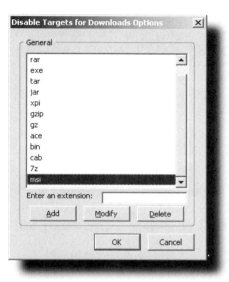

FIGURE 11-11: Disable Targets for Downloads Options window

Follow these steps to add additional filename extensions to the list for target disabling:

1. Install the Disable Targets for Downloads extension.

2. Restart your browser to finish the installation process.

3. Select the Extensions option from the main browser's Tools menu.

4. Locate and double-click the Disable Targets for Downloads entry on the list.

5. For each filename extension desired, type the filename's extension and click the Add button.

6. Click OK when you're done, and your settings are ready for use.

Note While most extensions are three letters, this is not a steadfast rule for all operating systems and applications, as you see with the .7z, .gz, and .gzip filename extensions.

Another real bonus of this extension is its ability to use regular expression pattern matching to remove the blank target windows for links matching the regular expression. Because the extension relies on regular expression pattern matching, this means that you are not restricted to just filename extensions. One example on this extension's site is to add the following entry, which removes the blank window opened by downloading a file in Gmail:

```
/gmail\?view=att/
```

Additionally, some sites open up just one too many tabs or windows when you are navigating from section to section, and although they are not necessarily blank, they are annoying. Some sites that I hack with this extension are `http://www.klitetools.com/` and `http://www.versiontracker.com/`. While these sites have great content and are updated frequently, they are annoying when they open two, three, or more windows. To alleviate this on the KLite Tools site, I have pinpointed the most common URL snippet to match on to remove these target windows, which is as follows:

`klitetools.com/comments.php`

Or enter just the root domain to eliminate all targeted links for the Version Tracker site:

`versiontracker.com`

Using these will successfully remove the target window for the specified page or the entire site.

Sorting Downloads to Directories with the Download Sort Extension

Once you have the Download Sort extension installed, you can begin a life of organized downloading. This extension allows you to add filename extensions or keywords to monitor and save files that match to the desired directory. As shown in Figure 11-12, the settings window for this extension allows full customization of each file extension, as well as the use of keywords in filenames.

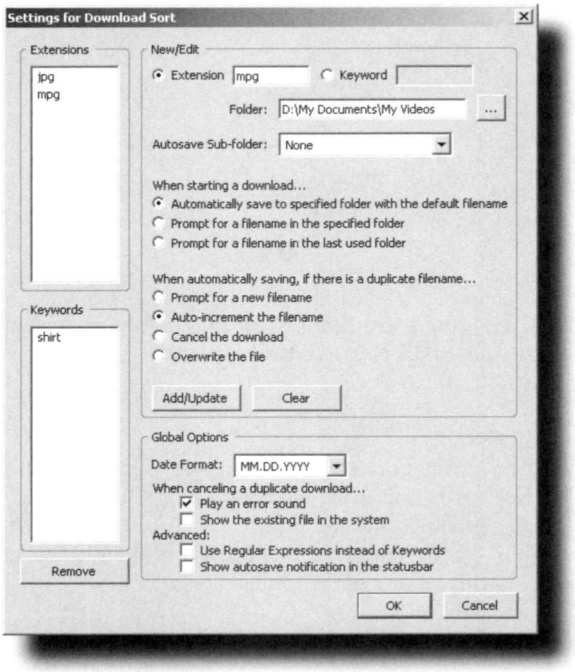

FIGURE 11-12: Main configuration settings for Download Sort

To open the settings window, open the Extensions Manager and double-click on the Download Sort entry listed. After entering or modifying an entry, make sure to click the Apply/Update button, and your settings will be saved.

Note For more information on the Download Sort extension, visit `http://downloadstatusbar` `.mozdev.org/downsort/`.

Hacking MIME Types

One of the key pieces of information that is communicated between a web server and a browser is a file's content type or MIME type. Multipurpose Internet Mail Extensions (MIME) were originally implemented for use with e-mails and aides in defining a header of information for nontext e-mail attachments. This standard was extended to the Web to define the format of incoming objects that are requested. This section covers how to sniff out the MIME type being sent by a server, as well as how to modify Firefox's behavior for these MIME types.

Understanding File MIME Types

The easiest way to explain MIME type is by using an example such as downloading an executable from a site. Most web servers will associate a Windows executable or .exe extension with a default MIME type of "application/octet-stream" or "application/exe." When the web server initiates the transfer back to the browser, it includes this information in the initial communication header and lets the browser handle the information as it sees fit. A typical prompt that Firefox would display after receiving this information is shown in Figure 11-13.

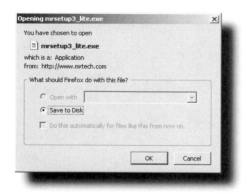

FIGURE 11-13: Default download confirmation window

As Figure 11-13 also shows, some prompts do not always have all available options enabled. Furthermore, some web servers spoof the MIME type to force downloading of files. Solutions and alternatives to each of these situations are covered in the following sections.

Using the Mimetype Editor and LiveHTTPHeaders Extensions

After the headaches caused by trying to figure out what the best MIME type handling setting are, I resorted to recommending a two-extension approach to dissecting the response headers and hacking MIME types from a web server.

The approach that has worked for me is to install both the LiveHTTPHeaders and Mimetype Editor extensions and to use the first to sniff out the MIME type or Content-Type and then add it using the editor. The best part of these extensions is that they are tucked away in the Tools menu until you are ready to use them; they do not add any visually obnoxious elements.

Using the LiveHTTPHeaders extension to detect the custom MIME type is a snap. The whole process of detecting the Content-Type may seem a bit overwhelming, but after your first run, you should have the hang of things. My approach is to do the following:

1. Navigate directly to the page that contains the offending MIME type download issue.
2. Launch the Live HTTP Headers tool from the Tools menu.
3. Switch back to the download page.
4. Click on the download link in question and then save or cancel the download.
5. Switch back to the Live HTTP Header window.

At this point, the window contains the header communication that was exchanged between the server and the browser. The entry to look for is the Content-Type, which is highlighted in Figure 11-14.

Tip

You can right-click and copy any of the individual lines presented. To copy multiple lines, you can click on the first entry, hold down the Shift key, and click the last entry desired; then release the Shift key, right-click the highlighted block, and choose Copy from the context menu.

Note

For more information on the LiveHTTPHeaders extension, visit `http://livehttpheaders .mozdev.org/`.

Once you have the Content-Type text, you can open the Mimetype Editor tool from Tool ⇨ Mimetypes, shown in Figure 11-15, to add the type and the default action that you would like to associate with this type.

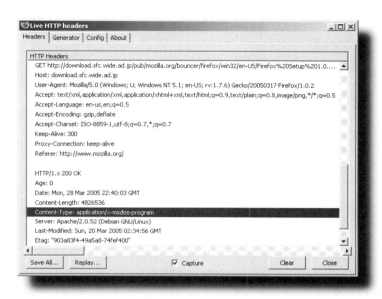

FIGURE 11-14: LiveHTTPHeaders extension capture window

FIGURE 11-15: Mimetype Editor options window

From our LiveHTTPHeaders Firefox download example, you can see that the MIME type or Content-Type in the header information is as follows:

```
Content-Type: application/x-msdos-program
```

Now you take this value and add it to the internal list of MIME types with the following steps:

1. Open Tools ⇨ Mimetype.

2. Click on the New Type button (shown in Figure 11-15), which opens the Edit Type window, shown in Figure 11-16.

3. Populate the MIME Type field with the Content-Type value of `application/x-msdos-program`.

4. Type a general description, such as **Program Files** or **Application**.

5. Enter **exe** in the Extension field, which corresponds to the filename extension.

6. Choose a default action for this type and then enable or disable the "Always ask me before handling files of this type" setting according to your preference.

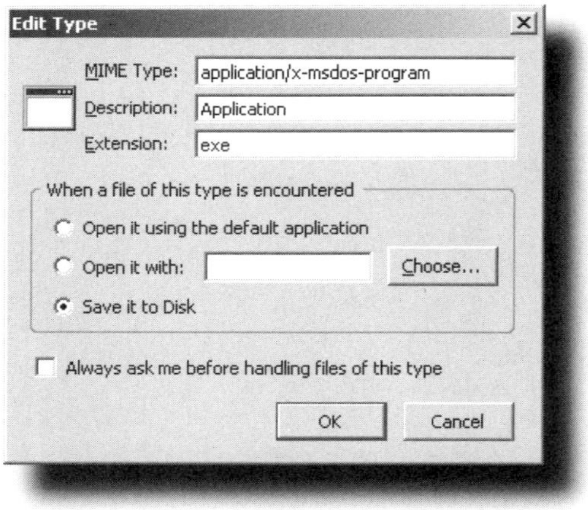

FIGURE 11-16: Mimetype Editor's Edit Type screen

This MIME type update is applied immediately and can be tested by redownloading the file in question. If the Opening dialog (shown in Figure 11-13) still pops up, make sure you have supplied the correct MIME Type without leading or trailing spaces and that you are using the correct filename extension.

What Is MIME Type Spoofing?

MIME type spoofing is commonly used by different software update sites to force a download, open, or save prompt. The technique they use is to create a custom header with the addition of a custom MIME type. Because the browser does not recognize the MIME type, it will bring up the Opening prompt and ask you how to handle the download. One possible spoof could look like this:

```
application/download-this
```

You would have to add this custom type and associate the default actions that you prefer. Using LiveHTTPHeaders, you are able to easily detect any MIME type spoofing practices by capturing the header information while the file is downloading.

 Note Installing via the Install link on the Mimetype Editor web page may not work; just choose the Download link, and it will prompt you to install.

Another key observation is that managing and using MIME types is internal to Firefox and not a function of the extension. This extension merely helps you manage the internal list that Firefox uses, which means that once you are content with changes to the different MIME types you need, you can disable or uninstall it without sacrificing the customizations that you have made to the MIME type list.

Custom MIME type definitions are stored with each profile in the mimeTypes.rdf file, which is formatted in standard RDF/XML syntax. While you can manually edit this file, I find it easier to use these extensions to modify MIME behavior. Another nice feature of this file is that it makes it easy to duplicate the customizations to another computer or profile by just copying it to the main profile directory of the profile that needs updating.

 Note For more information on the Mimetype Editor extension, visit `http://gratisdei.com/FF .htm#mtypes`.

Hacking External Download Managers

Most new Firefox converts have an existing arsenal of tools and utilities installed that help with anything from printing to downloading. Some tools that are used for managing downloads are GetRight, Mass Downloader, Download Express, and so on. While newer versions of these tools are smarter in detecting the presence of the Firefox installation, some have yet to update. This section covers two approaches to hooking Firefox to your external Download Manager by using either the Launchy or FlashGot extensions or by hunting down the needed files for full integration.

Using Launchy to Handle External Programs

One of the beautiful things about Launchy is its ability to detect and show installed applications via the right-click menu. This, coupled with the ease of integrating them with Firefox, makes it the easiest approach to merging installed program handling with Firefox. Launchy supports over 60 external applications and currently supports the following external download managers:

- GetRight
- LeechGet
- Mass Downloader
- Star Downloader
- Internet Download Manager
- ReGet Deluxe
- BitTorrent
- FlashGot
- WackGet
- Offline Explorer Pro

Additionally, Launchy supports many common external browsers, media players, FTP clients, and editors.

Figure 11-17 illustrates the automatic detection of the currently installed programs that it supports and the two download managers currently available on my system. Advanced configuration options are available, but right out of the box, this extension does a lot. To activate or use its features, just right-click on a link and select the desired external program from the Launchy submenu. To disable showing a detected application from the list, just uncheck it in the Launchy Options window.

FIGURE 11-17: Launchy Options window

Note

For more information or to download Launchy, visit `http://gemal.dk/mozilla/launchy.html`.

Using FlashGot to Handle External Programs

Another wildly popular extension used to handle external download programs is FlashGot. Much like the Launchy extension, FlashGot provides support and automatic detection of external download managers, but also merges in the functionality of extensions such as Linky and DownThemAll by allowing you to download all links from the page being viewed via the right-click menu. Another great feature that FlashGot provides, as shown in Figure 11-18, is that it adds an option to the standard Opening Firefox Setup dialog, which helps with MIME types that Firefox does not know how to handle. Using FlashGot, you can avoid the lengthy setup and detailed drudgeries involved with manually having to find and set up the default method to handle unknown MIME types.

FIGURE 11-18: The Opening Firefox Setup dialog with FlashGot feature

Note

For more information or to download FlashGot, visit `http://www.flashgot.net/`.

Seamless Download Integration

So what if you want seamless download integration with Firefox — integration that does not require intervention on your part? Then you have to dig a little deeper or check for a few settings. Newer versions of popular programs such as Download Express, Mass Downloader, and GetRight have added Firefox detection or provide a mechanism for seamless integration. MetaProducts has gone one step further and has created an official extension for Mass Downloader and Download Express to allow Firefox integration.

So what exactly are these programs doing to integrate themselves in the world of Firefox? Quite simply, just copying a plugin file to the Firefox Plugins directory. While I will cover plugins more in the next section, this introduction is a nice segue to help with downloads first.

Most download programs have code that comes bundled to help Firefox and other browsers with settings and options. This code, called a *plugin,* operates quite differently from extensions, and for the most part, these plugins are operating system–dependent. Again, while most updated version of these programs have this feature integrated into their options or settings, you can manually find the needed plugin DLL file(s) by doing a little digging. Once you have identified the program you want to dig into, all you have to do is find its default installation directory and hunt around for the corresponding DLL file. One key thing to note is that in the file's properties, the description provided may assist you in finding the correct plugin DLL. If you are not sure, hold on the side of caution and do not copy any of the files to the plugins directory.

To manually install a plugin file, close Firefox, copy the DLL file to the plugins subdirectory of your Firefox installation, and restart Firefox.

Note Plugins are also the technology implemented by Flash and Macromedia to extend Firefox's capabilities.

Table 11-2 lists the directory and plugin files for GetRight and Mass Downloader.

Table 11-2	GetRight and Mass Downloader	
	GetRight	*Mass Downloader*
Default directory	C:\Program Files/GetRight	C:\Program Files\Mass Downloader
Plugin filename	NPGetRt.dll	npmassdn.dll

Note You can find more information on external Download Manager integration for Windows by visiting http://plugindoc.mozdev.org/windows4.html.

Hacking Plugins

Plugins are compiled pieces of code that implement a standard connection or interface using the plugin architecture, which was originally used as far back as early Netscape versions. Using this interface, third-party developers have the capability of extending and enhancing the features of the browser to handle audio, video, custom filetypes, or processing of requests.

While the previous section briefly covered how to find the plugins file for a couple of the common download programs, this section helps you test your plugins configuration, find additional plugins that you may already have installed, and disable the default behavior from some of the currently installed plugins. Figure 11-19 is a sample plugins directory that contains support for Apple QuickTime, RealPlayer, and Macromedia Flash.

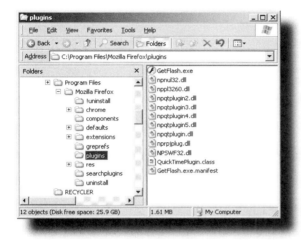

FIGURE 11-19: Sample plugins directory

Tip

The ultimate plugins reference for users is located at `http://plugindoc.mozdev.org/`.

Checking Installed Plugins with about:plugins

Firefox and its predecessors include a simple page that helps you see which plugins are currently installed and recognized. To access this page, just type **about:plugins** in the location bar and press Enter.

Figure 11-20 shows a sample page populated with all of the plugins that Firefox was able to automatically detect, based on operating system and configuration, in addition to the specific plugins located in the plugins subdirectory of your Firefox installation.

Tip

Because the Opera browser uses the same plugins programming interface, most, if not all, of the Opera plugins are compatible with Firefox.

FIGURE 11-20: about:plugins displayed information

For testing purposes, you can also display the full installation path for each of the programs listed in the about:Plugins page by modifying the following preference and setting it to `true`:

```
user_pref("plugin.expose_full_path", true)
```

Please keep in mind that showing the plugin's full path may open you to potential security risks, because most of these values are exposed to public web pages to help them detect if you have proper support for key features such as Flash and others. Use this option only for testing purposes, and make sure to reset this value to `false` once you are done.

Using Available Plugins without Reinstalling

Because several programs already have support for Mozilla or Firefox's plugins technology, reinstalling these programs would seem a tad redundant. This section shows you how to manually dig around Adobe Reader, Apple QuickTime, and RealPlayer plugins. When copying plugins to the Firefox\Plugins directory, it is generally safe to assume that you can replace existing files.

Note   When manually copying files, make sure Firefox is closed.

Finding the Adobe Reader Plugin

To see if your Adobe Reader installation supports the browser plugin, check the following directory, substituting for the question mark the version you have installed:

```
C:\Program Files\Adobe\Acrobat ?.0\Reader\Browser
```

Then copy the Plugin file listed to your Firefox\Plugins directory:

```
nppdf32.dll
```

Finding the Apple QuickTime Plugin

The required plugin files for QuickTime are located in the plugins directory (C:\Program Files\Apple\QuickTime\Plugins) of your QuickTime installation. Just copy all the files in that directory, which are gathered in the following list, to the plugins subdirectory:

- npqtplugin.dll
- npqtplugin2.dll
- npqtplugin3.dll (file may not exist)
- npqtplugin4.dll (file may not exist)
- npqtplugin5.dll (file may not exist)
- QuickTimePlugin.class

Then copy the following component files in the QuickTime plugins directory to the components subdirectory of your Firefox installation:

```
nsIQTScriptablePlugin.xpt
```

Finding the RealPlayer Plugin

RealPlayer may have two different directories that you need to tap into:

- C:\Program Files\Real\RealPlayer\Netscape6 can be the default location for both plug-ins and components.
- It can have a Plugins directory of C:\Program Files\Real\RealPlayer\Browser\Plugins and a Components directory of C:\Program Files\Real\RealPlayer\Browser\Components.

In either case, copy the following files to the corresponding Plugins subdirectory in Firefox:

- nppl3260.dll
- nprjplug.dll

Then copy the following components files to the components subdirectory of your Firefox installation:

- nppl3260.xpt

- nsJSRealPlayerPlugin.xpt

Caution

Because of security concerns and potential issues, Windows Media Player embedding with ActiveX should not be tampered with unless you have fully read the implications. For more information, visit the "Embedded Windows Media in Firefox" posting available at `http://forums.mozillazine.org/viewtopic.php?t=206213`.

Tip

A good reference for installing or configuring plugin support in Firefox for some common programs is available at `http://www.mozilla.org/support/firefox/faq#plugins`.

Disabling Plugin Support for Specific File Extensions

Because Firefox is designed to detect some common plugins, you may want to disable internal plugin handling of common file extensions Firefox has a configuration screen in the Downloads section of the Tools ➪ Options window. In Figure 11-21, you can see that just by unchecking the Enabled column of the file extension, you can customize internal extension handling. When you are done, click OK, and you are all set.

FIGURE 11-21: The Plug-Ins support options window

Summary

While this chapter covers a lot of the basic customizations that you can apply to Firefox to handle downloading, MIME types, and plugins, even more options are available. At this point, you should be able to change the visual and the internal functionality of each of these functions, in addition to knowing where Firefox stores the related keys files.

Extensions such as Download Statusbar, Disable Targets for Download, Mimetype Editor, and Live HTTP Headers have become daily staples for me; you may find other extensions, such as Download Sort and Download Manager Tweak, suit your needs better. Any combination of these extensions that are actively updated and supported should yield a great download and plugin experience when using Firefox.

Search Hacks

A web browser is an information-gathering tool. Sometimes you know where you need to go, so you use bookmarks and familiar links, but eventually you'll need to search the Web to look up new sites and sources of information. Firefox includes some excellent search tools and makes it easy for you to modify the browser to suit your search habits. And some nifty tricks can speed up your searches and help you find what you need right away.

Adjusting the Default Google Search

A fresh install of Firefox uses Google for all searches, whether from the location bar or the search box in the upper-right corner. If you enter your search terms in the location bar, Firefox checks with Google and then takes you to the top search result site. In other words, it's the same as if you searched from `http://www.google.com` and clicked the I'm Feeling Lucky button.

The search box in the upper-right corner behaves a little differently. When you enter your search terms there, Firefox treats it like a normal Google search and shows you a web page with all of the results. If you prefer to see all of your search results but like performing your searches from the location bar, you can adjust Firefox's default Google search through about:config.

From the about:config list, type **keyword** to filter out all but the two items related to keyword searches. You should see these two items:

```
keyword.URL
keyword.enabled
```

Leave the second one alone and focus on the URL setting. By default, it should look like this:

```
Keyword.URL    default    string
http://www.google.com/search?btnI=I%27m+Feeling+
Lucky&ie=UTF-8&oe=UTF-8&q=
```

Notice the words `I'm Feeling Lucky` in the URL? That setting tells Firefox to submit the search to Google and return the same result as if you'd clicked that button on their site. To adjust it so that a location bar search shows you all the results from Google, double-click on the item and change the URL to look like this instead:

```
http://www.google.com/search?&ie=UTF-8&q=
```

by Phil Catelinet

in this chapter

☑ Customize searches with Google

☑ Add search tools to context menus

☑ Search within pages using Find-As-You-Type

☑ Add toolbars to your browser to increase your searching power

Normally, changes you make to about:config take effect right away. However, because of a bug in Firefox (as of version 1.0.3), you'll need to restart Firefox for this particular change to take effect. After you restart Firefox, try a search from the location bar again. It should show you all of the search results this time.

Using Quick Searches

Firefox also lets you search different sites from the location bar by putting a letter or keyword in front of the search terms. These searches are in the default bookmarks under the Quick Searches folder. For example, to search for the definition of politics at Dictionary.com, type **dict politics** in the location bar and press Enter. Firefox takes you to Dictionary.com, displaying the results of your search.

You can add your own location bar searches to Firefox using any site with a search function. Here's how to add a Microsoft.com option to your browser.

1. Go to http://www.microsoft.com.

2. Locate the search box in the web page.

3. Right-click in the search box on the web page and select "Add a Keyword for this Search..."

4. An Add Bookmark popup window appears (see Figure 12-1). Fill in a name for your search and type a keyword (such as **ms**) in the Keyword field.

Tip You might want to prepend the keyword to the name of your bookmark so when you look in the Quick Searches bookmarks folder you don't need to check the properties of each bookmark to remember the keyword.

5. Select a folder for the bookmark. Click OK.

Tip You can put a Quick Search bookmark anywhere, but I suggest keeping them in the Quick Searches folder so you can find them later.

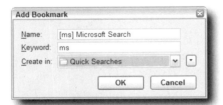

FIGURE 12-1: Adding a Quick Search to your bookmarks.

Now go back to your location bar. Type **ms windows bsod** and press Enter. Firefox searches Microsoft's web site using the terms "windows bsod" and shows you the results just as if you'd browsed to microsoft.com and used their search box.

Hacking the Search Box

The real power of searching with Firefox is in the built-in search box in the browser's upper-right corner. While Google is the default search engine, Firefox comes with several other search plugins in a fresh install: Yahoo!, Amazon.com, eBay, and others. To choose a different search plugin for a particular search, click on the icon in the window and select an engine from the drop-down list, as shown in Figure 12-2.

FIGURE 12-2: Firefox's built-in search engine options.

You can add new search engines to the list by clicking on the Add Engines link. You'll see a few popular search sites linked there; click on any of them and you'll be prompted to confirm the plugin installation. The new engine appears as a drop-down option immediately.

One of the best sites to find a wide variety of search engine plugins is Mycroft at `http://mycroft.mozdev.org`. Mycroft lists plugins by category and provides a search box for you to look up those hard-to-find sites that defy categorization. When you find the search plugin you want, just click on it and it will be added to your Firefox search box drop-down list. Firefox remembers the last search engine you used, so if you use the Yahoo! plugin then close and reopen the browser, Yahoo! will still be the selected search engine.

To remove a search plugin, browse to the searchplugins folder and delete the SRC and GIF files for the plugin, then restart Firefox.

Search plugins consist of two files:

- An SRC file that contains the code telling Firefox how to use search terms for that site.
- A GIF file that provides the icon for the search box.

These files are kept in the searchplugins subfolder of your Firefox installation directory (*not* your Firefox user profile directory). If you uninstall and reinstall Firefox, you will lose any plug-ins you downloaded from Mycroft or other sites.

The typical plugin SRC file has two or three sections, as shown in the following code example from Firefox's built-in Amazon.com search plugin:

```
# Search Plug-in for Amazon.com (http://www.amazon.com)
# by Paul Millar <dazzle@edazzle.net> created: 18 January 2003
# updated by Rafael Ebron <rebron@meer.net>

<SEARCH
    version = "7.1"
   name="Amazon.com"
   description="Amazon.com Search"
   method="GET"
   action="http://www.amazon.com/exec/obidos/external-search/"
>

<input name="field-keywords" user>
<input name="mode" value="blended">
<input name="tag" value="mozilla-20">
<input  name="sourceid" value="Mozilla-search">

</search>

<BROWSER

update="http://www.mozilla.org/products/firefox/plugins/amazondotcom.src"

updateIcon="http://www.mozilla.org/products/firefox/plugins/amazondotcom.png"
        updateCheckDays="3"

>
```

The SEARCH section defines the plugin and tells Firefox what site will be used for the search. The version number is the highest version of Netscape (*not* Firefox) with which the plugin has been tested. It's irrelevant for our purposes. The input tag with the word user tells the browser the actual user-entered search request.

The BROWSER section gives Firefox a way to automatically update the plugin if the site's search system changes and if the plugin author uploads a new version to the Mozilla site.

Some plugins also include an INTERPRET section between SEARCH and BROWSER that tells Firefox how to display the results it receives from the site.

Note Mycroft includes a detailed tutorial on plugin design; you can find it at http://mycroft .mozdev.org/deepdocs/quickstart.html.

Searching from the Web Page Itself

Admit it: sometimes you're lazy. When surfing you'll come across a word or phrase that you'd search the Web for if only that search box wasn't at the top of the screen. Now you don't have to type your search queries anymore. There are several search extensions available that let you right-click on terms in your web page and search the Web for those terms — no typing required.

Web Searches Using the Context Menu

Using the Context Search extension, you can add a search option to the right-click menu in a web page. After you install the extension, highlight a word or phrase, then right-click and select "Search Web for [your word or phrase will appear here]." Not only can you search the Web for the term, but you can also search using any of your installed search plugins. You can see Context Search in action in Figure 12-3. If your web page has a reference to George Washington and you want to see what books Amazon.com sells about him, just highlight George Washington, right-click on the selection, and choose Amazon.com from the search engine list. The results will appear in a new tab or window, depending on how you've configured those options.

Note You can get Context Search from http://www.cusser.net/extensions/ contextsearch/.

Define Words in Web Pages

I love using Dictionary.com to find definitions and synonyms, but sometimes it's a chore to go to the site and search, or even to use the Quick Search option with "dict [my word here]" in the location bar. You can get several extensions that add dictionary searches to your context menu, and two of them are covered here: DictionarySearch and DICT Search. Despite the similar names, they look up words in different ways.

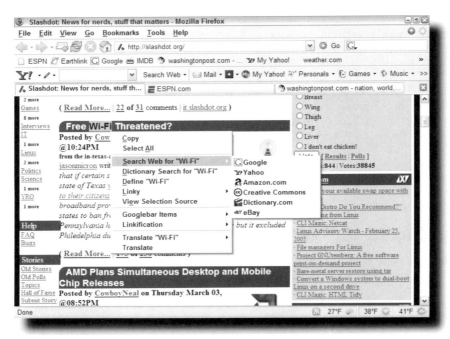

FIGURE 12-3: Context Search brings your search plugins right to the web page.

DictionarySearch adds a simple context menu option when you right-click on a highlighted word. Selecting "Dictionary search for [highlighted word]" brings up a new tab or window with the results from Dictionary.com. You can add other online dictionaries to the context menu from the extension's options window, shown in Figure 12-4.

FIGURE 12-4: User options for the DictionarySearch extension.

Note You can find the DictionarySearch extension at `http://dictionarysearch.mozdev` `.org/`.

DICT Search looks up words in online dictionaries using the DICT network protocol. Instead of searching for words in online versions of commercial dictionaries such as Merriam-Webster, DICT Search looks in user-maintained public dictionaries and online databases. Because it uses sites such as the Jargon File (`jargon.org`) and the Virtual Entity of Relevant Acronyms, DICT Search is particularly well suited for technical and computer terms. The method is the same as with DictionarySearch: highlight the word you want to define, then right-click and select Define [word]. The extension displays its results in a special popup window, which you can see in Figure 12-5.

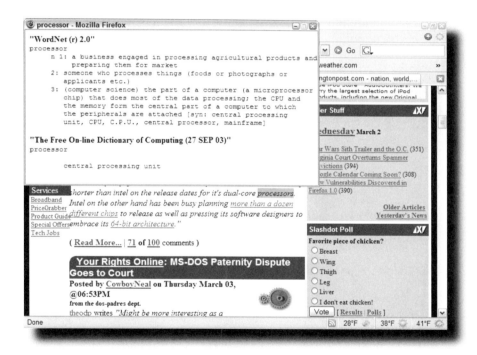

FIGURE 12-5: DICT Search results appear in a new window.

Note Get DICT Search at `http://dict.mozdev.org`.

Add Translation Tools to Your Menus

While web page translation systems are still in their infancy, sometimes reading a page translated by a computer from a foreign language to your own is better than not being able to read the page at all. Firefox doesn't come with any built-in translation offerings, but you can add your own easily via the Translate extension. It adds a Translate function to Firefox's Options menu and the web page context menu. The former translates an entire web page to English, while the latter will translate highlighted text and present the results in a new tab or window. Translate uses Altavista's Babelfish translation engine. If you'd prefer to translate pages from English to another language, Translate's Options window lets you change your preferred language to any of 12 others, including French, Italian, Russian, Korean, Japanese, Chinese, and more (see Figure 12-6).

FIGURE 12-6: Translate's list of available languages.

Note   The Translate extension is available at https://addons.update.mozilla.org/ extensions/moreinfo.php?id=181.

Put Your Search Results in a Sidebar

The sidebar is a feature of the Mozilla suite that lets you keep your bookmarks, history, search tools, and other functions on the side of your browser window. Firefox's sidebar functions are initially limited to just bookmarks, downloads, and history, but you can add new tools to the sidebar via extensions. One such tool is SearchStation, which gives you search and translator options.

SearchStation's web search sidebar performs web searches but keeps the results in the sidebar. That way you can refer back to them without having to switch away from your current web page. Figure 12-7 shows a Google search using SearchStation. When you click on a result, the page loads in the active tab in the same browser window. SearchStation uses your search plugins, so you can search Yahoo!, eBay, Amazon.com, and any other sites using plugins you've installed.

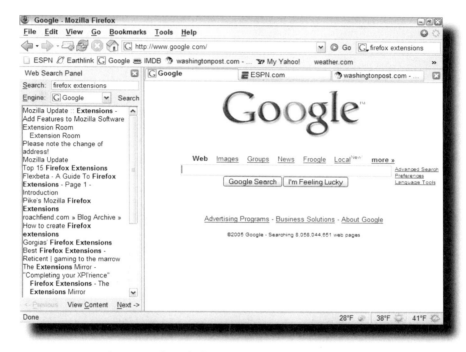

FIGURE 12-7: Searching Google with the SearchStation extension.

The Translator sidebar is like a miniature version of the Babelfish or Google translator sites. It translates text you type or cut and paste into the space provided, but not entire web pages. (You'll need the Translate extension I discussed earlier to do that.) You can choose among 15 languages (including English) to translate text in either direction, and you have three to five different translation engines at your disposal (depending on the languages you've selected — not all translation sites handle all 15 languages). You can see an example of the Translator feature in Figure 12-8.

Note You can get SearchStation from `http://members.lycos.co.uk/toolbarpalette/searchstation/index_en.html`.

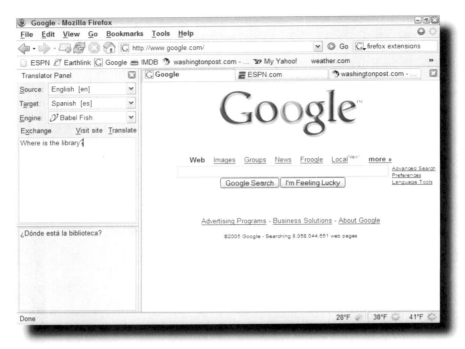

FIGURE 12-8: Translate text while browsing with the Translator sidebar.

Open Your Search Results Quickly with Linky

Search engines give you pages and pages of links as results for your queries. That's great, but you have to click on each link that you want to visit to open the site in a new tab. If you're interested in only one or two links, you're okay, but what if you want to see four or five links? Or all of the links on a page? That's where the Linky extension comes in. Linky adds the option to open some or all links in a page in new tabs or windows. Just right-click anywhere in the page and pick from the Linky menu, shown in Figure 12-9. If you first highlight a part of the page containing links, you will have the option to open either the selected links or all the links on the page.

Figure 12-10 shows the popup window that allows you to confirm which links you want to open. Linky can also show all images from a web page in a new tab or window, or open images from a list of image links.

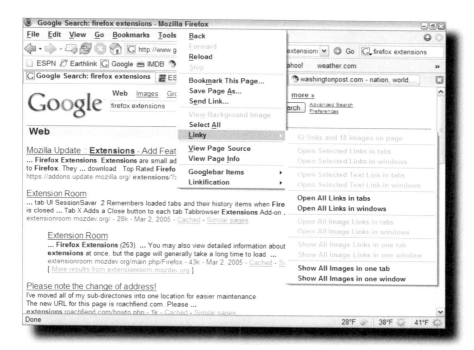

FIGURE 12-9: The Linky extension's context menu.

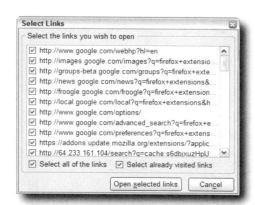

FIGURE 12-10: Linky's open links confirmation window.

Linky can get you through your search results in a hurry.

Note You can find the Linky extension at `http://gemal.dk/mozilla/linky.html`.

Turning Nonlinked Links into Linkable Links

Sometimes, in the course of your browsing, you'll wind up on a page with a URL that isn't a hyperlink. You'd like to go to that site, but you'd have to cut and paste the URL into the location bar or take your hand off the mouse and type it. When you find yourself in that situation, fear not, for you have the Linkification extension.

Linkification activates these text links and makes them clickable so you don't have to do any pesky typing or highlighting. Just right-click on the page, look for the Linkification context menu, and select Linkify Text. Any text links in the page will become clickable, ready for your browsing needs. There's also a feature-rich options menu for Linkification available from the Extensions list.

Figure 12-11 shows part of a Google results page with some links that are not clickable.

FIGURE **12-11: Text links that cannot be clicked.**

After using Linkification, some of those same links are now underlined and can be clicked, as shown in Figure 12-12.

FIGURE 12-12: The same links after applying Linkification.

Linkification may not work on all text links, but it should work on those with the standard http://www.foo.com format.

Note

Get Linkification from `http://www.beggarchooser.com/firefox/`.

Searching within the Web Page

You've been searching the web for information and you've finally found the page that contains what you need. The trouble is that the page is filled with text and you're not sure where your information is located. What you need now is a search tool that works inside the web page. You can access the Find command from the browser's Edit menu to bring up the search toolbar and look for your term. You can also press Ctrl+F to activate the search toolbar. Or you can just type the term using Firefox's Find-As-You-Type feature.

To use Find-As-You-Type, click in the web page, type a forward slash (/), then the text of your search. Firefox jumps to the first instance of the characters you type and highlight the text it finds. The search toolbar appears at the bottom of the browser window with your text in it, along with Find Next and Find Previous buttons (see Figure 12-13). To find text located in links on the page, type an apostrophe (') followed by the text.

If you really like the function, you can activate it all the time:

1. On the Options menu, under Advanced, look for the Accessibility items at the top of the list.

2. Check the box next to "Begin finding when you begin typing" and click OK.

Now you don't need to use the leading forward slash or apostrophe to start your search; just start typing in the web page and Firefox locates your terms.

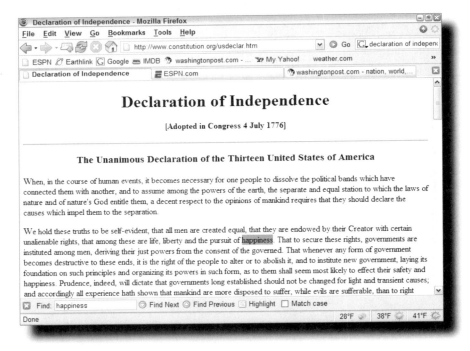

FIGURE 12-13: Firefox's Find-As-You-Type feature in action.

Once you stop typing your search terms, the toolbar disappears from the screen after a set time. You can change the amount of time the toolbar is displayed by adjusting the setting in about:config, as follows:

```
accessibility.typeaheadfind.timeout
```

The default is 5000 milliseconds (equal to five seconds), so if you want to show the toolbar for ten seconds instead, change the setting to 10000. You'll have to restart Firefox for this change to take effect.

Recommended Search Extensions

So far, we've discussed extensions that are behind the scenes, hiding until you need them. Now let's shift the focus to a few extensions that add visible search toolbars to Firefox and that go far beyond the search capabilities built into the browser.

The most popular Internet search portals — Google, Yahoo!, MSN, to name a few — have created toolbars for Microsoft Internet Explorer (IE) that give users enhanced search benefits and also provide shortcuts to the portals' special features. Firefox users were initially left out so extension authors stepped in to create versions of these toolbars for Firefox. While these unofficial versions don't provide 100 percent of the functionality of their IE counterparts, they do give Firefox users most of the same abilities as the IE versions.

Googlebar

One of the first add-on toolbars to appear was the Googlebar. It provides most of the same functions for Firefox as the official Google toolbar for IE does for that browser. Figure 12-14 shows the Googlebar in Firefox. You can search for information on any of Google's primary sites: Web, Images, News, and USENET newsgroups. There are drop-down menus to search Google for specific computer-related information or scour university web sites. There are even links to Google's nonsearch features such as Gmail and Blogger. Googlebar also provides context menu options within web pages and is highly configurable. For example, if you want to add a button to search Apple's web site for search terms, take the following steps:

1. Right-click on the Googlebar.

2. Select Computer Searches.

3. Select Mac Search.

An iMac icon appears on the toolbar. When you type your query into the search box and click the Mac button, Googlebar searches Apple's web site for your information. To choose a default university web site to search, click on the arrow next to the graduate cap icon and choose your preferred school from the alphabetical drop-down menu.

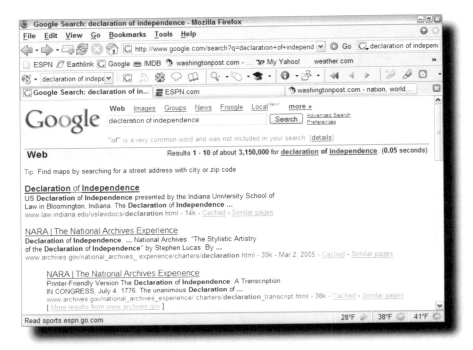

FIGURE 12-14: Googlebar expands your Google search options in Firefox.

More Googlebar configuration options can be found on the extension's Options window. If you prefer to search one of Google's international sites instead of the default U.S. engine, you can set the Googlebar to use a different site on the Google Site Options tab. This option is available for Google News, as well.

Note

Googlebar is available at `http://googlebar.mozdev.org`.

Ultrabar

The makers of Ultrabar looked at Googlebar and said, "That's great, but what if I prefer a different search engine?" Ultrabar is designed not only to allow you to choose different search engines within the toolbar, but also to give you easy access to tools to maintain your blog. In addition to a standard search-only toolbar, you can download Ultrabars for Blogger, LiveJournal, TypePad, and Bloglines blogs.

Once installed, Ultrabar looks and feels similar to Googlebar but with more search sites and fewer buttons. Figure 12-15 shows Ultrabar's typical layout and list of search engines.

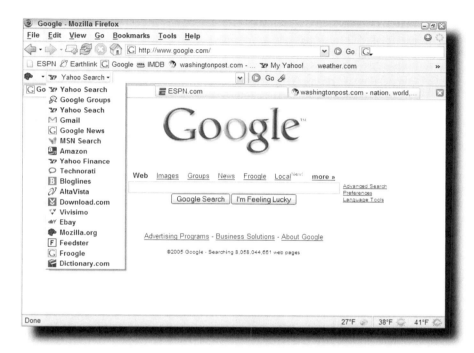

FIGURE 12-15: Ultrabar gives you more search options from the toolbar.

Note You can find Ultrabar at `http://www.firefoxtoolbar.com/download`.

Yahoo! Toolbar

Like Google, Yahoo! created its own toolbar for Internet Explorer that gave its users convenient access to searches, web mail, news, stock quotes, and many other features of their portal. Yahoo! has also developed a version of the Yahoo! Toolbar for Firefox. With the toolbar installed, you can sign into your Yahoo! account and configure the toolbar to show you the buttons for portal services that you use most often. For example, I play fantasy football through Yahoo!, so I configured my toolbar to put a Fantasy Sports icon next to the search box (see Figure 12-16).

FIGURE 12-16: Yahoo! Toolbar puts the portal's features within easy reach.

Note Yahoo! Toolbar is found at `http://toolbar.yahoo.com/firefox`.

Summary

This chapter explained different ways that Firefox can be modified to suit your searching habits. It looked at a plethora of tools and extensions that let you search the Web from anywhere in the browser, including search boxes, toolbars, and even within web pages. It also explained how to define words and translate pages with a few mouse clicks. You are now a web search master.

Installation, Automation, Tools, and Tricks

part

V

Hacking Installation and Deployment

by Mel Reyes

This chapter offers several options for customizing and deploying Firefox to more than one computer. Topics covered here include using command-line options, hacking the default setup options, creating custom installers, and hacking existing installers. For anyone who truly wants to replace their default browser with Firefox across multiple computers, this chapter should help in customizing the installation, as well as providing a mechanism for future updates.

Two factors that help with deploying Firefox are that there are minimal operating system dependencies and installation is highly customizable. When reviewing this chapter, keep your ultimate goal in mind and see if any of the techniques covered here will fit that goal. This chapter is not a complete deployment guide, but it will help in integrating to current systems. Each section includes examples and site references to great resources for customizing and deploying.

Built-in Installer Options

Running the Firefox installation in Standard mode selects most defaults and has minimal prompts, while the Custom installation type offers a few additional options. The Setup Type dialog is available after the Welcome and License Agreement windows, and choosing Custom allows you to modify the installation path, components to install, and which shortcut icons to create. While these options are good for single-user installations, the available command-line options can help in automating this process for multiple computer installations. Additionally, the foundations for extracting and hacking the installer are covered here.

Note Before beginning, download the latest installer from http://www.getfirefox.com.

in this chapter

☑ Built-in installer options

☑ Installation and profile customization options

☑ Creating a custom installer

Using Command-Line Options

The Firefox installer includes command-line options that can be used from a batch file, a script, Active Directory, Novell ZENworks, WinBatch, or any other custom installation process. Figure 13-1 highlights the available parameters that can be used while in command-line mode or in your script. To display this prompt, just run the Firefox installer with the -h parameter from the command prompt:

```
FirefoxSetup.exe -h
```

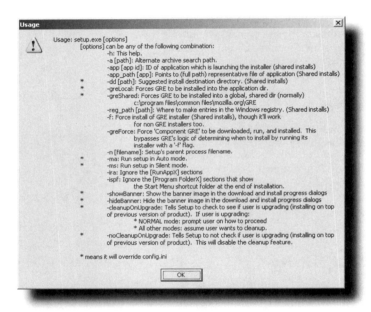

FIGURE 13-1: Custom setup installation options

The easiest parameters to use for purposes of automating the installation process are the -ms and -dd parameters. The -ms parameter specifies that the installer run in silent mode, installing with the default options enabled, thus silently installing or upgrading Firefox on each system without changing existing settings. The -dd parameter allows you to specify a custom installation or destination directory for the Firefox files.

To use the installer in silent mode, just type the following entry either in your script or at the command prompt:

```
FirefoxSetup.exe -ms
```

The combination of the silent mode and destination directory parameter are nice for customizing the basic installation process. To use these parameters together, just type the following:

```
FirefoxSetup.exe -ms -dd d:\Mozilla\Firefox\
```

You can substitute `d:\Mozilla\Firefox\` for the directory you wish to use. If the destination path includes spaces, try putting quotes around the path, as follows:

```
FirefoxSetup.exe -ms -dd "d:\Local Apps\Firefox\"
```

Note There is a space between the -dd parameter and the installation path name.

When using the −ms parameter to run in silent mode, the only dialog that is displayed is the setup-file extraction progress. This makes it difficult to alert the user that the installation is in progress. Status dialogs should be created and can be customized depending on the installation or scripting system used to automate the installation process. Additionally, running the installer in silent mode creates all the standard icons, desktop, Start menu, and Quick Launch toolbar; a postinstallation process will be needed to remove these if desired.

Extracting the Installer

Like many installers, the Firefox installer executable is really just a wrapper to the actual installer setup files. The main installer file contains the actual setup.exe and supporting installer files. To begin hacking through the installer, you must first extract the single installer file to gain access to the individual files contained within. For Windows-based systems, you can use compression extraction tools such as 7-Zip (http://www.7-zip.org/) or WinRar (http://www.rarlab.com/) to quickly view or extract these files.

Note On Linux-based systems, uncompressing the GZipped installer file gives you access to the installation files.

To extract the Firefox compressed tarball using Linux or UNIX-based systems, just issue the following commands in a console window, pressing Enter after each line:

```
tar -xzvf firefox-1.0.4.installer.tar.gz
cd firefox-installer
./firefox-installer
```

Figure 13-2 shows the contents of the installer using 7-Zip, but similar results are achieved using WinRar on the file.

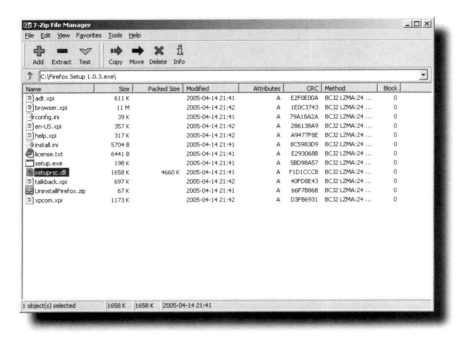

FIGURE 13-2: Firefox installer listing using 7-Zip

To extract the installer listing with 7-Zip or WinRar, follow these steps:

1. Open Windows Explorer to the path to which you have downloaded the installer.

2. Select the Extract files, Extract Here, or Extract To option from the right-click context menu.

3. Based on the option selected, follow the appropriate dialog to select the path to extract to.

Note   To open or just view the installer's contents with 7-Zip choose the Open archive option from the right-click context menu; for WinRar select Open with WinRar from the menu.

Command-Line Installer Extraction

To extract the installer file in command-line mode using 7-Zip you can use the following:

```
7z e -o"setup" "Firefox Setup.exe"
```

Just substitute the name `Firefox Setup.exe` for the name of the Firefox installer saved locally, and substitute `setup` for the subdirectory or full path where you want the files extracted to. In our example, a subdirectory will be created called `setup` in the current path.

Note There is no space between the -o and the directory path for extraction.

To have Windows find the 7z executable, the installation path for 7-Zip needs to be added to the `Path` environment variable. You can also accomplish this on the fly by issuing the following command in Windows just before running the 7-Zip extraction command:

```
set Path=%PATH%;C:\Program Files\7-Zip\;
```

The path of C:\Program Files\7-Zip\ should reflect the local installation path for 7-Zip.

The next section covers the options available in the config.ini file to create a customized install process.

Hacking the Configuration INI File

As illustrated in Figure 13-2, one file that is included with the Firefox installer is the configuration INI file config.ini. This file contains different sections for the installation process and default values associated with each section; this is where customizing the installation process can truly be achieved. With the multitude of options available, I want to focus on some of the critical options and detail those; they include the following:

- Disabling specific dialogs
- Running silently
- Changing the installation path

INI files have a standard structure that includes a header, or section, and then associated name-value pairs. INI files can be edited with any standard text editor. Additionally, you can include comments, which in the config.ini are prefixed with a semicolon, as shown in the following:

```
[General]
; Run Mode values:
;   Normal - Shows all dialogs.  Requires user input.
;   Auto   - Shows some dialogs, but none requiring user input.
It will
;            automatically install the product using default
values.
;   Silent - Show no dialogs at all.  It will install product
using default
;            values.
Run Mode=Normal
```

In this example, the header, or section, is `[General]`, and the variable name is `Run Mode` with a value of `Normal`. This format allows for human-readable parameters that can be modified easily to create a custom installation.

Disable Specific Dialog Windows

To begin customizing, I can review the headers associated with each dialog that can be enabled or disabled by setting the Show Dialog parameter to either TRUE or FALSE, as shown:

```
Show Dialog=TRUE
```

The headers are all prefixed with Dialog, are encapsulated with brackets, and include the following:

- Dialog Welcome
- Dialog License
- Dialog Setup Type
- Dialog Select Components
- Dialog Select Install Path
- Dialog Install Successful

To disable the Welcome screen dialog just change the Show Dialog value to FALSE, as follows:

```
[Dialog Welcome]
Show Dialog=FALSE
```

Because the file is over 1,100 lines, the easiest way I have found to edit it is to do a search for the header or value that you are looking for and then modify it accordingly. Later in this chapter, I show you how to bypass this task by using the Nullsoft installer to automate the update of the INI values.

Running in Silent Mode

Disabling each of the installer dialogs is nice but does not have to be done if you want to run the installer in silent mode. To have the installer run in true silent mode, with absolutely no dialogs, just change the value of the Run Mode in the [General] header to Silent, as shown:

```
[General]
Run Mode=Silent
```

After you make this change, the setup.exe will run with no dialogs and will use the default settings. Choosing a Run Mode of Auto does show the installation process, but the installation will not end properly, and the last dialog window will not close. Additionally, the command-line option -ma yields the same result as Run Mode=Auto.

Note

For more information on –ma support, visit the following Bugzilla posting: https://bugzilla.mozilla.org/show_bug.cgi?id=229706.

Modify the Installation Path

To modify the installation path just update the `Path` value in the `[General]` section. The default value is shown here:

```
Path=[PROGRAMFILESDIR]\Mozilla Firefox
```

`[PROGRAMFILESDIR]` is automatically parsed to reflect your program file's installation path. The INI file also highlights other system-related destination paths that it will recognize when placed in the `Path` value. These include WINDISK, WINDIR, and WINSYSDIR.

The `Path` value can easily also reflect a direct path, as shown:

```
Path= D:\Mozilla Firefox
```

The combination of running the installer in true silent mode and customizing the installation path is a great starting point to automating the installation process.

Installation and Profile Customization Options

My initial efforts in creating a customized image included using the zipped file distribution that was available up until the 1.0.2 release. With the zipped version no longer available, this section focuses on automating some of the supporting elements for using Firefox. These techniques include creating a profile, installation extensions, and themes globally; deploying plugins and profile templates; and using other tools.

Automated Profile Creation

This code allows you to create a profile, and if no directory is specified, a directory with a random `salt` prefix is created. This random salt string is used as an attempt to reduce profile name spoofing and tampering, and so on. All active profiles are listed in the profiles.ini file, usually located at %UserPath%\Mozilla\Firefox.

To automatically create a user profile you can use the `-CreateProfile` command-line option that is available. For ease of use, follow these steps:

1. Open a command console window.

2. Change into your current Firefox installation path.

3. Type **firefox.exe -CreateProfile MyProfile**.

In the preceding example, `MyProfile` is the name you want to call the profile; this name cannot contain spaces. The `CreateProfile` option can also accept a directory path, so the command would end up looking something like this:

For Windows:

```
firefox.exe -CreateProfile "MyProfile c:\Profiles\MyProfile"
```

On Windows systems, the default location for profiles is as follows: C:\Documents and Settings\User Name\Application Data\Mozilla\Firefox\Profiles.

For Linux:

```
firefox.exe -CreateProfile "MyProfile ~/.mozilla/firefox/"
```

It is important to note that the two parameters, the profile name and the directory paths, need to be quoted together, as together they are the single value that is used by the -CreateProfile instruction when you specify a custom path for the MyProfile directory.

For more information on other Mozilla Suite command-line options that may work with Firefox, visit http://www.mozilla.org/docs/command-line-args.html.

Adding Global Extensions and Themes

One interesting but somewhat limited set of features that is available is global installations of extensions and themes. These options are available as command-line options after Firefox has been installed, so they are Firefox options and not install file options. The -install-global-extension and -install-global-theme command-line options allow extensions and themes to be installed to the main directory in which Firefox is installed, much like the similar option in the Mozilla Suite. On the surface, these look to be ideal for deploying extension and themes, but in my experience a global extension installation might not be worth the hassle.

Before I dive into how to best use these, I will just cover the issues I have come across in trying to implement them. What I have found on Windows-based systems is that the extension parameter does not play nice when it comes to the location of the actual extension XPI file. After some testing, the only way to get extensions to install was to have the XPI file reside in the same directory as the Firefox.exe or the Firefox installation path. This makes deploying a tad annoying because the files have to be copied over the computer, the installation for each executed, and then cleaned up afterward. This, coupled with the fact that the Options dialog for globally installed extension is disabled, makes it difficult for users to customize extensions. All preference changes for globally installed extensions will have to be entered into the user.js or prefs.js file in the profile.

Installing themes globally, though, was a tad smoother, and I was able to get all my themes to install properly.

Installing extensions globally works best on brand-new Firefox installations with a new and clean profile. Profiles that already contain the same extension that will be installed globally may encounter issues. If the extension is installed in the profile, uninstall it and restart Firefox. Additionally, the directory associated to the GUID in the profile's extension directory needs to be deleted, as well as any references in the chrome.rdf file located in the profile's chrome directory.

To install an extension globally, you should make sure of the following:

- You have the extension XPI install file saved locally into the Firefox installation path.
- The user must have read and write access to the Firefox installation path.
- All instances of Firefox must be closed.

Once these have been satisfied, open a command prompt to the Firefox installation path and issue the following command:

```
firefox -install-global-extension "local_install.xpi"
```

 Note If the installation fails, try removing the quotes.

Though all of this seems straightforward, I have had several issues with getting extensions to register themselves properly, and I would recommend using the extension installation enhancements that are slated for the Firefox 1.1 release.

With less of a configuration headache, you can install themes by issuing the following command:

```
firefox -install-global-theme "D:\Firefox\apollo_fx.jar"
```

As you can see, having the themes in a different directory works and makes installing themes globally a more viable option.

For each extension and theme, Firefox will run and then exit, so on slower computers it will take longer to deploy using this method.

Deploying Plugins

We covered finding and fixing plugins in Chapter 11; here I show you how to automate the plugin installation and disclose where some of the required files are located.

Adding Macromedia Flash and Shockwave Support

To deploy Flash and Shockwave updates that support Firefox, simply run the latest Macromedia installers, and they will automatically add Firefox plugin support. Automating this is a little trickier, especially for the Shockwave installer.

To download the Flash installer, just visit the following Macromedia site using Firefox and download the installer: http://www.macromedia.com/go/getflashplayer.

The reason I specify "using Firefox" is if you go to download the installer using Internet Explorer, the site delivers and installs the ActiveX version of the plugin. When you download the Flash installer with Firefox, the Macromedia site provides support for Firefox, Opera, and Internet Explorer.

To download Shockwave just visit and download the installer using Firefox: `http://sdc .shockwave.com/shockwave/download/download.cgi?`.

Both installers have the ability to run in silent mode by specifying a command-line parameter of `/silent`, as shown for the Flash Installer:

```
flashplayer7installer.exe /silent
```

The only major problem is that the new Shockwave installer now also includes the Yahoo! Toolbar installation, and this will be automatically installed if you run the Shockwave installer with the command-line `/silent` parameter. Unless you have or want to use the Yahoo! Toolbar, the silent option will not work. An alternative approach to silent installation is to sign up for the Macromedia Distribution Program. The distribution program, found at `http:// www.macromedia.com/support/shockwave/info/licensing/`, gives you one installer for both Flash and Shockwave that can also be executed with the `/silent` parameter. Installation is a breeze; during the installation, an installer tray icon and the Shockwave extraction screen are visible, but the whole process is automated and works well to add Flash and Shockwave support to Firefox.

After you fill out the registration form for the distribution program, a download link is sent via e-mail. Once the installer has been downloaded, it can be run in silent mode with the following:

```
mm_fl_sw_installer.exe /silent
```

Adding Apple QuickTime and RealPlayer Support

Both QuickTime and RealPlayer come with components and plugin files that allow Firefox to offer embedded playback of these media file types. The newer QuickTime and RealPlayer installers automatically detect and copy the corresponding components and plugins if Firefox is already installed. Unfortunately, if Firefox is installed after these media tools, it will not have, nor will it be able to find, the plugins and components needed to allow them to work properly.

So you can either reinstall both media tools after installing Firefox or just copy the contents of the components and plugins directories associated with QuickTime and RealPlayer to the corresponding directories in the main Firefox application directory. The default Firefox path would be something like this:

- C:\Program Files\Mozilla Firefox\plugins
- C:\Program Files\Mozilla Firefox\components

The default path for RealPlayer browser plugin and component files is C:\Program Files\ Real\RealPlayer\Netscape6.

The default path for Apple QuickTime is C:\Program Files\Apple\QuickTime\Plugins.

Creating a script to automatically copy these over will always ensure that the plugins and components match the installed versions of QuickTime or RealPlayer.

Create a Custom Windows Desktop Icon

In a great posting on his site, Henrik Gemal has created Microsoft Windows Scripts to auto-mate the creation of Windows desktop icons for Firefox, Thunderbird, and Sunbird. The dif-ference between a desktop icon and a standard shortcut icon is that it implements Microsoft's namespace functionality to give the desktop icon enhanced right-click functionality, much like Microsoft Outlook and Internet Explorer. Figure 13-3 shows the key right-click context menu options available: Open, Open (Safe Mode), Options, and Profile Manager.

Note

For more information on the status of integrating this feature into the official Firefox installer, visit the following Bugzilla posting: `https://bugzilla.mozilla.org/show_bug .cgi?id=264889`.

FIGURE 13-3: Right-click menu
for Firefox desktop icon

To use this, just download and execute the Microsoft script file from `http://gemal.dk/ misc/desktop-firefox.vbs`, and a desktop icon will be created. Just remove the old Mozilla Firefox shortcut before running the script.

Note

You may have to refresh your desktop by switching focus to the desktop and pressing F5 or by logging off and then back on.

For more information on the desktop links from Henrik's site, visit `http://gemal.dk/ blog/2004/11/05/firefox_thunderbird_and_sunbird_desktop_shortcuts/`.

This script is also a good reference point to use if you want to extract the necessary registry information to create your own script to accomplish the same thing.

Hacking the Desktop Icon with Nullsoft Installer Script

Tapping into Henrik's script, I have converted it to a Nullsoft Installer script that you can com-pile with the Nullsoft Scriptable Install System (NSIS) installer engine. To download the NSIS visit its site at `http://nsis.sourceforge.net/`.

The script is designed to do the following:

- Remove previous registry entries.
- Add the appropriate registry entries for the desktop icon.
- Remove the standard Mozilla Firefox shortcut link from the desktop.
- Refresh the desktop to force the display of the newly created icon.

The script will automatically run in silent mode with no dialog windows and is available for download at `http://www.hackingfirefox.com/desktop-icon.nsi`.

For easier editing and compiling, I like to use HM NIS Editor, an open-source editing tool for NSIS scripts. This editor includes a great Help file and syntax highlighting for all the NSIS keywords, functions, and commands. Figure 13-4 displays the desktop-icon.nsi script using the HM NIS Editor.

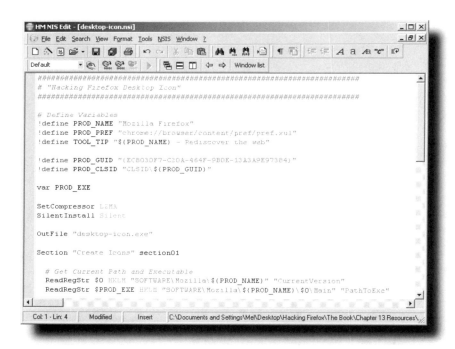

FIGURE 13-4: HM NIS Editor with desktop-icon.nsi script loaded

Following is a full listing of the desktop-icon.nsi source code:

```
################################################################
# Hacking Firefox: Desktop Icon - version 1.0
################################################################
```

```
# Define Variables
!define PROD_NAME "Mozilla Firefox"
!define PROD_PREF "chrome://browser/content/pref/pref.xul"
!define TOOL_TIP "${PROD_NAME} - Rediscover the web"

!define PROD_GUID "{EC8030F7-C20A-464F-9B0E-13A3A9E97384}"
!define PROD_CLSID "CLSID\${PROD_GUID}"

var PROD_EXE

SetCompressor LZMA
SilentInstall Silent

OutFile "desktop-icon.exe"

Section "Create Icons" section01

  # Remove old icon settings
  DeleteRegKey HKCR "${PROD_CLSID}"

  # Get Current Path and Executable
  ReadRegStr $0 HKLM "SOFTWARE\Mozilla\${PROD_NAME}"
"CurrentVersion"
  ReadRegStr $PROD_EXE HKLM
"SOFTWARE\Mozilla\${PROD_NAME}\$0\Main" "PathToExe"

  # Setup NameSpace Icon
  WriteRegStr HKCR "${PROD_CLSID}" "" "${PROD_NAME}"
  WriteRegExpandStr HKCR "${PROD_CLSID}" "InfoTip" "${TOOL_TIP}"

  WriteRegStr HKCR "${PROD_CLSID}\DefaultIcon" "" "$PROD_EXE,0"

  WriteRegStr HKCR "${PROD_CLSID}\Shell\Open" "" "&Open"
  WriteRegStr HKCR "${PROD_CLSID}\Shell\Open\command" ""
"$PROD_EXE"

  WriteRegStr HKCR "${PROD_CLSID}\Shell\Open (safe-mode)" "" "Open
(&Safe Mode)"
  WriteRegStr HKCR "${PROD_CLSID}\Shell\Open (safe-mode)\Command"
"" "$PROD_EXE -safe-mode"

  WriteRegStr HKCR "${PROD_CLSID}\Shell\Options" "" "Op&tions"
  WriteRegStr HKCR "${PROD_CLSID}\Shell\Options\Command" ""
"$PROD_EXE -chrome ${PROD_PREF}"

  WriteRegStr HKCR "${PROD_CLSID}\Shell\Profilemanager" ""
"&Profile Manager"
  WriteRegStr HKCR "${PROD_CLSID}\Shell\Profilemanager\Command" ""
"$PROD_EXE -ProfileManager"
```

```
  WriteRegBin HKCR "${PROD_CLSID}\ShellFolder" "Attributes"
32000000
  WriteRegStr HKCR "${PROD_CLSID}\ShellFolder"
"HideOnDesktopPerUser" ""

  # Show Icons
  WriteRegDWORD HKCU
"SOFTWARE\Microsoft\Windows\CurrentVersion\Explorer\HideDesktopIco
ns\NewStartPanel" "${PROD_GUID}" "0"
  WriteRegDWORD HKCU
"SOFTWARE\Microsoft\Windows\CurrentVersion\Explorer\HideDesktopIco
ns\ClassicStartMenu" "${PROD_GUID}" "0"

  # Create NameSpace Icon
  WriteRegStr HKLM
"SOFTWARE\Microsoft\Windows\CurrentVersion\Explorer\Desktop\NameSp
ace\${PROD_GUID}" "" "${PROD_NAME}"

  # Remove Old Shortcut
  Delete "$DESKTOP\Mozilla Firefox.lnk"

  SetShellVarContext all
  Delete "$DESKTOP\Mozilla Firefox.lnk"

  # Refresh Desktop to show newly created desktop icon
  System::Call 'user32.dll::RedrawWindow(i 0, i 0, i 0, i 0x0085)
i .r1'

SectionEnd
```

Other Notable Deploy Tools

Currently, there is only one initiative to create a deployable and customized Firefox installation for Windows, and that is FFDeploy. The tool itself is just a combination of Windows Scripts and other small executables, but the effort to automate this is not trivial, and kudos go out to Bob Templeton for his hard work.

 Note To get more information on FFDeploy, just visit `http://home.comcast.net/~ifrit/` `FFDeploy.html`.

Creating a Custom Installer

One issue I want to discuss without going too deeply into its logistics and semantics is the options available with different tools to create a custom Windows installer. The system used for deployment will determine what approach to take. Active Directory, ZENworks, and other systems have built-in mechanisms for detecting which versions and packages are installed and come with different options. While an entire book could be written on how to deploy Firefox with all these systems, the following sections focus on highlighting tools that you could use with these systems, including some short sample scripts to help with the automation process.

Custom Nullsoft Scriptable Install System Installer

The Nullsoft Scriptable Install System is a great scripting tool that I like to use to create full installers, as well as customized scripting executables that run silently. It supports all the key areas with file management, and registry and other great functions. Another great feature of this tool is that it supports LZMA, ZLIB, and BZIP2 compression of files that are included with the installers that it will create; and the NSIS installer itself adds minimal overhead to the size of the installer created. To download the core NSIS installer tool, visit `http://nsis .sourceforge.net/`.

After installing the main NSIS engine tool, files with .nsi extensions get two right-click context menu options, Complete NSIS Script and Complete NSIS Script (Choose Compressor). Either can be used to quickly create an installer from an existing NSIS script file. All NSIS scripts are text-based and can be edited with any standard text editor. To gain better control over editing and to get color syntax highlighting of NSIS keywords and functions (as shown in Figure 13-4), I like to use the HM NIS Edit tool, which can be downloaded from `http:// hmne.sourceforge.net/`. This free editor is a great companion to the NSIS engine and provides a nice interface to editing and compiling your source NSIS scripts.

Knowing that I could modify the config.ini from the extracted installer, I wanted to write a script that would automate specific config.ini settings that I wanted to create; this script would make future upgrades easier to deploy. The script that follows focuses on providing methods for modifying the run mode; updating the installation path; disabling specific dialogs (if running in normal versus silent mode); and providing a mechanism to create a full installer, versus a stub installer, that would run the setup from the extracted directory. To download this NSIS script example, visit `http://www.hackingfirefox.com/custom-installer.nsi`.

This script relies on the fact that the Firefox installer is extracted to a directory, as highlighted earlier in this chapter. To specify the path that the Firefox installer is extracted to, start by looking for the following line of code:

!define SOURCE_PATH "setup"

This current line looks for the config.ini and Firefox setup files in a subdirectory of `setup`. The `setup` path is a relative directory to the current location where the NSIS script is running from. To specify a different directory, just change this value, as in the following example:

```
!define SOURCE_PATH "d:\Firefox Extracted Files"
```

Note   The value for SOURCE_PATH has to be a directory and does not have to have a trailing slash. All files in this directory will be included with the full installer.

Trying to make the script as generic as possible, I have included sections of code that are commented out with semicolons, which can be used to further customize the script. To run the installer in normal mode and disable specific dialogs, change the Run Mode value of Silent to Normal, as follows:

```
WriteINIStr "${SOURCE_PATH}\config.ini" "General" "Run Mode"
"Normal"
```

Then add the dialog window registry edits that you want to disable. For example, to disable the welcome dialog, uncomment this line:

```
WriteINIStr "${SOURCE_PATH}\config.ini" "Dialog Welcome" "Show
Dialog" "FALSE"
```

Other installer dialogs include the following:

- Dialog Welcome
- Dialog License
- Dialog Setup Type
- Dialog Select Components
- Dialog Select Install Path
- Dialog Install Successful

Another option I wanted to add was the ability to create a full installer and a stub installer. The full installer would repackage the customized config.ini with all the original Firefox installation files, and the stub installer would just have the config.ini changes and would execute the installer from the directory it was extracted to.

The base script is designed to create a full installer. To modify it to create a stub installer, just switch the semicolon comments as follows:

```
# 1) Use this section to make single installer containing
# the complete installer
;File "${SOURCE_PATH}\*.*"
;ExecWait '"$INSTDIR\setup.exe"'

# 2) Use this for a stub installer with setup extracted
# to the SOURCE_PATH
ExecWait '"${SOURCE_PATH}\setup.exe"'
```

Following is the listing of the custom-installer.nsi source code:

```
###########################################################
# Hacking Firefox: Custom Installer - version 1.0
# Source: http://www.hackingfirefox.com/custom-installer.nsi
###########################################################
!define PRODUCT_NAME "Hacking Firefox Custom Installer"
!define SOURCE_PATH "setup"
!define CONFIG_INI "${SOURCE_PATH}\config.ini"

# Use ZLIB compression to create installer faster
# Use LZMA compression to create a smaller installer
SetCompressor ZLIB
```

```
Name "${PRODUCT_NAME}"
SilentInstall Silent

OutFile "hacking_firefox.exe"

# Create a random install path in Temp directory for single
# installer using the NSIS $PLUGINSDIR variable
InstallDir "$PLUGINSDIR"

Section "Options" SEC01

  # Run installer in Silent Mode - Default Value = Normal
  WriteINIStr "${CONFIG_INI}" "General" "Run Mode" "Silent"

  # Choose a custom installation path
  #    ex: "d:\My Custom Apps\Mozilla Firefox"
  # Other Destination Path values include:
  #    PROGRAMFILESDIR, WINDISK, WINDIR, WINSYSDIR
  ;WriteINIStr "${CONFIG_INI}" "General" "Path"
"[PROGRAMFILESDIR]\Mozilla Firefox"

  # Disable the Welcome Dialog: Uncomment if changing
  # "Run Mode" to Normal
  ;WriteINIStr "${CONFIG_INI}" "Dialog Welcome" "Show Dialog"
"FALSE"

  # Diable the License Dialog: Uncomment if changing
  # "Run Mode" to Normal
  ;WriteINIStr "${CONFIG_INI}" "Dialog License" "Show Dialog"
"FALSE"

  # 1) Use this section to make single installer containing
  # the complete installer
  File "${SOURCE_PATH}\*.*"
  ExecWait '"$INSTDIR\setup.exe"'

  # 2) Use this for a stub installer with setup extracted
  # to the SOURCE_PATH
  ;ExecWait '"${SOURCE_PATH}\setup.exe"'

SectionEnd

Function .onInit
  # Initialize the random Plugins Directory for installation
  InitPluginsDir
FunctionEnd
```

Other Notable NSIS Code

Another good source of NSIS code that I have tapped into in the past was created by Sébastien Delahaye. This code was written for the original Phoenix and Firebird builds, which were pre-release builds of Firefox. The code itself is dated but can be easily modified or updated to fit the current release builds. Some of the functionality that makes this script hold up is that it is localized into different languages, and it can download from the Mozilla servers. For more information or to download this script, visit `http://seb.mozdev.org/firebird/`.

Hacking Microsoft Windows Installers

Using a Microsoft Windows Installer (MSI) is one of the hottest topics when talking about deploying Firefox. The ease of integrating an MSI into corporate environments using Windows Active Directory makes using an MSI version of Firefox very desirable. An MSI file is a specific format chiseled out by Microsoft to create a standard installation package based on a simple database of parameters and options and bundled with the corresponding installation files. The benefits of using any MSI are to capitalize on the ability of Windows to allow repairing and managing the installation of needed files, as well as provide easy integration with deploy procedures such as Active Directory deployment.

Currently slated for the Firefox 1.1 release is an MSI installer version, shown in Figure 13-5, to accompany the existing Windows executable and other platform-specific installers. On the surface, this seems to be the solution to everything, but for corporate environments that want to deploy a version prior to 1.1, there are other options. These options include FrontMotion's MSI installer, shown in Figure 13-6, as well as the ability to create your own using MSI installer tools such as MaSaI or Microsoft's Installer Software Development Kit.

FIGURE 13-5: Official Firefox MSI installer

Note To track the progress of the official Firefox MSI installer, visit the following Bugzilla posting: `https://bugzilla.mozilla.org/show_bug.cgi?id=231062`.

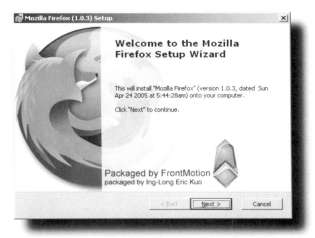

FIGURE 13-6: FrontMotion's MSI installer

Note For more information on FrontMotion's MSI installer, visit `http://www.frontmotion .com/Firefox/`.

Upon inspecting the official Firefox MSI installer, I found that the contents of the file were merely the extracted setup files, so in reality, the MSI installer from Mozilla is just a wrapper to the official installer. However, the installer available from FrontMotion uses all of the MSI capabilities in installing Firefox, and both MSI installers use the free MAKEMSI tool to build their installer.

Another nice feature of the FrontMotion installer is the inclusion of the integrated desktop icon (as mentioned earlier in this chapter) with right-click context menu options. This, coupled with the ability to use the MSI's repair functionality, makes it an ideal option for deployment in corporate environments.

For the latest technical support and help with FrontMotion's Firefox MSI installer visit this MozillaZine posting: `http://forums.mozillazine.org/viewtopic.php?t=138033`.

Hacking with MaSaI

One great tool that you can use to create or update MSIs is MaSaI Solutions' MaSaI Installer. While Microsoft has the Orca MSI editor as part of its Installer SDK, MaSaI offers some interesting options and an enhanced interface, as shown in Figure 13-7. While the full version of this tool is not free, if you want to get serious about creating, extracting, or updating MSIs, this is a viable option. The MaSaI tools offer the ability to extract MSI contents to a source path for easy updating and rebuilding without having to do this on the system that originally created the MSI. Additional features include MCE and ICE validation and verification, as well as a host of other advanced tools.

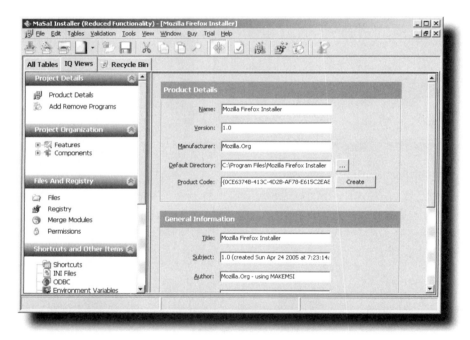

FIGURE 13-7: MaSaI Editor viewing the official Firefox MSI

Note   You can download the MaSaI Installer from `http://www.masaieditor.com/`.

Hacking with Microsoft's Orca

To download and install Microsoft's Orca tool from the Windows Software Development Kit SDK, just hop over to `http://www.microsoft.com/downloads/details.aspx?FamilyId=A55B6B43-E24F-4EA3-A93E-40C0EC4F68E5` or to the older link `http://www.microsoft.com/msdownload/platformsdk/sdkupdate/`, which redirects easily.

Special attention should be placed on the fact that this site is heavily Internet Explorer-specific and will prompt you to install an ActiveX control to manage the downloading and updates of the Installer SDK.

Once you have installed the full Installer SDK, you can dig through the directories to find the Orca.msi installer. The default directory that the installer uses is C:\Program Files\Microsoft SDK\Bin. This is where you can find the Orca.msi file.

The Orca installer creates an Orca shortcut in your Start ➪ Programs menu and launches a simple interface, as shown in Figure 13-8.

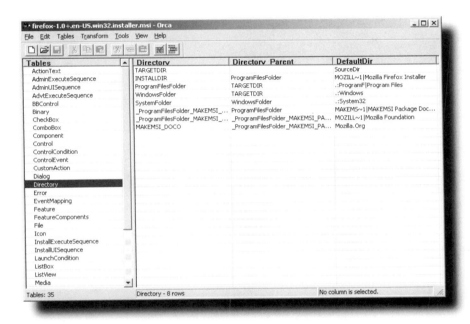

FIGURE 13-8: Microsoft's Orca MSI editor viewing the official Firefox MSI

Other Notable MSI Tools

Two additional tools that you can use for creating and updating are MAKEMSI and Advanced Installer. Each tool offers different features; MAKEMSI is an XML scripted tool, and Advanced Installer is a fully visual Windows application, as shown in Figure 13-9.

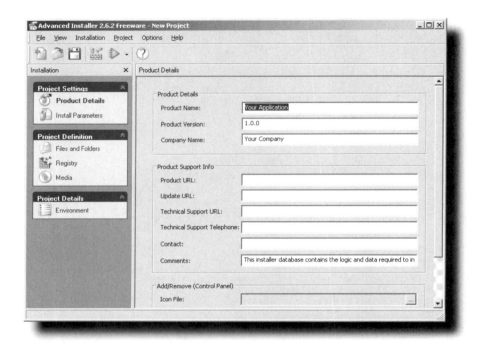

FIGURE 13-9: Advanced Installer's main window

Getting MAKEMSI

One nice feature of MAKEMSI is its ability to create an installer by just pointing it to a directory or registry file. To download the MAKEMSI installer tool, visit http://www .labyrinth.net.au/~dbareis/MAKEMSI.htm.

To make life easier when using MAKEMSI you can also download the MSIDIFF tool (http://www.labyrinth.net.au/~dbareis/msidiff.htm), which adds right-click context menu options for MSIs to extract MSIs to scripts, as well as to compare different scripts.

Getting Advanced Installer

While Advanced Installer lacks the import functionality needed to update an existing MSI, it does have a rather simple interface for creating a new installer. Once you have created this new installer you can save the setting as an Advanced Installer Project for future updating and redeploying.

Tip

To get your free copy of Advanced Installer, visit http://www.advancedinstaller.com/.

Summary

This chapter should help you deploy and manage a core Firefox installation across multiple computers. The chapter started by discussing hacking the installer and extracting the contents, moved on to configuration options, and finished with options and methods for building a deployable Firefox installer.

While this chapter is not meant to cover every possible installation or deployment option for Firefox, it does cover many of the more popular options available today.

Backing Up and Managing Your Profile/Settings

chapter

14

by Phil Catelinet

Firefox uses profiles to keep track of your browser preferences, extensions, themes, and cached data. They're stored apart from the browser's application files and can be managed separately from the program itself. This chapter looks at different ways you can manipulate your profiles for backup and portability. You'll find out how to preserve your profiles, move them to other computers, and restore them when the time comes.

in this chapter

☑ Use the hidden Profile Manager

☑ Create new profiles for different purposes

☑ Back up and restore your profiles

Before You Begin, Back Up

Because you're a seasoned Firefox user, you've personalized the browser to give yourself a familiar environment in which to work. We're going to hack your existing profiles in this chapter, and there's a chance that you could accidentally damage or destroy your settings. To prevent that, back up your current profiles now so that if you do mess them up, you can easily restore them and get your old Firefox settings back.

In Windows, profiles are stored in the following directory:

```
C:\Documents and Settings\[your username]\Application Data\
Mozilla\Firefox\Profiles
```

In Linux, the profile for each user is stored in the user's home directory, in the following path:

```
~/.mozilla/firefox/[Profile name]/
```

In Mac OS X, profiles are located in either of these directories:

```
~/Library/Mozilla/Firefox/Profiles/[Profile name]/
```

or

```
~/Library/Application Support/Mozilla/Firefox/Profiles/
[Profile name]/
```

Copy the entire Firefox folder to another location on your hard drive. Because the default disk cache location is in the profile, you can save time and space by launching Firefox and clearing the browser cache before copying the folder. If, at any time, you want to restore your profiles, close Firefox and copy the backup folder back to this directory.

Finding and Using the Hidden Profile Manager

If you used the Mozilla suite or an older browser like Netscape, you might remember the Profile Manager that would launch the first time you ran the browser. The Profile Manager lets you use different settings for different browser users without having to log out of the operating system and back on as another user. Firefox still contains the Profile Manager, but it's been hidden from view. When you start Firefox for the first time, it builds a profile for you based on its defaults, but you can start Firefox with the Profile Manager to create new profiles or delete existing ones.

To launch the Profile Manager in Windows, first make sure that Firefox is closed. Then click on Start ⇨ Run and type **%ProgramFiles%\Mozilla Firefox\firefox.exe -ProfileManager**. (You might need to enclose everything but the -ProfileManager switch in quotes.)

In Mac OS X and Linux, open a new Terminal session and type the path and switch at the command prompt. For Mac OS X, the command should be as follows:

```
/Applications/Mozilla.app/Contents/MacOS/mozilla -ProfileManager
```

For Linux, the path depends on where you installed Firefox, but the command line switch is the same:

```
~\[path to Firefox]\firefox -ProfileManager
```

You can also edit the shortcut for Firefox and add the -ProfileManager switch after the executable command. Note that the Profile Manager now launches every time you use the shortcut, so you might want to copy the original shortcut first, and then add the switch to the copy (and rename the shortcut appropriately). That way, you can launch Firefox with the Profile Manager when you need it, but start Firefox without it the rest of the time.

Creating and Deleting Profiles

The Profile Manager lets you create, rename, and delete profiles, as shown in Figure 14-1.

When you click on the Create Profile . . . button, the Profile Manager starts a new profile wizard that lets you configure two options: the profile name and its location (see Figure 14-2). The name of a new profile will always be "Default User" at first, and the location will be the Profiles folder we located earlier. You can choose a different name for your new profile and Firefox adjusts the profile path accordingly. If you prefer, you can create the new profile in a completely different location from your existing profiles by using the Choose Folder . . . button.

FIGURE 14-1: Firefox's Profile Manager.

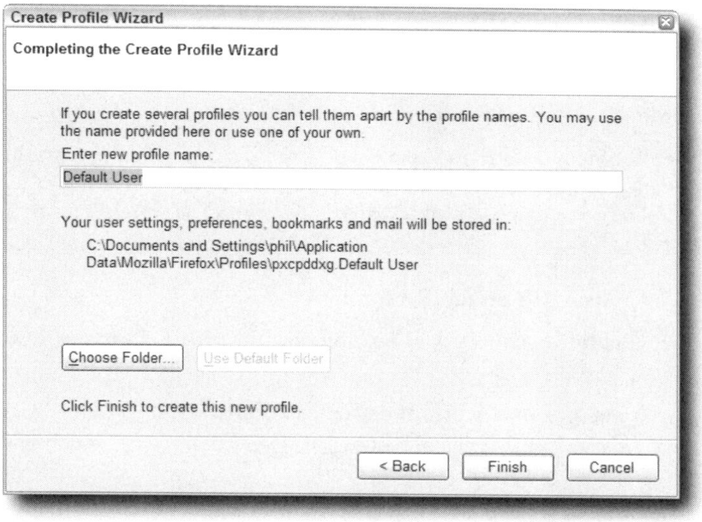

FIGURE 14-2: The Create Profile wizard.

From the Profile Manager screen, you can also rename an existing profile or delete it entirely. If you delete a profile, Firefox asks if you want to delete the files associated with the profile along with the name. Figure 14-3 shows the choices when deleting a profile. You have the opportunity to save any of the data stored in the profile — the bookmarks, cookies, saved passwords, and more — before deleting the profile for good. If you delete the files through the Profile Manager, they are gone forever, so know what you want before you click.

FIGURE **14-3: The Profile Manager gives you the chance to save the data before you delete a profile.**

One more thing to remember: Firefox always starts with the last profile used, unless you use the Profile Manager or a command line switch to select a different profile.

What's in a Profile?

Let's take a closer look at the files in a typical profile. We'll explore a new profile, then compare it with your working profile.

Launch Firefox with the Profile Manager and create a new profile. Start Firefox with this profile. Using your computer's file system, browse to the new profile's folder. Because this is a new profile, any files in the folder were automatically created by Firefox. You should find these files, among others, in the profile:

- **bookmarks.html**: Contains the default Firefox bookmarks.
- **compatibility.ini**: Checks for extension compatibility with currently installed version of Firefox.
- **components.ini**: Contains components listing for extensions.
- **compreg.dat**: Contains Firefox component Registry listing.
- **cookies.txt**: Contains cookies set while browsing.
- **defaults.ini**: Lists locations for some extensions in your profile.
- **history.dat**: Contains Firefox's browser history.
- **localstore.rdf**: Defines default window settings and toolbar sizes and positions.
- **mimetypes.rdf**: Lists default file MIME types for helper applications.
- **prefs.js**: This is Firefox's preferences file.
- **search.rdf**: Contains information on Firefox's search plugins.
- **xpti.dat**: This is a catalog for Component Object Model type library.
- **XUL.mfl**: This is a cache file of the Firefox user interface for quick load of browser.

A brand new profile will also have three directories:

- **cache**: Stores the Firefox browser disk cache.

- **chrome**: Contains userChrome-example.css and userContent-example.css files, which contain sample text for userChrome.css and userContent.css. If you create customized versions of userChrome.css and userContent.css, they will be kept in this folder.

- **extensions**: Where your extensions are kept. Some extensions may store their data outside of the extensions folder.

Your active profile may have many other files in it, but the additional files you should be most concerned with are as follows:

- **downloads.rdf**: Keeps track of your Download Manager data.

- **formhistory.dat**: Stores your autocomplete data for web forms.

- **signons.txt**: Holds any web page usernames and passwords you've saved while browsing. The usernames and passwords are encrypted for added security.

- **key3.db**: Works with the signons.txt file to save usernames and passwords.

- **parent.lock**: This file only appears when Firefox is using this profile. It indicates that the profile is in use.

- **user.js**: Contains user-added preferences (if you created this file yourself).

There are two other files located above the Profiles folder:

- **pluginreg.dat**: Registers installed plugins, and is created each time Firefox launches.

- **profiles.ini**: Tells Firefox where to find your profiles.

We'll take a closer look at profiles.ini in the next section.

Note   You can learn more about the files in a typical profile at `http://gemal.dk/mozilla/ files.html`.

Move Your Profiles Around

The default location for profiles works for most people, but you're not most people. Maybe you have a network file share that you'd like to use for your profile, so that the profile gets backed up automatically each night by the file server. Or perhaps you want to take your profile with you and use it on another computer. Knowing how to move your profile can come in handy.

Launch Firefox with the Profile Manager, select your regular profile, and start Firefox. Then close the browser. Now open your profiles.ini file for editing. It should look like this:

```
[General]
StartWithLastProfile=1

[Profile0]
Name=default
IsRelative=1
Path=Profiles/u31g6nph.default
Default=1

[Profile1]
Name=firefox2
IsRelative=0
Path=C:\Documents and Settings\username\My Documents\firefoxprofiles\firefox2
```

Your current profile will have the variable `Default=1` listed under it. Make a note of the path to that profile. The random-looking code in the path will vary according to which version of Firefox the profile was created with, but, as long as you know the path, the name of the folder doesn't matter. You'll need to know it when you move the profile.

Moving a Firefox profile is not difficult, but it takes a bit of care.

1. Create a new folder on your hard drive named MovedProfile and place it somewhere other than your current Profiles folder.

2. Start Firefox with the Profile Manager.

3. Create a new profile with the name MovedUser. Change the path of the profile to your MovedProfile folder. Click Finish.

4. The main Profile Manager window appears, with the MovedUser profile selected. Click the Start Firefox button to launch Firefox with the MovedUser profile. Firefox opens with the default home page and bookmarks — a new, blank profile. Close Firefox.

5. Browse to your old Firefox Profiles folder and look for the exact folder you noted earlier. Copy everything in that folder to your MovedProfile folder. If your operating system prompts you to overwrite existing files, do so.

6. In the MovedProfile/Chrome folder, edit the file chrome.rdf with a text editor. Look through the file for the path to your old profile location. It will be listed in codes for each installed extension. Manually, or using your text editor's find and replace feature, change each occurrence of the old path to the path to your MovedProfile folder.

   If your old profile was in

   ```
   C:\Documents and Settings\username\Mozilla\Firefox\Profiles\xxxxxxx.default
   ```

   (where xxxxxxx is the random text in the profile folder name), search for

   ```
   C:/Documents%20and%20Settings/username/Mozilla/Firefox/Profiles/xxxxxxx.default
   ```

(because chrome.rdf is an XML file and can't contain spaces or backslashes in URLs) and replace it with

```
C:/MovedProfile
```

assuming that the MovedProfile folder was on drive C:.

7. Start Firefox again, this time without the Profile Manager. If all has gone well, Firefox should launch with your normal bookmarks, extensions, and themes intact. To make sure you are using your new profile location, look in the MovedProfile folder for the parent.lock file. Its presence indicates that the profile is active.

You will need to keep your old Firefox Profiles folder around, because Firefox looks at profiles.ini located there to find your profiles. However, if you're pressed for space, you can browse to the subfolder where your original profile was located and delete it. Before you empty your trash, launch Firefox again to make sure that it isn't still using that old profile for anything. If you have any problems, look in your chrome.rdf file again to see if you missed a path.

Note For more information on formatting URLs with special characters, go to `http://academ.hvcc.edu/~kantopet/xhtml/index.php?page=writing+the+url&parent=xhtml+hyperlinks`.

Creating a Portable Profile

If you're using Firefox on two or more computers, you might want to maintain the same bookmarks and preferences on both machines. A portable profile lets you take your most important settings with you but keeps things small and simple, so it will work on any Firefox installation. Bear in mind that a portable profile should be easy to move around, so don't plan to use extensions or themes in this configuration.

1. Start Firefox with the Profile Manager. Create a new profile named Portable. Change the directory name to PortableProfile.

2. Firefox will start with the new, blank profile. Close Firefox.

3. Copy these files from your regular profile to the PortableProfile folder, overwriting the existing copies. (You'll see why these files are important in the next section.)

   - bookmarks.html
   - prefs.js
   - cookies.txt
   - chrome/userChrome.css (if present in your profile)
   - chrome/userContent.css (if present in your profile)

4. Start Firefox again and the Portable profile should be in use. Your bookmarks and existing preferences will be in place, but you won't have any of your extensions.

5. Under Tools ➪ Options ➪ Privacy, change the size of the disk cache from 50,000 to a much smaller number, such as 5000. Because you'll be moving this profile around, the disk cache should not be allowed to grow to 50 MB. Close Firefox.

6. Copy this PortableProfile folder to a USB key, a floppy disk, or other removable medium.

7. On another machine with Firefox installed, plug in your USB key or copy the profile to the hard drive. Access the profile by starting Firefox with the -profile switch, like so:

```
"c:\Program Files\Mozilla Firefox\firefox.exe" -profile F:\PortableProfile
```

F: is the drive letter where the profile directory is located. You can make sure that Firefox is using the portable profile by checking the directory for the parent.lock file.

Manually Backing Up Critical Data

You've already seen how you can move or copy your entire profile and use it from a different location. However, that's not really a backup, it's just a copy. To think of it as a backup, you'd have to move it off your computer or at least off your primary hard disk and leave it alone. Then you'd copy it again after each time you use the browser, because the files in your profile change every time you access something with Firefox. But copying the entire profile by browsing to the profile's location and selecting the right directory can be time-consuming and overkill, depending on your needs. Maybe you're interested only in keeping your Firefox bookmarks safe in case of catastrophic data loss. Or it could be that you need to have your preferences available when you reinstall Firefox.

That's the first question to consider when it comes to backing up your data: what information is most important to you? If your computer were to crash and lose your files, which ones would you need most desperately to get up and running again? Those files are the ones you should back up and keep handy in case you have a problem with the originals. Data backup at the consumer level doesn't get much attention because it's not interesting or fun. It's like insurance: you only need it when something bad happens, and who wants to worry about things going wrong? Yet when you lose data, either through a software or hardware problem, that's when you'll be glad you keep current and accurate backups of your crucial information. If your personal Firefox settings are important to you, you should include elements of your profile in your ongoing backup strategy, whatever that may be.

Earlier in this chapter, we went through a list of the files in your profile. Now we'll look at some of those files from a backup point of view, in order of importance.

- **bookmarks.html**: For most users, this file is the most important one in the profile. If you have built a set of bookmarks over the years, you'd probably be lost if this file were to disappear. I keep several copies of my bookmarks on different computers and on different storage media, just in case.

- **prefs.js**: If you've changed your preferences with about:config or by manually editing this file, you might want to keep an extra copy around.

- **chrome/userChrome.css** and **userContent.css**: If you've created or edited either of these files, you should probably keep backups of both.

- **cookies.txt**: You might want to keep this file if you regularly use web sites that store information in cookies, such as newspaper web sites that set cookies with your registration data. Without cookies.txt, if you use a new profile and browse to these sites, you'll have to log in or register again.

- **signons.txt and key3.db**: Copy these files to save your stored username/password combinations for any sites that require you to log in.

- **formhistory.dat**: If you don't want to lose any data that you've entered in web forms, make a copy of this file.

- **downloads.rdf**: Back up this file if you don't want to lose your downloaded files history.

There are many other files in a typical profile, but these will get you working again should your profile become damaged or unusable. Copy these files to another location, on your computer or on removable media, as often as you want and you're insured against the loss of your Firefox data and preferences.

Automatic Backups of Critical Files

If you already make frequent backups, you probably have special software just for the task. You don't need any extra software or hardware for backups, but they both help make the task easier. Using your existing backup software, just add the files listed in the previous section (or your entire profile, if you really want the whole thing) to your normal automatic backup process and keep the backups in a safe place.

If you want to start making regular backups, your operating system should include a decent backup program that will get the job done. For example, Microsoft's Backup utility will let you select individual files for backup and schedule the backups using the Windows Scheduled Tasks function. There are also many commercial backup options available that include more features and use different types of backup media. If you're interested in cheaper solutions that can get the job done, search Google for "freeware shareware backup software" and take your pick, but remember that you get what you pay for.

The other important thing to keep in mind regarding backups is that they need to be tested occasionally. If you can't restore any data from your backups, they won't be of much help to you when you need them. So, once in a while, restore some information from your backups and make sure you can use it.

Unofficial Mozilla Backup Tool

For Windows users, there's a free backup utility designed specifically to back up and restore Mozilla, Firefox, and Thunderbird profiles. Mozbackup backs up and restores bookmarks, saved passwords, web forms data, and cookies with ease. It gives you a quick way to save the major elements of your profile to a compressed file that can be moved or copied to other media for safekeeping. However, Mozbackup doesn't back up the chrome folder or work well with extensions.

Mozbackup uses a wizard for every backup and restore operation. It lets you back up different profiles, password-protect your backup file, and select which items from your profile to include in the backup (see Figure 14-4). Unfortunately, the program has only this wizard interface, so it's not great for scheduled backups using the Windows Scheduled Tasks function, unless you don't mind setting a time for the wizard to run each day and ask you to respond. However, for the occasional profile backup, emergency restore, or quick move of profile data from one PC to another, Mozbackup is an effective tool.

FIGURE 14-4: Mozbackup stores all of this information in one file for easy backup.

Note

Mozbackup is available at `http://mozbackup.jasnapaka.com/`.

Backing Up Plugins and Other Components

Browser files and search plugins aren't part of the user profile, so they aren't touched by any of the backup tools or methods discussed so far. Plugins live in Firefox's application directory and are available for all Firefox users, whereas extensions and themes, which are stored in the profile, are only available for users who have installed them.

To back up the file plugins, make a copy of the Plugins folder in the Firefox application directory or mark that folder as part of your normal automated backup process. If you need to uninstall and reinstall Firefox, you can restore the file plugins by copying the contents of this folder into the new, empty plugins folder. Firefox registers available plugins when the browser launches, so you don't need to adjust any other settings to activate the restored plugins. To make sure Firefox sees the plugins as available, you can check the browser's registered plugins by typing **about:plugins** in the location bar.

Search plugins can be backed up by copying or marking the searchplugins folder in the Firefox application directory. After reinstalling Firefox, copy the contents of the backup searchplugins folder to the new searchplugins folder in the Firefox application directory. While some of the plugins come with Firefox, any plugins you have installed yourself will be restored to the browser.

Recommended Extensions for Backups

Because Firefox doesn't come with any built-in backup tools, extension authors have created some useful applications that provide limited backup and restore functions. None of these tools offers as much capability as a straightforward backup of your profile folder, but they will do the jobs for which they are intended.

Bookmark Backup

This extension saves a backup of your bookmarks and several other files to a folder every time Firefox closes. By default, the backup folder is located in the current profile, but there is an option to change that. You can also select a number of other files to be backed up along with the bookmarks, as shown in Figure 14-5. Bookmark Backup keeps its backups separated by subfolders named for the days of the week, so you can go back up to seven days to retrieve an older version of a file.

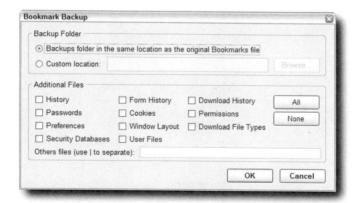

FIGURE 14-5: Bookmark Backup copies your bookmarks and more.

The advantage of Bookmark Backup is that it runs automatically every time you close Firefox. So it's great if you don't want to bother with scheduling backups through another utility. However, because it only backs up certain files, you should plan to use Bookmark Backup as a quick-restore for critical files, and continue to make regular backups of your entire profile.

Note Bookmark Backup can be found at `http://www.pikey.me.uk/mozilla/`.

Bookmarks Synchronizer

If you run Firefox on more than one computer (for example, an office computer and a home PC), you have probably wanted your office bookmarks at home at one time, and vice versa. Because a bookmarks file is usually less than a megabyte, you could just e-mail it to yourself, but you'd have to do it every day to keep up with any changes. That's where Bookmarks Synchronizer comes in.

This extension can be configured to upload a set of bookmarks to an Internet-accessible FTP or web server, or download bookmarks from these servers. So, you can set up one computer at work to upload your bookmarks every time the browser closes. At home, you configure your other computer to download the bookmarks from the server when Firefox launches. Bookmarks Synchronizer can overwrite existing bookmarks with the changes from the server or merge two different sets of bookmarks into one set. It doesn't account for duplicate bookmarks, so you might get doubles if you select the merge option. You can even select a subfolder within your bookmarks if you need to synchronize only part of the overall bookmarks collection. Figure 14-6 shows the configuration options for Bookmarks Synchronizer. All you need to get started is access to a web or FTP server on the Internet. Your ISP usually provides a certain amount of web space for a personal home page, so you should be able to store your bookmarks there.

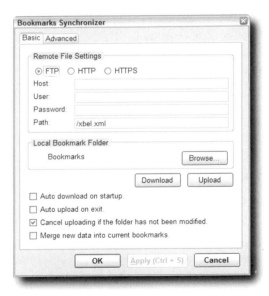

FIGURE 14-6: Bookmarks Synchronizer helps you manage bookmarks on different computers.

The bookmarks are stored in an XML file on the server, which can be read by any modern web browser. Therefore, uploading your bookmarks to an HTTP or HTTPS web site may make them visible to anyone who explores the site. If you're a stickler for security or just want to keep your bookmarks private, you may want to keep your backup file on an FTP site or a web site that is password-protected or closed to the public Internet.

Note You can get Bookmarks Synchronizer from `http://cgi29.plala.or.jp/mozzarel/`.

fireFTP

fireFTP isn't a backup extension per se, but a full-fledged FTP client right in your Firefox browser window. With fireFTP, you don't need to install a separate FTP client or open a command prompt window to access FTP sites. Upon installation, fireFTP becomes a menu option under Tools and, when accessed, will open in a new tab, by default, though you can change it to use a new window if you prefer. It does all of the following:

- Provides a two-pane interface.
- Supports active and passive FTP connections.
- Automatically detects binary versus ASCII files.
- Will resume broken downloads if the site supports resuming.
- Works across all three Firefox-supported operating systems.

You can see fireFTP in action in Figure 14-7.

The implication for profile backup and restoration is that you can use fireFTP to upload your MozBackup files or zipped profiles to an FTP site for safekeeping.

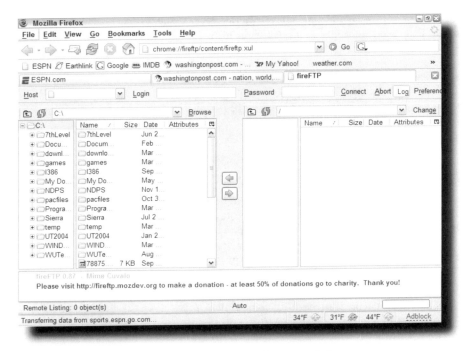

FIGURE 14-7: fireFTP puts FTP access right in your browser window.

Summary

The ability to customize Firefox is one of the key features that sets it apart from other web browsers. The profile is the method by which the browser stores and tracks preferences. Profile management is a vital aspect of deploying and using Firefox across different systems. Using the skills from this chapter, you can back up, move, and restore your profiles. You know how to create portable profiles that let you take your settings with you. The tools listed here let you manage your profiles the way you want, with the flexibility you've come to expect from Firefox.

Hacking Tools for Web Programmers

O ne of the main reasons why I love to use Firefox is for the bountiful number of extensions that are available for all facets of web programming. With a base installation, sans extensions, Firefox delivers pure HTML rendering, CSS support, some JavaScript validation functions, tab browsing, and easy search functionality. Add to this a great collection of extensions, and web programming or debugging is raised to a whole new level.

by Mel Reyes

This chapter focuses on the most popular and best-maintained extensions that I and many other folks have used for web programming. The topics covered in this chapter include the following:

- HTML
- Link
- JavaScript
- XUL
- Page validation tools

I cover what I have found to be the most useful features of some of the most popular extensions and how I tap into them.

Configuration Hacking

Two key extensions that I want to cover that don't fit in any of the main topics are configuration and managing research references. One thing that I have always done is to configure my settings to make debugging or coding as easy as possible. Historically, I have used different sets of extensions to accomplish this or have made the changes manually. Lately, I have been tapping into the excellent work done with the Configuration Mania extension, shown in Figure 15-1. This extension adds a self-titled menu option to the Tools menu and contains many useful setting for all users.

The Configuration Mania window options are divided into categories on the left panel and option groupings on the right. The most useful tweaks are in the Browser, HTTP Network, and Debug categories. While the extension does have other great features, these are the ones that I find the most beneficial when setting my coding environment.

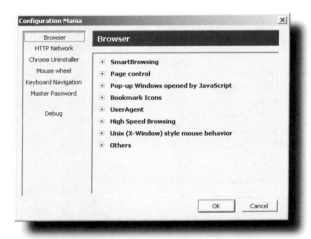

FIGURE 15-1: Configuration Mania tweaking window

Browser

In the Browser category, I like to focus on three of the groupings:

- **UserAgent:** The UserAgent section allows me to manipulate the strings that are automatically sent to web servers when browsing. This value is used by web pages to determine what the browser's capabilities are and can be modified to spoof or trick a web page to allow you access to specific content or areas. While many sites have been updating to support real standards, this feature is still rather handy.

- **High Speed Browsing:** While I normally adjusted these manually, this interface gives me the ability to make changes with ease when doing high-speed testing.

- **Others:** The Others section allows me to disable modal error messages, change the throbber's link, and enable the tab browsing Single Window Mode in the base Firefox Options menu.

HTTP Network

The HTTP Network category allows us to add some additional tuning of the number of connections, as well as set the HTTP connection type. Making changes to these settings breaks away from known standards but can yield some incredible web page downloading performance.

Cross-Reference   For more information on these settings and values, see Chapter 5.

Debug

The Debug category is the section that I use when I want to use Firefox's built-in feature to help me debug existing JavaScript code. Enabling JavaScript strict warnings assures tight alignments with JavaScript standards and usually highlights some of the most obviously overlooked bugs that pop up. Additionally, when coding or creating Firefox extensions, enabling "Enable JavaScript dump() output" and "Show Chrome JavaScript errors & warnings" will help to pinpoint extension-specific syntax issues.

Note   For more information or to install Configuration Mania, visit `http://members.lycos` `.co.uk/toolbarpalette/confmania/index_en.html`.

Tip   The following preference settings can be set to enable the same debug features using the about:config screen:

—Enable Strict JavaScript warnings: `javascript.options.strict = true`

—Enable dump() output: `browser.dom.window.dump.enabled = true`

—Show Chrome Errors and warnings: `javascript.options.showInConsole =true`

Organizing Web Research

One of the most troubling issues that I have to deal with is organizing web research that I am doing for a specific project. Whether it is a link to reference materials, code snippets, or forum posting, organizing and having them readily available is a monumental task, and that's when ScrapBook comes to the rescue. ScrapBook has to be one of the best organizational tools I have used for collecting page snippets or whole pages.

This extension adds an entry to the Tools menu, a shortcut-key combination of Alt+K, and right-click context functionality to capture selected text or whole page. As you can see from Figure 15-2, ScrapBook has the capability to create folders and subfolders, and edit saved content. All contents captured with ScrapBook are saved locally, along with such web page support elements as images, HTML, and CSS files.

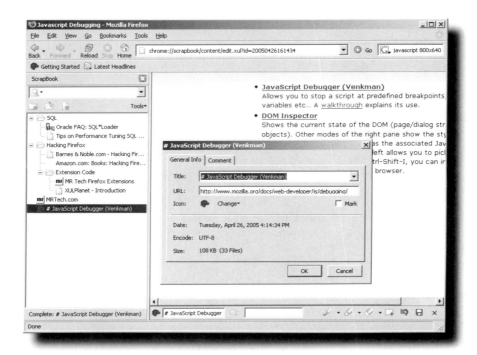

FIGURE 15-2: ScrapBook extension with content loaded

An entry's property also contains the original URL or link back to the source of the captured content. Another interesting feature highlighted in Figure 15-2 is ScrapBook's ability to edit the locally saved content, as shown by the Edit toolbar below the main window.

Note   To download and install ScrapBook, visit `http://amb.vis.ne.jp/mozilla/scrapbook/`.

The Godfather of Web Programming Extensions

Finding Internet or web programming tools can be a real hassle; however, with Chris Pederick's Web Developer extension, web programming just got a lot easier. The Web Developer extension has so many features that this entire chapter could have been dedicated to using it. In a nutshell, this extension allows you to edit, disable, enable, show, or hide key page features such as cookies, images, JavaScript, style sheets, and form values. It can also help you validate your documents for standards, show page element information, reset sessions or cookies, and a whole lot more. As shown in Figure 15-3, Web Developer installs itself in three ways:

- A toolbar of options with dropdown menus
- A right-click context menu
- A matching Tools menu option

Any of these can be disabled by using the extension's option panel. The extension also adds a toolbar button that you can use to toggle the Web Developer toolbar itself and can find by choosing Customize from the View ⇨ Toolbars menu.

FIGURE 15-3: Web Developer extension toolbar and Tools menu

Key Web Developer Features

One of the key abilities that I like to tap into includes live Cascading Style Sheet editing, which can be accessed by choosing Edit CSS from Web Developer's CSS menu or by pressing Ctrl+Shift+E. This feature alone warrants installing this extension, as it will allow you to modify style sheet properties and view the changes on the fly.

The next feature I want to highlight allows you to validate your HTML or other pages against the World Wide Web Consortium standards on the W3C web site. To access this feature, just navigate to the page you want to validate and choose Validate HTML from Web Developer's Tools menu. The current web page address is submitted to W3C's validation scripts, and the results are displayed accordingly. Running this every now and then helps with reducing page-rendering inconsistencies across systems or browsers and will keep your code in line.

A third Web Developer extension feature that I cannot live without is the window resize feature, which is available from the Web Developer's Resize menu. By default, it comes with 800 × 600 as an option for resolution testing, but you can add any custom entries from the Options menu. This feature allows for quick testing of different resolutions without having to manually switch your display's properties for testing.

These are just a few of the many features wrapped up in the Web Developer extension. The more you use it, the more you'll love it.

Note To download and install Web Developer, visit `http://chrispederick.com/work/firefox/webdeveloper/`.

Hacking Tools of the Trade

When putting this list together, I wanted to make sure that I included just the right extensions, even if I did not use them. I pulled together a list of my most recommended tools, scoured the forums and download sites for comments, and then added a few more. While this list is not a comprehensive list of every possible extension, it is a list of great extensions that you can use for hacking HTML, links, JavaScript, and XUL and for validating web pages. You can search the ever-evolving and -updated Mozilla Update site, `https://addons.update.mozilla.org/`, for more extensions and goodies.

To help with installing extensions listed in this chapter, use my MR Tech's Local Install extension, which allows installing extensions (or themes) from the local disk. For more information or to install MR Tech's Local Install, visit `http://www.mrtech.com/extensions/`.

Additionally, you can make your Extension Manager listing much more manageable by installing the Slim Extension List extension, which will sort and trim the amount of space each extension uses on the list. For more information or to install Slim Extension List, visit `http://v2studio.com/k/moz/`.

HTML Hacking Tools

The section is full of goodies to help with the everyday tasks a web programmer may come across. This chapter contains extensions and information on sniffing out MIME types, validating stored cookies, selecting colors, and changing the User Agent string to use a different editor to view a page's source. It's a nice arsenal of HTML tools to get you started loving Firefox more and more.

Hacking with LiveHTTPHeaders

Hacking with the LiveHTTPHeaders extension is great when you need to sniff out the communication between the browser and the web server to extract details. The information collected, as shown in Figure 15-4, includes all the details for requests and responses that are made from the browser and web server. When dealing with different servers, configurations, and third-party tools, this extension really comes in handy. It also helps with projects that require download prompting and triggering specific file MIME type actions, and is a must-have if you are diving into projects like these.

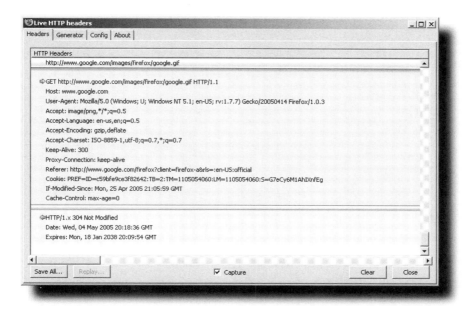

FIGURE 15-4: LiveHTTPHeaders with style sheets enabled

This extension can be opened from the LiveHTTPHeaders option in the Tools menu and will collect information only while the window is open and the Capture option is selected, so having this extension installed should have no impact on the performance of download content when it is not in use.

Note For more information or to install LiveHTTPHeaders, visit `http://livehttpheaders.mozdev.org/`.

Hacking with View Cookies

This extension makes it easy to view, temporarily remove, or permanently remove cookies that you might be working with. This extension is good for all users and adds a new information tab panel to the page details. To access the panel, shown in Figure 15-5, just choose the Page Info option from the Tools menu or right-click on the page and choose View Page Info. All the default page information tabs will be populated with the addition of a new tab that contains cookie information.

FIGURE 15-5: View Cookies information tab

Caution should be taken when using the Remove Cookie forever feature, as it will add that domain to the Cookies block list, and no further cookies for that domain will be added. To undo this change, follow these steps:

1. Open the Firefox Options window from the Tools menu and select the Privacy section on the option's icon bar.

2. Expand the Cookies section and select the Exceptions option.

3. Find the domain you just blocked from this list and remove it.

After you do this, setting cookies will be reenabled for that domain.

Note

For more information or to install View Cookies, visit `http://www.bitstorm.org/extensions/`.

Hacking with ColorZilla

The ColorZilla extension is great and has the following features listed on the site, among other colorful goodies:

- Advanced Eyedropper
- ColorPicker
- Page Zoomer

After installation, a new eyedropper icon is placed to the far left of the status bar. Left-clicking will activate the eyedropper crosshairs to find colors, and right-clicking will give you the options available. The eyedropper tools extracts the color codes from whatever you move the crosshairs over and can also be activated by pressing Shift+Esc. The status bar is updated with color information corresponding to the location of the eyedropper crosshair; then, clicking on the final location will lock those values, which are accessible by right-clicking the status bar icon. The Page Zoomer feature can be used in combination with the eyedropper to pinpoint a specific color. Unlike Firefox's built-in text zoom function, this Page Zoomer feature also increases the size of images, making it easier to find specific pixels that you may want to use the eyedropper on, and so on. For web color matching work, this extension is in a league of its own.

Note

For more information or to install ColorZilla, visit `http://www.iosart.com/firefox/colorzilla/`.

Using User Agent Switcher Extensions

From the maker of the fantastic Web Developer extension comes another interesting tool, User Agent Switcher. This tiny extension allows you to spoof or trick web sites into thinking that you are running different browsers. Based on my experience, this tool helps in two ways:

- It enables Firefox to bypass annoying or outdated Internet Explorer-only sites that really do not have Internet Explorer-only content but are just too lazy to add support for real standards.
- It enables me to quickly test browser-specific features that I may have created.

The user agent string or value is a standard browser feature that is discussed in RFCs 1945 and 2068, which basically involves having your browser send the web server a string to help with detecting the type of browser you are currently using. This is helpful when having to code for specific projects or feature sets and is universally used and accepted. The values that are submitted to the web server, though, do not have to meet any hard rules, and this extension lets you dynamically change this string. The three default strings that User Agent comes with are listed in Table 15-1.

Table 15-1 Default User Agent Values

Option	User Agent String Value
Default	Firefox's current User Agent String value (This varies based on operating system and version of Firefox running.)
Internet Explorer	Mozilla/4.0 (compatible; MSIE 6.0; Windows NT 5.1)
Netscape 4.8	Mozilla/4.8 [en] (Windows NT 5.1; U)
Opera 7.54	Opera/7.54 (Windows NT 5.1; U) [en]

Additional values can be added and customized to your liking by using the extension's Options panel window.

Note To download and install User Agent Switcher, visit `http://chrispederick.com/work/firefox/useragentswitcher/`.

Hacking with ViewSourceWith

ViewSourceWith is a simple, well-thought-out extension that allows you to add a list of different editors via its Options window, shown in Figure 15-6, which will then be made available via the Source View option in Firefox's View menu, as "View source with" in the right-click context menu, or as an optional toolbar button. The uses for this extension quickly materialize when working with simple local HTML pages that require quick editing. Additionally, pulling page source code into my favorite editors is a nice added bonus when reviewing or skimming through code.

FIGURE 15-6: ViewSourceWith configuration screen

Note To download and install ViewSourceWith, visit `http://dafizilla.sourceforge.net/viewsourcewith/`.

Navigation and Link Hacking Tools

Three tools that are used for handling or working with links and their HTML code are Mouse Gestures, ieview, and BBCode. All have different tasks and are extremely useful when navigating from page to page or when posting link information on web forums and sites.

Hacking with Mouse Gestures

While this tool is not necessarily web programming–specific, once you review all the available options and features you will see how it can save you tons of time when navigating through the Internet — for example, to look up reference code or code snippets. By default, you can right-click and drag your mouse in several directions to execute a specific navigation command. (For example, right-clicking and dragging from right to left anywhere on the page jumps you back to the previous page; doing the reverse from left to right jumps you forward one page in your browsing history.) This extension is highly configurable but comes with some very easy-to-learn basic gestures, which, coupled with the Gesture Exchange link on their site, will have you customizing things to your liking or just leaving things as they are and enjoying quick navigation.

Tip To visually enhance the benefits of this little puppy, activate the mouse trails in the extension's options window, and you will see your mouse gestures as you do them.

For more information or to install Mouse Gestures, visit `http://optimoz.mozdev.org/gestures/`.

Hacking with ieview

As much as I hate to admit it, there are still sites, including both public and corporate intranets, that rely heavily on Internet Explorer technology. So, whether for testing or pure outright need, this extension allows a quick way to load a link from Firefox into Internet Explorer. For most users this need revolves around Windows Updates, Office Updates, Microsoft Java VM, or other Microsoft media-rich sites — basically, sites that are Microsoft ActiveX–dependent and have been absorbed into the Microsoft collective. If you want to help with the migration pain of using Firefox until sites wake up and smell the Mozilla coffee brewing, you can use this extension as a one-time option from the right-click context menu or to permanently add sites that will launch in Internet Explorer.

The two options that are added to the right-click context menu include "Open Link Target in IE" and "Always Open Linked Site in IE." The first is for one-time use or testing, and the second will add the link to a list that will automatically launch in Internet Explorer after selecting this. To make changes to the "Always Open" list, open the Extension Manager and choose the Options for ieview to make configuration changes.

Note For more information or to install ieview, visit `http://ieview.mozdev.org/`.

Hacking with BBCode and BBCodeXtra

Without getting into extreme detail on how to use either one of these extensions, I can tell you that they can definitely help in filling out responses in forums or forms and with creating links and image tags for HTML, BBCode, and XHMTL. BBCode is the universally accepted markup language for just about all major online user forums. BBCode markup language has a much smaller subset of available formatting tags than HTML, and tags are usually delimited with brackets instead of the normal HTML tags, which are delimited with less than (<) and greater than (>) signs. Options that make either of these extensions great are their ability to create links from selected text or clipboards into an input form and to add text-formatting syntax, as needed. Either one of these extensions is a must-have if you intend on posting forum requests with links or have your own online forum that you use to support your applications, and so on.

Note For more information or to install BBCode, visit `http://jedbrown.net/1.0/mozilla/`.

For more information or to install BBCodeXtra, visit `http://www.extenzilla.it/bbcodextra/index.php?lang=eng`.

JavaScript and XUL Hacking Tools

JavaScript and XUL programming can be used in tandem to create great Firefox extensions and applications. This section focuses on tools that will help with inspecting the Firefox interface, help debug JavaScript, and provide JavaScript tools and XUL packaging features. These tools vary in level of difficulty and may have a steep learning curve, but all should be worth the effort required.

Hacking with the DOM Inspector

The DOM Inspector is easily the best tool to use when working with Firefox and trying to create extension overlays by picking apart a window's or dialog's XUL elements. Using the combination of File ➪ Inspect a Window and Search ➪ Select Element by Click, you can easily extract a window's or an element's id to use within your code. This is how I originally extracted the "throbber-box" and "search-container" ids that I later used and modified in my local userChrome.css file, as described in Chapter 2. Using this technique of selecting a window or dialog to inspect and then walking through the document tree also gives you a better understanding of the different elements that are used or are available with XUL interface programming.

Installing the DOM Inspector is covered in Chapter 1 in greater detail, but suffice it to say, you will need to redownload the Firefox installer to get this little gem. After that, you can just follow the Custom installation options to enable Developer Tools when prompted.

Hacking with JavaScript Console and Debugger

The JavaScript Console and JavaScript Debugger are two different tools that are miles apart with respect to features and ease of use. The Console is a default install with Firefox and can be configured to show JavaScript errors and warnings from web pages, as well as errors from extensions or XUL applications. The entries that get added here are errors, warnings, and messages.

While this native feature of Firefox is good, some crave more control over JavaScript coding, and that is where Venkman or JavaScript Debugger comes in handy. Venkman is the project code name for the JavaScript Debugger extension, which includes an extremely rich and robust editing and debugging environment specifically geared toward JavaScript debugging, as shown in Figure 15-7.

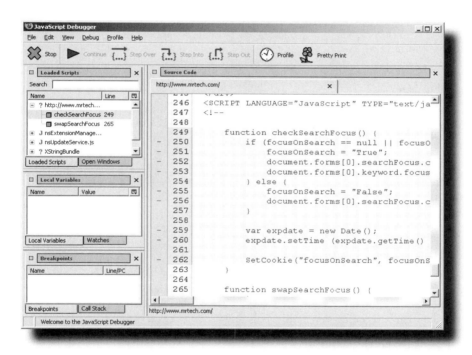

FIGURE 15-7: JavaScript Debugger window

This extension may be overwhelming for the faint of heart at first, but once you have gotten over the initial shock, the utilitarian features become very evident.

Note

For more information or to install Venkman, visit `http://www.hacksrus.com/~ginda/venkman/`.

Hacking with Extension Developer's Extension

This extension is a nice compilation of quick tools that can make creating extensions a smooth ride. The extension comes with the following features:

- Extension Builder
- install.rdf Editor
- JavaScript Shell
- JavaScript Environment
- Live XUL Editor
- Live HTML Editor
- Toggle Debugging Preferences
- Reload All Chrome

An Extension Developer menu is added to Firefox's Tools menu, and all of these features are accessible there.

Some of these features are mini–XUL applications that you can also use directly from Firefox without having to install them separately. While some of the features are really diamonds in the rough, the overall usefulness of this extension can quickly be reaped by novice or serious extension developers.

Note For more information or to install Extension Developer's Extension, visit `http://ted .mielczarek.org/code/mozilla/extensiondev/`.

Page Validation Hacking Tools

While the Web Developer extension includes a couple of online validation service features, I want to also recommend two other extensions that may be of use: HTML Validator and Checky. These extensions offer different sets of features, but both can be tapped into to clean up any nonstandard coding that may be lingering in the HTML closet.

Hacking with HTML Validator

When I first used this extension on some of my pages, I was truly shocked and ashamed that it found so many errors and warnings. The core is based on Tidy, which was originally created by the W3C and has been updated and extended as an open-source project. Tidy's core functionality focuses on analyzing specific strict standards and formatting for HTML code.

The latest version of HTML Validator, which taps into Tidy's core features, adds a color-coded icon to display the status of the current page that is loaded to the status bar. The real functionality comes with the information that it displays when you view a page's source code from

View ⇨ Page Source. This is where HTML Validator adds a split panel, shown in Figure 15-8, to the bottom of the view source screen. The bottom-left panel provides a list of errors and warnings, and the bottom-right panel contains generic details and possible resolutions for the selected error or warning. A nice feature of this extension is that when in view source mode, clicking on an entry in the bottom-left panel jumps you to the offending code within the source code in the main code window above it, making it easier to track bugs within the code.

Another feature that I have not really tapped into, but definitely will, is the Cleanup feature, which is available as a button on the bottom of the Page Source window or from the right-click context menu from the extension's icon on the status bar. This feature steps you through proposed fixes for the offending page with source and browser views for the original as well as the newly cleaned HTML.

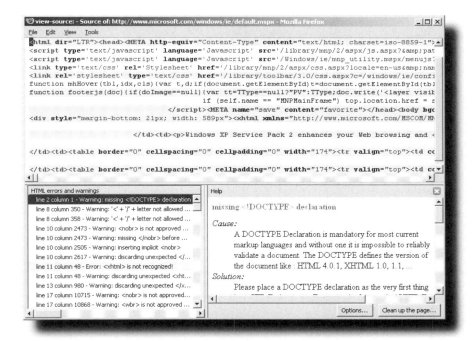

FIGURE 15-8: HTML Validator list of errors and warnings in view source window

Note   For more information or to install HTML Validator, visit `http://users.skynet.be/mgueury/mozilla/`.

Hacking with Checky

Another notable extension for page validation is Checky, which is more centered on using online web validation services but comes with tons of options. This extension also has the ability to create an *agent*, which automates several validation checks and caches the results locally.

Note For more information or to install Checky, visit `http://checky.sourceforge.net/` `extension.html`.

Summary

This chapter highlights how to quickly make local configuration changes, discusses using ScrapBook to organize notes and web pages, and finally recommends the mother of all web developer extensions to get the boat rockin'. After that, the chapter dives into a few extensions that help with hacking HTML, links, JavaScript, XUL, and validating web pages. The chapter's main goal is to provide well-rooted and actively supported extensions that can really make an impact on the day-to-day web programming drudgeries that usually pop up.

Creating Extensions and Themes

part

VI

Understanding Mozilla Programming

by Alex Sirota

This chapter introduces you to the wonderful world of Mozilla programming. You get to know the main Mozilla technologies and see how these technologies work together. After getting acquainted with the various concepts and terms, we take our first look at the exciting possibilities found in creating new browser extensions.

What makes Mozilla programming and especially Mozilla *extension* programming so great? You can quickly achieve quite a lot with a simple text editor and some imagination. Moreover, Mozilla is truly cross-platform. For example, the vast majority of Firefox extensions can run on many different operating systems with no modifications whatsoever. Finally, Mozilla is open source. This means that you can see exactly what is happening behind the curtains in each and every component you want to enhance or modify. It also means that there are more people in the community who know the inner workings of the various Mozilla parts and can help you on your development quest.

Understanding Mozilla Technologies

This section provides an overview of the various Mozilla technologies, beginning with XML User Interface Language (XUL), the language Mozilla uses to describe user interfaces (UI). Then we'll discuss JavaScript, a programming language used to implement the logic behind the user interface. You'll also see how to use Cascading Style Sheets (CSS) to define the appearance of your HTML and XUL documents and how to programmatically access these documents using the Document Object Model (DOM) interfaces. The section concludes with a short overview of the Cross Platform Component Object Model (XPCOM).

XUL: XML User Interface Language

XML User Interface Language (XUL) is the language used in Mozilla to describe user interfaces. Being an XML language, it has all the advantages of XML: it is simple, text based, cross-platform, and very flexible. You can create an advanced user interface with XUL in minutes using a simple text editor. You don't need to compile anything or to learn any platform-specific concepts or tools. This makes creating user interfaces with Mozilla as straightforward as creating regular web pages, and similarly to a web page, your XUL user interface works on any platform supported by Mozilla.

Note XUL is pronounced "zool" (rhymes with "cool").

XUL can be used to create both simple and complex user interfaces, starting with simple dialogs all the way to full-featured applications. In fact, the Mozilla applications — Firefox, Thunderbird, and the Mozilla Suite — are all built using XUL. There are several other XUL-based applications, including the Internet Relay Chat (IRC) client named ChatZilla.

User interfaces created with XUL can be easily skinned, extended, and localized. For example, you can change the visual theme of your UI or translate it to another language by simply changing a few text files. Another nice feature is that you can open XUL documents inside your browser's content area — exactly as you would open an HTML document. You can even run your XUL-based application directly from the Internet. This makes creating web applications as easy as creating web pages.

A XUL user interface definition is an XML file that contains the UI elements and their hierarchal structure. For instance, your interface may consist of a window that contains two boxes. Each box can in turn have any number of child widgets (entry boxes, buttons, labels, and so on).

In the following sections, we create and lay out some simple widgets, and finally create a complete XUL document.

Tip If you want to test the XUL code in the following examples, you can create a file with a .xul extension and the following contents:

```
<?xml version="1.0" encoding="UTF-8"?>

<window align="start"

xmlns="http://www.mozilla.org/keymaster/gatekeeper/there
.is.only.xul">
    .
    .
    .
    [Your XUL widgets go here]
    .
    .
    .
</window>
```

Once you create the file and insert some XUL elements, you can open it in Firefox using File ⇨ Open File. The `align="start"` part makes sure your XUL widgets are shown correctly when opened inside the browser window.

XUL Widgets

The basic element of a XUL document is a *widget*. Buttons, text boxes, menu items, and so on are all widgets. A widget is created by inserting an appropriate element into your XUL document. The attributes of this element determine the various properties of your widget. For example, the following defines a simple button:

```
<button label="Go"/>
```

The `label` attribute determines the text that appears on the button.

A button by itself isn't much of a user interface, so let's add a text box:

```
<textbox value="Enter you text here"/>
```

The optional `value` attribute defines the default text that initially appears inside the text box.

Tip

You shouldn't put text labels directly in a XUL file. If you do, you won't be able to use Mozilla's localization mechanisms to translate this text into other languages. If you use XML entities instead of literal text strings, the translation will become virtually effortless. You learn about Mozilla localization in the next chapter.

XUL elements can have many optional attributes. For example, some of the attributes that a text box can have follow:

- `maxlength`: The maximal number of characters that can be entered into the text box.

- `readonly`: Setting this attribute to `true` makes the entry box read-only.

- `type`: You can create special-purpose entry boxes with this attribute. For example, setting the value of this attribute to `password` creates a password entry box, one that doesn't display what is being typed.

XUL Layout

We have seen how individual widgets can be specified using XUL. Now it is time to see how XUL handles layout.

XUL uses a scheme called the *box model* to specify how the elements are oriented, aligned, and positioned. The user interface is divided into boxes. A box can contain UI elements or other boxes. Each box specifies whether its child elements are horizontally or vertically aligned. By grouping your elements into boxes, adding spacers, and specifying the flexibility of your elements, you can achieve the wanted layout for you user interface.

For example, the following specifies that we want three buttons to be arranged in a row:

```
<hbox>
    <button label="Red"/>
    <button label="Green"/>
    <button label="Blue"/>
</hbox>
```

Figure 16-1 shows the horizontally arranged buttons.

FIGURE 16-1: Horizontally arranged buttons

As you can see, to create a horizontal layout, we placed the three buttons inside an hbox element. Similarly, to create a vertical layout, you place the elements inside a vbox:

```
<vbox>
    <button label="Red"/>
    <button label="Green"/>
    <button label="Blue"/>
</vbox>
```

Figure 16-2 shows the vertically arranged buttons.

FIGURE 16-2: Vertically arranged buttons

An example of a complete XUL document follows:

```
<?xml version="1.0"?>

<window orient="horizontal"
        xmlns="http://www.mozilla.org/keymaster/gatekeeper/there.is.only.xul">
    <textbox value="Enter you text here"/>
    <button label="Go"/>
</window>
```

Note The xmlns="http://www.mozilla.org/keymaster/gatekeeper/there.is.only .xul" line specifies that the window children are XUL elements.

RDF in XUL Applications

Resource Description Framework (RDF) is a technology for describing Internet resources. It is typically implemented as an XML file having a special syntax. RDF is a complex topic outside the scope of this book. In the following sections, you can see some Mozilla configuration files written using this format, but understanding RDF is not required — all the examples include the necessary explanations and clarifications.

Note The RDF specification is maintained by the World Wide Web Consortium (W3C). For more information about this technology in Mozilla visit the Mozilla RDF page: `http://www .mozilla.org/rdf/doc/`.

Additional XUL Resources

Following are two additional XUL resources that might come in handy:

- **Mozilla XUL project page:** This page contains the XUL specification and links to additional XUL resources: `http://www.mozilla.org/projects/xul/`.

- **XUL Planet:** This site is dedicated to XUL programming. It has several very helpful tutorials and a lot of reference material: `http://www.xulplanet.com/`.

We now know what XUL is and how we can use it to create user interfaces. But XUL by itself isn't very useful; we have merely created a bunch of elements and placed them together. We need a way to add some functionality to our user interface. This is usually done with JavaScript, which leads us to the following section.

JavaScript

JavaScript is a powerful scripting language most widely used for creating dynamic web pages. Mozilla also uses JavaScript to implement the logic behind XUL user interfaces. Like many other technologies used in Mozilla, JavaScript is very easy to master; you don't have to be an experienced programmer to start writing JavaScript programs.

 Note JavaScript and Java are two completely different languages. They both have syntax somewhat similar to C, but other than that, they don't really have much in common. JavaScript is a lightweight scripting language created by Netscape, while Java is a more complex, compiled language developed by Sun Microsystems.

JavaScript is an interpreted language. This means that the program is executed directly from the source code; there is no need to first compile it into binary form. This also means that programs written in JavaScript are usually open source by definition — they are just plain-text pieces of code, located either in separate files or embedded in HTML or XUL documents.

The JavaScript language is standardized by the ECMA-262 standard under the name ECMAScript.

Syntax

When it comes to syntax, JavaScript is similar to C, Perl, PHP, and many other programming languages.

Tip

If you want to test the JavaScript examples that follow, you can create an HTML document with the following contents:

```html
<html>
  <body>
    <script type="text/javascript">
    <!--
        .
        .
        .
        [Your JavaScript code goes here]
        .
        .
        .
    //-->
    </script>
  </body>
</html>
```

Insert your JavaScript code into the `<script>` element and open the HTML page inside the browser to see what it does.

Conditional Statements

Similar to most programming languages, JavaScript has an `if...else` statement:

```javascript
if (i == 1) {
    alert("i is 1");
} else {
    alert("i is not 1");
}
```

As with many other programming languages, the `else` part of the `if` statement is optional.

Tip

You can use the `alert` function to display a dialog with a custom message.

JavaScript also has a `switch` statement that allows executing different blocks of code, depending on the expression value:

```javascript
switch (i) {
    case 1:
        alert("i is 1");
        break;
    case 2:
        alert("i is 2");
        break;
    default:
        alert("i is neither 1 nor 2");
}
```

Loops

JavaScript has several different looping statements. For example, the following loop will be executed four times:

```
for (i = 0; i < 4; i++) {
    alert(i);
}
```

In the preceding statement we want i to be initialized with 0 and to be incremented by 1 on each loop iteration. The loop will be executed as long as the value of i is less than 4.

Variables

Variables in JavaScript are created by either assigning a value to a new variable or by declaring it using the var keyword:

```
var i;
```

Variables declared inside a function have a local scope, meaning that they can be used only inside that function. Variables that were defined outside any function are global and can be used anywhere in the script.

Functions

You can define new functions using the function keyword:

```
function add(a, b) {
    return a + b;
}
```

The preceding function receives two arguments, a and b, and returns their sum.

Scripting the User Interface

As previously mentioned, we will be using JavaScript in Mozilla to implement the logic behind the user interface. Each user interface element can trigger several events. For example, a button can trigger an event when it is pressed. If we attach a JavaScript function to such an event, it will be executed each time the event is triggered. A function attached to an event is called an *event handler*.

Note If you are familiar with HTML, you may find the XUL events and their handlers very familiar. In fact, Mozilla handles XUL and HTML events in an almost identical fashion.

Let's create a simple XUL user interface — two entry boxes and a button (see Figure 16-3):

```
<hbox>
    <textbox id="first-box"/>
    <textbox id="second-box"/>
    <button label="Add" oncommand="calculateSum()"/>
</hbox>
```

FIGURE 16-3: A primitive calculator

Each time the button is pressed, our `calculateSum` function is executed. Let's look at how this function might be implemented:

```
function calculateSum() {
    var firstBox  = document.getElementById("first-box");
    var secondBox = document.getElementById("second-box");
    var a = parseInt(firstBox.value);
    var b = parseInt(secondBox.value);
    alert(a + b);
}
```

Step by step, the preceding function does the following:

1. Find the two entry boxes elements using `getElementsById`. This function is a part of the DOM interface. (See the DOM section later in this chapter for details.)

2. After finding our entry boxes, we get their value by examining their `value` property.

3. Convert the value to integer using the `parseInt` function.

4. After we have a numerical representation of the contents of our textboxes, we can calculate the sum and present it to the user in a popup box.

To see the previous example in action, you can create the following XUL document and open it in Firefox:

```
<?xml version="1.0" encoding="UTF-8"?>

<window align="start"
        xmlns="http://www.mozilla.org/keymaster/gatekeeper/there.is.only.xul">
    <script type="application/x-javascript">
    <![CDATA[
        function calculateSum() {
            var firstBox  = document.getElementById("first-box");
            var secondBox = document.getElementById("second-box");
            var a = parseInt(firstBox.value);
            var b = parseInt(secondBox.value);
            alert(a + b);
        }
    ]]>
    </script>
```

```
<hbox>
    <textbox id="first-box"/>
    <textbox id="second-box"/>
    <button label="Add" oncommand="calculateSum()"/>
    </hbox>
</window>
```

Note

In the previous example, we embedded some JavaScript code directly in the XUL document. In such cases, the JavaScript code should be placed inside a CDATA section, so the XML parser doesn't try to parse it. Otherwise, characters that have a special meaning in XML (such as >) can confuse the XML parser.

After reading this section, you should have a basic idea about what JavaScript is and how you can use it to add some logic to your user interface. Chapter 17 continues exploring the possibilities while examining several additional examples.

Additional JavaScript Resources

Following are some additional JavaScript resources that might be useful:

- The WebReference JavaScript Section has many articles and tutorials on JavaScript programming: http://www.webreference.com/js/.

- The JavaScript Guide, while a bit outdated, is still a good reference: http://wp .netscape.com/eng/mozilla/3.0/handbook/javascript/.

- The official JavaScript (ECMAScript) specification can be found on the Ecma web site: http://www.ecma-international.org/publications/standards/ Ecma-262.htm.

- Here is a good JavaScript tutorial: http://www.tizag.com/javascriptT/.

- Here is a nice article about the history of JavaScript: http://www.howtocreate .co.uk/jshistory.html.

Cascading Style Sheets

Cascading Style Sheets (CSS) is a mechanism for specifying the appearance of HTML, XUL, and other documents. With CSS, you can specify colors, fonts, sizes, and other style elements. CSS is a World Wide Web Consortium (W3C) specification.

CSS allows you to separate your document content from its presentation. For example, your XUL document can specify that your user interface contains an entry box and two buttons. A style sheet can then be used to specify the size of the entry field, the color of the buttons, and the font of their labels. There are many advantages to separating the document style from its content. The first and possibly the most important benefit is flexibility. If you define all the presentation-related information in a separate style sheet, you will be able to easily modify the style of your user interface without needing to adjust the document content. Your HTML or XUL files will become much more readable and clean.

Suppose that you have created a large project with dozens of XUL documents. Then, after working with your program for a while, you notice that changing the font of all the labels will greatly improve their readability. In a world without style sheets, you would have to search all your XUL documents for `label` elements and add an appropriate attribute to each and every one of them. What would happen if you decided to experiment with several different fonts to see which one looked the best? With style sheets, this task becomes trivial. If all your documents use the same style sheet (and if they are part of the same project, they probably should), you can just add a line to this style sheet specifying the new font of your label elements.

A typical CSS definition is a list of rules. A rule has a selector that specifies the elements the rule applies to and a list of style declarations. For example, a rule for changing the appearance of all the `label` elements might look like this:

```
label {
    font-family: arial;
    font-weight: bold;
    color: blue;
}
```

In this rule, `label` is a *selector;* it specifies that the rule applies to all the `label` elements. After the selector comes a block enclosed in curly braces that specifies the styles that should be applied to the selected elements. The block is a semicolon-separated list of `property: value` pairs. In this example, the `color` property will receive the value `blue`, meaning that the text of all our labels will be blue.

There are many places in which both the author of the document and its reader can specify their preferred style rules. For example, styles can be defined in external style sheets, embedded in the document, or specified inline by setting an element's style attribute. Users can further change these styles by changing the browser settings or adding their own custom style sheets. This means that several, often-conflicting style definitions can be applicable to the same element. The "cascading" in CSS allows these conflicts to be resolved by specifying the order in which the rules are evaluated. For example, the author-specified rules have higher priority than the reader-specified ones, and the more specific rules will override ones that are more general.

Each element in our HTML or XUL document can have a `class` attribute that can be used to specify that several elements are related to one another in some way. Elements can also have an `id` attribute. Unlike the `class` attribute, the element's `id` should be unique throughout the document — it will be used to identify the specific element. Let's look at a fragment of a XUL document to clarify things a bit:

```
<button id="play-button" class="control" label="play"/>
<button id="stop-button" class="control" label="stop"/>
```

In the preceding example, both buttons belong to the `control` class. This will be useful if you want to apply some style to all the elements belonging to this class. For example, you might want to make all your control buttons bigger than the others. You can see that both buttons are uniquely identified by their respective `id` attributes. You can use this to apply a specific style only to one element (the play button, for example) without affecting all the other elements. The `id` attribute will also become handy if you want to find a specific element using JavaScript.

Let's see a few examples of the various style declarations we can apply to our documents and specifically to the two buttons from the previous example.

To specify a style for all the button elements in your document, you can use the following rule:

```
button { border: 1px solid red; }
```

This rule will draw a 1-pixel-wide red border around all the buttons in your document.

You can style all the elements having a specific class:

```
button.control { color: blue; }
```

This rule selects the buttons having a `control` class and makes their label text blue. If you want the rule to apply to all the elements that belong to the `control` class and not only buttons, you can omit the `button` part of the selector, as follows:

```
.control { color: blue; }
```

Now let's change the label font of the stop button to bold by selecting it using its id, `stop-button`:

```
#stop-button { font-weight: bold; }
```

The preceding examples, while simple, demonstrate the power of CSS. There is, of course, much more to style sheets; there are additional selector types, inheritance, and many useful style properties. The important principle you should have gotten from this section is that you should always separate your document content from its presentation by using style sheets.

Additional CSS Resources

Following are some additional CSS resources that might be helpful:

- The CSS specification can be found on the W3C site: `http://www.w3.org/TR/REC-CSS1` (Level 1), `http://www.w3.org/TR/REC-CSS2` (Level 2).

- The Web Design Group (WDG) site has a nice guide to CSS: `http://www.htmlhelp.com/reference/css/`.

The Document Object Model

The DOM is a collection of interfaces for working with HTML and XML documents. The document is represented as a tree of elements. The DOM defines methods for navigating and searching this tree, retrieving information about the various elements, modifying the tree structure by removing and inserting elements, manipulating individual elements, and so on.

Note

The DOM isn't a language or a software library. It is a World Wide Web Consortium (W3C) specification for an interface. So how does it actually work? Software vendors, in our case Mozilla, implement the DOM standard interfaces and allow them to be used from various programming languages. When developing Mozilla extensions, we will typically be using JavaScript to call the DOM methods.

The following sections provide some examples of what you can do with the DOM interfaces. This isn't intended as a complete DOM reference but is rather meant to give you a taste of the possibilities.

Assume that you have an HTML document that contains the following table:

```
<table id="my-table" border="1">
    <tr>
        <th>First Name</th>
        <th>Last Name</th>
    </tr>
    <tr>
        <td>John</td>
        <td>Doe</td>
    </tr>
</table>
```

This table will typically be rendered by the browser, as shown in Figure 16-4.

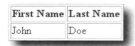

FIGURE **16-4: The sample table rendered by the browser**

The DOM representation of this table is shown in Figure 16-5.

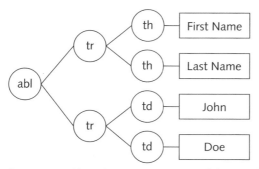

FIGURE **16-5: The DOM representation of the sample table**

Tip

You can use the DOM Inspector extension to see the exact tree structure. You can inspect and modify the elements, their attributes, styles, and much more. See Chapter 15 for more details on the DOM Inspector.

Navigating and Searching the Document Tree

The following JavaScript code searches the document tree for our table using the table's id attribute `my-table`:

```
var myTable = document.getElementById("my-table");
```

Note

The `document` object represents the root element of our document tree. It can be used to access all the other elements.

In all of the following examples, assume that we have already found our table using the `getElementById` method and assigned it to the `myTable` variable.

After successfully locating the table, you can find all the table header (`th`) elements of that table:

```
var headers = myTable.getElementsByTagName("th");
for (var i = 0; i < headers.length; i++) {
    alert(headers[i].innerHTML);
}
```

The preceding code displays two popup dialogs, the first saying "First Name" and the second saying "Last Name."

To see this example in action, create an HTML document with the following contents, open it in the browser, and click the Test button. You can later modify the body of the `test` function inserting the code of the following examples.

```
<html>
  <head>
    <script type="text/javascript">
    <!--
        function test() {
            var myTable = document.getElementById("my-table");
            var headers = myTable.getElementsByTagName("th");
            for (var i = 0; i < headers.length; i++) {
                alert(headers[i].innerHTML);
            }
        }

    //-->
    </script>
  </head>
  <body>
    <table id="my-table" border="1">
        <tr>
            <th>First Name</th>
            <th>Last Name</th>
        </tr>
        <tr>
```

```
            <td>John</td>
            <td>Doe</td>
        </tr>
    </table>
    <br>
    <button type="button" onclick="test()">Test</button>
  </body>
</html>
```

Given a tree element, you can easily get its child elements:

```
var firstChild  = myTable.firstChild;
var lastChild   = myTable.lastChild;
var allChildren = myTable.childNodes;
```

After retrieving the wanted element, you can in turn get its children and so on. This allows you to navigate your way through the tree structure.

Modifying the Document Tree Structure

Let's use the DOM methods to dynamically insert an additional row of data in our table. First, we need to create the new row:

```
var newRow = document.createElement("tr");
```

Now create two new table cells (td elements):

```
var firstName = document.createElement("td");
var lastName = document.createElement("td");
```

We can now fill the new table cells with data:

```
firstName.innerHTML = "Jane";
lastName.innerHTML = "Smith";
```

Let's add the new cells to the new row:

```
newRow.appendChild(firstName);
newRow.appendChild(lastName);
```

Finally, add the new row to our table:

```
myTable.appendChild(newRow);
```

Figure 16-6 shows the updated table.

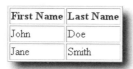

FIGURE 16-6: The table with the dynamically inserted row

The updated document tree is shown in Figure 16-7.

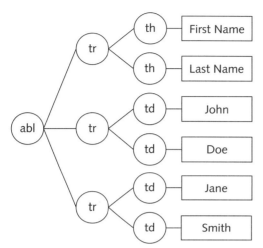

FIGURE 16-7: The document tree after a new row is dynamically inserted

Note The table example was intentionally simplified to keep things clear. The actual DOM structure might include a few elements that are added by the browser. You can examine the complete DOM structure and see if the preceding examples need any adjustments; I'll leave that exercise to you.

Tip If your HTML or XUL document is displayed on-screen, you do not have to instruct the browser to update its view after you modify the document tree. The browser determines automatically whether the update is needed and performs all the necessary redraws.

Changing Element's Attributes

For a final DOM example, let's change the `border` attribute of our table, making it four times wider:

```
myTable.setAttribute("border", "4");
```

Note We have demonstrated the use of the DOM methods on an HTML document. As previously mentioned, the same techniques can be used to access and modify an XML document. For example, the browser UI is implemented using XUL, meaning that you can use the DOM interfaces to dynamically access and modify the Mozilla user interface.

Additional DOM Resources

Following are some additional helpful resources for the DOM:

- The Mozilla DOM Reference is a great DOM resource: `http://www.mozilla.org/docs/dom/domref/`.

- The Mozilla DOM Documentation page has a lot of information on the DOM and its implementation in Mozilla: `http://www.mozilla.org/docs/dom/`.

XPCOM: Cross Platform Component Object Model

Components are software modules with well-defined functionality. They are the application building blocks that can be combined in a program at runtime.

There are many benefits to developing software that employs components. Two of these benefits are listed here:

- Using components allows us to ignore their implementation; in fact, we need know nothing about implementation. All we need to know is the component interface — its set of methods and properties. The component author can change the way the component performs some action, or fix a bug, and provide a new version of the component. As long as the interface remains the same, our program doesn't have to change to accommodate the new implementation.

- The same component can be seamlessly used from many different software environments. The component interface doesn't assume anything about the operating system, programming language, or a program that will use the component. For example, Cross Platform Component Object Model (XPCOM) components in Mozilla can be used from C++, JavaScript, and other environments. Typically, these components can be reused in all Mozilla products without your needing to rewrite them for any specific target application.

Mozilla's Component Object Model, XPCOM, allows building cross-platform components and later using them in Mozilla-based applications. This book focuses on using XPCOM components rather than creating them.

Note Mozilla XPCOM technology is somewhat similar to Microsoft COM. Both technologies share the principles of component-based design, but while XPCOM is an open-source and cross-platform framework, Microsoft COM can be used on Windows only. The two technologies are not compatible; COM components cannot be used as XPCOM components and vice versa.

When you are writing a program in Mozilla you have access to a wide range of components and interfaces. In fact, almost any functionality you might need will be available to you as an XPCOM component. Some of the component categories are as follows:

- **Browser:** These interfaces allow you to access the browser history, autocomplete, download, and other functionalities.

- **Clipboard:** Interfaces that allow you to programmatically cut and paste content to the clipboard.

- **File:** A set of components and interfaces that can be used to access, list, and modify files and directories.

- **DOM:** These interfaces mostly correspond to the W3C DOM interface definitions.

- **Network:** Interfaces that allow you to open network connections, transfer information, and more.

- **Preferences:** These interfaces can be used to retrieve and modify the user preferences.

Note Mozilla is a dynamic platform; things are updated and improved with every new release. Unfortunately, this sometimes means that some interfaces change from time to time, and your program will need to be modified accordingly. Many Mozilla interfaces are defined as "frozen," meaning that they are not going to change in future versions of Mozilla. If your program relies only on such interfaces, you can be sure that it will work with future versions of Mozilla.

Following is an example for using XPCOM from JavaScript. We will use the preferences interface to determine the user's default text color. First, we need to obtain the XPCOM preferences service object:

```
var prefs = Components.classes["@mozilla.org/preferences-service;1"];
prefs = prefs.getService(Components.interfaces.nsIPrefBranch);
```

First, we use the `classes` array that is a part of the `Components` object to find the specific XPCOM component. The elements of this array are indexed by a contract id, a string that uniquely identifies each component. In our case, `@mozilla.org/preferences-service;1` identifies the preferences service, the component used for accessing the user preferences. After finding the wanted component, we can get the specific component object by using the `getService` method and specifying the wanted interface, in our case `nsIPrefBranch`.

Note Some components are defined as *services* (or singletons), meaning that only one instance of the component exists in the application. These components are obtained using the `getService` method. Nonservice components can have many different instances. To create a new component instance, use the `createInstance` method. The component documentation should state whether the component is a service.

After obtaining the wanted interface, we can call one of its functions. For example, we can use the `getCharPref` method of the `nsIPrefBranch` interface to obtain the value of a user preference:

```
var color = prefs.getCharPref("browser.display.foreground_color");
```

This code retrieves the default text color specified by the user in the browser Options dialog.

This section demonstrated the principles and the advantages of component-based design. Mozilla XPCOM technology uses these principles and provides a framework for developing, registering, and using components in your Mozilla-based programs. You saw some examples of the available XPCOM components and how you can use these components in your JavaScript code.

Additional XPCOM Resources

Some helpful XPCOM resources follow:

- The Mozilla XPCOM page has links to many additional resources: `http://www.mozilla.org/projects/xpcom/`.

- A great reference of the available XUL components and interfaces can be found on the XUL Planet XPCOM Reference page: `http://www.xulplanet.com/references/xpcomref/`.

Introduction to Firefox Extension Programming

The previous sections provided some basic explanations of the main Mozilla technologies. Armed with that understanding, you can consider writing your first Mozilla-based product, a Firefox extension. This section introduces you to the main concepts of extension programming.

What Are Firefox Extensions?

Firefox extensions are Mozilla-based programs that can be integrated into the browser and that enhance it in many ways. As you have seen in the previous sections, the Mozilla platform is very flexible and extensible by nature. This means that almost anything in your browser can be modified, tweaked, or extended using the extension mechanisms. Some extensions go one step further by introducing new and innovative features while seamlessly integrating them with the browser.

 Note The term *plugin* is sometimes mistakenly used for Mozilla extensions. In Mozilla, there is a distinction between extensions and plugins. A *browser plugin* is a small program designed to handle a specific types of content (MIME types) that can be embedded in the browser. For example, the Adobe Acrobat Reader plugin handles PDF files, the Macromedia Flash plugin enables seeing Flash content in HTML pages, and the Apple QuickTime plugin allows playing embedded QuickTime video and audio files.

Extensions play an important role in Firefox philosophy. The browser itself is very lean and free of clutter, which makes it exceptionally compact and user friendly. Extensions are the optional building blocks that allow users to construct their personal dream browser, the one that has all the needed features and none of the unwanted ones. This philosophy is somewhat similar to hi-fi component systems — you can get the best amplifier and CD player that money can buy. If at some later point you decide you want to give your old vinyl records a spin, you can get a nice turntable and hook that in. The idea is that you are in control of your system; you can add and remove any component at any time, always making sure that each component is of the highest quality. This also allows the maker of each component, or in our case, extension, to focus on that specific component and provide the best set of features possible.

What Extensions Can Do

Following is a list of some examples of what extensions can do:

- **Extend the existing functionality:** There are many extensions that enhance the bookmarking, downloading, tabbed browsing, and other components of the browser. For example, extensions can allow you to download several files at once or to reorder the tabs using drag-and-drop.

- **Assist web developers:** Extensions can assist you with inspecting, creating, modifying, and validating HTML documents, style sheets, JavaScript programs, and so on. The browser is the perfect platform for performing these tasks, and the Mozilla framework provides the necessary tools for creating such extensions.

- **Make editing web forms more convenient:** There are extensions that can spell-check your posts, insert formatting tags for various forum systems, and even automatically fill out some forms to save you time.

- **Navigation and accessibility:** Extensions make browsing more convenient by adding new and alternative ways of doing routine things. There are *mouse gesture* extensions that allow you to perform many tasks by simply moving your mouse in a special way. Some extensions add useful context menu items and toolbar buttons for easy navigation between search results, opening new windows and tabs, and so on.

- **Page display modification:** Extensions can be used to change the way the browser displays web pages. There are extensions that block ads and other unwanted content, add screenshots and similar useful information to search results, enlarge some elements of the page, and much more.

- **Search and web site integration:** Extensions allow your browser to be tightly integrated with web sites and search engines. For example, some extensions allow you to easily post to your blog, search for some term using your favorite search engine, or translate the current page with your preferred web translation site.

- **Applications:** Extensions are not limited to creating small browser tweaks and enhancements. Complete applications have been implemented as Mozilla extensions. I already mentioned the ChatZilla IRC client. There are also an FTP client, a Calendar, several RSS readers, and many other XUL applications that can be installed into the browser. There is an ongoing project called XULRunner that allows such applications to be used in a standalone mode without needing a browser.

- **Various user experience enhancements:** Extensions can be used to do many useful things not directly related to the Web or browsing. For example, there are extensions that can conveniently display the current time, weather forecasts, or even control the music playing on your computer from the browser window.

As you can see, extensions can do almost anything and can greatly enhance your browsing experience. Hundreds of extensions have already been developed. But there is always room for creativity and innovation — with some imagination, the sky is the limit.

Extension Ingredients

So what are the basic ingredients of an extension? Extensions are created using Mozilla technologies introduced in previous sections of this chapter. This means that you can create a full-featured extension using only your text editor.

Most extensions will need to interact with the user on some level, meaning that they will need a user interface. The user interface is defined in one or more XUL documents. Mozilla has a mechanism called *dynamic overlays* that allows a XUL document to be overlaid with another XUL document to either extend or modify it. Typically, an extension will use this mechanism to extend the browser XUL.

The extension uses JavaScript to implement its functionality. More advanced extensions contain custom XPCOM components written either in JavaScript or C++.

The extension can have a skin. A *skin* is a set of style sheets (CSS files) and graphics that determine how the user interface of the extension looks.

An extension can have any number of *locales*. As mentioned earlier, all text strings that a XUL interface presents to the user should be defined in a separate file, and the XUL document should contain references to these strings only. This allows the user interface to be easily translated to other languages. Extensions can use this mechanism; they can contain several sets of translated strings, and the browser will determine which language is the most appropriate for the user.

So basically, an extension is a set of XUL-user interface definitions, JavaScript files that define the extension functionality, CSS and image files that define the extension presentation, and some string tables that allow the extension to be translated into other languages.

The Extension Manager

The Extensions dialog allows you to install, update, configure, disable, and uninstall extensions. In Firefox, you can open the Extensions dialog by selecting Extensions in the browser Tools menu. Figure 16-8 shows the Extensions dialog.

Note that while the dialog is named simply Extensions, it is frequently referred to as Extension Manager on Firefox wiki, forums, and elsewhere in this book.

FIGURE 16-8: The Extensions dialog

An extension is a regular ZIP archive file with an XPI extension. The archive contains all the extension files: XUL documents, style sheets, and so on. It also contains files with some extension metadata, including its name and version number, its skins, locales, components, and so on. You don't have to write any installation code for your extension; you specify only the contents of your extension package, and the Extensions Manager takes care of the actual installation for you. You learn about the structure of the extension package and its metadata in the next chapter.

An extension can be installed either directly from the Internet by clicking an appropriate install link or by first downloading it to your computer and then opening it with your browser. When installing an extension, the Extensions Manager first checks whether the extension is compatible with the user's Firefox version. The extension must specify the Firefox version number range it is compatible with, and by examining this information, the Extensions Manager can determine whether the extension is compatible.

After verifying that the extension is compatible, the Extensions Manager copies it to its final destination folder (typically the user profile folder), extracts the needed files, and registers the extension with the browser.

Note   Currently, Firefox must be restarted to complete the extension installation process. Future Firefox versions may support installing and registering extensions on the fly.

After the extension is installed, it is visible in the Extensions dialog. You can use this dialog to get some information about the installed extensions, their version number, author, home page, and so on. Some extensions implement an Options dialog that can be used to configure the extensions. This dialog is also accessible from the Extensions dialog.

Firefox has an update mechanism that allows new extension versions to be automatically downloaded and installed when they are available. An extension can specify a URL of a configuration file with information about the latest available version of the extension. Firefox periodically queries this file and sees whether a new extension version is available. If it finds a new version, it displays a dialog that informs the user about the new version. If the user decides to update the extension, Firefox automatically downloads and installs the new version.

 Note If an extension doesn't specify a custom update file URL, Firefox tries to query the Mozilla Update site for a new version of the extension.

You can manually check whether a new extension version is available by opening the extension context menu in the Extensions dialog and choosing Update.

When you no longer need an extension, you can either disable it or completely uninstall it from your browser. Both operations can be performed in the Extensions dialog. When an extension is uninstalled, it is first unregistered from the various browser configuration files, and then its files are removed.

The next chapter provides further details about the Extensions dialog, the structure of an extension package, and other extension-related Mozilla mechanisms.

Summary

This chapter provided an overview of the main Mozilla technologies and explored the possibilities of Firefox extension programming. Get ready to dive deeper into the process of creating Firefox extensions in the next chapter.

Creating Extensions

This chapter explains how to create a fully functional Firefox extension from the ground up. The extension performs a simple but useful task — it monitors a specific web page and notifies you when the page content changes.

We start by creating the extension user interface and implementing its basic functionality. When the coding is finished, you learn how to package the extension, test it, and release it to the public. The last section introduces additional extension programming concepts and techniques you might find useful when developing your own extensions.

Tools for Creating Extensions and Themes

Before you can start working on your first extension, you will need to get a few programs and utilities: a text editor, a ZIP compression tool, and a graphics editor. You probably already have these tools installed on your computer, but if you don't, there are many excellent freeware programs available.

Text Editor

As you saw in Chapter 16, most of the Mozilla technologies are text-based. XUL user interfaces, JavaScript programs, and CSS style sheets are plain-text files that are created using a text editor. While any program that is capable of creating plain-text files will do, there are several features to look for in a good programming-oriented text editor:

- **Syntax highlighting:** The editor highlights different elements of your document with different colors. For example, in XUL documents, the tags, attributes, and the actual content are easily distinguishable because they are highlighted with three distinct colors. This feature greatly improves the readability of your documents.

Most text editors won't recognize XUL files as XML by default. You should look for an editor that can highlight XML and in which you can specify that XUL files are actually XML files.

- **Automatic indentation:** If you want to create readable XML documents, JavaScript programs, or any other structured text files, you should use indentation to emphasize the hierarchical structure of the document elements. For example, in XML files, the child elements should have greater indentation than their parent element:

```
<box>
    <button label="one"/>
    <button label="two"/>
</box>
```

  Editors with an autoindentation feature automatically indent the elements of your document according to its type.

- **Parentheses matching:** A good text editor warns you if you forget to close a previously opened parenthesis. This can save you a lot of debugging time further along the way. Some editors also allow you to see the correspondence between the opening and the closing parentheses, which can be a great troubleshooting tool.

- **Line numbering:** If there are problems or errors in your document, the browser (or a validation program) typically reports them along with the line number on which the error was encountered. A good text editor will display the current cursor position within the document and allows jumping directly to any given line number.

There are many excellent freeware text editors available:

- **JEdit:** A multiplatform programmer's text editor
- **VIM:** A flexible text editor that works on many operating systems
- **Crimson Editor:** Source editor for Windows
- **Nedit:** A multipurpose text editor for the X Window System

Dozens of additional text editors are available on the Web.

ZIP Format Compression Tool

Extensions are packaged using the ZIP compression format. There are a lot of great ZIP compression tools, many of which are free. If you are on Windows, you might want to look at one of the following programs:

- 7-Zip
- WinZip
- WinRar

Tip   If you want to automate the packaging process, you should get a ZIP tool with a command-line interface. For example, the free 7-Zip file archiver has a command-line utility called 7z.exe. You will see an example of how it can be used to automatically package your extension later in the chapter.

Graphics Editor

If you want your user interface to have icons, images, or any other graphic elements, you need to create them using a graphics editor. Similar to the other software tools mentioned, a great variety of graphics editors is available, starting with simple and lightweight utilities and going all the way to full-featured applications.

You will want your graphics editor to have several features. First, it should be able to handle GIF, PNG, and JPG image formats. The program should also be able to save transparent GIF and PNG files and give you some control over the saved format parameters, such as the number of colors in the GIF image palette. For creating more elaborate graphics, you might want an application that supports special effects such as drop shadow, emboss, and so on.

Some of the most popular graphics editor applications are as follows:

- **GIMP:** An advanced, free, multiplatform image editor
- **Adobe Photoshop:** A professional image editing application
- **Adobe Photoshop Elements:** A simplified (and much more affordable) version of Photoshop with most of the needed functionality
- **Corel Paint Shop Pro:** An advanced image editing application for Windows

Building Your First Extension

This section is a tutorial for creating, packaging, and deploying Firefox extensions. You will learn how to create a fully functional extension, how to test and troubleshoot it, and finally, how to deploy it by publishing it on your web page and on other extension-related sites.

The extension we will create in this section is called SiteLeds. The idea is to have an icon, or a *status led,* on your Firefox status bar that displays the state of a given web page — whether it is available or not and, if so, whether it was recently changed. Such an extension has several uses: You can monitor your own website and make sure the server is up and running, or alternatively, you can watch some web page for changes and get a notification whenever the page is updated.

Introduction to Chrome

As you should know by now, the process of building applications with Mozilla is very similar to building dynamic web pages. Typically, a web page is an HTML document that defines the page contents, a JavaScript program that adds some functionality to the page, and a CSS style sheet that determines its appearance. Building applications with Mozilla is very similar. The XUL document defines the user interface, the JavaScript makes it dynamic, and a style sheet specifies its presentation. Figure 17-1 demonstrates this concept.

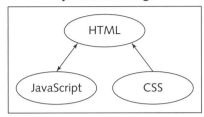

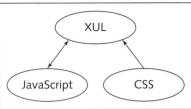

FIGURE 17-1: A comparison between a web page and a XUL application

To specify the address of any specific web resource, an HTML page, a CSS file, and so on, you use a Uniform Resource Locator (URL). For example, if you want to specify the official Firefox page, you can use its URL, `http://www.mozilla.org/products/firefox/index.html`. The `http` part means that the page should be fetched from the Web using the HTTP protocol. Similarly, when specifying application resources (XUL documents, CSS style sheets, and many other components of our application), you will use a `chrome` URL. The Web is the place where all the web pages are found. Similarly, the chrome contains all the elements of our application user interface. Figure 17-2 further clarifies this concept. One example of a chrome resource is the Firefox Options dialog, which can be found at the following address: `chrome://browser/content/pref/pref.xul`.

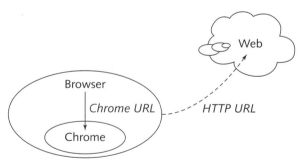

FIGURE 17-2: Web versus chrome resources

 Note As mentioned in the previous chapter, XUL applications can be run directly from the Web. We will be using the regular HTTP URLs to reference such applications. Chrome addresses are used to reference the components of the locally installed application, such as the browser itself or any of its extensions. Because XUL applications that are run directly from the Web can be potentially malicious, they have some security restrictions imposed on them by the browser. Installed components accessed through the chrome URL do not have such restrictions.

Let's use our web address analogy to introduce some additional concepts. For the browser to be able to find a web page using its URL, the page domain (`mozilla.org` in our previous example) must be first registered in a *domain registry*. Similarly, for Mozilla to locate the files that define a XUL application, the packages that contain these files must be first registered in the *chrome registry*. When a browser receives a chrome URL, it looks into the chrome registry, obtains the installation locations of the needed files, and then loads the documents from these locations. Using this method for accessing our application resources allows us to be independent of the physical location of the files, as long as the chrome registry contains the correct information.

A typical chrome URL looks like this:

```
chrome://<package name>/<type>/<filename>
```

Take a closer look at the different parts of the chrome URL:

- `chrome:`: This means that we want a chrome resource.

- `package name`: The package of the wanted file. Typically, every Mozilla application is split into several packages. For example, Firefox consists of browser, mozapps, help, and so on. An extension is usually a separate package with its own package name.

- `type`: There are three chrome resource types:

    - **content:** XUL and JavaScript documents are located in the content part of the package. This part contains the definition of the user interface and its behavior.

    - **skin:** This part contains the files that determine the appearance of the user interface, typically CSS style sheets and images. Separating this part from the content allows having several skins in the same package. The browser can determine which skin to display based on the user's current browser theme.

    - **locale:** All user interface strings and messages should be located in this part of the chrome package. Separating them from the content part allows the package to contain several sets of strings, each translated into a different language. The browser determines which translation to use based on its current user interface language. The string resources are usually specified in XML Document Type Definition (DTD) and JavaScript property files (more on this later in this chapter).

Figure 17-3 demonstrates the structure of a typical chrome package.

Note   You don't have to keep the content, locale, and skin parts packaged in the same physical file. While this is often the case, a logical package specified in the chrome URL can actually be composed of several physical chrome package files. For example, you can add a translation to an existing logical package by installing and registering a separate locale package file.

Some examples of chrome URLs follow:

- `chrome://browser/content/browser.xul`: The browser.xul file defines the user interface of the main browser window. As you can see, it is a part of the browser package and located in the content part of this package, as expected.

- `chrome://inspector/content/inspector.xul`: The main window of the DOM inspector extension is defined in the inspector.xul file. This file is a part of the inspector package.

- `chrome://browser/skin/browser.css`: This is the main browser style sheet. If there are several sets of skins in the browser package, each containing a different browser.css file, the correct one will be used, according to the current browser theme.

- `chrome://browser/locale/browser.dtd`: This is the address of the main browser string table. Note that nothing specifies the specific language or locale in the URL. If the locale part of the browser package contains several browser.dtd files (each in a different language), the URL is resolved to the string table file that contains the strings in the user's language.

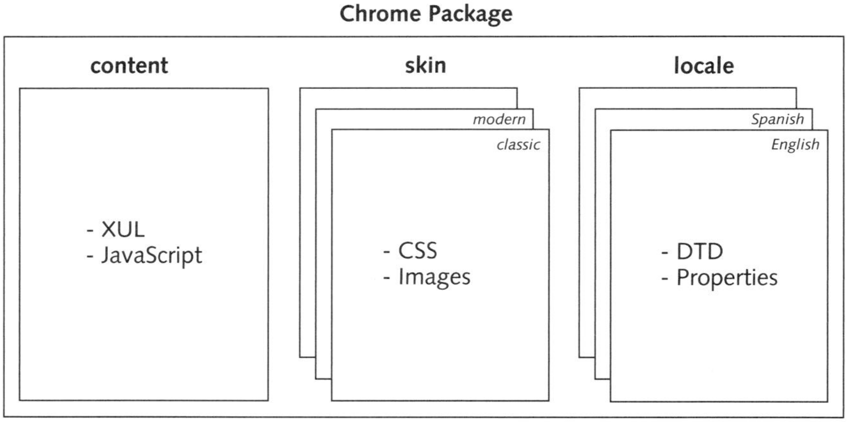

Chrome Package

FIGURE 17-3: The structure of a typical chrome package

Creating the SiteLeds Extension

In this section, we create the first fully functioning version of our extension. We create the various components of the extension: its XUL user interface definition, its functionality written in JavaScript, and its CSS style sheet. Then you see how to package these components and create the final installable extension file.

Building the User Interface

The user interface of our first extension is extremely simple. Because we want to add an icon to the status bar, our user interface consists of a single `statusbarpanel` element:

```
<statusbarpanel class="statusbarpanel-iconic"
                id="siteleds-statusbar-panel"/>
                tooltiptext="SiteLeds Status Icon"
                sitestate="unknown"/>
```

We are using the `statusbarpanel-iconic` class to specify that the status panel will display an icon. Also, we gave our status bar panel a unique id so we can find it later, using the DOM methods from JavaScript, and apply different styles to it, using CSS.

The `tooltiptext` attribute specifies the text that will appear on the panel tooltip.

We have added a new private attribute called `sitestate` to our panel. This attribute specifies the current site status and is useful in applying different styles to our panel widget.

Integrating the New Element into Firefox

Now that we have created our user interface element, how do we let the browser know that we want this new element to appear on the status bar? Mozilla has a mechanism called *dynamic overlays* that allows the user interface to be modified dynamically without changing the actual document that defines it. In our example, we add an element to the Firefox status bar without modifying the browser XUL definition file.

The procedure for creating a dynamic overlay is straightforward:

1. Create a separate XUL document that specifies all the needed additions and modifications to the original user interface.

2. The root element of the new XUL document is `overlay`. This specifies that the children of this element are inserted into a target document (or are overlaid on top of it).

   Define any number of child elements under the `overlay`. The `id` attribute of these elements will be matched against the ids of the elements in the document being overlaid, and if there is a match, the two elements will be merged.

3. You need to perform one additional step to let Mozilla know which XUL documents are overlays and what their target documents are. The following sections explore how this is done.

Let's modify our XUL definition to specify that we want our status bar panel to appear on the main browser status bar:

```
<overlay id="siteleds-overlay"
        xmlns="http://www.mozilla.org/keymaster/gatekeeper/there.is.only.xul">
    <statusbar id="status-bar">
        <statusbarpanel class="statusbarpanel-iconic"
                id="siteleds-statusbar-panel"
                tooltiptext="SiteLeds Status Icon"
                sitestate="unknown"
                insertbefore="statusbar-display"/>
    </statusbar>
</overlay>
```

Let's see exactly what we have done:

■ We have defined an `overlay` element. Its `id` attribute uniquely identifies it, and the value of the `xmlns` attribute specifies that the default name space of our XML document is XUL, meaning that all its children are XUL elements.

- We have created a child `statusbar` element in the `overlay` node. Its `id` is `status-bar`, which is identical to the `id` of the main Firefox `statusbar` element. This means that our status bar is overlaid on top of the Firefox status bar.

- Because our status bar element is merged into the Firefox status bar, all the child elements of our status bar — in this case, a single `statusbarpanel` element — are added to the child elements of the Firefox status bar. We can use the `insertbefore` attribute to specify the exact position at which the new status bar panel is inserted. In this case, we want it to be inserted just before the element with the `statusbar-display` id, which is the element that displays the current browser status. Figure 17-4 shows the position of the new status bar panel.

The SiteLeds status panel

FIGURE 17-4: The position of the new status bar panel

Note Dynamic overlays can be used not only to add new elements to existing ones but also to modify the attributes of the existing elements and to add new top-level elements to the target window.

Defining the Appearance

We want our status bar panel to display different icons, depending on the current state of the monitored site. Table 17-1 specifies the various icons that are displayed according to the `sitestate` attribute of our `statusbarpanel` element.

Table 17-1   Displayed Icons

State	Icon	Icon Filename	Meaning
unknown		state-unknown.png	The site state is unknown.
ok		state-ok.png	The page is reachable and hasn't been modified.
error		state-error.png	There was an error connecting to the site.
modified		state-modified.png	The monitored page has been modified.

Our style sheet document, siteledsOverlay.css, will therefore look like this:

```
#siteleds-statusbar-panel[sitestate="unknown"] {
    list-style-image: url("chrome://siteleds/skin/state-unknown.png");
}

#siteleds-statusbar-panel[sitestate="ok"] {
    list-style-image: url("chrome://siteleds/skin/state-ok.png");
}

#siteleds-statusbar-panel[sitestate="error"] {
    list-style-image: url("chrome://siteleds/skin/state-error.png");
}

#siteleds-statusbar-panel[sitestate="modified"] {
    list-style-image: url("chrome://siteleds/skin/state-modified.png");
}
```

As you can see, we are selecting our status bar panel by its id attribute (`siteleds-statusbar-panel`), and specifying which icon to display by defining different rules for different values of the `sitestate` attribute. The icon we want to appear on the status bar is specified using the CSS `list-style-image` attribute.

Adding the Functionality

We want our extension to try to load a given web page. If this load operation succeeds, the extension checks whether the page was modified by comparing its content with the one saved during the previous request. Our JavaScript code then sets the value of the `sitestate` attribute of our status panel according to the result of this operation.

We will create the JavaScript implementation file named siteledsOverlay.js.

First, let's define some global variables:

```
var gSiteLedsLastRequest = null;
var gSiteLedsLastContent = null;
```

These variables contain the last HTTP request object and the contents of the last loaded page.

The main function that initiates the page load request is called `siteLedsCheckPage`:

```
function siteLedsCheckPage() {
    var pageURL = 'http://www.iosart.com/firefox/siteleds/index.html';
    gSiteLedsLastRequest = new XMLHttpRequest();
    gSiteLedsLastRequest.onload = siteLedsPageLoaded;
    gSiteLedsLastRequest.onerror = siteLedsPageError;
    gSiteLedsLastRequest.open('GET', pageURL);
    gSiteLedsLastRequest.send(null);
}
```

This function does the following:

1. Creates a new `XMLHttpRequest` object. This object is used to perform HTTP requests.

2. Adds two event handlers. The `siteLedsPageLoaded` function is called when the server responds to our query, and the `siteLedsPageError` function is executed in case an error occurs during the HTTP request.

3. Initializes and sends an HTTP Get request for the specified web page.

Our error handling function looks like this:

```
function siteLedsPageError() {
    var ledElement = document.getElementById('siteleds-statusbar-panel');
    ledElement.setAttribute('sitestate', 'error');
    setTimeout(siteLedsCheckPage, 900000);
}
```

This function is called if there is an error during the attempt to load the monitored web page (for example, if the network connection is down). We first find our status panel element using the DOM `getElementById` method. Then we set the value of the `sitestate` attribute to `error`. This, along with our style sheet definitions, will make the error icon appear on the status bar. Finally, we call the `setTimeout` function to try to perform the same test again after 900,000 milliseconds (15 minutes).

If the server responds to our HTTP request, the `siteLedsPageLoaded` function is called:

```
function siteLedsPageLoaded() {
    var ledElement = document.getElementById('siteleds-statusbar-panel');

    if (gSiteLedsLastRequest.status == 200) {
        var prevContent = gSiteLedsLastContent;
        gSiteLedsLastContent = gSiteLedsLastRequest.responseText;
        if ((prevContent != null) && (prevContent != gSiteLedsLastContent)) {
            ledElement.setAttribute('sitestate', 'modified');
        } else {
            ledElement.setAttribute('sitestate', 'ok');
            setTimeout(siteLedsCheckPage, 900000);
        }
```

```
    } else {
        ledElement.setAttribute('sitestate', 'error');
        setTimeout(siteLedsCheckPage, 900000);
    }
}
```

First, we check whether the server returned HTTP status code 200 (OK). If so, the page was loaded correctly, and we can check whether it has changed since the last time we successfully loaded it. We compare the contents of the current and the previously loaded pages and, depending on the outcome of this comparison, set the current state to either ok or modified. If the server returned a status code other than 200, we set the state of our panel to error. Also, if the page wasn't modified, we schedule a new test to 15 minutes from now by calling the setTimeout function.

After defining all the needed functions, we must tell Firefox to start the site checking cycle when it loads by adding the following line at the top level of our JavaScript file:

```
window.addEventListener("load", siteLedsCheckPage, false);
```

This adds an event handler for the window load event, meaning that our siteLedsCheckPage function will be called after the main Firefox window is first opened and initialized.

Note The JavaScript functions and global variables we have defined are evaluated in the global namespace along with the other Firefox JavaScript code. This means that if one of our functions or variables has the same name as an existing identifier, we will have a name collision. To avoid this situation, you should always create a unique string ("siteLeds" in our case) and use it as a prefix for all your global identifiers. The following sections describe another technique for avoiding such conflicts.

The final siteledsOverlay.js file is as follows:

```
var gSiteLedsLastRequest = null;
var gSiteLedsLastContent = null;

function siteLedsCheckPage() {
    var pageURL = 'http://www.iosart.com/firefox/siteleds/index.html';
    gSiteLedsLastRequest = new XMLHttpRequest();
    gSiteLedsLastRequest.onload = siteLedsPageLoaded;
    gSiteLedsLastRequest.onerror = siteLedsPageError;
    gSiteLedsLastRequest.open('GET', pageURL);
    gSiteLedsLastRequest.send(null);
}

function siteLedsPageError() {
    var ledElement = document.getElementById('siteleds-statusbar-panel');
    ledElement.setAttribute('sitestate', 'error');
    setTimeout(siteLedsCheckPage, 900000);
}
```

```
function siteLedsPageLoaded() {
    var ledElement = document.getElementById('siteleds-statusbar-panel');

    if (gSiteLedsLastRequest.status == 200) {
        var prevContent = gSiteLedsLastContent;
        gSiteLedsLastContent = gSiteLedsLastRequest.responseText;
        if ((prevContent != null) && (prevContent != gSiteLedsLastContent)) {
            ledElement.setAttribute('sitestate', 'modified');
        } else {
            ledElement.setAttribute('sitestate', 'ok');
            setTimeout(siteLedsCheckPage, 900000);
        }
    } else {
        ledElement.setAttribute('sitestate', 'error');
        setTimeout(siteLedsCheckPage, 900000);
    }
}

window.addEventListener("load", siteLedsCheckPage, false);
```

Making the Extension Localizable

As mentioned in the previous chapter, XUL documents shouldn't contain any literal strings that are presented to the user. Instead, you should define all such strings in a separate file and make your XUL document reference them. This allows the extension to be easily translated to a different language. All you need to do is to provide an additional file with the translated strings.

Currently, our XUL element looks like this:

```
<statusbarpanel class="statusbarpanel-iconic"
                id="siteleds-statusbar-panel"/>
                tooltiptext="SiteLeds Status Icon"
                sitestate="unknown"
                insertbefore="statusbar-display"/>
```

As you can see, the "SiteLeds Status Icon" string is in English. If we want to translate our extension into a different language, we will need to modify the XUL file and provide two different versions of our extension. What if the extension is translated into a dozen languages?

Luckily, there is a better way. First, we define all the strings in a separate DTD file. DTD files are usually used to define the structure of XML elements, but they can also contain *entities*, which are XML variables that define common strings and allow them to be reused. Let's define our string as an XML entity in the siteledsOverlay.dtd file:

```
<!ENTITY siteLeds.tooltip "SiteLeds Status Icon">
```

We need to modify our XUL element accordingly:

```
<statusbarpanel class="statusbarpanel-iconic"
                id="siteleds-statusbar-panel"/>
                tooltiptext="&siteLeds.tooltip;"
                sitestate="unknown"
                insertbefore="statusbar-display"/>
```

We have replaced the literal string `"SiteLeds Status Icon"` with an XML entity reference `"&siteLeds.tooltip;"`.

The Final XUL File

We have created the CSS style sheet, the needed JavaScript functions, and a string table DTD file. How can we specify that our XUL document should use all these files? Look at the final version of our siteledsOverlay.xul document:

```
<?xml version="1.0"?>
<?xml-stylesheet href="chrome://siteleds/skin/siteledsOverlay.css"
                 type="text/css"?>

<!DOCTYPE overlay SYSTEM "chrome://siteleds/locale/siteledsOverlay.dtd">

<overlay id="siteleds-overlay"
         xmlns="http://www.mozilla.org/keymaster/gatekeeper/there.is.only.xul">

    <script type="application/x-javascript"
            src="chrome://siteleds/content/siteledsOverlay.js"/>

    <statusbar id="status-bar">
        <statusbarpanel class="statusbarpanel-iconic"
                id="siteleds-statusbar-panel"
                tooltiptext="&siteLeds.tooltip;"
                sitestate="unknown"
                insertbefore="statusbar-display"/>
    </statusbar>
</overlay>
```

An explanation of what's been added follows:

1. The `xml-stylesheet` XML instruction associates the siteledsOverlay.css style sheet with our XUL document. Please note that we are using chrome URLs, meaning that the extension package needs to be properly installed and registered before we can test our extension. You will see how this is done in the following sections.

2. The `DOCTYPE` declaration associates an external DTD file named siteledsOverlay.dtd with our XUL document.

3. The `script` element specifies that the document should import and use the siteledsOverlay.js JavaScript file.

Packaging the Extension

This section explains where the files we have created in the previous sections should be located and how they should be packaged to create an installable extension file.

In addition to the extension files already created, we need to create an install manifest and several configuration files for correctly registering our extension package in the chrome registry.

Extension Directory Structure

In the "Introduction to Chrome" section, you saw that the chrome package has three logical parts: content, skin, and locale. During the development process, the physical directory structure of our extension will follow this logical partition. The top-level directory in the extension directory tree will contain the install manifest file named install.rdf (more on this shortly) and a directory named chrome. The chrome directory contains three subdirectories:

- **content:** Contains XUL documents and JavaScript files.

- **skin:** Contains one or more skin sets, each in a separate subdirectory. A skin is any number of CSS style sheet files and images. Our extension contains only one skin located in the subdirectory named classic.

- **locale:** Contains one or more locale sets, each containing a different translation of the user interface and located in a separate subdirectory. The string tables are located in DTD files (for strings used in XML documents) and Property files (for strings used in JavaScript programs). Our extension initially contains only English strings located in a subdirectory named en-US.

Figure 17-5 shows this directory structure.

```
⊟ 🗀 siteleds
    ⊟ 🗀 chrome
        🗀 content
    ⊟ 🗀 locale
        🗀 en-US
    ⊟ 🗀 skin
        🗀 classic
```

FIGURE 17-5: The extension directory structure

Note The directory structure described in this section is only a suggestion. Arranging your files in this directory hierarchy during development is convenient and allows easy packaging of your extension at the later stages, but as you see in the following sections, the extension mechanism doesn't assume anything about the locations of your chrome directories. You can change the locations of these directories and their names, as long as your manifest files are adjusted to reflect these changes.

Creating Old-Style Chrome Manifest Files

If we merely package together all the files we have created, Firefox has no way of knowing how to register them in the chrome registry. We need to provide additional files called *chrome manifests* that describe the package contents. There are two styles of chrome manifest. The old-style files, used in Firefox versions prior to 1.1, are RDF files called contents.rdf. The new-style manifest mechanism introduced in Firefox 1.1 greatly simplifies matters by requiring a single plain-text chrome manifest file. This section covers the old-style manifests, and the new manifest is described in the following sections.

Each directory that contains a chrome package part, in our case `content`, `skin/classic`, and `locale/en-US`, must contain a file named contents.rdf. Each contents.rdf file describes the contents of the package directory and is used during the extension installation for registering the package in the chrome registry, so the files can be accessed using chrome URLs.

Note The following examples use the name siteleds to denote our package. When creating a new extension, give it a unique name and replace all the occurrences of siteleds with the name of your extension.

The contents.rdf file is an XML document with a special syntax. Look at the contents.rdf located in our content directory:

```
<?xml version="1.0"?>

<RDF:RDF xmlns:RDF="http://www.w3.org/1999/02/22-rdf-syntax-ns#"
         xmlns:chrome="http://www.mozilla.org/rdf/chrome#">

    <RDF:Seq about="urn:mozilla:package:root">
        <RDF:li resource="urn:mozilla:package:siteleds"/>
    </RDF:Seq>

    <RDF:Description about="urn:mozilla:package:siteleds"
            chrome:displayName="SiteLeds"
            chrome:author="Alex Sirota"
            chrome:name="siteleds"
            chrome:extension="true"/>

    <RDF:Seq about="urn:mozilla:overlays">
        <RDF:li resource="chrome://browser/content/browser.xul"/>
    </RDF:Seq>

    <RDF:Seq about="chrome://browser/content/browser.xul">
        <RDF:li>chrome://siteleds/content/siteledsOverlay.xul</RDF:li>
    </RDF:Seq>

</RDF:RDF>
```

Now look more closely at the different parts of this file:

- The following lines introduce a new package named siteleds that should be merged into the chrome registry:

```
<RDF:Seq about="urn:mozilla:package:root">
    <RDF:li resource="urn:mozilla:package:siteleds"/>
</RDF:Seq>
```

- Next, we describe the new package and its attributes:

```
<RDF:Description about="urn:mozilla:package:siteleds"
            chrome:displayName="SiteLeds"
            chrome:author="Alex Sirota"
            chrome:name="siteleds"
            chrome:extension="true"/>
```

- Now we specify that we are interested in overlaying the main browser user interface document `browser.xul`:

```
<RDF:Seq about="urn:mozilla:overlays">
    <RDF:li resource="chrome://browser/content/browser.xul"/>
</RDF:Seq>
```

- Finally, we specify which document will overlay the browser UI, in our case, `siteledsOverlay.xul`:

```
<RDF:Seq about="chrome://browser/content/browser.xul">
    <RDF:li>chrome://siteleds/content/siteledsOverlay.xul</RDF:li>
</RDF:Seq>
```

The manifest file located in the skin directory, `skin/classic/contents.rdf`, is simpler because it doesn't contain any overlay information:

```
<?xml version="1.0"?>

<RDF:RDF xmlns:chrome="http://www.mozilla.org/rdf/chrome#"
        xmlns:RDF="http://www.w3.org/1999/02/22-rdf-syntax-ns#">

    <RDF:Seq about="urn:mozilla:skin:root">
        <RDF:li resource="urn:mozilla:skin:classic/1.0" />
    </RDF:Seq>

    <RDF:Description about="urn:mozilla:skin:classic/1.0">
        <chrome:packages>
            <RDF:Seq about="urn:mozilla:skin:classic/1.0:packages">
                <RDF:li resource="urn:mozilla:skin:classic/1.0:siteleds"/>
            </RDF:Seq>
        </chrome:packages>
    </RDF:Description>
</RDF:RDF>
```

Here, we are specifying that our `siteleds` package includes a skin part that should be registered in the chrome registry.

Finally, here is the locale `contents.rdf` file, located in the `locale/en-US` directory:

```
<?xml version="1.0"?>

<RDF:RDF xmlns:chrome="http://www.mozilla.org/rdf/chrome#"
        xmlns:RDF="http://www.w3.org/1999/02/22-rdf-syntax-ns#">
```

```
<RDF:Seq about="urn:mozilla:locale:root">
    <RDF:li resource="urn:mozilla:locale:en-US"/>
</RDF:Seq>

<RDF:Description about="urn:mozilla:locale:en-US"
                 chrome:author="Alex Sirota"
                 chrome:displayName="English(US)"
                 chrome:name="en-US">
    <chrome:packages>
        <RDF:Seq about="urn:mozilla:locale:en-US:packages">
            <RDF:li resource="urn:mozilla:locale:en-US:siteleds"/>
        </RDF:Seq>
    </chrome:packages>
</RDF:Description>
</RDF:RDF>
```

This `contents.rdf` file specifies that our `siteleds` package contains an English (en-US) locale information.

Packaging the Chrome Files

When all your chrome files — XUL documents, JavaScript scripts, CSS style sheets, and so on — are ready, and you have created all the needed chrome manifest files, you should package the contents of the chrome directory, which typically contains three subdirectories (content, skin and locale), into a single ZIP archive. You should give this ZIP archive the same name as your extension package (in our case, siteleds) and a .jar extension. Figure 17-6 shows the contents of our siteleds.jar archive.

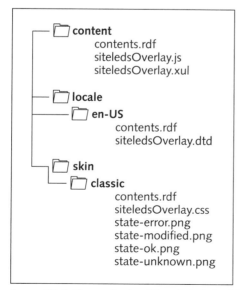

FIGURE 17-6: The contents of the siteleds.jar file

Creating the Install Manifest

The install manifest is a file that contains various information about the extension — its name, author, version number, what versions of Firefox it is compatible with, and so on. This file is called install.rdf, and it is located in the root directory of the extension directory tree.

The following code listing shows the SiteLeds install.rdf file:

```
<?xml version="1.0"?>

<RDF xmlns="http://www.w3.org/1999/02/22-rdf-syntax-ns#"
     xmlns:em="http://www.mozilla.org/2004/em-rdf#">

    <Description about="urn:mozilla:install-manifest">
        <em:id>{E1B2492D-E6AC-4221-A433-C143E3A1C71E}</em:id>
        <em:version>0.1</em:version>
        <em:name>SiteLeds</em:name>

        <em:description>Site Status Monitor</em:description>
        <em:creator>Alex Sirota</em:creator>
        <em:homepageURL>http://www.iosart.com/firefox/siteleds</em:homepageURL>

        <em:targetApplication>
            <Description>
                <em:id>{ec8030f7-c20a-464f-9b0e-13a3a9e97384}</em:id>
                <em:minVersion>0.9</em:minVersion>
                <em:maxVersion>1.1</em:maxVersion>
            </Description>
        </em:targetApplication>

        <em:file>
            <Description about="urn:mozilla:extension:file:siteleds.jar">
                <em:package>content/</em:package>
                <em:skin>skin/classic/</em:skin>
                <em:locale>locale/en-US/</em:locale>
            </Description>
        </em:file>
    </Description>
</RDF>
```

Take a closer look at the various parts of this file:

- The em:id property specifies the extension Globally Unique Identifier (GUID). GUID is a 128-bit number that uniquely identifies the extension. You should generate this unique number for every new extension you create. There are several utilities that can generate a GUID for you. On Windows, there is a guidgen utility that is available for download from the Microsoft site. On UNIX, there is a similar utility called uuidgen. There are also a number of websites that can be used to generate a GUID. If you have an IRC client installed, you can generate a GUID by visiting the #botbot channel on the irc.mozilla.org server and typing **botbot uuid**:

  ```
  <em:id>{E1B2492D-E6AC-4221-A433-C143E3A1C71E}</em:id>
  ```

- The `em:version` property specifies the version of your extension. The version should be in Firefox Version Format (FVF): major.minor.release.build[+]. Only the major part of the version number is mandatory, so 2, 1.1, 3.4.5, and 7.0.1.20050313 are all valid version numbers:

```
<em:version>0.1</em:version>
```

- The `em:name` specifies the name of the extension for being displayed in the user interface:

```
<em:name>SiteLeds</em:name>
```

- The `em:description`, `em:creator`, and `em:homepageURL` properties are optional and specify the extension description, its author, and home page. This information will be displayed in the Extension Manager dialog after the extension is installed:

```
<em:description>Site Status Monitor</em:description>
<em:creator>Alex Sirota</em:creator>
<em:homepageURL>http://www.iosart.com/firefox/siteleds</em:homepageURL>
```

- The `em:targetApplication` property specifies the application the extension is intended for and the range of versions of this application it is compatible with. The target application is specified using its GUID. For example, SiteLeds is compatible with Firefox versions 0.9 to 1.1:

```
<em:targetApplication>
    <Description>
        <em:id>{ec8030f7-c20a-464f-9b0e-13a3a9e97384}</em:id>
        <em:minVersion>0.9</em:minVersion>
        <em:maxVersion>1.1</em:maxVersion>
    </Description>
</em:targetApplication>
```

- The `em:file` property specifies the jar file that contains the extension chrome files and the various parts of the chrome package (content/skin/locale). For example, the SiteLeds chrome files are packaged into a siteleds.jar file, which contains `content`, `skin/classic`, and `locale/en-US` subdirectories:

```
<em:file>
    <Description about="urn:mozilla:extension:file:siteleds.jar">
        <em:package>content/</em:package>
        <em:skin>skin/classic/</em:skin>
        <em:locale>locale/en-US/</em:locale>
    </Description>
</em:file>
```

The `em:file` property isn't needed when using the new-style plain-text `chrome.manifest` chrome manifest.

Creating a New-Style Chrome Manifest File

In Firefox 1.1, there is a much simpler chrome manifest mechanism. All the information needed to describe the chrome contained in an extension package is specified in a single plain-text file named chrome.manifest and located in the root directory of the extension tree. When using the new manifest, you no longer need to create the contents.rdf files or specify the `em:file` property in the install.rdf install manifest.

The SiteLeds `chrome.manifest` file contains only four lines:

```
content siteleds jar:chrome/siteleds.jar!/content/
locale siteleds en-US jar:chrome/siteleds.jar!/locale/en-US/
skin siteleds classic/1.0 jar:chrome/siteleds.jar!/skin/classic/
overlay chrome://browser/content/browser.xul @ta
chrome://siteleds/content/siteledsOverlay.xul
```

The file structure is very simple and straightforward:

- Content package:

  ```
  content <package name> <path to files>
  ```

- Locale package:

  ```
  locale <package name> <locale name> <path to files>
  ```

- Skin package:

  ```
  skin <package name> <skin name> <path to files>
  ```

- XUL overlay:

  ```
  overlay <chrome://file to overlay> <chrome://overlay file>
  ```

Creating the Extension Installation Package

After creating the chrome JAR archive and the install.rdf install manifest, you can finally create the extension package that can be installed into Firefox. This package file will have an XPI extension, but just like the chrome JAR file, it is actually a regular ZIP archive.

Create a ZIP archive that contains the install.rdf file and the chrome directory at its root, and give it an XPI extension. The chrome subdirectory contains the chrome JAR file. If you are using the new-style chrome manifests, there should also be a chrome.manifest file at the topmost level of the XPI archive.

Preferably, give your XPI file a meaningful name, one that includes the extension name and its version. Figure 17-7 shows the contents of the SiteLeds_0.1.xpi archive.

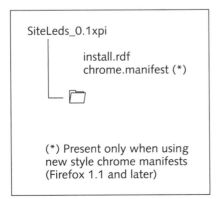

FIGURE 17-7: The contents of the SiteLeds XPI package

Later in this chapter, you will see how to automate the packaging process. If you want to package the extension manually, you can do the following:

1. Create a directory named build somewhere on your hard disk.

2. Copy the install.rdf file into this directory.

3. If using new-style chrome manifests, copy the chrome.manifest file into this directory.

4. Create a subdirectory named chrome under the build directory.

5. Copy the siteleds.jar file you created earlier into the newly created chrome directory.

6. Go to the build directory and zip up the install.rdf, chrome.manifest, and the chrome directory into the SiteLeds_0.1.xpi file.

Once your extension XPI package is ready, you can install it into Firefox and give it a try.

Tip

There are several ways to install a local XPI file into Firefox. You can open it using File ⇨ Open File . . . , or just drag your XPI file and drop it into the Firefox window.

Testing and Debugging Your Extension

As with any other program, there is a good chance that you will initially run into some problems with your extension. Things might work differently from what you were expecting or not work at all. There are several mechanisms you can use to troubleshoot your extension and help you find and fix those annoying bugs.

Tip

Some bugs in your extension, its packaging, or its chrome registration may break your browser and make it either partially or completely unusable. You can usually solve these problems by starting Firefox in safe mode (by using the -safe-mode command-line switch, for example) and uninstalling the extension, or by creating a new user profile.

Tip

If you see an error dialog saying "Chrome Registration Failed" when trying to install your extension, verify that the content of your manifest files is correct and that you have packaged all the needed files using the correct directory structure. Also, pressing the View Details button in this dialog can provide useful clues about the problem. For example, you can see whether the problem was in the content, skin, or locale part of your extension's chrome.

Preferences Settings

Several preferences settings in Firefox can assist you with the debugging process:

- `javascript.options.showInConsole`: Setting this preference to `true` instructs Firefox to show errors that originate in chrome files in the JavaScript Console. For example, a JavaScript function might be silently failing inside your extension, and, without seeing the error message, it may be very hard to pinpoint the problem.

- `javascript.options.strict`: When this preference is set to `true`, Firefox displays JavaScript warnings in the JavaScript Console. A warning usually means that you are doing something illegal or nonstandard in your code, and that might cause unexpected behavior or other problems. It is always recommended to solve all such problems before releasing your extension. Enabling this preference causes all the warnings, not only those originating in your extension, to be reported to the JavaScript Console. Many extensions have warnings in their code, and having several such extensions installed while trying to debug your own code might make finding only the relevant warnings difficult.

- `browser.dom.window.dump.enabled`: You should set this preference to `true` if you want to use the `dump()` function to print messages to the standard console. More information on this appears later in this chapter.

Tip

As with other preference settings, you can type **about:config** in your Firefox address bar and use the Preferences window to create new preferences and modify the existing ones. Other methods for setting preferences, such as modifying the prefs.js file, will also work.

Logging

Logging is a simple but very efficient method for debugging your code. Printing the values of your variables, the received messages, return codes, and so on can help you figure out where the problem is and how it can be solved. Logging can also be used to report major events and errors in your application, and looking at these messages can help you make sure that the application is actually doing what you expect it to do.

There are several logging mechanisms in Mozilla:

- **Standard Console:** You can use the `dump()` function to print messages to the standard console. Similar to the `alert()` function, `dump()` expects a single string argument. By default, the standard console is disabled in Firefox. To enable it, set the value of the `browser.dom.window.dump.enabled` preference to `true` and start Firefox with the `-console` command-line flag.

- **JavaScript Console:** This console can be opened using Tools ➪ JavaScript Console. To print a line to this console, you first obtain the `nsIConsoleService` interface and then call its `logStringMessage` method:

```
var consoleService = Components.classes['@mozilla.org/consoleservice;1']
                .getService(Components.interfaces.nsIConsoleService);
consoleService.logStringMessage("Testing 1 2 3");
```

Remove the debug messages before releasing your extension to the public. Having a lot of such messages printed can slow your code down and create an unnecessary clutter in the console window. You can create your own wrapper function that will determine whether the debug message should be printed:

```
function myPrintDebugMessage(message) {
    if (gMyDebugging) {
        dump(message);
    }
}
```

If you use the preceding function to print all your debug messages, toggling the value of the global `gMyDebugging` flag turns all the messages on and off.

Tip

You can often use the `alert()` function for basic debugging without needing any of the preceding logging mechanisms. Temporarily inserting a call to this function in the problematic piece of code can sometimes help you quickly figure out what the problem is.

Developer Extensions

Several extensions can be used to troubleshoot your extension. Some of these are listed here:

- The **DOM Inspector** can be used to examine the DOM structure of your documents, their styles, and much more.

- **Venkman** is an advanced Mozilla-based JavaScript debugger.

- **Extension developer's extension** can be used to quickly run JavaScript code snippets, edit XUL, HTML, and much more.

- **ColorZilla** can be used to quickly get various pieces of information about XUL elements, including their colors, ids, class names, and so on. You can also use ColorZilla to quickly launch the DOM Inspector on the selected element.

There are probably many other extensions you might find useful during the extension development process, and many new ones are being released all the time.

Deploying Your Extension

You have created your extension, packaged it, and fixed all the bugs found. Your creation is now ready for release to the public.

Most authors create a home page for their extension. The page typically contains some information about the extension, its author, and the latest version of the extension available for download. In addition, you will probably want your extension to be listed on one or more sites that host Mozilla extensions.

Note

The Mozdev.org site allows you to host your Mozilla extension project on their servers and provides many useful tools for managing the development process and collaborating with other developers. Your extension must be released under an Open Source license to qualify for being hosted at Mozdev.

Configuring Your Server

Firefox allows extensions to be installed directly from the Web without their having to be downloaded to the local disk first. Giving your file an XPI extension and putting it on a web server isn't enough for it to be installable directly from your site. Your web server should send this file using the correct MIME type, `application/x-xpinstall`. With Apache, this can be achieved by creating an `.htaccess` file that has the following line:

```
AddType application/x-xpinstall xpi
```

Inserting the preceding directive into an .htaccess file and placing this file in a directory on your server allows you to change the MIME settings for this directory only, including all its subdirectories. Adding a similar line to the main httpd.conf file can make the setting global. Also, many web hosting providers won't give you access to the main http.conf file of your web server but will allow you to place local .htaccess files in your directories.

Creating JavaScript Installer Links

You can create a direct link to your XPI file on your web page, and if the file is sent using the `application/x-xpinstall` MIME type, clicking this link triggers the Firefox install mechanism:

```
<a href="http://www.iosart.com/firefox/siteleds/SiteLeds_0.1.xpi"
    title="Install SiteLeds (right-click to download)">Install SiteLeds 0.1</a>
```

There is an alternative way of triggering the extension installation process. A global object called `InstallTrigger` is available to scripts running in web pages. You can use this object's methods to trigger the installation process and to verify that the extension was indeed successfully installed. Using this method also allows you to specify a custom icon that will appear in the installation dialog.

An example of using `InstallTrigger` follows:

```
<script type="text/javascript" language="JavaScript">

    function installCallback(name, result) {
     alert('The installation of ' + name +
             ' finished with a result code of ' + result);
    }

    function installExtension(aEvent) {
     var params = {
       "SiteLeds": { URL: aEvent.target.href,
                     IconURL: 'http://www.iosart.com/firefox/siteleds/logo.png',
                     toString: function () { return this.URL; }
       }
     };

     // trigger the installation process:
     var res = InstallTrigger.install(params, installCallback);
     if (!res) {
         alert('Error calling install');
     }

     return false;
    }

</script>

<a href="http://www.iosart.com/firefox/siteleds/SiteLeds_0.1.xpi"
    title="Install SiteLeds (right-click to download)"
    onclick="return installExtension(event);">Install SiteLeds 0.1</a>
```

Take a closer look at what we have done:

1. Adding an `onclick="return installExtension(event)` to the anchor HTML element causes the `intallExtension` function to be called when the link is clicked. The `onclick` handler returns `false`, preventing the default anchor click action from being performed.

2. Inside the `installExtension` function, we define the parameter object for the `install` method. This object contains the URLs of the extension XPI package and its icon.

3. We then call the `InstallTrigger.install` function. The second parameter is the name of the function that will be called when the installation completes (or in case the user cancels the installation).

4. If `InstallTrigger.install` returns a zero result, there was a problem starting the installation process. For example, your site may not be on the user's white list for sites that are allowed to install extensions. In this case, the user should see a Firefox notification, but you can further explain the situation by displaying an appropriate popup message or redirecting the user to an explanation page, for example.

5. When the installation process finishes or is cancelled by the user, the `installCallback` function is called. This function receives two parameters: the URL of the extension package and the installation result code. A zero result code means successful installation.

Getting Your Extension Listed

There are several sites that list Mozilla extensions. Users often visit these sites to check out the new extensions or when they are looking for an extension with a specific functionality. If you want people to notice your new extension, you should have it listed on one or more of the following sites:

- **Mozilla Update** (`addons.mozilla.org`): This is the official Mozilla extensions site. The Extension Manager dialog links to it, and this makes it the first place that the users look for new extensions. The site contains a FAQ with information about getting your extension listed.

- **The Extension Mirror** (`www.extensionsmirror.nl`): A very active site with the largest index of the existing extensions. The site administrators actively look for new extensions on the Web and on the MozillaZine forums and publish them on the site, so theoretically you don't have to do anything to get your extension listed. The Extension Mirror has an Announcements forum where you can announce your extension to make sure it is noticed by the administrators.

- **The Extension Room** (`extensionroom.mozdev.org`): A popular index of Mozilla extensions. The site has instructions for getting your extension listed.

- **The MozillaZine Extensions Forum** (`forums.mozillazine.org`): Many extension authors announce their extensions on this forum, which is read by many members of the Mozilla community. You can start a new topic, letting people know about your new extension and its purpose. People can comment on this post, providing valuable feedback, comments, and bug reports.

Extension Programming Techniques

The previous sections have shown how you can create a simple extension. This section introduces additional techniques that can be useful for creating extensions that are more elaborate.

Understanding the Browser Chrome

You saw that to extend a XUL user interface you need to know its structure: the elements you want to overlay, their hierarchy, ids, and so on. If you want to extend the browser, it is important to have a basic understanding of the browser chrome: its XUL windows and dialogs, style sheets, and JavaScript code. There are several ways to learn about these components:

- The DOM Inspector can help you navigate through the document hierarchy and examine the user interface elements, their properties, and styles.

- You can learn a lot by looking at the browser code; just like your extension, the browser's chrome is composed of XUL, CSS, and JavaScript files you can examine.

- The Web offers a lot of useful information, including documentation, references, tutorials, and so on. See the "Online Resources" section, later in this chapter, for some useful links,

- Finally, you can use the Discussion Forums and the IRC to ask for help from your fellow community members. The "Online Resources" section lists some popular forums and IRC channels.

Using the DOM Inspector

The DOM Inspector is launched by choosing Tools ⇨ DOM Inspector in your browser. The main window is divided into two panes, as shown in Figure 17-8. The left pane displays the DOM tree, a hierarchical structured view of the document elements. The right pane displays detailed information about the selected element (its DOM attributes, style sheets, properties, and much more).

 Note The DOM Inspector is included in the Firefox installer, but you may need to choose the Custom installation option and select Developer Tools to have it installed.

To start examining a XUL window, make sure it is open and then select it from the File ⇨ Inspect a Window list in the DOM Inspector. Once the desired window is selected, its URL appears on the DOM Inspector address bar, and the left pane is updated to reflect its DOM structure. You can now explore the document tree in the left panel by expanding and collapsing the tree elements. When you select a visible UI element in the tree, it is highlighted by a blinking red border in the target window.

You can search for specific elements by their tag name, id, or attribute by choosing Search ⇨ Find Nodes . . ., as shown in Figure 17-9.

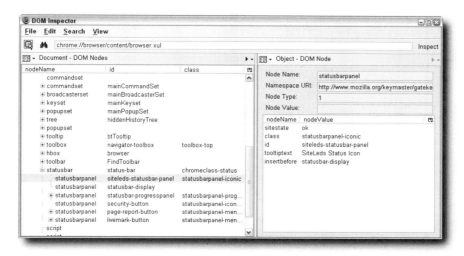

FIGURE 17-8: The DOM Inspector window

FIGURE 17-9: The DOM Inspector Find Nodes dialog

You can also find a visible user interface element by choosing Search ➪ Select Element By Click and then clicking on the desired element in the window you are examining. If the DOM Inspector successfully finds the element you clicked on, the element is highlighted by a blinking red border for a few seconds and then selected in the DOM Inspector tree view.

Tip

If you want to examine a specific visible element when the DOM Inspector isn't open, you have to open the DOM Inspector, select the desired window, choose Select Element By Click, return to the window, click on the wanted element, and then return to the DOM Inspector dialog. With the ColorZilla extension, there is a faster way of achieving the same thing. Click on the ColorZilla status bar icon, click on the desired element, and then choose DOM Inspector . . . from the ColorZilla context menu. The DOM Inspector will be launched with the desired element selected in the left pane.

Once you have selected the element you want to inspect in the left pane, the right pane can be used to examine it more closely. You can use the drop-down list above the right panel to select the type of information you are interested in, as shown in Figure 17-10.

FIGURE 17-10: The various types of information provided by the DOM Inspector

Here's a brief overview of the available information types:

- **DOM Node:** This displays some basic information about the selected DOM node, including its tag name, attributes with their values, and so on.

- **Box Model:** Displays the element's layout information, including its position, dimensions, margins, and so on.

- **XBL Bindings:** XUL elements can be extended using Extensible Binding Language (XBL). This view displays information about the XBL definitions that were applied to the selected element.

- **CSS Style Rules:** Displays all the CSS rules that are applicable to the selected element and information about the style sheets and the selectors that contributed these rules.

- **Computed Style:** After the various CSS rules applicable to the selected element are merged and all the conflicts are resolved according to the cascading order, an element receives its final set of styles. This set of styles, called the *computed style,* is displayed in this view.

- **JavaScript Object:** Every element is an object with a set of properties and functions that can be accessed using JavaScript. This view displays these properties and their values.

Besides allowing you to examine the selected elements, the DOM Inspector allows you to modify them dynamically. For example, you can modify and delete the existing element's attributes or even add new ones by using the context menu in the DOM Node view, as shown in Figure 17-11. By using the context menu in the left pane, you can manipulate the selected element (delete it, duplicate it, set its pseudo-classes to hover, active, or focus, and so on).

The DOM Inspector is a very powerful tool that can be used both for learning and for troubleshooting purposes. If you learn to use it, you will surely find it indispensable.

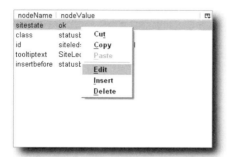

FIGURE 17-11: Dynamically changing the node's attributes

Examining the Source Code

One of the great things about the Mozilla platform is that it is open source. If you are not sure about how something works, you can always take a look at the code and see exactly what is happening behind the scenes.

Typically, you will want to understand how some part of the browser works by looking at its XUL and JavaScript files. You can use the DOM Inspector to find out what XUL file defines a specific part of the UI. Just open the wanted window with the DOM Inspector and look at its address bar. For example, when examining the Options dialog you will see the following: `chrome://browser/content/pref/pref.xul`. This means that this dialog is defined in the `pref.xul` file inside the `browser` chrome package.

There are several ways to find the needed source files and examine them, including the following:

- If you have Firefox installed, you already have all the browser chrome XUL, CSS, JavaScript, and other files on your machine. They are located in the chrome subdirectory under the main Firefox application folder. In this directory, you will find several JAR files (browser.jar, toolkit.jar, and so on). These files are very similar to the chrome JAR file we created for our extension in the previous sections; they contain the chrome that the browser itself is built of. For example, if you want to look at the browser.xul file found at `chrome://browser/content/browser.xul`, you should look inside the browser.jar file that contains the browser package. Looking inside the installed-chrome.txt file in the chrome directory can give you an idea about the installed browser chrome packages and the JAR files that contain them.

  We already mentioned that JAR files are regular ZIP archives. You can extract all the files from a JAR archive and examine them, perform a search for specific keywords, and so on. Also, many ZIP programs allow you to take a quick look at a file inside an archive without needing to extract it first.

- The Mozilla Cross-Reference site, located at `http://lxr.mozilla.org`, contains all the latest Mozilla source code. You can browse and search this code until you find the needed information. For example, the browser.xul file can be found here:

  `http://lxr.mozilla.org/mozilla/source/browser/base/content/browser.xul`

  The site is very useful if you want to see the file history, including when the file changed, who changed it, and what bugs were fixed in the process. Another useful feature is that you can easily create a link to a specific line in any file — the line numbers in the code listing pages are actually links — and use this link elsewhere, for example, to create a bookmark, report a problem, or ask questions about the code.

- You can download the complete Firefox source code and extract it to a local directory. For example, Firefox 1.0 source code is a 31MB archive that can be downloaded from here:

  `http://ftp.mozilla.org/pub/mozilla.org/firefox/releases/1.0/source/firefox-1.0-source.tar.bz2`

  You can browse the Mozilla FTP site (`http://ftp.mozilla.org/pub/mozilla.org/`) and find the source code package that is most appropriate for your needs.

  Once the code is extracted, you will get a directory tree very similar to the one found at the Mozilla Cross-Reference site.

Note The Mozilla source code package is compressed using the BZIP2 format. Many compression programs (7-Zip is one) support this format and can be used to open such archives.

Online Resources

If examining the document structure and looking at the code didn't get you closer to understanding how things work, you can try finding more information on the Web or asking your fellow Firefox hackers for help. This section lists the most useful online resources for extension developers.

- **XULPlanet** (`http://www.xulplanet.com/`): An excellent resource packed with Mozilla-related guides, tutorials, and examples. The site has several reference sections covering everything from XUL to XPCOM components.

- **Mozilla.org** (`http://www.mozilla.org`): Has a lot of useful information for developers. Most of it is linked from the documentation page at `http://www.mozilla.org/docs/`, but there are many additional resources scattered around the site. You can do a site search to try to find the needed information.

- **MozillaZine.org knowledge base** (`http://kb.mozillazine.org`): A user-contributed wiki with many useful articles, guides, and links to additional resources. The Development section has a lot of information on extension programming.

- **MozillaZine forums** (`http://forums.mozillazine.org/`): Post your questions and comments here. The site has a Mozilla development section with a forum dedicated to extensions.

- **netscape.public.mozilla newsgroups** (`http://www.mozilla.org/community/developer-forums.html`): You can search the newsgroups for the wanted information or post your Mozilla development-related questions. The Mozilla.org site has a list of the available newsgroups and their topics.

- **Internet Relay Chat (IRC)** (`irc://irc.mozilla.org/`): There are several IRC channels you can visit to chat with your fellow Mozilla developers in real time. Several developer channels, including `#developers`, `#mozilla`, and others, can be found on the Mozilla.org IRC server.

More XUL

This section introduces several additional XUL-related techniques you might find useful in the process of extension development.

More XUL Elements

After reading the XUL section in Chapter 16 and going over the various examples in this chapter, you should have a pretty good understanding of how XUL elements can be used to create a user interface. This section provides some additional examples of the basic XUL widgets and is intended to give you a taste of the most common UI elements and their XUL representations.

Tip

If you want to test the XUL code in the following examples, you can create a file with an .xul extension and the following contents:

```
<?xml version="1.0" encoding="UTF-8"?>

<window align="start"

xmlns="http://www.mozilla.org/keymaster/gatekeeper/there
.is.only.xul">
    .
    .
    .
    [Your XUL widgets go here]
    .
    .
    .
</window>
```

Once you create the file and insert some XUL elements, you can open it in Firefox using File ➪ Open File. The `align="start"` part makes sure your XUL widgets are shown correctly when opened inside the browser window.

Buttons

A `button` element creates a button that can be pushed to trigger some action (see Figure 17-12):

```
<button label="Test" oncommand="alert('Testing 1 2 3');"/>
```

FIGURE 17-12: A simple button

A `toolbarbutton` is a special button that is usually a part of a `toolbar` and typically has an image (see Figure 17-13):

```
<toolbarbutton id="home-button"
               class="toolbarbutton-1"
               label="Home"
               onclick="BrowserHomeClick(event);"/>
```

FIGURE 17-13: A toolbarbutton XUL element

 Note The toolbar button image is usually specified in a CSS style sheet, rather than directly in the XUL document.

Text Labels

A `label` element can be used to display a short string, often used as a label for another element (see Figure 17-14):

```
<label value="Your first name:"/> <textbox id="first-name"/>
```

Your first name: [   ]

FIGURE 17-14: A label element next to a text box

Larger pieces of text that can optionally wrap to multiple lines should be placed inside a description element (see Figure 17-15):

```
<description>
She Sells Sea Shells by the Sea Shore.
</description>
```

FIGURE 17-15: A description element

The text of the description element wraps to multiple lines only when necessary—for example, when the parent element isn't wide enough. You can resize the window and make it narrow to see the wrapping, as in Figure 17-15.

Text Entry Boxes

A textbox element can be used to create a text entry box like the one shown in Figure 17-14.

If you want to allow entering multiple lines of text, set the multiline attribute to true (see Figure 17-16):

```
<textbox multiline="true" rows="4" cols="10"/>
```

FIGURE 17-16: A multiline text entry box

Checkboxes and Radio Buttons

A checkbox is a UI element that can have either an on or an off state (see Figure 17-17):

```
<checkbox label="Add sugar" checked="false"/>
<checkbox label="Add cream" checked="true"/>
```

FIGURE **17-17:** A couple of checkboxes

Radio buttons can also have two states, but unlike checkboxes, they usually make more sense when grouped. When the user turns on a radio button that is a part of a group, all the other radio buttons in that group are automatically turned off.

You can use a `radio` element to create a radio button and a `radiogroup` element to group several radio buttons (see Figure 17-18):

```
<radiogroup>
    <radio label="Jazz"/>
    <radio label="Rock" selected="true"/>
    <radio label="Blues"/>
</radiogroup>
```

◯ Jazz

◉ Rock

◯ Blues

FIGURE **17-18:** A group of radio buttons

List Boxes

A `listbox` element is used to create a list of items (`listitem` elements) that can be selected by the user (see Figure 17-19):

```
<listbox rows="3">
    <listitem label="Red"/>
    <listitem label="Green"/>
    <listitem label="Blue"/>
    <listitem label="White"/>
</listbox>
```

FIGURE **17-19:** A simple list box

You can use a `menulist` element to create a drop-down list (see Figure 17-20):

```
<menulist label="Tuesday">
  <menupopup>
    <menuitem label="Sunday"/>
    <menuitem label="Monday"/>
    <menuitem label="Tuesday" selected="true"/>
    <menuitem label="Wednesday"/>
    <menuitem label="Thursday"/>
    <menuitem label="Friday"/>
    <menuitem label="Saturday"/>
  </menupopup>
</menulist>
```

FIGURE **17-20: A drop-down list**

Menus

A menu is usually created by defining a `menu` element that displays the menu title and a `menupopup` element that defines the contents of the menu popup window. This window can have any number of `menuitem` elements, `menuseparator` separators, and other menus.

```
<menu label="Tools" accesskey="T">
    <menupopup>
        <menuitem label="JavaScript Console"/>
        <menuitem label="DOM Inspector"/>
        <menuseparator/>
        <menu label="ColorZilla">
            <menupopup>
                <menuitem label="Eyedropper"/>
                <menuitem label="Color Picker"/>
            </menupopup>
        </menu>
    </menupopup>
</menu>
```

Figure 17-21 shows a multilevel menu.

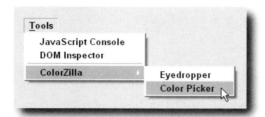

<small>FIGURE **17-21:** A multilevel menu</small>

This section merely scratched the surface of what can be done with XUL. The XULPlanet site has a complete reference of all the available elements, their attributes, and many more examples of their usage.

Introduction to Events

The event mechanism allows your JavaScript functions to be called in response to events that occur in the browser. For example, you can attach a script to handle a mouse click or a keyboard button press, or to have it called every time Firefox loads a web page. Events are essential for creating dynamic user interfaces because they are the primary mechanism for adding behavior to otherwise static elements. For example, it is hard to imagine a user interface having a button that does nothing when clicked.

XUL and HTML events in Mozilla are very similar because they both use the same World Wide Web Consortium (W3C) DOM events specification (`http://www.w3.org/TR/DOM-Level-2-Events/`). If you have worked with dynamic HTML in the past, you will find the concepts introduced in this section very familiar.

The simplest way to attach your script to an element is by adding an appropriate attribute to its XUL definition:

```
<label value="I'm a clickable label" onclick="alert('Label clicked');"/>
```

Each time the user clicks on the preceding label, the script defined by the `onclick` attribute is executed. The name of the attribute is the event name (`click` in our example) prefixed by `on`.

Note The JavaScript functions referenced in the event attribute should be defined when the script is executed. For example, you can define your functions in an external JavaScript file and include this file in the XUL document using the `script` tag. An explanation of how this is done is provided in previous sections.

The most common events and their attributes are listed here:

- Mouse events

    - `click`: Occurs when a mouse button is clicked on an element. This is even triggered when the mouse button is pressed and then released over the same screen location. In that case, three events occur: `mousedown`, `mouseup`, and `click`. When handling a button press or selection of a menu item, you should use the `command` event instead, because the user may also use the keyboard to trigger these actions.

- mousedown: Occurs when the mouse button is pressed on an element.
- mouseup: Occurs when the mouse button is released over an element.
- mouseover: Occurs when the mouse pointer is moved onto an element (enters it).
- mousemove: Occurs when the mouse is moved while it is over an element.
- mouseout: Occurs when the mouse pointer is moved away from the element (leaves it).

■ Keyboard events

- keypress: Occurs when a keyboard key is pressed and then released.
- keydown: Occurs when a keyboard key is pressed (before being released).
- keyup: Occurs when a keyboard key is released.

■ Focus events

- focus: Occurs when an element receives focus either because the user clicked on it with a mouse or navigated to it using the keyboard.
- blur: Occurs when an element loses focus.

■ Document events

- load: Occurs when all content in a document (HTML page, XUL window, and so on) is finished loading and initializing.
- unload: Occurs when the document is unloaded or a XUL window is being closed.
- resize: Occurs when a document view is being resized.
- scroll: Occurs when a document view is being scrolled.

■ General event

- command: Occurs when an element is being activated in some way. For example, this event is triggered whenever a button is pressed or a menu item is selected. As previously mentioned, you should handle this event in these cases rather than the mouse click events, because there are several alternative ways a user can activate a button or use a menu.

When an event handling function is called, its first parameter is the event object that contains additional information about the event that occurred. For example, the target property of this object contains the element that triggered the event:

```
<label value="I'm a clickable label" onclick="handleLabelClick(event);"/>
```

Our handleLabelClick function is defined as follows:

```
function handleLabelClick(event) {
    alert(event.target.value);
}
```

When we click on the label, our `handleLabelClick` function is called. We can obtain the label element that triggered the event from the `target` property of the `event` parameter. When the user clicks on the label, the alert box (similar to the one shown in Figure 17-22) is opened.

FIGURE 17-22: An alert box displaying the value of the label element

To allow additional flexibility, several elements can receive notifications when a certain event occurs. This notification process is called *event propagation* and is divided into two phases. First, the event is sent to every ancestor element on the document hierarchy path, starting with the top-level document and moving all the way down to the element that triggered the event (the target). If any element above the target node has a registered capturing handler for the event (see the Note that follows), the handler will be executed during this *capturing phase*. Any event handler can prevent further event propagation by calling the `stopPropagation` method of its `event` parameter.

Note Event handlers defined using the element event attributes (such as `onclick`) are noncapturing. Further, as you will see in this section, you can use the `addEventListener` method to dynamically define a capturing event handler.

The second part of the event propagation process is called the *bubbling phase*, and it is the reverse of the capturing phase. During event bubbling, the event is sent to every ancestor of the target element, starting with the parent of the target node and moving all the way up the element hierarchy, ending with the top-level document node. Any event handler can prevent further bubbling by calling the `stopPropagation` method of its `event` parameter.

An example of the bubbling phase follows:

```
<box id="top-box" onclick="handleClick(event);">
    <box id="inner-box" onclick="handleClick(event);">
        <button id="button-element"
                label="Test"
                onclick="handleClick(event);"/>
    </box>
</box>
```

We defined the following element hierarchy:

top-box ⇨ inner-box ⇨ button-element

We attached the same event handler to all three elements. Let's define our `handleClick` function:

```
function handleClick(event) {
    dump(event.currentTarget.id + '\n');
}
```

When the user clicks on the button, three lines will be printed on the console:

```
button-element
inner-box
top-box
```

We are witnessing the bubbling phase. First, the button's event handler is called; then the one attached to the inner box; and finally, the event handler defined on the top-level box.

To see the previous example in action, you can create the following XUL document and open it in Firefox:

```
<?xml version="1.0" encoding="UTF-8"?>

<window align="start"
        xmlns="http://www.mozilla.org/keymaster/gatekeeper/there.is.only.xul">
    <script type="application/x-javascript">
    <![CDATA[
        function handleClick(event) {
            dump(event.currentTarget.id + '\n');
        }
    ]]>
    </script>

    <box id="top-box" onclick="handleClick(event);">
      <box id="inner-box" onclick="handleClick(event);">
        <button id="button-element"
                label="Test"
                onclick="handleClick(event);"/>
      </box>
    </box>
</window>
```

Note The `currentTarget` property contains the element that defined the executing event handler, and the `target` property contains the element that triggered the event (the button, in our example). If we used the `target` property in our last example, we would see the "`button-element`" line printed three times.

There is an additional way of registering event handlers. You can use the DOM `addEventListener` method to attach an event handler to an element. This method is more flexible because it allows you to attach event handlers dynamically, define more than one handler for a given element, and define capturing events. Let's continue our previous example by attaching a capturing event handler to our `top-box` element:

```
var topBoxElement = document.getElementById('top-box');
topBoxElement.addEventListener("click", handleClick, true);
```

The third parameter of the `addEventListener` method specifies whether the attached event handler will capture events during the capturing phase. We can attach an event handler by using the `addEventListener` function at any time — during the UI initialization, as a result of some user action, and so on. After we attached the capturing event handler, pressing the button produces the following output:

```
top-box
button-element
inner-box
top-box
```

As you can see, the first line is printed during the capturing phase, before the button itself receives the event; all the other lines that are printed during the bubbling phase remained the same, as in the previous example.

Figure 17-23 demonstrates the two phases of the event propagation process.

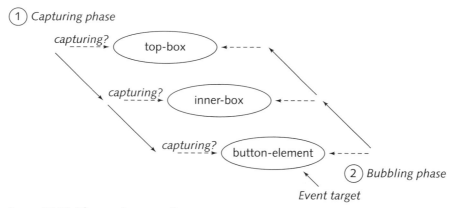

FIGURE **17-23: The event propagation process**

Tip Some events have default actions associated with them. These actions, which are implemented internally by the browser, can be cancelled from any event handler by calling the `preventDefault` method of the `event` object passed to it as a parameter.

Dialogs

In the previous sections, we saw a XUL document that defines an overlay, a portion of the user interface that will be merged with another document. An overlay document has an `overlay` element at its root. Documents having a `window` element as their root define stand-alone, top-level application windows, such as the Bookmarks Manager or the JavaScript Console.

Dialogs and windows have several things in common, but there are several conceptual differences between them:

- Dialogs usually perform a temporary function, such as asking for a password, letting the user change some aspect of the program, or displaying a message.

- A dialog often has buttons that allow the user to close it. Many dialogs have an OK button that closes the dialog while accepting the user input and a Cancel button that closes the dialog without performing any action.

- Dialogs are typically smaller than the top-level application windows.

- A dialog can be *modal,* meaning that the user cannot resume using the application until the dialog is closed.

In XUL, a dialog is defined by creating a document having the `dialog` element at its root.

An example of a simple dialog follows:

```
<?xml version="1.0" encoding="UTF-8"?>
<?xml-stylesheet href="chrome://global/skin" type="text/css"?>

<dialog xmlns="http://www.mozilla.org/keymaster/gatekeeper/there.is.only.xul"
        id="test-dialog"
        title="Test Dialog"
        buttons="accept,cancel"
        ondialogaccept="return dialogOK();"
        ondialogcancel="return dialogCancel();">

  <script type="application/x-javascript"><![CDATA[
    function dialogOK() {
        alert("OK pressed");
        return true;
    }

    function dialogCancel() {
        alert("Cancel pressed");
        return true;
    }
  ]]></script>

  <label value="Testing 1 2 3"/>
</dialog>
```

Figure 17-24 shows the dialog we have created.

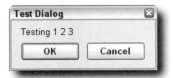

FIGURE **17-24: A simple dialog**

Let's look at our dialog code more closely:

- The `dialog` element specifies that our XUL document is in fact a dialog.

    - The `title` attribute specifies the dialog title.

    - The `buttons` attribute specifies the comma-separated list of buttons that will appear in the dialog. In our case, we want two buttons: OK and Cancel. Notice that we specified only the wanted buttons and didn't have to create the button elements. The buttons are created automatically, and their position and appearance are determined by the user's operating system conventions.

    - The `ondialogaccept` and `ondialogcancel` attributes define functions that will be called when the user presses OK and Cancel, respectively.

- The `script` element defines our JavaScript code. Notice that while all our examples until now demonstrated the use of external JavaScript files, you can have your scripts embedded directly in the XUL document.

- A single `label` element is used to display a line of text. Obviously, real dialogs often have more complex user interfaces.

Once our dialog implementation is ready, we can add it to our chrome package. Let's name our dialog file `testDialog.xul` and add it to the siteleds package. We can now open it using the `window.openDialog` method like so:

```
window.openDialog("chrome://siteleds/content/testDialog.xul",
                  "_blank",
                  "chrome");
```

The first parameter specifies the URL of the dialog XUL file; the second, the name of the dialog. The third parameter specifies some optional flags — the `chrome` flag means that the document is a chrome window and doesn't need to be wrapped by a browser component, like an HTML document, for example. You can specify the `modal` flag to make the opened dialog modal.

Preferences and Persistent Information

The preferences mechanism allows the browser to store user modifiable application settings. For example, when a user changes the browser's home page in the Options dialog, the new value is saved as a user preference.

The preference name is typically a dot-delimited list of words. For example, the home page user preference is `browser.startup.homepage`. You can see each word in the preference name as a *branch*. For example, all browsing-related preferences are located under the browser main branch, all the preferences that are related to the browser startup are located under the startup subbranch of the browser branch, and so on. This way, all the user preferences can be viewed as a tree (see Figure 17-25). When a new component or an extension creates its own preferences, it should give them a unique main branch name to avoid conflicts. For example, our sample extension might save and use a preference named `siteleds.monitor.url`.

Tip   There is a convenient user interface for examining, modifying, and creating preferences. You can open it by typing **about:config** in your browser address bar.

There are three main preference data types: string, integer, and Boolean. Also, each preference can have two optional values: default and current. When the user modifies the default preference value or creates a new preference, the new value is saved as a current value and is highlighted in bold in about:config. When the system tries to retrieve a preference value, it does the following:

1. Checks whether the preference has a current value and, if so, returns it.

2. If there is no current value, it checks whether there is a default value and, if there is, returns it.

3. If neither current nor default value can be found, an exception is thrown.

Note   If you are trying to retrieve a preference of a specific type, and a preference having a different type is found, an exception is thrown. For example, if you are trying to retrieve the string value of the user home page preference (`browser.startup.homepage`) and a Boolean value is found instead, the call will throw an exception.

There are several XPCOM components and interfaces for working with preferences. You can specify the preference names using these interfaces in two ways. You can obtain an interface to the root branch and specify the full preference names (such as `browser.startup.homepage`). Alternatively, you can get an interface to a specific subbranch, which will allow you to omit that branch prefix from the preference names. For example, if you are working with the browser branch, you can use the `startup.homepage` string to access the `browser.startup.homepage` preference.

Here's how to get an interface to the root branch:

```
var prefs = Components.classes["@mozilla.org/preferences-service;1"].
             getService(Components.interfaces.nsIPrefBranch);
```

After we have the root branch, we can access a preference by specifying its full name:

```
var homePage = prefs.getCharPref("browser.startup.homepage");
```

If we want to work with a specific subbranch, we can use the `getBranch` method of the `nsIPrefService` interface:

```
var prefs = Components.classes["@mozilla.org/preferences-service;1"].
             getService(Components.interfaces.nsIPrefService);
var prefsBranch = prefs.getBranch("browser.");
```

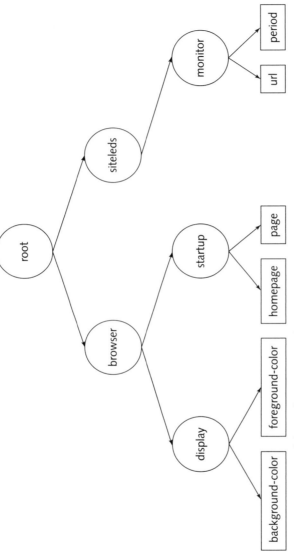

FIGURE 17-25: Some of the preferences viewed as a tree

Now we can omit the `browser` prefix from all the preference names:

```
var homePage = prefsBranch.getCharPref("startup.homepage");
```

To modify a preference or create a new one, you can use one of the `setCharPref`, `setBoolPref`, or `setIntPref` methods (for string, Boolean, and integer preferences, respectively). For example, the following changes the user's home page preference (`prefsBranch` should contain a reference to the browser branch):

```
prefsBranch.setCharPref("startup.homepage", "http://www.iosart.com/firefox/");
```

To retrieve a preference value, you can use one of the `getCharPref`, `getBoolPref`, or `getIntPref` methods.

Note

As mentioned earlier, the methods that retrieve preference values can throw exceptions if the preference is not found or has the wrong type. You can use the `prefHasUserValue` and `getPrefType` methods of the `nsIPrefBranch` interface to make sure that the preference exists and has the expected type or you can wrap your preference retrieval calls in `try`/`catch` JavaScript blocks.

A related Mozilla mechanism allows saving the state of XUL elements across browser sessions. For example, a dialog can remember its size, so if the user resizes it, the correct size will be retained even after the browser is restarted. One way to accomplish this is to manually save the current state of the various elements as user preferences. Mozilla has a persistence mechanism that greatly simplifies this task. The following will make the size of a dialog persistent:

```
<dialog xmlns="http://www.mozilla.org/keymaster/gatekeeper/there.is.only.xul"
        id="test-dialog"
        title="Test Dialog"
        buttons="accept,cancel"
        ondialogaccept="return dialogOK();"
        ondialogcancel="return dialogCancel();"
        width="400"
        height="200"
        persist="width height">
```

We have added a new `persist` attribute to our `dialog` element and specified a space-delimited list of element attributes that we want to be saved. Now, each time these attributes change (the dialog is resized), their new values are saved by the browser. Next time the dialog is displayed, the `width` and `height` attributes will receive the saved values, rather than the initial ones.

You can use the data persistence mechanism on any XUL element that has an `id` attribute. The mechanism is typically used to save element visibility, position, size, and so on, but you can make any attribute persistent, and any number of element attributes can be saved using this technique.

Localized Strings in JavaScript

As mentioned in the previous sections, all the strings that are displayed to the user should be defined in a separate string table file, which will allow easy translation of the user interface. You saw how this can be accomplished in XUL files using XML entities and DTD files.

Often, element labels and other displayed strings aren't static; they can change during the program execution. For example, a status bar can display many different messages, and the text of these messages is typically set by a JavaScript code. A mechanism similar to XML entities is needed so the messages and strings that originate in JavaScript can be easily localized.

JavaScript isn't an XML language. Unlike XUL, it cannot use XML entities to specify string variables. Mozilla has an additional mechanism called *property files* that allows having variable localizable strings in JavaScript. Let's extend our SiteLeds example to include this mechanism. First, we define a property file that is located in the same directory as our siteledsOverlay.dtd file and contains all the UI strings that need to be accessed from JavaScript. The contents of the siteledsOverlay.properties file are as follows:

```
pageModified=The monitored page was modified.
pageError=There was an error retrieving the monitored page.
```

Now we include the property file we have created in our XUL document (siteledsOverlay.xul) using a stringbundle element:

```
.
.
.
<!DOCTYPE overlay SYSTEM "chrome://siteleds/locale/siteledsOverlay.dtd">

<overlay id="siteleds-overlay"
         xmlns="http://www.mozilla.org/keymaster/gatekeeper/there.is.only.xul">

<script type="application/x-javascript"
        src="chrome://siteleds/content/siteledsOverlay.js"/>

<stringbundle id="siteleds-strings"
              src="chrome://siteleds/locale/siteledsOverlay.properties"/>
.
.
.
```

Finally, we can get a specific string from our JavaScript code by finding the stringbundle element and calling its getString method:

```
var stringBundle = document.getElementById("siteleds-strings");
var pageErrorString = stringBundle.getString("pageError");
alert(pageErrorString);
```

To translate the user interface, you will need to translate all the DTD and property files.

Firefox Customization Options

This section shows some additional examples of how Firefox can be customized and enhanced using the extensions mechanism.

Adding Main Menu and Context Menu Entries

An extension can add menu entries to the main Firefox menu and to the context menu of the browser content area (the place where the web pages are displayed).

First, let's add a new menu entry to the browser Tools menu using a dynamic overlay. With the help of the DOM Inspector, we can find out that the id of the Firefox Tools menupopup element is menu_ToolsPopup. We can add the following to our overlay:

```
<menupopup id="menu_ToolsPopup">
    <menuitem id="my-menu-item"
            label="My Menu Item"
            accesskey="y"
            insertbefore="menu_preferences"
            oncommand="alert('Testing 1 2 3');"/>
</menupopup>
```

The new menu item is shown in Figure 17-26.

FIGURE 17-26: The new menu item

Tip

You can control the exact position of the new menu item in the overlaid menu by specifying insertafter, insertbefore, or the position attributes of the new element.

You can add menu items to the context area menu by overlaying the contentAreaContextMenu element:

```
<menupopup id="contentAreaContextMenu">
    <menuitem id="my-context-menu-item"
            label="My Context Menu Item"
            accesskey="y"
            oncommand="alert('Context Testing 1 2 3');"/>
</menupopup>
```

You can dynamically determine whether to make your new menu item visible:

1. Add an initialization function that will be called when the Firefox window is loaded along with your overlay:

```
window.addEventListener("load", initMyOverlay, false);
```

2. In the initialization function, attach a `popupshowing` event handler to the `contentAreaContextMenu` menu:

```
function initMyOverlay() {
    var contextMenu = document.getElementById("contentAreaContextMenu");
    contextMenu.addEventListener("popupshowing", myContextPopupshowing, false);
}
```

This handler will be called every time the context menu is about to become visible.

3. In the `myContextPopupshowing` handler, test some condition and set the visibility of your menu item accordingly:

```
function myContextPopupshowing() {
    var contextMenuItem = document.getElementById("my-context-menu-item");
    if (contextMenuItem) {
        contextMenuItem.hidden = !gContextMenu.isTextSelected;
    }
}
```

The preceding code shows our new menu item in the context menu only if some text is selected on the web page. As you can see, we first find our menu item using the DOM `getElementById` method. We then determine whether some text is selected by examining the `isTextSelected` property of the global `gContextMenu` object and hide our menu item if no text is selected. The `gContextMenu` object has several useful methods and properties that can help you determine whether your menu item is appropriate for a given context. Some examples follow:

- `target`: The element on which the user clicked to open the context menu.
- `isTextSelected`: Determines whether there is some text selected on the web page.
- `onLink`, `onTextInput`, `onImage`, `onTextInput`: Allow you to determine the type of element that the context menu was opened on.
- `linkText()`, `linkURL()`: If `onLink` is true, provides additional information about the link element that the context menu was opened on.

Adding Keyboard Shortcuts

In XUL, shortcut keys are defined using the `key` element. Several `key` elements are typically grouped in a `keyset` element. The Firefox keyboard shortcuts are defined in a `keyset` element that has an id of `mainKeyset`. You can overlay this element to create additional keyboard shortcuts. For example, you can add the following to your dynamic overlay:

```
<keyset id="mainKeyset">
    <key id="my-key-test"
        key="T"
        modifiers="accel,shift"
        oncommand="alert('Testing 1 2 3');"/>
</keyset>
```

When the user presses Ctrl+Shift+T (Cmd+Shift+T on Macintosh), the oncommand script is executed. See the key element documentation for further details on specifying shortcuts in Mozilla.

Tip

When adding new global shortcut keys, you should verify that your keys aren't conflicting with the existing shortcuts, defined either in Firefox itself or in other popular extensions. It is always a good idea to implement some functionality in your extension that will let the user reconfigure the default extension shortcut keys.

In addition, similar to text strings, it is recommended to define shortcut keys as XML entities rather than directly in the XUL file. Shortcut keys often correspond to the name of the action (for example, Ctrl+S for Save). If the extension is translated into another language, the default shortcuts may no longer make sense. If the shortcuts are specified inside a DTD file along with the other strings, they can be easily modified to correspond to the translated name of the action.

Adding Toolbars and Toolbar Buttons

A toolbar is created using the toolbar XUL element. All Firefox toolbars are located inside a single toolbox element. The id of this element is navigator-toolbox, and by overlaying it, we can add a custom browser toolbar, as demonstrated in the following example:

```
<toolbox id="navigator-toolbox">
    <toolbar id="my-test-toolbar"
            class="chromeclass-toolbar"
            toolbarname="My Test Toolbar"
            accesskey="T"
            context="toolbar-context-menu"
            hidden="false"
            persist="hidden">
        <toolbarbutton id="my-toolbar-button-1"
                    tooltiptext="First Button"
                    label="Button 1"
                    oncommand="alert('Testing Button 1');"/>
        <toolbarbutton id="my-toolbar-button-2"
                    tooltiptext="Second Button"
                    label="Button 2"
                    oncommand="alert('Testing Button 2');"/>
    </toolbar>
</toolbox>
```

Let's take a closer look at what we have done:

■ We created a toolbox element with navigator-toolbox id in our overlay. The specified id attribute ensures that this toolbox will overlay the main Firefox toolbox and our toolbar will be added to the browser.

- The `toolbar` element defines our new toolbar. Let's examine its attributes:

  - `class`: The `chromeclass-toolbar` class specifies that the XUL element should be styled as a standard Firefox toolbar.

  - `toolbarname`: The name of the toolbar as it appears in the View ⇨ Toolbars menu.

  - `accesskey`: The keyboard key that can be used to trigger the toolbar visibility in the Toolbars menu. The specified letter will be underlined, similar to other menu keyboard shortcuts.

  - `context`: The id of the context menu that appears when the user right-clicks over the toolbar. You can create your own custom menu or specify `toolbar-context-menu`, which is the id of the default Firefox context menu that allows toggling the visibility of the various toolbars.

  - `hidden`: The value of `false` specifies that the toolbar is initially visible.

  - `persist`: By setting this attribute to `hidden`, we are instructing the browser to remember the visibility state of our toolbar across sessions.

- Inside the `toolbar` element, we have defined a couple of toolbar buttons. As we mentioned earlier, the `toolbarbutton` element is similar to a regular button but typically has a different style. In addition to toolbar buttons, we can place any elements on our toolbar (checkboxes, text boxes, drop-down lists, and so on).

Figure 17-27 shows our new toolbar.

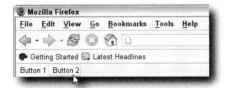

FIGURE 17-27: A simple toolbar

If you want to add a single toolbar button rather than a complete toolbar, you must use a slightly different technique. In Firefox, the user can customize a toolbar by choosing View ⇨ Toolbars ⇨ Customize and dragging the wanted toolbar buttons and other elements from the toolbar palette to the target location. By adding our toolbar button to the customization palette, we can allow the user to later add this button to one of the toolbars.

Note It is possible to add a toolbar button directly to one of the browser toolbars, rather than to the customization palette, but this requires a somewhat more complex technique.

To add our `toolbarbutton` to the customization palette, we need to overlay the Firefox main `toolbarpalette` element, which has an id of `BrowserToolbarPalette`:

```
<toolbarpalette id="BrowserToolbarPalette">
    <toolbarbutton id="my-toolbar-button-3"
                   class="toolbarbutton-1"
                   tooltiptext="Third Button"
                   label="Button 3"
                   oncommand="alert('Testing Button 3');"/>
</toolbarpalette>
```

Note We have set the `class` of our `toolbarbutton` element to `toolbarbutton-1`. This ensures that the button will be displayed correctly in both Icons and Text toolbar modes.

We now want to specify an icon for our `toolbarbutton`. Because toolbars can have two sizes, big and small, we will have to define two icons for our toolbar button. The big icon is 24 × 24 pixels, and the small one is 16 × 16 pixels.

Let's look at the style sheet that defines the toolbar button icon:

```
#my-toolbar-button-3 {
    list-style-image: url("chrome://my-extension/skin/button_3_large.png");
}

toolbar[iconsize="small"] #my-toolbar-button-3 {
  list-style-image: url("chrome://my-extension/skin/button_3_small.png");
}
```

As you can see, the `iconsize` attribute of the parent toolbar element determines whether the small or the large icons are displayed.

Changing the Appearance of Web Pages

An extension can modify the appearance of web pages that are loaded into the browser content area. You can define an event handler function that will be called each time a new web page is loaded. In this function, you can examine and modify the DOM structure of the loaded page.

This is accomplished with the following steps:

1. Add an initialization function that will be called when the Firefox window is loaded along with your overlay:

```
window.addEventListener("load", initMyOverlay, false);
```

2. In the initialization function, find the browser content element using its id (`appconten`) and attach a `load` event handler to it:

```
function initMyOverlay() {
    var appContent = document.getElementById("appcontent");
    appContent.addEventListener("load", myNewWebPageLoaded, true);
}
```

This event handler (myNewWebPageLoaded) will be called each time a new page is loaded inside the browser.

3. The myNewWebPageLoaded function can examine and modify the loaded page using the DOM interfaces. For example, we can create a function that will add a tooltip with the link target URL to every link found on the web page:

```
function myNewWebPageLoaded(event) {
    var webPage = event.originalTarget;
    var allLinks = webPage.getElementsByTagName("A");
    for(var i=0; i < allLinks.length; i++) {
        var link = allLinks[i];
        link.setAttribute("title", link.href);
    }
}
```

As you can see, we obtain the root element of the loaded web page from the originalTarget property of the event parameter. Then we get a list of all the links using the getElementsByTagName DOM method. Finally, we go over all the link (anchor) elements and set their title attribute to the value of their target URL. Now, when you hover over a link on the web page, you will see a nice tooltip displaying the link target URL (see Figure 17-28).

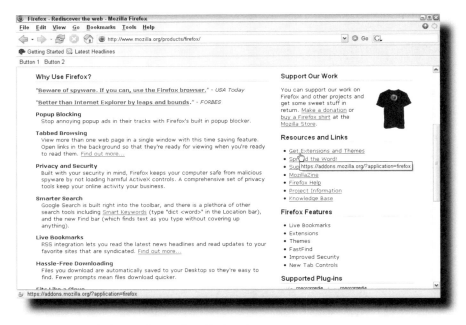

FIGURE 17-28: A link with the newly added tooltip

Note

Something similar can often be achieved by creating a *bookmarklet,* a small JavaScript snippet that is saved as a bookmark and that when clicked can examine and modify the current page. The mechanism we introduced in this section is much more powerful and flexible.

Advanced Packaging

This section explores additional packaging-related options and techniques.

Optional Install Manifest Items

You should already know how to create the install manifest file (install.rdf). Several optional items can be added to this file. Let's extend the install.rdf file of our SiteLeds extension:

```xml
<?xml version="1.0"?>

<RDF xmlns="http://www.w3.org/1999/02/22-rdf-syntax-ns#"
    xmlns:em="http://www.mozilla.org/2004/em-rdf#">

    <Description about="urn:mozilla:install-manifest">
        <em:id>{E1B2492D-E6AC-4221-A433-C143E3A1C71E}</em:id>
        <em:version>0.1</em:version>
        <em:name>SiteLeds</em:name>

        <em:description>Site Status Monitor</em:description>
        <em:creator>Alex Sirota</em:creator>
        <em:homepageURL>http://www.iosart.com/firefox/siteleds</em:homepageURL>

        <em:contributor>First Contributor</em:contributor>
        <em:contributor>Another Contributor</em:contributor>
        <em:optionsURL>chrome://siteleds/content/settings.xul</em:optionsURL>
        <em:aboutURL>chrome://siteleds/content/about.xul</em:aboutURL>
        <em:iconURL>chrome://siteleds/skin/logo.png</em:iconURL>
        <em:updateURL>http://iosart.com/firefox/siteledsUpdate.rdf</em:updateURL>

        <em:targetApplication>
            <Description>
                <em:id>{ec8030f7-c20a-464f-9b0e-13a3a9e97384}</em:id>
                <em:minVersion>0.9</em:minVersion>
                <em:maxVersion>1.1</em:maxVersion>
            </Description>
        </em:targetApplication>

        <em:file>
            <Description about="urn:mozilla:extension:file:siteleds.jar">
                <em:package>content/</em:package>
                <em:skin>skin/classic/</em:skin>
                <em:locale>locale/en-US/</em:locale>
            </Description>
        </em:file>
    </Description>
</RDF>
```

Let's examine the items we have added:

- You can specify one or more `em:contributor` properties for every person that contributed to the extension.

- The `em:optionsURL` property specifies the chrome URL of the extension Options dialog (sometimes called Settings). The document found at this URL is a XUL dialog that typically lets the user change the various extension settings and saves these settings as user preferences. If this property is specified, the Options dialog can be opened from the Extensions Manager window.

- The `em:aboutURL` property allows you to create a custom About dialog for your extension. By default, this dialog is created automatically and displays the extension name, version, author, home page, and so on. You can create a custom About dialog and specify its chrome URL in the install manifest.

- You can create a custom icon for your extension and specify its chrome URL using the `em:iconURL` property. This icon should be 32 × 32 pixels, and when defined, it is displayed in the Extension Manager window instead of the default icon.

- Firefox can automatically check if a new version of your extension is available and, if found, show a notification message and let the user update the extension. By default, Firefox contacts the Mozilla site (`addons.mozilla.org`) to see if an update is available. By using the `em:updateURL` property, you can specify a custom URL that will be queried instead. More information on this file appears in the following section.

Custom Update File

As previously mentioned, by specifying the `em:updateURL` property in your install manifest file you can have Firefox query a custom URL to see whether updates are available for your extension. At this URL, the browser expects to find an RDF file that specifies the available extension versions.

Note The server must send the RDF file as `text/rdf` for the update mechanism to work. With the Apache web server, this can be achieved by creating an .htaccess file and adding the following line to it: `AddType text/xml rdf`.

Take a look at a sample update.rdf file:

```
<?xml version="1.0"?>

<RDF:RDF xmlns:RDF="http://www.w3.org/1999/02/22-rdf-syntax-ns#"
         xmlns:em="http://www.mozilla.org/2004/em-rdf#">

  <RDF:Description ⊃
    about="urn:mozilla:extension:{E1B2492D-E6AC-4221-A433-C143E3A1C71E}">
    <em:updates>
      <RDF:Seq>
```

```
        <RDF:li resource= ⟳
    "urn:mozilla:extension:{E1B2492D-E6AC-4221-A433-C143E3A1C71E}:0.2"/>
        </RDF:Seq>
    </em:updates>

    <em:version>0.2</em:version>
    <em:updateLink>http://www.iosart.com/firefox/siteleds/SiteLeds_0.2.xpi⟳
    </em:updateLink>
  </RDF:Description>

  <RDF:Description ⟳
    about="urn:mozilla:extension:{E1B2492D-E6AC-4221-A433-C143E3A1C71E}:0.2">
    <em:version>0.2</em:version>

    <em:targetApplication>
      <Description>
       <em:id>{ec8030f7-c20a-464f-9b0e-13a3a9e97384}</em:id>
       <em:minVersion>0.9</em:minVersion>
       <em:maxVersion>1.1</em:maxVersion>
       <em:updateLink>http://www.iosart.com/firefox/siteleds/SiteLeds_0.2.xpi
@ta </em:updateLink>
      </Description>
    </em:targetApplication>
  </RDF:Description>

</RDF:RDF>
```

As you can see, the update RDF file specifies that version 0.2 of the extension with GUID E1B2492D-E6AC-4221-A433-C143E3A1C71E is available for download from http://www.iosart.com/firefox/siteleds/SiteLeds_0.2.xpi. It also specifies that version 0.2 of the extension is compatible with Firefox (by specifying its GUID) versions 0.1 to 1.1. If, for example, a user has version 0.1 of the SiteLeds extension installed in Firefox 1.0, the update procedure will detect that there is an available update (version 0.2 of the extension) and display the appropriate notification.

Automating the Packaging Process

As noted in the previous sections, you must perform several operations each time you want to create an XPI package for your extension. You need to package the contents of the chrome directory into a JAR file and then package it along with the install.rdf file into an XPI archive. You can create a simple script that will automate this process for you. All you need is a ZIP utility with a command-line interface and a scripting language.

This can be done as follows, using the 7-Zip utility and a simple Windows batch script:

```
cd chrome
del siteleds.jar
7z a -tzip -mx=0 -r siteleds.jar *
cd ..
del SiteLeds_0.1.xpi
7z a -tzip -mx=9 SiteLeds_0.1.xpi install.rdf chrome\siteleds.jar
```

We can put the preceding script in a file named package.bat at the top-level directory of our extension (in the same directory as the install.rdf file). Clicking on this file creates a fresh SiteLeds_0.1xpi package in the current directory. As you can see, the script performs a couple of very simple tasks: It first compresses the contents of the chrome directory and then creates the final XPI package by compressing the chrome JAR file along with the install.rdf install manifest.

You can create more elaborate packaging scripts that will automatically update the version number in all the needed files, upload the extension package to your web server, and perform additional tasks you are routinely doing when packaging and releasing your extensions. The point is that even a very simple script can be used to make the process much more efficient.

Developing an Extension without Repackaging

We have seen that you need to install your extension into the browser before you can test it. This means that you have to constantly repackage and reinstall your extension while developing it. This process is highly inefficient and frustrating. There is a simple way you can avoid having to repackage your extension each time you make a change. The idea is that during development, you change your manifest files to use plain directories instead of the JAR file and then install this modified extension into the browser. Now you can work directly on the installed files without having to repackage anything.

If you want your extension to work with plain directories, you need to change a few things:

1. Instead of packaging the content, skin, and locale directories into the siteleds.jar file, create a siteleds subdirectory inside the chrome directory and copy the content, skin, and locale folders to this new directory. Basically, you are creating a directory at the same place your JAR file would be and with exactly the same contents.

2. Change the following line in the install.rdf file

   ```
   <Description about="urn:mozilla:extension:file:siteleds.jar">
   ```

   to

   ```
   <Description about="urn:mozilla:extension:file:siteleds">
   ```

   If you are using the new-style chrome registration manifest, you should apply similar changes to your chrome.manifest file instead.

3. Create your XPI file as usual, by compressing the install.rdf file and the chrome directory (which now contains the siteleds subdirectory and not the siteleds.jar file), and install it into the browser.

Figure 17-29 shows the contents of the modified XPI package.

Now you can locate your extension installation directory (typically in your profile folder) and work directly on the installed files. You don't have to continually repackage your extension to see the changes. You might have to restart the browser, though, to see the changes made to the overlay elements.

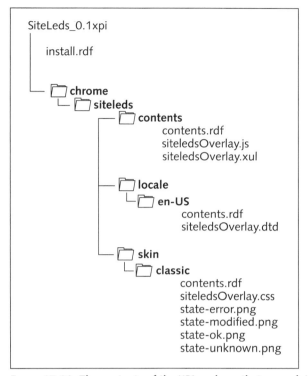

```
SiteLeds_0.1xpi
    │
    install.rdf
    │
    │
    └── 📁 chrome
            └── 📁 siteleds
                    ├── 📁 contents
                    │       contents.rdf
                    │       siteledsOverlay.js
                    │       siteledsOverlay.xul
                    │
                    ├── 📁 locale
                    │       └── 📁 en-US
                    │               contents.rdf
                    │               siteledsOverlay.dtd
                    │
                    └── 📁 skin
                            └── 📁 classic
                                    contents.rdf
                                    siteledsOverlay.css
                                    state-error.png
                                    state-modified.png
                                    state-ok.png
                                    state-unknown.png
```

FIGURE 17-29: The contents of the XPI package that uses plain directories

There is one additional thing you can do to avoid restarting the browser when modifying nonoverlay XUL documents (such as windows and dialogs). By default, Mozilla caches all XUL documents, meaning that once it loads a XUL file, it won't be read again from the disk until you restart the browser. To disable this XUL caching mechanism, set the `nglayout .debug.disable_xul_cache` preference to `true`.

Tips and Tricks

This section provides various techniques that can prove useful in the extension development process.

Avoiding JavaScript Name Collisions

As mentioned earlier, the JavaScript identifiers we define in overlays are evaluated in the global scope, meaning that if we are not careful, we can give our function or variable a name that is already taken by another component. This situation causes a name collision and should be avoided. To solve the problem, we used unique prefixes for all our global identifiers. This solution works, but you need to constantly be aware of the problem and remember to add the prefix to each and every identifier. This also makes the code less readable.

There is a better way of handling this situation. You can put all your JavaScript code inside an object. All the global identifiers, both functions and variables, become members of this object. Now, as long as the name of this one object is unique, you don't have to worry about name collisions.

Let's rewrite our SiteLeds JavaScript code to use this technique:

```
var SiteLeds = {
    _siteLedsLastRequest: null,
    _siteLedsLastContent: null,

    pageLoaded: function () {
      ...
    },

    pageError: function() {
      ...
    },

    checkPage: function() {
      ...
    }
}

window.addEventListener("load", SiteLeds.checkPage, false);
```

Testing Your Code without Creating an Extension

JavaScript code that uses XPCOM components and other browser APIs needs to have certain privileges to be able to run in the browser. When such code runs from a chrome URL, meaning that it is a part of the browser or an extension, it has such privileges. Does this mean that you have to create a chrome package and register it every time you want to experiment with JavaScript? There is a way to run a privileged JavaScript code from a simple HTML file, as long as it is located on the local file system.

The trick is to enable the necessary privilege before attempting to use XPCOM and other restricted interfaces. To enable access to XPCOM from a script, call the `netscape .security.PrivilegeManager.enablePrivilege` function with the `UniversalXPConnect` parameter. Now you can create a simple HTML file that contains your JavaScript code and test it without needing to create a chrome package.

An example for working with the preferences XPCOM objects using this technique follows:

```
<html>
  <head>
    <script>
      function getHome() {
        netscape.security.PrivilegeManager.
                          enablePrivilege("UniversalXPConnect");
        var prefs = Components.classes["@mozilla.org/preferences-service;1"].
                      getService(Components.interfaces.nsIPrefBranch);
        var homePage = prefs.getCharPref("browser.startup.homepage");
        alert(homePage);
      }
```

```
    </script>
  </head>
  <body>
    <button onclick="getHome();">Get Home</button>
  </body>
</html>
```

When you click on the Get Home button, the script retrieves the user Home Page preference using the Preferences Service XPCOM object.

 Note When a local file requests a privilege using the preceding mechanism, a security dialog is displayed, and you must explicitly grant this privilege before the script execution can be resumed. You should be very careful when granting such privileges and make sure that you know exactly which file is requesting them.

 Tip As you saw earlier, you can also experiment with your XUL files without installing them into your browser first. Create a XUL file and open it with your browser just as you would open a local HTML document. Your XUL interface will appear in the browser content area. If the UI looks stretched, add `align="start"` to the root element of your XUL document (`window`, `overlay`, and so on).

Hacking Existing Extensions

There is no better way to understand how some component works than to look at its source code. Extensions are no different. Because they are developed using mainly text-based technologies such as XML and JavaScript, they are open source by their nature. You can learn a lot by looking at the code of existing extensions and playing around with them.

Suppose that you have a great idea for an extension, but even after you read through all the available documentation you still can't figure out how to get started. For example, let's assume that you want your extension to add a context menu item that sends the selected text to some website, and you are not sure how you can modify the context menu, get the selected text, or open a connection to a remote site. There are already dozens of extensions that perform very similar operations, and looking at their code will get you on the right track.

Some of the things you can do to start hacking existing extensions are as follows:

- Find an extension that does something similar to what you are trying to accomplish.

- Install the extension and play around with it for a while. See how it works and whether it indeed has the needed functionality.

- Extract the extension using your favorite ZIP utility and start looking at its code. Examine the structure of the XUL files and overlays, see how different elements are styled using CSS, and learn how the extension does things by looking at its JavaScript code.

■ If there are still things you don't completely understand, you can do some real hacking — you can modify the extension, comment things out, and add your own pieces of code. You can add `dump()` and `alert()` calls to examine the value of JavaScript variables, see how different functions are invoked, and so on. Also, you can use the technique that allows you to modify an installed extension (described earlier in this chapter) to make the hacking process more efficient.

One of the greatest benefits of knowing how extensions work is being able to tweak existing extensions to better suit your needs. You can modify the extension UI to make it prettier or to change some of its JavaScript code to slightly adjust its behavior. If you believe that your changes might be useful to anyone besides yourself, you can contact the extension author and suggest these improvements or even offer your help with the project.

Note   If you want to use in your own work the code you found in another extension or to modify it in any way, first make sure that the extension license allows it. Many extensions have licenses that allow you to use their code in your extension under different conditions. Always credit the original authors for their work. Many licenses specifically require that, but this is really a matter of courtesy. Also, if you think that an existing extension is missing some pieces of functionality, consider contacting the author and suggesting a contribution to the existing extension before creating your own derivative product.

Summary

This chapter explained everything you need to know to start writing your own extensions. You should now know how extensions are created, packaged, and distributed; how different parts of Firefox can be customized using extensions; and where to get further documentation and help.

Once you see how simple the process of creating Firefox extensions is, you might be tempted to start writing your own extension right away. Don't resist this temptation! Extensions are among the things that make Firefox the best browser out there, and I'm sure that your new extension can make it even better.

Creating Themes

I started creating themes for Mozilla around August 2002 but didn't release my first theme for Firefox (known then as Firebird 0.7) until November 2003. As with extensions, the Firefox theme process is a work in progress. Those that started creating themes for Firefox when it was still in beta stages know this all too well. Now that Firefox 1.0 has been released, changes are coming more slowly, but they're still coming.

The following section details the theme creation process from start to finish, from defining the files to publishing your theme. Some of the concepts are the same as those used in creating and modifying extensions.

Tools for Creating Themes

You probably have most if not all of the software required to create a Firefox theme already installed on your computer. There are no theme-specific tools required for theme creation. Themes consist of the following file types:

- CSS
- Images
- RDF
- XML

All these files are packaged into the final product, known as a compressed archive. You will need the following tools to create a theme for Firefox:

- A text editor
- An image/graphics editor
- A compression tool

Text Editor

Most files in themes are simple text files (.txt). You can use any text editor to edit them. I use a Windows-based operating system, and depending on the level of complexity involved, I use Notepad, WordPad, or even Microsoft Visual Studio .Net. Notepad and WordPad are great basic text editors, but when I want to do something like a find/replace in multiple files, I use Visual Studio .Net because it allows multiple files to be open at once. The beauty of the Mozilla theme engine lies in its cross-platform compatibility. If you weren't already aware of this, different operating systems use different ways to store line breaks. Windows-based systems use carriage return plus line feed (CR/LF), UNIX-based (including Linux) systems use only LF, and Macintosh systems use only CR. This can cause problems if the software isn't able to detect the line-break style of a file. The Mozilla theme engine is able to detect different line-break styles and accommodate them. That means that you can use any text editor, regardless of operating system, as long as the file is saved as plain text. Bottom line, use a text editor that you're comfortable with.

Image/Graphics Editor

As with text editors, the choice is up to you. Generally, most images in themes are either GIF or PNG format because of their transparency options. Any image/graphics editor that allows you to save images with transparency is acceptable. My favorite is Jasc Paint Shop Pro. You can also use Adobe Photoshop or any similar tool for your operating system. I don't recommend editors as simple as Microsoft Paint, as they generally don't handle transparency properly.

ZIP-Format Compression Tool

A ZIP-compatible compression tool is required to create the JAR file, which is the compressed archive file. Feel free to use any compression tool that you are comfortable with to create the JAR file when ready to test or make your theme public. I use WinZip, but your favorite, if different, should work too. Another great tool is 7-Zip. 7-Zip is free and comes with command-line options built in. With WinZip, command-line tools are an add-on.

Note The only exception to "use any ZIP-compatible compression tool you want" is Zipmagic; I've heard reports from some folks that it's incompatible with the JAR file format.

You can go to `http://www.winzip.com` to get a copy of WinZip and to `http://www.7-zip.org` for a copy of 7-Zip.

Building Your First Theme

So you're ready to create a Firefox theme? Now that you know all the tools required, it's time to roll up your sleeves and get to work. The best way to get started is to use the default Firefox theme as a template.

Define and Create Your Theme's Core Files

While it may sound simplistic to say that a theme is composed of images and text files, there are a great many files, and the Firefox theme engine looks for specific files in specific places. You should never try to write all the files yourself. No theme author that I know of ever created a theme that way. It's better to begin by modifying the default theme. Browse to the location where you installed Firefox. Up until the release of Firefox 1.0.2, there were zipped versions of Firefox available for download. Now that those have been discontinued for official releases, you will need to be able to locate the folder where you installed Firefox.

For those of you using Windows, the default install location for Firefox is C:\Program Files\ Mozilla Firefox.

Mac users have two ways to access the Firefox folder. You can Ctrl+click the Firefox application package and select "Show Package Contents," or you can browse to the /Applications/ Mozilla.app/Contents/MacOS/ folder.

For the Linux users out there, there does not seem to be a standardized location yet for the Firefox installation. The install location depends on which distribution you are running. I know the install locations for three popular Linux distributions. Gentoo installs Firefox to the /usr/lib/MozillaFirefox directory, Debian to the /usr/lib/mozilla-firefox directory, and Fedora to the /usr/lib/mozillafirefox directory.

The default theme file is named classic.jar, located in the Firefox\chrome directory. If you have not been able to locate your Firefox directory yet, now is the time to search your computer for the classic.jar file. You'll need to open classic.jar with your ZIP format compression tool and extract the files. After extraction, you should have a directory structure similar to that shown in Figure 18-1.

FIGURE **18-1: Classic.jar directory structure**

Because the default theme is installed during the Firefox installation process, it has a different directory structure from that of themes that require installation on their own. You'll need to move some files around and create some yourself. Figure 18-2 shows the directory structure that your theme will need.

FIGURE 18-2: Your theme's directory structure

Both the preview.png and icon.png files are used in the Themes window. The preview.png file traditionally shows what the theme looks like when in use, and the icon.png file is displayed to the left of the theme's name, as shown in Figure 18-3.

FIGURE 18-3: Themes Manager

Creating the install.rdf File

You might have noticed that the default theme doesn't have an install.rdf file. This is one of the files that you need to create. The following is the install.rdf file from my Smoke theme:

```
<?xml version="1.0"?>
<RDF xmlns="http://www.w3.org/1999/02/22-rdf-syntax-ns#"
     xmlns:em="http://www.mozilla.org/2004/em-rdf#">

<Description about="urn:mozilla:install-manifest">
<em:id>{3646e22c-5e51-43fb-b8a4-9ebaf7eb11f2}</em:id>
<em:version>1.5</em:version>

<em:targetApplication>
<Description>
```

```
<em:id>{ec8030f7-c20a-464f-9b0e-13a3a9e97384}</em:id>
<em:minVersion>0.8</em:minVersion>
<em:maxVersion>1.0</em:maxVersion>
</Description>
</em:targetApplication>

<em:name>Smoke</em:name>
<em:description>Based on the Orbital icon set by Florian Freundt
(http://www.freundt.org/florian)</em:description>
<em:creator>Aaron Spuler</em:creator>
<em:contributor>Icons by Florian Freundt</em:contributor>
<em:homepageURL>http://www.spuler.us</em:homepageURL>
<em:updateURL></em:updateURL>
<em:internalName>smoke</em:internalName>
</Description>

</RDF>
```

Creating the contents.rdf File

The default theme also handles the contents.rdf file differently. Instead of one contents.rdf file, it has four — one in each subdirectory. You'll need to delete all four of the contents.rdf files. After you have deleted all four contents.rdf files, you must create one file and place it in the root directory of the theme, as shown in Figure 18-2. The following is the contents.rdf file from my Smoke theme:

```
<?xml version="1.0"?>

<RDF xmlns="http://www.w3.org/1999/02/22-rdf-syntax-ns#"
     xmlns:chrome="http://www.mozilla.org/rdf/chrome#">

<Seq about="urn:mozilla:skin:root">
<li resource="urn:mozilla:skin:smoke"/>
</Seq>

<Description about="urn:mozilla:skin:smoke" chrome:name="smoke">
<chrome:packages>
<Seq about="urn:mozilla:skin:smoke:packages">
<li resource="urn:mozilla:skin:smoke:global"/>
<li resource="urn:mozilla:skin:smoke:browser"/>
<li resource="urn:mozilla:skin:smoke:mozapps"/>
</Seq>
</chrome:packages>
</Description>

<Description chrome:skinVersion="1.5"
about="urn:mozilla:skin:smoke:global"/>
<Description chrome:skinVersion="1.5"
about="urn:mozilla:skin:smoke:browser"/>
<Description chrome:skinVersion="1.5"
about="urn:mozilla:skin:smoke:mozapps"/>

</RDF>
```

For the moment, you can use these files as they are, but you'll want to edit them later. If you already know the name you want for your theme, replace all instances of Smoke with your theme's name. You should probably also change the creator name and URL right now. If you don't have a web site, you can leave that portion blank, as I've done with the em:updateURL section. (The update URL is discussed later in this chapter.)

Note For more information on RDF files, see `http://www.xulplanet.com/tutorials/mozsdk/rdfsyntax.php`.

Generate a Custom GUID

A Globally Unique Identifier (GUID) is a 128-bit random number. The number of unique ids is so large that the chances of generating the same 128-bit number twice are virtually nonexistent. There are two GUIDs in the preceding sample install.rdf posted. One is for Firefox (`ec8030f7-c20a-464f-9b0e-13a3a9e97384`), and the other is for the Firefox version of the Smoke theme (`3646e22c-5e51-43fb-b8a4-9ebaf7eb11f2`). A GUID is used to avoid causing confusion by guaranteeing that no two themes or extensions have the same name. You'll need to generate a GUID for your theme. This will replace the Firefox Smoke GUID on the line `<em:version>1.5</em:version>` in the sample code previously provided. I use the following tool, available on the Web, to generate GUIDs for themes: `http://www.hoskinson.net/webservices/guidgeneratorclient.aspx`, shown in Figure 18-4. The Rain theme is shown in the screenshot.

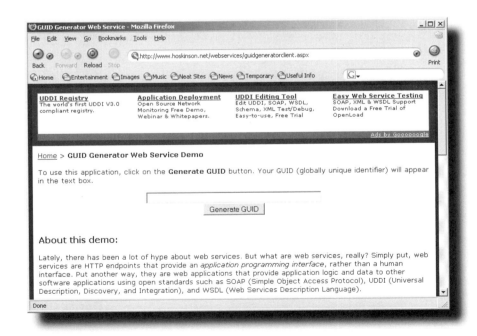

FIGURE 18-4: GUID Generator

This web site is very simple to use: Simply click the Generate GUID button, and the text box above the button will be populated with a GUID. If you need to create more than one, just click the button as many times as needed.

Customizing Chrome

Chrome is the user interface portion of the application window that lies outside a window's content area. Toolbars, menu bars, progress bars, and window title bars are all examples of elements that are typically part of the chrome. Every part of the chrome is defined through CSS files. All the files in your theme contain declarations for objects in the chrome. The most important CSS file for Firefox is browser\browser.css. This file controls the main display that's visible while using the browser. All of the standard buttons (back, forward, stop, reload, print, go, and so on) are defined in this file. In order to change the attributes for an element, you need to know its internal id.

Using the DOM Inspector

The DOM Inspector is without a doubt the most useful tool involved when constructing a theme. I didn't know about it when creating my first few themes, and believe me, I wish I had. Without the DOM Inspector, it became a guessing game, and my guesses were wrong more often than not. With the DOM Inspector, you can find out anything you want to know about every portion of the browser window. It will tell you the CSS id for any button, what file the button attributes are defined in, and even in what line the definition starts.

To start using the DOM Inspector, follow these steps:

1. Go to the Tools menu and select DOM Inspector. This opens the DOM Inspector in a new window.

2. Go to the File menu, select Inspect a Window, and then select the Mozilla Firefox window. If you've done that correctly, the text box at the top of the page will read as follows: chrome://browser/content/browser.xul.

3. Click the Inspect button. The bottom half of that window should display the browser window. Figure 18-5 shows the progress so far. My Smoke theme is shown in the screenshot.

Now you can start to explore the code to generate browser elements. Directly underneath the File menu is a button that looks like a mouse pointer hovering over a button. This button allows you to click on a browser element and see its attributes. To activate this feature, click on the button (it turns darker when you do this); then click on a browser element in the lower pane. Try that now. Click on the Reload button (it will briefly flash red). In the upper-left pane, the Reload button will be selected in the DOM tree, and in the upper-right pane, information about the Reload button will be populated. Clicking the button to the left of the text "Object - DOM Node" brings up a menu with six items. The one that we are interested in at this time is the CSS Style Rules menu item (see Figure 18-6).

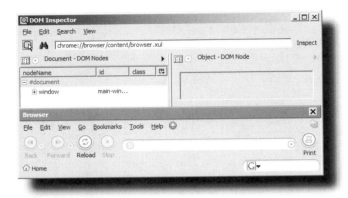

FIGURE 18-5: DOM Inspector

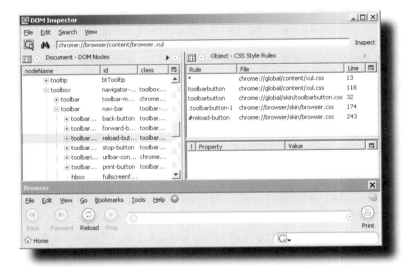

FIGURE 18-6: Reload button, CSS Style Rules

Now that the CSS rules are shown, you can actually see what code controls the Reload button. The first two lines in the CSS Style Rules pane are irrelevant. The third item details the styles applied to all buttons. This deals with margins, padding, borders, and text colors. The fourth, fifth, and sixth items — `.toolbarbutton-1` — are general properties that deal with the main toolbar buttons only. The following buttons are part of the `.toolbarbutton-1` group:

- Back
- Forward
- Reload
- Stop

- Print

- Downloads

- History

- Mail

- Bookmarks

- New Tab

- New Window

- Cut

- Copy

- Paste

The last line, `#reload-button`, details properties that are specific to the Reload button.

Understanding CSS

Because the entire user interface is defined through Cascading Style Sheets, you'll need to know something about CSS to create a Firefox theme. I had never heard of CSS when I started creating Mozilla themes, and that made the process (unnecessarily) difficult. I still don't know all that much about CSS, but I know enough to get around. If you don't know any CSS, now might be a good time for a bit of research. A Google search for "CSS Tutorial" will bring up lots of useful sites to get you started. If you're interested in a quick tutorial, visit the following sites:

- `http://www.htmlhelp.com/reference/css/`

- `http://www.w3schools.com/css/`

Creating Needed Graphics

To make your theme truly unique, you'll need to replace the graphics associated with the default theme. A great majority of the buttons are found in the files browser\toolbar.png and browser\toolbar-small.png.

Tip

PNG is an extensible file format for the lossless, portable, well-compressed storage of raster images. PNG is a replacement for GIF because PNG allows for true color (24-bit) images with alpha transparency, as opposed to GIF, which allows for 256-color images with indexed transparency. Indexed-color, grayscale, and true-color images are supported, plus an optional alpha channel for transparency. The PNG format was sought as a replacement for the GIF format when Unisys requested royalties from GIF-supporting software for the use of its patents on the LZW compression algorithms in 1994.

See `http://www.webcolors.freeserve.co.uk/png` for more information on the PNG format.

Overlay Default Icons

If you want to use the same size buttons as the default theme (24 × 24 pixels for large buttons, 16 × 16 pixels for small buttons), you can simply open the image files and replace them with your own images in your image editor. I would recommend this method to anyone unfamiliar with CSS.

The default theme uses one large image file to hold all the large toolbar button images and another for the small toolbar button images. In Figure 18-7, the buttons are all laid out on a single *.png image.

FIGURE 18-7: Toolbar.png

The top row of icons is for the normal state (not disabled, not hovered). The second row holds the icons displayed when you hover over a button with your mouse. The third row is the icons shown when a button is disabled. You'll notice that there is only one icon on the fourth row — that is the bookmarks icon, which has four states in the default theme. When you click on the bookmarks button, Firefox displays your bookmarks along the left side of the screen. The icon on the fourth row is displayed while the bookmarks are open.

Personally, I don't like to use one large image file to hold all the toolbar images. It's hard to edit files when they're stored this way because of image alignment issues. I store each button in a different image, with three button states per image, as shown in Figure 18-8. The only downside to storing each button in a different image is that compression is generally better when all buttons are stored in a single image, as in Figure 18-7. The compression issues should not affect your theme at all during normal use — only the size of the jar file.

FIGURE 18-8: Separate images for each button

The normal button image is on top, in the center is the button when hovered over, and on the bottom is the disabled state image. I do not specify a fourth state for the bookmarks icon while open. I modified the code to display the hover state for the icon when the bookmarks are visible.

Keep in mind that there is no correct way to lay out images; you can simply choose the method that works best for you. As long as the code you write is valid CSS and points to valid images, it will work properly.

Layered Images

The easiest way for me to align all the different image states was to put each state on a separate layer. That way, I could manipulate each layer individually. Another method that might prove helpful is the use of gridlines.

I use Jasc Paint Shop Pro to edit images while creating themes. To overlay the default theme's images, open browser\toolbar.png, as shown in Figure 18-9.

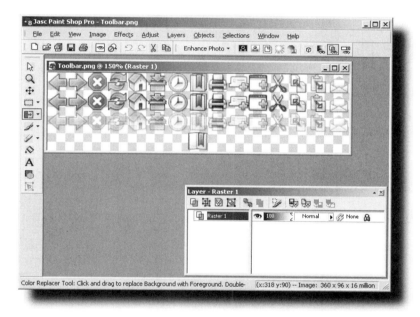

FIGURE 18-9: Paint Shop Pro

Because the default theme uses 24 × 24 pixel images for large icons, you need to have your images the same size. Open up the image that you would like to use for the Back button and then copy the image by pressing Ctrl+C, or selecting Edit ➪ Copy. To paste your image as a new layer, press Ctrl+L or select Edit ➪ Paste ➪ Paste As New Layer. You can then select the new layer in the layer properties window (it will be called Raster 2), and use the Move tool to drag your icon over to where the Back button resides in the default icon set. Once you complete that step, your display will look similar to Figure 18-10. The Back button on layer 2 is the Back button from the Smoke theme.

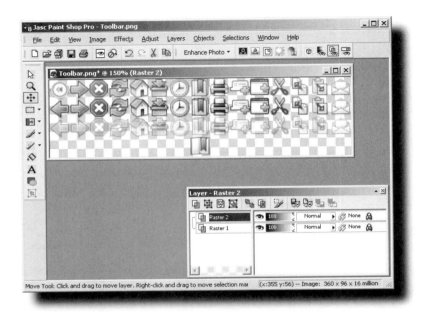

FIGURE 18-10: Paint Shop Pro, layered overlay

Simply repeat the process until you have covered all images from the default theme with the images you want to appear in your theme. If you put each individual image on its own layer, you can easily manipulate them later on to correct alignment issues. When you are finished editing, select the Raster 1 and then press the Delete key on the keyboard to remove the default images. When saving the image, you might be asked if you want to merge all layers. Select Yes to finish saving the file.

If you are using separate images for each button, as I choose to do, the process is similar. You can skip the step on deleting the layer containing the default images, but make sure to put each state of the images on a different layer to help with alignment.

Most image editors have the capability to display gridlines behind the images to aid with alignment. In Figures 18-9 and 18-10, the gridlines are shown as the gray and white squares visible on the background of the images.

An easy way to create the small toolbar icons is to simply resize the large toolbar icons. If you've already completed the large toolbar icons, you can press Shift+S or choose Image ⇨ Resize to shrink your image and then save it as a different name than the large toolbar icon. If you don't use a different name, you will lose the large toolbar icon because the file will be overwritten.

Different image editors handle things slightly differently, but all have the ability to display gridlines and resize images. If you are unsure how to perform an action, consult the help file for your image editor for more information.

Graphics Locations

If you are familiar with CSS, you can modify attributes freely. The majority of the buttons that you see while using Firefox are defined within the browser\browser.css file. I would say that about 90 percent of the Firefox interface that you see from day to day is defined in that file. If you are ever unsure of where a button's image is located, refer to the DOM Inspector example to find which CSS file the button's code resides in; then you can look at that CSS file to find out the exact location of the image.

Main Toolbar

The majority of the buttons you see when using Firefox are defined within the browser\browser.css file. Browsing through this file will give you the location of all the images used, and you can modify attributes for buttons here. Figure 18-11 displays the main toolbar of the Atlas theme.

FIGURE **18-11:** Main toolbar

Extensions Window

The Extensions window requires a few graphics of its own, and they are defined in the mozapps\extensions\extensions.css file. If you wish to put icons on the buttons in the lower left, that is possible. I do not provide icons for those buttons in my themes. Figure 18-12 displays the Extensions window of the Mars theme.

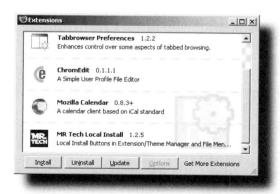

FIGURE **18-12:** Extensions window

Options Window

The Options window requires a few icons for the option categories. The code that governs them resides in the browser\pref\pref.css file. Figure 18-13 displays the Options window of the Apollo theme.

FIGURE 18-13: Options window

In Firefox 1.1, the location of the code that handles the Options window will be changing. The new location is the browser\preferences\preferences.css file. Figure 18-14 displays the new Options window of Firefox 1.1 with the Neptune theme.

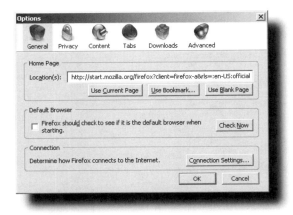

FIGURE 18-14: Options window, Firefox 1.1

Bookmarks Manager

The Bookmarks Manager has seven buttons to theme. The code defining the buttons is in the browser\bookmarks\bookmarksManager.css file. Figure 18-15 shows the Bookmarks Manager window of the Pluto theme.

FIGURE 18-15: Bookmarks Manager

Help Window

The icons for the Help window are not actually included within the classic.jar file; they are in the Firefox\Chrome\help.jar file. To theme the Help window, I recommend using the DOM Inspector to find out the CSS id of each button and then adding the code to theme the buttons at the bottom of the global\global.css file. Be sure to set the !important flag after defining any styles for the Help window buttons so that your styles will be used instead of the default. Figure 18-16 shows the Help window of the Playground theme.

FIGURE 18-16: Help window

Icon Conversion

I did not draw any of the images in my themes. I am somewhat of a novice when it comes to creating images. The method I used to create the button images in my themes was to find existing icon sets. After receiving permission from the icon creator to use his or her work, I converted the ICO files to PNG files.

To create a PNG image from an ICO file, I use a product from Axialis IconWorkshop (see Figure 18-17). This is not a free program, and it is available for Windows users only. After opening the ICO file with IconWorkshop, you'll need to select the size that you want to export as PNG from the list on the right. After selecting the image size, press Ctrl+Shift+T, or select File ➪ Export ➪ PNG with Transparency.

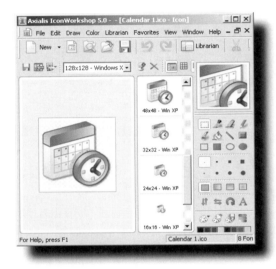

Figure 18-17: IconWorkshop

A Linux utility called ImageMagick will convert ICO files to PNG format. You can find more information at `http://www.imagemagick.org/`.

A Mac program called IconBuilder can convert ICO files to PNG format. You can find more information at `http://www.iconfactory.com/iconbuilder.asp`.

Supporting Popular Extension Buttons

While not a requirement, supporting the buttons of popular extensions does enhance a theme. Theming the buttons of an extension is handled slightly differently from theming the standard buttons of Firefox. To theme an extension's button, you need to find out the button's CSS id. This can be done one of two ways: with the DOM Inspector or by manually opening up the extension's JAR file and looking at the code. Either way will work, but I prefer to open the JAR file and look in the CSS there for any button ids. That way, I'm certain that I'll theme all buttons of the extension. After locating the button ids and creating images, you'll need to add lines of code to your theme to support the extension's buttons. The best way to do this is to open global\global.css and insert lines of code at the bottom of this file. Add the code for all of the extension's buttons to the bottom of global.css and point the button ids to your images.

To ensure that your image is shown, you must specify the `!important` flag in the line of code identifying the button image. The `!important` flag means that once an attribute is defined as `!important`, it can never be changed, even if the element is redefined in another CSS file. Here is an example of its use:

```
#extension-button {
 list-style-image: url("chrome:\\browser\skin\extension_button.png") !important;
}
```

Let's look at a real-world example. I'll show you how to support the Basics extension, available at my web site: `http://www.spuler.us`. The Basics extension does only one thing: adds a button to the left side of the tab bar that opens a new tab when clicked. This emulates the behavior of the New Tab button that resides in the tab bar for Mozilla and Netscape. The Basics extension utilizes a 16 × 16 pixel image — anything taller than 16 pixels would not fix properly on the tab bar. By default, I have the image for the button set to look identical to the small version of the New Tab button, because many users will be using the default theme. Figure 18-18 shows the default theme with the Basics extension installed.

FIGURE 18-18: Default theme, Basics extension

I support the Basics extension in all my themes. If I had left out the code for the Basics extension, the iCandy Junior theme would have looked like something was not quite right, because the Basics button would display the icon that is bundled with the extension — the icon from the default Firefox theme, as shown in Figure 18-19.

FIGURE 18-19: iCandy Junior theme, Basics extension not supported

To add support for the Basics extension, I needed to add some code to the browser\browser.css file. This approach generally works for most extensions, but remember to specify the attributes as !important. If you come across an extension where this method does not work, add the code to the global\global.css file instead. The code that I needed to add to browser\browser.css for the Basics extension is as follows:

```
.tabs-newbutton {
    list-style-image: url("chrome://browser/skin/icons/basics.png") !important;
}
```

After you add that code to the browser\browser.css file and supply the necessary image, the button is themed appropriately, as demonstrated in Figure 18-20.

FIGURE 18-20: iCandy Junior theme, Basics extension supported

By now, you can see how adding support for extensions to your themes can enhance them. However, just because you don't provide support for an extension doesn't mean that the extension will not work. The extension will still work, but without support for it, the extension's buttons will not be themed to match the rest of the icons used throughout your theme. Listed are a number of popular extensions that I support on my Firefox themes:

- Basics
- Calendar
- Chromedit
- CuteMenus
- Download Manager
- Google Bar
- JavaScript Debugger
- Quicknote
- Search Button
- Scrollable Tabs
- Tabbrowser Preferences
- Toolbar Enhancements

- Translation Panel
- Web Developer Toolbar

Packaging the Files

Now that you've customized the graphics and modified your code, you can take care of the last remaining tasks before creating the JAR file archive for your theme.

The install.rdf file needs to be modified to reflect your theme. Replace the GUID of Smoke (3646e22c-5e51-43fb-b8a4-9ebaf7eb11f2) with the custom GUID you created earlier. The following also need to be changed:

- name
- description
- creator
- contributor (optional)
- homepageUrl (optional)
- updateURL (optional)
- internalName

Any optional elements can be left blank. The name element is the theme's name. The internalName element will need to be identical to the theme's name, but lowercase.

Earlier, you used the contents.rdf file from the Smoke theme. The only modification left is to change every instance of smoke to the internalName in your install.rdf file.

Creating an Update Definition File

If you would like users to be able to automatically update the theme without having to go to your web site and reinstall, you can specify an updateURL in the install.rdf file. I prefer that users know what has changed in my themes, so I don't utilize this feature. If you wish to use this feature, you will need to create a file, named updade.rdf, and place it on a web site. Specify the URL of the update.rdf file in the updateURL field of the install.rdf file. A sample update.rdf file follows:

```
<RDF:RDF xmlns:RDF="http://www.w3.org/1999/02/22-rdf-syntax-ns#"
        xmlns:em="http://www.mozilla.org/2004/em-rdf#">


<RDF:Description
about="urn:mozilla:extension:{88060a48-addf-4060-87db-c9aec3e5615a}">
<em:version>1.5.1</em:version>
<em:updateLink>http://www.website.com/theme.jar</em:updateLink>
</RDF:Description>

</RDF:RDF>
```

The GUID listed in the `urn:Mozilla:extension` field must be the GUID of the theme. The `em:version` is the version of the theme located online, the most recent version number. When Firefox looks for an update to a theme, it will query the URL of the update.rdf file and compare the version number in the update.rdf file to the version number of the theme currently installed. If the version number in update.rdf is greater than what is currently installed, Firefox will update the theme with the file located in the `em:updateLink` field.

Now that all files are ready, you can create the JAR file for your theme. Using your ZIP-format compression tool, create an archive named theme.jar, replacing "theme" with the name of your new theme. Make sure that you do *not* select the "Save Path Info" option if it is offered.

Testing

To install your new theme, open the Themes window from within Firefox by selecting Tools ⇨ Themes. You can drag your theme JAR file on the left pane of the Themes window or use the Local Install extension mentioned in Chapter 3. MR Tech's Local Install extension can be found at `http://www.mrtech.com/extensions`. If the theme doesn't install, check to see that the install.rdf and contents.rdf files are formatted properly. Also, verify that the JAR file directory structure matches that previously shown in Figure 18-2.

Note
On a Mac, the drag-and-drop functionality is disabled, and the Local Install extension is the only method of installing a theme stored locally.

Using the DOM Inspector

If your theme installs properly but you still need to make minor adjustments, you can once again use the DOM Inspector. For any element not displaying as expected, you can view its attributes in the DOM Inspector, using the same process that you used earlier to locate button ids and attributes. You can examine the attributes in use and correct any mistakes in your CSS files. After making corrections, repackage the JAR file. Repeat this process as many times as necessary to get the theme exactly as you want it. If you are stuck on something and can't figure it out, the greatest source of information that I know of for Firefox themes is the MozillaZine Themes forum (`http://forums.mozillazine.org/viewforum.php?f=18`). Many theme authors visit this forum regularly to get help and offer advice to others.

A quicker way to see your changes without reinstalling the theme is to replace the file manually. Navigate to your profile folder, as described in Chapter 1. Then navigate to the extensions folder and locate the folder that is named after the GUID of your theme. Opening that folder will show the theme file; you can replace this with the newly corrected version. You'll have to exit Firefox before replacing the file, but afterwards you can open Firefox and see the changes immediately. Another advantage of this method is that when you install the theme multiple times, multiple copies of the jar file are stored in the profile directory.

Deploying Your Theme

Once you feel that the theme is ready for general use, you need to deploy it. There are two ways of deploying a theme: hosting it on your web site or hosting it on the Mozilla Update web site. There are pros and cons to each method.

Hosting your theme on the Mozilla Update site means that many people will be able to see it, but you won't be able to manage your files. One popular complaint is that there can be two versions of your theme available to the public if you host the file on Mozilla Update and on a personal site — the most recently updated copy on your web site and a possibly outdated copy on the Mozilla Update site. The site administrator does all file management on Mozilla Update, and you have to file a bug in Bugzilla (http://bugzilla.mozilla.org) in order for changes to take place. This process usually takes several weeks. The Mozilla Update site has been known to be out of commission for long periods. Many theme authors like having control over their files and thus don't post them on the Mozilla Update site. To find out more information, visit https://addons.update.mozilla.org/about.

Hosting your theme on your web site gives you total control over your files, but it may or may not get as much visibility as the Mozilla Update site. I used to host my files on both Mozilla Update and http://www.spuler.us, but now I prefer to manage my own files. (Currently, my site is averaging 2.2 million hits and 45GB of bandwidth traffic per month.)

Creating JavaScript Installer Links

Hosting the theme on your web site requires some JavaScript to provide a clickable install link for the theme. Otherwise, users will have to download the theme and then use a local install method. The following is a sample install link:

```
<a href = "javascript:void (InstallTrigger.installChrome
(InstallTrigger.SKIN,'icandyjr_fb.jar','iCandy Junior.'))">Install</a>
```

You will need to modify the link to match your theme name and filename. That link will pop up a dialog in Firefox like that shown in Figure 18-21.

FIGURE 18-21: JavaScript install confirmation

Making Your Theme Public

After you've hosted your theme on a web site, you need to get the word out. A few web sites where you can post your theme release include the following:

- `http://www.mozillazine.org`
- `http://www.gfxoasis.com`
- `http://www.neowin.net`

All of these sites have dedicated Mozilla/Firefox theme forums for postings. After all, the more people who know about the theme, the better.

Supporting Different Operating-System Platforms

One of the underlying goals of the Mozilla organization is cross-platform compatibility. Unfortunately, there is a bug with themes. On themes using native scroll bars (meaning that the scroll bars are drawn by the operating system rather than themed), the code is slightly different for the Mac operating systems than for all other operating systems. The default theme, as well as all of my own themes, suffer from this bug. This means that you'll have to maintain two versions of your theme: one for Mac users and one for those who use Windows, Linux, and all other operating systems that run Firefox. I submitted a bug to Bugzilla in October 2003 and progress has been slow, but it finally looks like a solution may be near. Keep an eye out for updates at `https://bugzilla.mozilla.org/show_bug.cgi?id=222654` for the most up-to-date information. For compatibility with all operating systems, I recommend making both a Mac and a non-Mac version of your theme available to users until bug 222654 is fixed.

Note There are quite a few differences between the two scrollbars.css files, so it is not feasible to list the differences between them at this time. You can obtain a copy of both files by visiting `http://www.hackingfirefox.com/themes`.

Hacking Existing Themes

If you wish to modify existing themes, you should be able to do that easily. Now that you know the process for creating a theme from the default theme, modifying an existing theme will be much easier. You don't have to redefine the install.rdf and contents.rdf files, and the directory structure will already be set up properly for you.

Using the method to extract the contents of the default jar file, do the same for the existing theme you wish to hack. Then you can go ahead and modify images or attributes in CSS files as you did when creating your theme. When you finish, you can re-create the JAR archive for the existing theme. Then replace the unhacked version in your profile folder, using the method I suggested. After you restart Firefox, your hacked version of the preexisting theme will load instead of the unhacked version.

Summary

This chapter covers the core topics for creating a Firefox theme. The chapter starts by defining the necessary tools and then moves on to describe the procedure for using the default theme as a base. Definition of core files, CSS, and image customizations are covered. Package and deployment of your theme are discussed. Information for supporting multiple operating systems and to hack existing themes is also provided.

While this chapter covers the basics, there will be a lot of work on your own to customize the graphics and CSS files to your liking.

Index

IF YOU ENJOYED THIS EXTREMETECH BOOK YOU'LL LOVE...